THE ALL-INCLUSIVE GUIDE TO JUDICIAL CLERKING

■ ■ ■

Abigail L. Perdue

Associate Professor
Wake Forest University School of Law

AMERICAN CASEBOOK SERIES®

American Casebook Series is a trademark registered in the U.S. Patent and Trademark Office.

© 2017 LEG, Inc. d/b/a West Academic
    444 Cedar Street, Suite 700
    St. Paul, MN 55101
    1-877-888-1330

West, West Academic Publishing, and West Academic are trademarks of West Publishing Corporation, used under license.

Printed in the United States of America

ISBN: 978-1-63460-822-0

To my beloved parents, best friends, and teachers,
Janet Lynn and David Perdue,
and to my judges,
The Honorable Jimmie V. Reyna and
The Honorable Mary Ellen Coster Williams,
without whom this work would not have been possible.

ACKNOWLEDGMENTS

First and foremost, I acknowledge my Heavenly Father with whom all things are possible. Throughout the arduous creative process, it has become increasingly clear to me that, taken together, each of the oft-confusing twists and turns of my professional life not only prepared me to produce this important work but also placed me in the ideal position to do so.[1] As a result, my grateful heart "[g]ive[s] thanks to the Lord, for He is good. His faithful love endures forever. Let the redeemed of the Lord tell their stories . . . "[2] This book is now part of mine.

This work would not have been possible without my incredible family who has encouraged, supported, and guided me throughout my life in every way imaginable—my mom and dad, Janet and David Perdue;[3] my Mamaw and Papaw, Mary and Hoover Asbury; my grandparents, Maxine and Herbert Perdue; my sister, Rachel, and brother-in-law, Sandy; my cherished nephews, Heath and Wyatt; my aunt and uncle, Christine and Turner Smith; and especially my four-legged best friend and faithful companion, Violet Sofia. I am so blessed and grateful for each of you.

I am especially indebted to my beloved mother, Janet Lynn Asbury Perdue, whose generosity, compassion, wisdom, and faith have inspired me to carry on through difficult times and strive to be the best possible version of myself—the version that is most like her. I feel privileged to come from a long line of very gifted teachers—my mother, my Mamaw, and my Grandmother. I carry their wisdom, strength, and passion for helping others with me, and it permeates every page of this book.

I am also extremely grateful to the handful of close friends so exceptional that I have come to love them like family—Amber Thompson Foster, who is always there for me; Nicole Davol Rhoads, whose unceasing positivity uplifts me; and Emily Barker, who brings out the best in me. An astute observer will notice that the names of my loved ones frequently appear throughout the book; this is my small way of honoring and thanking them for all of the love and support they have shown me through the years.

I am also forever thankful to The Honorable Jimmie V. Reyna of the United States Court of Appeals for the Federal Circuit and The Honorable Mary Ellen Coster Williams of the United States Court of Federal Claims. I had the great honor to serve these outstanding judges at a formative stage in my life and learned more from them than I ever could have imagined. They exemplify excellence and integrity in all they do, ever guided by their unwavering devotion to justice. Working beside these brilliant jurists was a life-changing experience for which I am eternally grateful.

Likewise, I owe an enormous debt of gratitude to the invaluable members of my extended Chambers family—Maria Martinez-Reyes, Trudy Black, Derek McCorquindale, Tara Ward, Collin Swan, Natalie Bennett, Jayna Rust, Travis Annatoyn, Jack Kelly, and many more. I am particularly grateful to my friend, colleague, and former co-clerk Dan Brean, Assistant Professor of Law at the University of Akron School of Law, for providing invaluable feedback and research assistance on portions of the book.

I also thank my colleagues at Wake Forest University School of Law whose support enriched this work, especially Christine Coughlin, Laura Graham, Sally Irvin, Kim Fields, Francie Scott, John Korzen, Mark Hall, Luellen Curry, Harold Lloyd, Jonathan Cardi, Gregory Parks, Michael Green, Wilson Parker, Dean Suzanne Reynolds, and former Dean Blake Morant. I especially appreciate Laura and Sally's willingness to serve as expert readers for portions of the book.

I am also exceptionally grateful to my legal writing colleagues around the globe from whom I have learned immeasurably much. Their mentorship and pedagogical innovation have significantly impacted my teaching and scholarship, which in turn has strengthened the book. I am especially thankful to my mentor Rosa Kim, Professor of Legal Writing at Suffolk University Law School, who has supported me at every turn, thoughtfully reviewed my work, and fostered my professional growth and development in every way possible.

I also acknowledge the important contributions of my outstanding research assistants and teaching assistants, both past and present: Amanda Brahm, Cate Berenato, Samantha Poon, Yawara Ng, Karon Fowler, Taryn Walker, Brittany Colton, Samer Roshdy, Stephen White, David Hopper, Katye Jobe, Joey Greener, Kaitlin Price, Crissy Dixon, Stephen Frost, Kayleigh Butterfield, Alexis Iffert, Evan Leadem, Tee Hassold, John Allen Riggins, Michael Herman, Kelsey Mellan, and Vanessa Garrido. Their research, editing, feedback, and most importantly, their enthusiasm for learning have truly enriched the book. I have learned more from these amazing students than I could ever hope to teach.

The book is a direct result of my development of the D.C. Summer Judicial Externship Program at Wake Forest University School of Law. Thus, I am also extremely grateful to the many individuals who have generously volunteered their time, efforts, and mentorship to make the Program a reality. I am particularly grateful to Judge Paul Friedman, Carolyn Corwin, Elliot Berke, Katie Simon, Jocelyn McIntosh, Jeff Minear, Kristina Wolfe, Stephen Jobe, Jennifer Richwine, and many more. My development of the Program ultimately inspired the book, so I am forever grateful for your contributions.

Finally, I am so thankful for the enthusiasm, patience, support, and guidance of my very capable editors—Tessa Boury and Elizabeth Eisenhart—at West Academic, gifted production specialists, Greg Olson and Daniel Buteyn, and my exceptionally talented cover art designer, Carol Logie. Thank you for giving me this opportunity.

Notes

[1] "A person plans her way, but the Lord directs her steps." Proverbs 16:9.

[2] Psalm 107:1–2.

[3] Whenever I have felt afraid or discouraged in my life, my dad has infused me with strength by praying a prayer with me drawn from 2 Timothy 1:7: "For God has not given us a spirit of fear, but [a spirit] of power and love and of a sound mind."

INTRODUCTION TO THE FOREWORD

I am incredibly honored that *my* judge—The Honorable Jimmie V. Reyna—agreed to author the Foreword to my book. Judge Reyna is a brilliant jurist who approaches legal issues with a singular perspective informed by his wealth of practical experience, unique personal background, and distinct judicial philosophy. At the heart of that philosophy lies his unwavering concern for "The Forgotten Man" at the heart of each decision. More than that, Judge Reyna is a truly remarkable human being who exemplifies integrity in every aspect of his life. He cares tremendously for each member of his Chambers family and offers invaluable mentorship and friendship to all those fortunate enough to know him. For this reason, he has become *my* North Star—the standard of humanity and professionalism to which I aspire and a light in the sky with which I navigate the darkness. Clerking for Judge Reyna was an honor and a blessing that has enriched my life in ways I could never have imagined.

FOREWORD BY THE
HONORABLE JIMMIE V. REYNA

I am honored that Professor Perdue asked me to write this Foreword for her book on judicial clerking. After all, I am a great believer that those seeking to develop a skill must gather tools and devices useful towards that growth. Look about the master of any craft, and you will see tools of their trade. This book is similarly a worthy tool, but I leave it to Professor Perdue to address its best use, she being the master. Instead, I dedicate the few lines of this Foreword to write about my most surprising discovery since becoming a Circuit Judge on the U.S. Court of Appeals for the Federal Circuit: the federal judge-law clerk relationship.

The relationship between federal appellate judges and their law clerks eludes singular definition. But over the years, I have discerned three common traits. First, the relationship offers both the judge and clerk a distinct opportunity for personal and professional growth. Second, the relationship imbues mentorship of the best kind. Finally, the work of both the clerk and judge is essential to the American system of justice.

There is no doubt that the relationship is special and, in many ways, complicated. Unlike a law firm, Chambers life is a sequestered setting. I recall how my prior law firm life routinely involved working with and coordinating among lawyers at my firm, outside counsel, administrative and judicial tribunals, and, of course, the client. Now, my days are spent ensconced in a quiet setting necessarily removed from crisis wrought deadlines, unpredictable schedules, and a steady stream of intrusions. Unlike most federal appellate judges, I am fortunate to have my Chambers in the same courthouse as my colleagues, for it provides opportunity for regular contact. Yet my daily dose of interaction remains almost entirely within my Chambers. This consistent, day-to-day interaction while working toward a single purpose forges a bond between the judge and law clerk.

The judge-clerk bond is key to appellate decision-making, which is a cyclical, collaborative process. While trial judges need only convince themselves of a legal conclusion, appellate judges sitting on panels must convince each other, and as a result are tied together as members of the Court. I was appointed to exercise my judgment, but I cannot shape the immediate outcome of a case without consensus among my colleagues; there is no panel of one. Like most appellate courts, we hear oral argument during a one-week period each month. Once oral argument is scheduled, three judges are assigned to each panel. Upon confirmation by the panel members, the briefs are distributed to the respective chambers. We prepare for and hold oral arguments, engage in deliberations, exercise our respective judgment, and embark on the opinion writing process. The process starts anew each month. The work is daunting: I run before an avalanche of law, secure that it will not consume me only because I do not run alone.

My law clerks run with me. Given the volume of briefing and the breadth of issues we confront each month, my law clerks build a foundation that enables me to focus on the issues essential to deciding cases. The bench memo provides the law clerk with an opportunity to assimilate large volumes of information into a singular document and to demonstrate judgment on which critical issues deserve the most attention. I read every brief, but I also value critical thought on the latent issues lurking in a case that may not be apparent from the briefs or exposed by the arguments. I practiced law for many years, and I trust my insight, instincts, and intuitions from that experience. Yet my clerks' fresh and varied perspectives invariably help me reach my judgment.

In many respects, my clerks are less scribes than counselors at law. The close-quarters setting in Chambers and intense preparation for each case requires teamwork between judges and their law clerks. Undoubtedly, the judge and law clerk become familiar companions as contentious issues surface and hard decisions are tended. In my Chambers, we spend significant time thinking about each case and discussing how to resolve disputes in a manner faithful to law and precedent. Whether on case law, legal doctrine, or a sense of justice, our continued discussions, some even passionate, are all incredibly interesting and enjoyable, moments that to my taste are delicious.

Throughout the process, my law clerks learn about me and my experiences, and I learn about their experiences and hopes for the future. We get to know each other, our upbringings, and perspectives. Inside jokes become the norm, and mutual respect develops. Over the course of the one-year term, I take great satisfaction in witnessing my clerks grow professionally and personally. What starts as a traditional apprenticeship morphs into a bond with invaluable meaning for both the judge and clerk. Gratitude becomes the overwhelming reciprocal emotion.

For judges who hire term clerks, the clerkship experience marks the passing of seasons. I feel sadness when a term expires, but I delight in seeing my clerks go on to practice in the profession to which I have dedicated my life. I get excited upon learning of their successes and triumphs, and I encourage them when things could have gone better. Reunions with former clerks are always fun. I have even been honored in officiating weddings of former clerks.

Given these dynamics, it is not unusual for judges to comment among each other on their appreciation for their clerks. A question often asked by non-judges is whether we could do our job without the clerks. The answer is yes, but the job would be much harder, and the work less productive. And since discovering how meaningful the judge-clerk relationship can be, I am not sure I would want to do the job without them. I speak only for myself, but I am fairly certain this sentiment is shared by many of my colleagues throughout the federal judiciary.

Very few relationships in the legal profession capture the dynamic of the relationship between a judge and law clerk. That the relationship is part apprenticeship and part familial makes clerking a unique experience rewarding for them and me. If there is any single truth in the experience, it is that my law clerks make me a better judge. That is why I firmly believe that the judicial clerkship is an essential element in our system of justice.

ABOUT THE AUTHOR

Abigail L. Perdue is an Associate Professor at Wake Forest University School of Law where she serves as Founding Director of the D.C. Summer Judicial Externship Program. She also teaches a variety of courses, including *Judicial Clerking*, and serves on her law school's Clerkship Committee. Prior to joining the faculty of Wake Forest, Professor Perdue practiced labor and employment law at the New York City office of Proskauer Rose LLP, and taught at Washington and Lee University and School of Law. She also clerked for The Honorable Mary Ellen Coster Williams at the United States Court of Federal Claims and The Honorable Jimmie V. Reyna at the United States Court of Appeals for the Federal Circuit. She graduated *summa cum laude* from Washington and Lee University and obtained her law degree at the University of Virginia School of Law.

Professor Perdue's clerkship experiences were so incredible that only a few months after she joined Wake Forest's faculty, she founded Wake Forest's D.C. Summer Judicial Externship Program, which places selective law students into unpaid summer judicial externships. In addition to the externship component, participants meet weekly with Professor Perdue to take a course tailored to judicial clerking. The course, which she designed, thoroughly explores many aspects of clerking, such as judicial ethics, confidentiality, professionalism, and judicial drafting. Students draft an 11-day memo, a bench memo, and a judicial opinion. They study a pending case and attend oral argument in the case. The course enriches their externship experience and improves their performance as externs.

The All-Inclusive Guide to Judicial Clerking is a direct result of the culmination of Professor Perdue's collective professional experiences: her clerkships, her teaching, and her subsequent development of the D.C. Summer Judicial Externship Program. In drafting the book, she has consulted with legal practitioners, law clerks, judicial externs, professors, students, alumni, and of course, judges.

TABLE OF CONTENTS

THE ALL-INCLUSIVE GUIDE TO JUDICIAL CLERKING

CHAPTER 1

DECIDING WHETHER TO CLERK

■ ■ ■

A *law clerk* is a member of a judge's personal staff.[1] The practice seems to have originated in the 1870s when Justice Horace Gray of the Massachusetts Supreme Court began hiring graduates of Harvard Law School to assist him with his mounting caseload.[2] When Justice Gray joined the Supreme Court of the United States in 1881, he brought the innovative concept of clerking with him. The idea soon caught on, and just five years later, Congress authorized each justice to hire one "stenographic clerk."[3] In 1919, Congress permitted each justice to hire one "law clerk" as well as one "stenographic clerk."[4]

Today, law clerks serve trial and appellate judges at every level of the federal and state judiciary. Clerks come in several varieties. *Term* (or *elbow*) *clerks*, which are the most common, are hired to serve a judge for a set term, such as one year.[5] Less often, judges hire a *career clerk* who serves in the same capacity as a term clerk but has no set term. Career clerks often serve a dual role as the judge's judicial assistant and as such, manage the business of Chambers, oversee term clerks, and assist the judge in resolving his or her caseload. A *staff attorney* serves the entire court, rather than a single judge, and is usually hired for an indefinite period of time. Staff attorneys sometimes handle diverse matters, but other times, they specialize, perhaps only handling *pro se* matters filed at the court. In special circumstances, a judge may hire a *temporary law clerk* to fill an unexpected, short-term vacancy, such as a clerk's departure due to serious illness. Some Chambers also hire short-term *temporary assistant clerks*; these positions are often unpaid and are limited to recent graduates who have not yet secured permanent employment. They are akin to a post-graduate internship. A *judicial externship* is an unpaid, short-term position in a judge's Chambers for which a student receives academic credit; by contrast, a student does not receive academic credit for an unpaid *judicial internship*. For the most part, the guidance contained in this book is equally applicable to any prospective or current clerk, extern, or intern whether at the state or federal level.

A. TYPICAL ROLE OF A LAW CLERK

Among other things, clerks assist the judge in completing the business of Chambers, whether by producing draft opinions and bench memoranda or by helping the judge prepare for an upcoming hearing. As such, clerks play a vital, albeit largely invisible, role in the functioning of the American judicial system.

Despite the critical importance of law clerks, they still play only a *supporting* role in Chambers, always serving at the pleasure of the judge. Judges decide cases and author opinions, not clerks. Judges are appointed or elected;[6] clerks are not. Clerks typically come and go every one to two years, but a judge may have lifetime tenure. Thus, a clerk's main purpose is to assist his or her judge however and whenever possible.

In this regard, clerks are often the first line of defense for the judges they serve. Trial court clerks assess newly assigned cases, communicate with parties, and manage the docket to ensure an expeditious and just resolution of each case. In addition, both appellate and trial court clerks often act as sounding boards for their judges, discussing complex legal issues in pending cases. It is a clerk's duty to objectively present all sides of an issue to the judge and to perform supplemental research as necessary to answer his or her judge's lingering questions.

Given the unique and important nature of these responsibilities, a clerk often enjoys a special relationship with his or her judge—one based on trust and accountability. Judges confide in their clerks and must know beyond a doubt that clerks will never disclose that information outside Chambers, even after the clerkship concludes. Judges depend on clerks to conduct thorough, thoughtful research and to produce an accurate, objective analysis.

Clerks also provide a fresh perspective on issues, drawing from their experience and expertise. They provide new ideas and innovative solutions, analyze legal issues, and work to ensure that their conduct as well as their work product will bolster their judge's reputation and improve public perception of the judiciary. Most importantly, clerks become a critical part of a Chambers family. They work alone or collaboratively, as necessary, to assist their judges in making the right decision and communicating it in the most effective way.

In return, a clerk receives immeasurable benefits that last a lifetime. As an extension of one's legal education, clerking imparts substantive knowledge, practical skills, and confidence in a relatively short period of time. Most importantly, clerks forge lasting friendships with their judges and fellow clerks, which ultimately foster professional development and personal growth. Perhaps unsurprisingly, in the National Judicial Clerkship Study (2000), 33% of respondents rated their clerkship(s) as a 10, the highest rating possible, while 95% rated it as a 7 or above.[7] Moreover, 97% of respondents stated that they would clerk again should the opportunity arise.[8] Speaking from personal experience, clerking was among the most formative and enriching stages of my career. As a direct result of the skills gained and the incredible mentorship received during my clerkship, I emerged a stronger lawyer and more well rounded human being.

B. DUTIES OF A LAW CLERK

A clerk's responsibilities vary significantly based on both the judge and the type of clerkship. However, broadly speaking, clerks generally possess the following responsibilities: (1) judicial drafting; (2) research and verification; (3) preparation for judicial procedures, such as oral argument, trials, and hearings; (4) editing; (5) case management; and (6) administrative duties. Each of these responsibilities will be discussed in more detail below. Trial court clerks may have additional obligations, such as managing the docket, communicating with the parties, and filing orders.

Judicial Drafting: The most important responsibility of each law clerk is judicial drafting. Law clerks, whether at the trial or appellate level, spend the bulk of their time drafting judicial documents for their judge to review. Then they will expend additional hours incorporating their judge's suggested revisions. A trial court clerk drafts orders,[9] jury instructions, and minute entries as well as lengthier bench memoranda[10] and judicial opinions. Because appellate courts exclusively handle appeals and have no trial functions, appellate clerks spend the vast majority of their time drafting bench memoranda to prepare their judges for upcoming oral arguments. Appellate clerks also provide critical support during and after oral argument and work collaboratively with their judges to draft opinions. As part of that process, clerks usually convert bench memoranda into draft opinions, although the opinion-drafting process varies by Chambers.[11] In addition, both appellate and trial court clerks will occasionally assist in other less traditional drafting projects, such as speeches, journal articles, or book chapters. In everything, however, the clerk merely plays a supporting role; the judge is always the author, and as such, the clerk should strive to draft in the judge's voice to the maximum extent possible. Every draft should reflect the judge's ideals and personal style.

Research and Verification: Another critical clerkship duty is research and verification. Due to the judge's heavy caseload, he or she is usually unable to thoroughly research each and every issue pending before the court. Thus, that task falls to the parties first and to the law clerks second. For example, it is counsel's responsibility to apprise the court of all relevant controlling case law and to present the case law and material facts in a truthful manner. However, the depth, quality, and veracity of briefing vary significantly from one attorney to another. Some briefs are the product of very thorough research; other briefs, particularly those produced by practitioners with less experience or more limited resources, may be less thorough and thoughtful as a result. Whether intentionally or inadvertently, some attorneys may even omit or overlook relevant controlling case law, particularly if a new case has recently been issued. In addition, some attorneys, perhaps in a misplaced attempt to zealously advocate for clients, mischaracterize facts and case law. As a result, clerks use the parties' briefing as a *starting* point for research, but a clerk's research and verification responsibilities do not end there. To the contrary, a clerk must use the Record or Appendix to verify any factual assertions made in the briefing; the clerk must correct any inaccuracies or misrepresentations, providing an objective discussion of the evidence, and also note any factual discrepancies. Likewise, clerks must also track the litigation history of each case cited to ensure that it remains good law. They must read each case to ensure, among other things, that it stands for the proposition asserted, is not factually or legally distinguishable from the case pending before the court, and that the language relied upon is taken from the majority opinion, rather than from dicta or a dissent. For more information on research and verification, see Chapter 16.

Preparation for Judicial Proceedings: Clerks also play a vital role in helping judges prepare for judicial proceedings, such as hearings, trials, or oral argument. After drafting a bench memo and conducting research, the clerk usually meets with the judge to discuss issues raised in the bench memo as well as to address the judge's lingering questions. In trial courts, a judge may ask a clerk to orally brief him or her on a time-sensitive issue because time does not permit the clerk to draft a lengthy bench memo. As such, a clerk must possess strong oral communication skills and be able to clearly and succinctly articulate his or her ideas and reasoning to the judge both orally and in writing. Moreover, trial court clerks may further assist the judge by scheduling or setting up for judicial proceedings and by drafting orders that clarify the scope and purpose of such proceedings.

Editing: Clerks play a significant part in editing their own work and that of others. Thoughtful editing is crucial in part because opinions may be precedential; as such, every word and punctuation mark may have lasting implications. Even a minor typographical error could cause confusion among practitioners and lower courts or diminish public perception of the court's competency. As a result, in many Chambers with multiple clerks, before an opinion issues, the other law clerks must proofread and spade the opinion. In some appellate courts, each Chambers has a certain period of time to review each opinion before it issues.[12] This requires the clerk to peruse the draft opinion with a fine-toothed comb, noting typographical, grammatical, spelling, citation, and stylistic errors. Clerks check the graphical history of each case cited. They note points where the word choice is imprecise, inaccurate, or unclear. Correct any citation errors. They ensure each quote is accurate. Clerks also review each cited source to verify that it supports the proposition for which it is cited. Especially when editing others' work, understand the scope of the review at the outset. Be diplomatic and constructive in offering suggested revisions. Before you commence review, determine the timeline by which you must provide edits so that the drafter has sufficient time to incorporate suggested revisions. For more information on editing, see Chapter 12.

Case Management: Clerks also play a pivotal role in case management. When Chambers receives a new case, the judge or judicial assistant, typically the latter, will assign it to a clerk. Once the clerk receives the case, he or she must take proactive steps to manage it effectively. For trial court clerks, this involves setting up electronic case filing alerts to track developments in the case, creating email and document folders related to the case where case-related documents and correspondence may be stored, and reviewing the case to assess what needs to be done. For instance, if a plaintiff has filed a motion to dismiss, the clerk should review the motion, note the deadlines by which a response must be filed, and commence work as necessary. At appellate courts, when a case is assigned to Chambers and assigned to a clerk, the clerk should follow steps to assess whether the case will be argued or submitted on the briefing alone.[13] Then the clerk should determine whether the case requires a bench memo, warrants dismissal for jurisdictional purposes, etc. If no oral argument will be held in the case and authorship has been assigned to the Chambers, then the clerk should begin preparing a draft opinion. In sum, it is the clerk's responsibility to make sure that no case goes overlooked and that any and all necessary steps are being taken to expeditiously and accurately resolve each matter. For more information on docket and case management, please review Chapter 7.

Administrative Duties: To a lesser extent, clerks will sometimes be responsible for performing courtroom duties and administrative tasks. This varies by court and by Chambers. It also hinges in large part upon the type of clerkship you possess; trial court clerks and career clerks tend to bear more administrative responsibilities than appellate clerks. For example, trial court clerks will often answer the phone, update the calendar, upkeep the Chambers' library, water dispenser, or coffee station, organize records, make the judge's travel plans, mail packages for Chambers, and schedule appointments for the judge. Some clerks even perform purely personal tasks for the judge, such as picking up the judge's dry cleaning or lunch. In all things, the clerk serves at the pleasure of the judge and must be willing to help out whenever and however possible, even with unglamorous, non-law-related duties. This is particularly true in the case of a career clerk who is not hired for a set term. Career clerks often play a dual role as judicial assistant and law clerk, and as such, perform many more administrative and courtroom duties than term clerks.

As a direct result of the function of appellate courts, administrative duties tend to comprise a much smaller part of appellate clerkship responsibilities. For the most part, however, appellate clerks are usually not actively involved in managing the courtroom or handling administrative duties. In such courts, those duties are primarily handled by the Clerk of the Court and/or the judicial assistant.

No matter the type of clerkship, it is important to take measures to ensure that the main Chambers telephone is covered at all times. For example, even if Chambers includes a judicial assistant, clerks may be responsible to take lunch at a different time during the day than the judicial assistant so that the clerks can answer the phone while the judicial assistant is unavailable. In Chambers without a judicial assistant, clerks should take staggered lunches, so that someone is always available to greet individuals in Chambers, answer the telephone, etc. In addition, in some Chambers, clerks are required to stay later than the judicial assistant and handle administrative tasks until the close of Chambers. For example, the judicial assistant may be permitted to leave at 5pm, and clerks may need to handle administrative tasks, such as answering the phone or greeting guests to Chambers, from 5pm until the close of the court's operational hours. Confer with your judge or senior clerk at the outset of the clerkship to determine whether this is required.

In conclusion, there is no "typical day" for a law clerk. Each day presents new and different opportunities for continued growth and development.

C. PROS AND CONS OF CLERKING

Clerking is an incredible opportunity, but it is not for everyone. In deciding whether to clerk, carefully consider the advantages and disadvantages and make a fully informed decision. The chart below summarizes some of the pros and cons of clerking, but it is non-exhaustive. Moreover, the pros and cons particular to a clerkship depend in large part upon the judge and court with whom one clerks. For this reason, some clerkships are far more beneficial and enjoyable than others.

Pros and Cons of Clerking

The non-exhaustive chart below outlines some of the pros and cons of clerking. The value assigned to a pro or con will differ from one person to the next. Notably, the pros and cons are listed in no specific order, and the pro identified in Column One may not directly correlate to the con noted in Column Two.

Pros	Cons	Notes
A clerkship enables you to develop expertise on substantive areas of the law within the court's jurisdiction that you may never have studied during law school or practiced. This, in turn, will make you attractive to prospective employers and help you acquire connections in an area of law. It may also help you determine which area of law you wish to practice once your clerkship concludes.[14]	A clerkship may require you to move to an undesirable location or to be separated from family, friends, or loved ones for one to two years.	Applicants can avoid separation from friends and family by limiting the scope of their clerkship search to locations that offer a preexisting support network. In addition, many clerks who move to new locations quickly acclimate in part due to the collegiality and hospitality of their fellow clerks who provide an instant support network.
Clerking will enhance your understanding of court rules and procedure, including civil procedure, appellate procedure, and evidence. This knowledge is valuable in every practice.	A clerkship does not usually pay as generously as other entry-level attorney positions.	A clerk who has practiced prior to clerking will receive compensation commensurate with that experience. In addition, some courts provide metro subsidies. Clerkship salaries are also quite comfortable for individuals who clerk in areas with a lower cost of living, such as

		a small or mid-sized city, or those who share living expenses with a roommate or significant other. Most importantly, the non-economic benefits of a clerkship far outweigh any disadvantages, and an eventual clerkship bonus may offset any initial salary disparity.
Clerking provides consistent opportunities to study examples of effective and ineffective oral and written advocacy. This, in turn, will help you become a stronger writer and oral advocate.	Clerks receive a tremendous level of responsibility but less oversight and training than they would receive at a law firm.	One of the most common complaints among young practitioners is difficulty in securing substantive responsibility early in their careers. Especially in sizeable practice groups at large and mid-sized law firms, young attorneys receive significant oversight and often spend much of their time conducting document review.
Clerking will significantly improve your oral and written communication skills. After all, not only are you practicing these skills each day, but you are receiving thoughtful feedback from an expert writer—your judge.[15]	A clerk working alone in Chambers for a single judge may find the position lonely and isolating. He or she may miss opportunities for collaboration or find the workload overwhelming.	A clerk with no co-clerks may form bonds and relationships with clerks in other Chambers or, in the alternative, may form an especially close-knit bond with the judge whom he or she serves.

Clerking will strengthen your research ability, which is a fundamental legal skill that any subsequent employer will highly value.	Due to the close familial atmosphere of Chambers, a clerk may not find the position fulfilling if he or she is not a good personality fit with the judge and the other clerks. This is a far greater risk for small environments like Chambers than in larger environments like a law firm or government agency.	Clerks can usually avoid ending up in a Chambers that is not a good fit by thoughtfully researching each judge before clerking, being truthful and honest during the clerkship application process, and immediately withdrawing an application or politely declining an offer to clerk if the clerk did not perceive that Chambers would be a good fit.
Clerking hones your editing skills and ability to give and receive constructive feedback.	A clerk may experience intense pressure since work product not only becomes public record but may also become precedential. Every word counts.	Notably, this burden is tempered somewhat because the judge is the decision-maker, and no opinion bears the law clerk's name. Not all opinions are precedential.
Clerking teaches how to work well under pressure and tight time constraints. This will prove particularly useful for clerks who plan to pursue careers in litigation.	Law clerks may work very long hours, particularly if the judge has a very busy docket. In addition, at trial courts, each day is quite unpredictable. A motion or bid protest may be filed without notice, disrupting the clerk's plans. This can be taxing on the clerk and on his or her personal relationships.	Appellate clerks tend to have a more predictable, steady flow of work. Judges who have senior status usually have less busy dockets.

Clerks become more succinct, efficient, and precise.	A clerk usually receives little or no oversight or micromanagement. Individuals who wish to be told how to complete tasks step-by-step may not be comfortable clerking.	Applicants who prefer more oversight may feel more comfortable clerking after several years of practice or serving in a Chambers with a supervising Career Clerk.
Clerks acquire other important professional and practical skills, such as discernment, resilience, and stress management.	Not all clerkships lead to clerkship bonuses from prospective employers.	
Clerks cultivate meaningful relationships and acquire helpful mentors that last a lifetime.[16]	Some cases and litigants can be emotionally taxing, particularly criminal and family law matters.	An applicant who prefers to avoid emotionally taxing, human-oriented cases can exclusively apply to specialty courts, such as the United States Court of International Trade.
Clerking opens doors. Because of the incredible skills and knowledge clerks acquire, clerks are highly appealing to prospective employers in both the private and public sectors.[17] Thus, clerking enhances your credentials and significantly improves your employability. In fact, many law firms offer former clerks sizeable clerkship bonuses to	As opposed to other legal positions, most clerks receive limited, if any, vacation days given the short nature of the clerkship term.	Plan the start date of your clerkship and start date of any post-clerkship position such that you are able to take a lengthy vacation before the clerkship commences and after it concludes. Most judges will permit law clerks to take additional days off for unforeseen circumstances, such as a death in the family, the birth of a child, a marriage, or

reward them for their clerkship experience. Some firms even permit clerks to enter the firm at a higher associate level that takes the clerkship into account. Many firms value clerking so much that they will even permit individuals to defer joining the firm to clerk or allow current associates to leave the firm for a year to clerk.[18] Government agencies and the Department of Justice also heavily recruit former clerks.[19] Moreover, other positions, such as law school teaching, often require that applicants have completed at least one clerkship.		a serious illness. However, try not to schedule events such as weddings or honeymoons during the clerkship term unless you have disclosed these dates to the judge prior to the clerkship and obtained his or her approval. Accommodate your judge's schedule; do not ask him or her to accommodate yours.
Clerks enjoy varied, meaningful, important, and fulfilling work. The job is challenging, rewarding, and interesting.	As compared to law firm positions, clerkships do not offer "perks," such as paid meals or transportation when working late.	
Clerks have an opportunity to serve the public in a significant way. Your work matters not just to the parties but to the public.	Clerks do not receive year-end bonuses, and sometimes the government is operating under salary freezes that prevent clerks from receiving raises.	

Clerks gain invaluable insight into the decision-making perspective behind the bench. As Professor Debra Strauss observes, "[a] clerkship offers a unique opportunity to glimpse behind the scenes of a courtroom into the practical workings of a judge's chambers. Unless you become a judge yourself someday, you will never again have the chance to gain this perspective on how judges make decisions and how the system of justice operates."[20]	Courts do not cover moving expenses, bar-related expenses, transportation, etc.	
Each clerk enjoys a unique, close relationship with his or her judge. As such, clerks benefit tremendously from the one-on-one mentorship they receive. The judge may later serve as a reference or recommender.	Clerks lack support staff, such as paralegals, to assist them.	Because clerks have little or no support staff, they often handle every aspect of a case and become more self-reliant. Moreover, attorneys in other positions, such as those working for the government or at a non-profit, may also lack support staff, so clerking is good training for subsequent government work.
As a result of the skills acquired during a clerkship, clerks gain confidence,		

maturity, and credibility. They emerge far stronger attorneys and usually more well rounded human beings.		
Clerks often forge lasting bonds with their fellow co-clerks and learn a tremendous amount from their peers.		
Clerks usually enjoy a better work-life balance than law firm associates or government attorneys.		
Clerking cultivates important attributes, such as resilience, which foster subsequent success in any workplace environment.		
For many clerks, the clerkship year is among the most formative experiences of their legal careers.		
Clerking provides a transitional year between law school and entering the practice. In addition, it serves as an apprenticeship of sorts that permits a new attorney to amass a broad array of skills in a relatively short period of time.		

As the non-exhaustive chart above illustrates, the benefits of clerking last a lifetime and far outweigh any disadvantages. Furthermore, clerks can avoid many disadvantages in four primary ways: (1) thoughtfully self-assess whether clerking is right for you *before* you apply; (2) if you do apply, thoroughly research the judge and court to choose the right fit for you;[21] (3) narrow the scope of your applications to positions that will be the best personal and professional fit; and (4) immediately and politely withdraw your application or courteously decline an offer to clerk as soon as you believe that the clerkship is not a good fit. Be mindful, however, that another opportunity to clerk may not arise.

How do you determine whether to clerk?

As noted above, despite the countless benefits of clerking, it is not for everyone. The first step in securing a successful clerkship is determining whether clerking is right for you based on your personality, aptitudes, and interests. In light of that, below is a short self-evaluation that will help you better assess whether you should clerk, and if yes, which *type* of clerkship might be most enjoyable and beneficial for you.

Self-Evaluation: Should I Clerk?

If you answer yes to most of the questions below, then clerking may be a great opportunity for you. As you respond, be honest with yourself. Otherwise, the results of your self-assessment will be meaningless.

Ask yourself . . .	Answer truthfully . . .	Consider this . . .
Do I enjoy writing and wish to strengthen my writing skills?		Clerks spend most of their time writing and editing, often for hours at a time in isolation.
Do I enjoy research and wish to improve my research skills?		Clerks spend a significant amount of time researching and verifying case-related information. They must be thorough and patient, conducting exhaustive searches to make sure that the judge has all relevant information necessary to make a well reasoned decision that will withstand an appeal.

Am I a strong editor who hopes to refine my editing skills?		Clerks spend a sizeable amount of time editing their own work and that of others.
Do I work equally well alone or with others?		Clerks often write alone but collaborate with others in various ways. Thus, clerks must be team players with strong interpersonal skills.
Am I comfortable working with little or no oversight?		Clerks handle cases from beginning to end with little or no micromanagement.
Do I take initiative? Am I self-motivated?		The general lack of micromanagement in Chambers means that clerks must take initiative, drafting a decision even before the judge asks them to do so.
Does the prestige of a clerkship matter more than the type of work I will be doing?		Appellate clerkships are generally viewed as more prestigious than trial court clerkships. Likewise, federal clerkships are usually viewed as more desirable than state court clerkships. Both clerkships provide countless opportunities for knowledge acquisition and skill refinement. *Tip:* Rather than worrying about perceived prestige, choose the clerkship

		that is the best fit for you.
Am I effective at managing my time and stress?		Clerks have busy dockets, and unexpected filings can occur at any time in trial courts. Thus, clerks must be able to effectively manage their time and stress levels without becoming overwhelmed or irritable.
Do I prefer to serve a single judge or work for the entire court?		Generally, clerks serve a single judge. However, staff attorneys work for the entire court, instead of a single judge. At the Office of Special Masters, a clerk may serve multiple special masters.
Do I orally communicate ideas in a clear and articulate manner and wish to further hone my oral communication skills?		Clerks must often communicate their research and analysis orally to the judge or to fellow clerks.
Do I plan to practice litigation in the future?		While many skills acquired or strengthened during a clerkship are transferable to any practice area, clerking is probably most valuable for individuals who plan to litigate. *Tip:* Although any kind of clerkship will

		help you develop skills critical to litigation, trial court clerkships offer greater insight into every aspect of the litigation process, including discovery, the motion practice, and trials. Appellate clerks only see oral argument and focus almost exclusively on high-level review of complex legal issues.
Do I handle constructive criticism well?		When a clerk provides a draft to his or her judge or co-clerk, he or she will likely receive significant feedback. The clerk must be resilient and mature enough not to take this constructive criticism personally, no matter how it is delivered. In the end, the judge is the author of the document, not the clerk. There is simply no room for ego in a functional Chambers family.
Do I keep confidences with little or no difficulty? Am I trustworthy?		A clerk is privy to much confidential information, including the judge's decision-making process. The judge must be able to share his or her thoughts openly with his or her law clerks without

		fear that they will disclose that information, even after the clerkship concludes. Some individuals find it quite difficult to keep confidences from friends, family, or significant others. Such individuals may not be suitable for clerking.
Am I introverted or extroverted?		Given the long hours of quiet writing and research, introverts may enjoy clerkships more than extroverts, particularly in Chambers that have only one clerk or that do not entail communicating with the parties. *Tip:* Extroverted individuals should apply to Chambers who hire multiple clerks or courts where all Chambers reside in the same location, such as the United States Court of Federal Claims.
Do I seek significant levels of courtroom exposure in my clerkship?		Trial court clerks usually enjoy tremendous courtroom exposure, while appellate clerks are only exposed to oral argument.
Do I prefer long periods of time to write and edit, or do I		Trial court clerks tend to have shorter periods of time to

write well under tight time constraints?		draft judicial documents, such as orders and sometimes even opinions. Appellate clerks have relatively short periods of time to draft bench memoranda but longer amounts of time to draft judicial opinions.
Do I view law as a scholarly endeavor and enjoy thinking deeply about novel issues?		Appellate clerkships permit more time for in-depth thinking and contemplation of legal issues. Many clerks describe appellate clerkships as more "academic" than trial court clerkships. Perhaps for this reason, some law schools will not hire teaching faculty who have not completed a clerkship unless the faculty will teach non-litigation courses.
Do I enjoy a fast or slow pace during the day? On a given day, would I prefer to handle a diverse array of small matters or devote the entire day to deeply exploring a single issue?		Trial court clerks usually experience a more fast-paced day and a less predictable flow of work than their appellate counterparts. Trial court clerks often juggle many small and varied responsibilities throughout the day, while an appellate clerk might spend the entire day

		researching a single issue.
Would I enjoy interacting with attorneys?		Trial court clerks typically enjoy greater interaction with counsel.[22] Appellate clerks have little or no interaction with attorneys.
Would I enjoy traveling regularly for work?		Most federal circuit court judges travel once per month to hear cases for an entire week. For example, judges on the United States Court of Appeals for the Fourth Circuit travel to Richmond, Virginia, one week each month. Clerks usually travel with the judge. Other courts, such as the United States Court of Appeals for the Federal Circuit, hear cases in Washington, D.C., the same place where the court resides. *Tip:* Trial court clerks typically do not travel for work, but exceptions exist. For instance, the United States Court of Federal Claims enjoys nationwide jurisdiction. Although the court is located in Washington, D.C., judges on the court sometimes travel

		across America to hear cases in locations more convenient to the parties.
Is one of my primary goals in clerking to learn more about the litigation process, particularly discovery and evidentiary issues?		Trial court clerks gain exposure to every aspect of litigation, including discovery and evidentiary issues. By contrast, appellate clerks only see oral argument and are not involved in issues related to legal fact-finding, discovery disputes, etc.
Do I enjoy discussing complex legal issues with others, including those who have opposing points of view? Am I diplomatic?		Clerks spend a significant amount of time thinking about and discussing legal issues. They must be able to see issues from all angles, even anticipating opposing points of view. They must be able to diplomatically discuss these issues with those who see things differently, including their judges.
Am I interested in pursuing a specialized area of practice after my clerkship?		Most trial courts and appellate courts possess general jurisdiction. They hear criminal and civil cases on a diverse array of topics. As such, a law clerk in such a court would become a veritable jack-of-all-

		trades, knowing a little about many different legal issues. However, some specialty courts, such as the Court of International Trade, offer clerks an opportunity to become subject matter experts in a narrow area of law.
Am I efficient?		Given the hectic nature of the court docket, efficiency is essential to effective clerking. There is no room for procrastination in Chambers. Chambers is only as efficient as its least efficient member, and all members must work to expedite matters before the Court.
Do I enjoy thinking on my feet and working under pressure?		Clerks, particularly at the trial level, will often be required to work under pressure and tight time constraints, as when the judge needs an immediate answer to a legal question raised during a hearing or trial. *Tip:* If you dislike working under pressure, an appellate clerkship may be more enjoyable for you. There are little

		or no unexpected emergency filings.
Am I flexible? Am I willing to sacrifice my time to accommodate the needs and schedules of others?		An effective law clerk is able to accommodate the varying needs of Chambers.
Am I a quick learner who can easily teach myself difficult concepts?		Clerks often encounter novel issues and must be able to quickly master an entirely new area of law.
Do I have a strong work ethic? Am I dependable?		As a member of a judge's personal staff, a clerk serves at the pleasure of the judge. A clerk usually arrives before the judge and stays until he or she leaves, if not later. In sum, clerks work very, very hard and must occasionally be available on evenings and weekends. They also enjoy limited, if any, vacation time.
Am I a team player?		Clerks usually function as part of a tight-knit family unit.
Do I require recognition or affirmation to find my work satisfying?		Clerks receive no acknowledgement for work product to which they have contributed. A clerk's name will never appear on an issued opinion. A clerk likely will not be able to share the names of

		cases upon which he or she worked absent the judge's permission. Nor may a clerk use an issued opinion as a writing sample absent the judge's permission; as will be discussed in a later chapter, such permission would rarely be granted.
Will I feel comfortable drafting a document that espouses a viewpoint with which I disagree?		Judges *decide* cases and *author* opinions. Clerks merely play a supporting role. On occasion, your judge may disagree with your recommendation. You must still be able to serve the judge effectively and craft the strongest draft opinion possible; after all, it is the judge's opinion, not yours.
Am I organized?		Clerks must possess strong organizational skills to manage a busy docket without letting any case or correspondence slip through the cracks. *Tip:* Trial court clerkships usually require even stronger organizational skills than appellate clerkships given the unpredictable nature of the docket and additional administrative duties.

Do I enjoy working for long periods in solitude?		If you prefer to work alone for long periods, you may find an appellate clerkship more appealing.
Am I interested in learning more about judicial decision-making?		Clerks gain tremendous perspective from behind the bench.
Do I spot issues quickly and effectively?		Clerks must be adept at spotting issues, such as lack of jurisdiction, that parties may have missed. This is especially true when handling *pro se* filings, which are discussed in Chapter 18.
Am I a strong analyst who hopes to improve my analytical skills?		Clerks must provide their judges with a thoughtful, clear analysis of each issue pending before the court.

In summary, the decision to clerk is a personal one. For the right candidate, clerking will be one of, if not the most, rewarding professional experiences of your life. A clerkship will enhance your practical skills, foster professionalism, and cultivate meaningful relationships. Trial court clerkships offer more insight into the litigation process, a faster pace, and more varied work under high-pressure circumstances and tighter time constraints. Appellate clerkships provide a more academic, isolated environment and a more predictable workflow that permits clerks to explore novel issues more deeply. Clerking at a specialty court will enable you to develop subject matter expertise, while courts of general jurisdiction expose clerks to diverse areas of law. Finally, due to the unparalleled benefits inherent in clerking, clerkships are highly valued by prospective employers and as such, open doors to highly coveted positions in the public and private sectors as well as in Academia.

D. SUPPLEMENTAL RESOURCES

1. REBECCA COCHRAN, JUDICIAL EXTERNSHIPS: THE CLINIC INSIDE THE COURTHOUSE (4th ed. 2016).

2. David Crump, *How Judges Use Their Law Clerks*, N.Y. ST. B.J. 43 (May 1986).

3. MARY L. DUNNEWOLD, BETH A. HONETSCHLAGER, & BRENDA L. TOFTE, JUDICIAL CLERKSHIPS: A PRACTICAL GUIDE (2010).

4. J. Daniel Mahoney, *Law Clerks: For Better or Worse?*, 54 BROOK. L. REV. 321 (1988).

5. Todd C. Peppers, Micheal W. Giles, & Bridget Tainer-Perkins, *Inside Judicial Chambers: How Federal District Court Judges Select and Use Their Law Clerks*, 71 ALB. L. REV. 623 (2008).

6. DEBRA M. STRAUSS, BEHIND THE BENCH: THE GUIDE TO JUDICIAL CLERKSHIPS (2002).

Notes

---

[1] For purposes of this book, a "law clerk," "clerk," and "judicial clerk" refer to the same general position and will be used interchangeably. In most Chambers, the position is referred to as a law clerk.

[2] Most of the new hires were former students of Justice Gray's half-brother, John Chipman Gray, who taught at Harvard Law School for many years. TODD C. PEPPERS, COURTIERS OF THE MARBLE PALACE: THE RISE AND INFLUENCE OF THE SUPREME COURT LAW CLERK 44–45 (2006). In 1873, Justice Gray hired Louis D. Brandeis to assist him. Justice Brandeis later served as an Associate Justice of the U.S. Supreme Court from 1916 to 1939. *Federal Judicial Center: Louis Brandeis* 2009–12–12. For more information on the history of clerking, see J. Daniel Mahoney, *Foreword Law Clerks: For Better or Worse?*, 54 BROOK. L. REV. 321 (1988).

[3] MARY L. DUNNEWOLD, BETH A. HONETSCHLAGER, & BRENDA L. TOFTE, JUDICIAL CLERKSHIPS: A PRACTICAL GUIDE 20 (2010).

[4] *Id.*

[5] Term clerks are alternatively known as "elbow clerks." *Id.* at 9.

[6] Some state and local judges are elected. Federal judges are not elected as discussed in Chapter Two.

[7] *Courting Clerkships: The NALP Judicial Clerkship Study,* NAT'L ASS'N FOR LAW PLACEMENT (Oct. 2000), http://www.nalp.org/clrktb46_66#63.

[8] *Id.*

[9] An *order* is a ruling on a motion. Orders can be oral or in writing, although the latter are more common. Orders are discussed in more detail in Chapter 14.

[10] A *bench memorandum* is a memo that summarizes briefing on a motion or appeal and recommends a disposition. Bench memos are discussed in more detail in Chapter 16.

[11] Opinion drafting is discussed in Chapter 17.

[12] This process is discussed in more detail in Chapter 15.

[13] More detailed instructions regarding how to assess a case are contained in Chapter 16.

[14] DEBRA M. STRAUSS, BEHIND THE BENCH: THE GUIDE TO JUDICIAL CLERKSHIPS 11 (2002) (quoting former Second Circuit and U.S. Supreme Court clerk John Elwood who stated, "[c]lerking

has made me a better lawyer, by broadening the areas of law to which I have been exposed and providing me the opportunity to work closely with experienced judges and bright young lawyers . . . Clerking permitted me to see litigation in many different fields of the law, which helped me decide which area I wanted to work in . . . I think it's much easier to decide what interests you while clerking.").

15   In NALP's National Judicial Clerkship Study (2000), respondents "reported that the skills most significantly enhanced [through their clerkships] were writing/drafting opinions, or memoranda and knowledge of court procedure, and other skills such as self-confidence, communication and supervisory skills, diplomacy, and a sense of social responsibility. Also listed by the majority as significantly or moderately enhanced were general knowledge/experience, general legal ability/judgment, legal reasoning and analysis, and knowledge of case law/statutes." *Id.* at 14–15. 96% of respondents stated that the "skills gained in their clerkships met or exceeded their initial expectations." *Id.* at 15.

16   In the National Judicial Clerkship Study (2000), respondents reported "a positive development of relationships and contacts, particularly with their judge and with the other law clerks and administrative staff in their own judge's chambers." *Id.*

17   Nearly half of the respondents in the National Judicial Clerkship Study (2000) stated that "their clerkship helped a great deal in obtaining their post-clerkship position." *Id.* According to one individual, "the same firms who had turned their noses up at me after my first year were pursuing me—the only real difference on my resume was the clerkship." *Id.* at 16.

18   *Id.* at 10 (quoting James Prendergast of Hale & Dorr who remarked, "[t]he fact that you have judicial clerks in your roster often is an enhancement to the prestige of the law firm. At our firm in the past couple of years, between 15 and 25% of our incoming . . . class have been or are going to be judicial law clerks. . . . [M]ost firms look[ ] to recruit judicial clerks.")

19   *Id.* at 8 (noting that one-third of the new hires in the Department of Justice Honors Program are former federal law clerks).

20   *Id.* at 7.

21   For more information on helpful tools to research judges, please see Chapter 2.

22   A trial court clerk "generally acts as a liaison between the judge and the attorneys or litigants." *Id.* at 6.

CHAPTER 2

AN OVERVIEW OF THE AMERICAN JUDICIARY

■ ■ ■

Sources of American law include statutes, regulations, precedent, and the United States Constitution. Among these, the U.S. Constitution is indisputably the most important. Indeed, the Constitution's Supremacy Clause declares it to be the supreme law of the land. No statute or judicial ruling may contravene it. Judges and public officers swear to uphold it. It is the glue that holds together our government, our legal system, and arguably even our society. But where did it come from, and what does it say?

To learn more about the origins of the Constitution, we must understand the extraordinary historical context in which it was drafted as well as the collective experiences of its drafters—men who have come to be known as the Framers of the Constitution and Founding Fathers of America. These men included George Washington, Commander-in-Chief of the Continental Army and America's first President; Thomas Jefferson, author of the Declaration of Independence and third President of the United States; and James Madison, the so-called "Father of the Constitution" as well as the fourth U.S. President. Indeed, as Madison once warned, "Do not separate text from historical background. If you do, you will have perverted and subverted the Constitution, which can only end in a distorted, bastardized form of illegitimate government."[1] Perhaps for this reason, Americans cannot understand who we are or where we are going until we fully understand where we have been and how far we have come. With that in mind, this chapter will first briefly discuss the historical events that shaped the development and design of America's sources and systems of law and then explore the general structure of our judicial system.

Much of the land mass now known as the United States began as nothing more than a British colony. Popularized as "The New World," many disenchanted British citizens flocked to its shores seeking land, gold, and adventure. Despite these lofty expectations, the first settlers instead often encountered hostility and violence from the Native Americans on whose lands the settlers had encroached. Most settlers were also woefully unprepared for the sacrifice and hard labor necessary to survive and faced famine, harsh weather, and disease. For instance, inhabitants of

Jamestown, Virginia, endured a dark period that has come to be known as *The Starving Time*, eating whatever they could to survive.[2] The colonists who survived were also constantly in conflict with the Powhatan Indians sharing the area. Finally, John Rolfe introduced tobacco to Virginian colonists and made peace with the Powhatan in part by marrying the Chief's daughter, Pocahontas. Her later visit to England transformed attitudes toward the New World.

Other settlers, like the Pilgrims, simply sought freedom from religious persecution. The Pilgrims were a group of Protestants who wanted to separate from the Church of England. Like the Jamestown settlers under Rolfe's guidance, the Pilgrims made peace with the local Wampanoag tribe, and that peaceful collaboration proved essential to their survival. In 1621, only a year after landing, the Pilgrims in Plymouth, Massachusetts, gathered with the Wampanoag for an autumn harvest celebration and three-day meal that has come to be known as the first Thanksgiving.

In the decades that followed, more settlers flooded America, and 13 colonies emerged: Delaware, Pennsylvania, New Jersey, Georgia, Connecticut, Massachusetts, Maryland, South Carolina, New Hampshire, Virginia, New York, North Carolina, and Rhode Island. Virginia also included the wild and wonderful landscape now known as West Virginia.

For the first time, men and women were born in the colonies, and some felt little or no connection to their sovereign across the sea. This feeling of disconnectedness and isolation intensified the colonists' outrage that they paid taxes to the British government but had no right to send colonial representatives to the British Parliament—taxation without representation. They were being governed by individuals who lived an ocean away most of whom had never even visited the colonies—parliamentarians largely unaware of and insensitive to the struggles of daily life in colonial America.

Not surprisingly, protests and dissention swept through the colonies, occasionally erupting in violence. For example, during The Boston Massacre, British soldiers shot several colonists, including African American Crispus Attucks who is oft-called the first casualty of the American Revolution. Yet the most famous protest was likely the Boston Tea Party on December 16, 1773, when the Sons of Liberty destroyed several hundred chests of tea from the British East India Company in defiance of a Tea Act, which granted the East India Company a monopoly on tea sales in the colonies.

The Boston Tea Party and similar activism eventually spurred disillusioned colonists to convene the First Continental Congress in 1774. Fifty-six delegates from 12 of the 13 colonies attended; Georgia sent no representatives.[3] The delegates debated the most effective ways to respond to the *Intolerable Acts*, objectionable legislation Britain had recently imposed. Ironically, the representatives' collective outrage over the acts both unified and mobilized them. As Virginian delegate, Patrick Henry, observed: "The distinctions between Virginians, Pennsylvanians, New Yorkers, and New Englanders are no more. I am not a Virginian but an American."[4]

The delegates initially sought a peaceful resolution. They petitioned King George III to redress their grievances, but in response, he sent troops to America. On April 19, 1775, the first shots of the American Revolution, also known as the American War of Independence, were fired. The Revolution had begun.

The delegates ultimately convened the Second Continental Congress in Philadelphia. On July 4, 1776, they adopted the Declaration of Independence, which reads in pertinent part:

> We hold these truths to be self-evident, that all men are created equal, that they are endowed by their Creator with certain unalienable Rights, that among these are Life, Liberty and the pursuit of Happiness. . . . [W]henever any Form of Government becomes destructive of these ends, it is the Right of the People to alter and to abolish it. . .

Although their actions constituted high treason punishable by death, their courage altered the course of history. America was born.

Unfortunately, words do not win wars; people do. And the Revolution did not end quickly. It waged on for eight long years from 1775 until 1783. But from this war emerged many of our nation's greatest heroes, including a talented general, George Washington, who would eventually become our first president and for whom our nation's capital is named.

Even before the war's dramatic conclusion, the former colonies—now states still in their infancy—acknowledged the need for a unifying system of government. Thus, in 1781, the states ratified the *Articles of Confederation*, a faulty precursor to the Constitution.[5] Still fighting to secure freedom from British tyranny, the states designed a system of government that permitted them to act as separate sovereigns, yet that excessive state sovereignty is exactly why the Articles ultimately failed. For example, under the Articles, Connecticut and New Jersey were conspiring to attack New York because New York taxed goods that went in and out of the state.[6] The final straw was Shays' Rebellion when a Revolutionary war veteran, Daniel Shays, led thousands of angry Massachusetts farmers, still reeling from bad harvests, in a military revolt against state and local enforcement of tax collection, foreclosures, and evictions.[7]

After the Revolutionary War, the fledgling federal government owed millions but had no way of raising those funds since the Articles only permitted states to tax their citizens.[8] Nor was there a central executive branch from which Massachusetts could seek immediate assistance in quashing the revolt. These and other issues made the need for a stronger national government readily apparent.

In response, state delegates convened the Constitutional Convention in Philadelphia in 1787. Although the Convention's original purpose was merely to revise the Articles of Confederation, the delegates soon decided to instead start from scratch. George Washington, now a celebrated war hero, presided over the Convention.[9] In the days and weeks that followed, James Madison and his fellow Framers debated, discussed, and finally drafted the United States Constitution. Its Preamble announces:

> We the People of the United States, in Order to form a more perfect Union, establish Justice, insure domestic Tranquility, provide for the common defense, promote the general Welfare, and secure the Blessings of Liberty to ourselves and our Posterity, do ordain and establish this Constitution for the United States of America.

These are the noble goals of the Constitution: solidarity, justice, tranquility, national security, promoting the public welfare, and ensuring liberty and freedom for all Americans. Liberty is the heart of America; everything we stand for and everything we fight for aims to promote it.

Still today, the Constitution remains the supreme law of the land. It contains six articles and, to date, 27 amendments, including the first 10 amendments that comprise the *Bill of Rights*.[10] Notably, the U.S. Constitution is the oldest extant constitution in the world.[11] Though our national identity has evolved through the centuries, our Constitution has endured largely unaltered, demonstrating the foresight of its visionary drafters.

A. THE STRUCTURE OF
THE U.S. CONSTITUTION

Art. I: Legislative
Art. II: Executive
Art. III: Judicial
Art. IV: Miscellaneous & States' Relationships
Art. V: Amendment Process
Art: VI: Miscellaneous & Supremacy Clause
Bill of Rights (10 Amendments)
Other Amendments (17)

Sir John Dalberg-Acton once quipped, "absolute power corrupts absolutely."[12] In carefully crafting the Constitution, this is exactly what the Framers feared. The Father of the Constitution, James Madison, opined, "all men having power ought to be distrusted"[13] and "the people are the only legitimate fountain of power."[14] Taken together, these beliefs led the Framers to devise a novel system of governmental checks and balances, which vested the people with more power than any other form of government then in existence. Given the hardship Americans had endured to secure freedom from British sovereignty, the last thing they wanted to do was trade one form of tyranny for another, vesting too much power in the hands of a single person or entity. Accordingly, the Constitution establishes three, independent branches of government each with the authority to check the power of the other branches to ensure that no single branch grows too strong.

B. THE THREE BRANCHES
OF THE U.S. GOVERNMENT

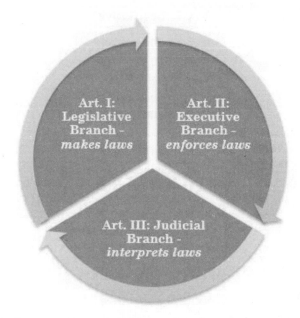

Article I—the first and longest article—establishes the Legislative Branch, which is comprised of the Senate and House of Representatives (collectively "Congress"). Congress is primarily tasked with drafting, enacting, amending, and repealing federal statutes. The Framers envisioned this body of elected lawmakers as constituting the strongest branch of government because it was the branch most directly derived from and representative of the American people. Article One has ten sections that enumerate the Legislative Branch's various powers and responsibilities.

Article II, which has only four sections, creates the Executive Branch. The Executive Branch, primarily comprised of the President, enforces laws, but in special circumstances, it can also issue executive orders that apply with the force of law to government agencies. Notably, the President can issue such an order without Congressional approval, but executive orders are still subject to judicial review.[15]

Article III establishes the Judicial Branch. Specifically, Section One states that the "judicial power of the United States, shall be vested in one Supreme Court, and such inferior courts as the Congress may from time to time ordain and establish."[16] The judiciary's original purpose was primarily to address disputes between the states and legal issues involving foreign treaties. The Framers likely thought it was the weakest branch, but over time the judiciary would grow both in strength and reputation. Article I gave Congress the authority to enact statutes that, among other things, would establish lower federal courts as necessary. Accordingly, in 1789, Congress enacted the Judiciary Act of 1789, which clarified the composition and procedures of the Supreme Court of the United States and also formally established the federal circuit and district courts.[17] President George Washington appointed John Jay to serve as America's first Chief Justice of the Supreme Court.[18] Jay and his five associate justices enjoyed lifetime tenures likely to better preserve their decision-making autonomy.[19]

The Judicial Branch may have remained the weakest branch if not for the appointment of Chief Justice John Marshall to the U.S. Supreme Court in 1801.[20] Two years later, the Marshall Court decided *Marbury v. Madison*,[21] which articulated the doctrine of *judicial review*. Judicial review permits the federal judiciary to invalidate federal statutes and actions of the Executive Branch if they are unconstitutional. Although the Constitution nowhere expressly grants this authority to the judiciary, as a result of *Marbury*, judicial review has become a foundational tenet of the American legal system perhaps because it better enables the judiciary to check the power of the Executive and Legislative Branches. Notably, the Judicial Branch used this power sparingly at first but has increased its use in recent years.[22] As a result, some critics of these invalidations have accused federal judges of *judicial activism* or *legislating from the bench*, which critics believe is beyond the scope of the judiciary's intended role.

In addition to statutory interpretation and invalidation, the Judicial Branch also produces *common law*—precedential judicial opinions announcing legal principles that resolve issues for which no statute, regulation, or codified rule exists. Under the principle of *stare decisis*, precedential, on-point decisions from a higher court are controlling on lower courts within the same jurisdiction. Stare decisis effectively gives these decisions the force of law unless and until the relevant law-making body, such as Congress, enacts a statute superseding or codifying the common law rule or a higher court overrules it.

As noted above, the Framers established three branches of government to guard against tyranny. As Madison cautioned, "[t]he accumulation of all powers, legislative, executive, and judiciary, in the same hands, whether of one, a few, or many, and whether hereditary, self-appointed, or elective, may justly be pronounced the very definition of tyranny."[23] Thus, the Constitution created a government where power is allocated throughout independent institutions, rather than concentrated in a single person or entity. This allocation aims to better ensure a balance of power.

As key figures in the Judicial Branch, federal judges play a critical role in the American legal system. As a result, they undergo a rigorous selection process. With regard to Article III judges,[24] when a vacancy occurs, the President selects a nominee.[25] For district court vacancies, the President may confer with *home-state senators*—those from the state in which the judge will serve.[26] Next, the candidate is thoroughly vetted and, required to complete a detailed Senate Judiciary Questionnaire among other things.[27] In addition, the American Bar Association's Standing Committee on the Federal Judiciary will rate the candidate as "well qualified," "qualified," or "not qualified." This process can last anywhere from months to years. Once the President finalizes his or her nomination, the Senate Judiciary Committee holds a hearing where senators hear witness testimony about the nominee and question him or her.[28] Then the Committee votes. If a nominee receives a majority vote, the nomination is forwarded to the Senate floor for consideration, and the Senate Majority Leader schedules a full vote in the Senate.[29]

With regard to state judges, the selection method differs. In some states, judges are elected and serve limited terms. In other states, an appointing authority, such as the governor or the state legislature, appoints a new judge. As with the federal judiciary, state judicial candidates possess significant relevant legal experience and exemplify high moral character.[30]

C. JUDICIAL PHILOSOPHY

Judicial philosophy is the way that a judge approaches and thus, interprets the law. Countless scholars have explored whether and to what extent, if any, a judge's personal experience and belief system impact his or her judicial decision-making.[31] For example, a judge's political leanings may correlate with his or her voting patterns, particularly on social issues. By way of illustration, the late Justice Antonin Scalia, a vocal conservative, believed that the text of the Constitution should be interpreted strictly; in other words, if the Constitution does not clearly and explicitly vest Congress with a specific power or protect a particular right, then the exercise of that power or protection of that right is up to the states.[32] In stark contrast, Justice Scalia's friend and colleague, Justice Ruth Bader Ginsburg, often took the opposite approach, particularly on social issues. Both in practice and on the bench, she pushed the Supreme Court to interpret the Constitution more expansively.[33] By comparison, The Honorable Jimmie V. Reyna of the U.S. Court of Appeals for the Federal Circuit has been described as "a faith-driven moderate whose story of excellence and overcoming obstacles both inspires and informs his experience as a sitting court judge. His 180 written opinions evidence an unparalleled work ethic and provide a clear insight into his . . . singular ideology: devotion to justice."[34] The same article observed: "At the heart of

Judge Reyna's judicial philosophy is his unwavering sensitivity to 'The Forgotten Man'—the person at the heart of each case and the countless lives each decision will impact."[35]

Although a full discussion of competing judicial philosophies exceeds the scope of this chapter, the examples above illustrate the importance of recognizing that judges do not approach judging in the same way. Instead, each judge possesses a distinct judicial philosophy that the judge leaves like a fingerprint on each opinion he or she issues. At the outset of your clerkship, if not before you apply, research your judge's biographical information and read his or her opinions to discern that philosophy. Most importantly, sit down with your judge at the outset of your clerkship to discuss his or her approach to decision-making so that your work product adequately reflects it.

D. JUDICIAL DIVERSITY

The judiciary has historically been comprised of affluent, white men, but that has changed dramatically through the years. Yet diversity, both on and behind the bench, remains an issue of paramount importance.

U.S. Supreme Court: Perhaps nowhere is this evolution more easily discernable than in the U.S. Supreme Court. From 1789 to 1981, every Supreme Court Justice was male.[36] Justice Sandra Day O'Connor was the first female Supreme Court justice followed in 1993 by Justice Ruth Bader Ginsburg, a long-time advocate for equal rights. In 2009, the Senate confirmed President Barack Obama's Supreme Court nominees—Elena Kagan and Sonia Sotomayor. Although there has never been a female Chief Justice, the fact that three women are members of the current Supreme Court is extraordinary given that in 1873, a majority of the court on which they now sit upheld Illinois' decision to prohibit women from admission to the bar solely due to sex.[37]

With regard to the racial and ethnic diversity of the Supreme Court, Justice Thurgood Marshall was the first African American Supreme Court Justice,[38] and he served on the Court from 1967 through 1991 when another African American, Justice Clarence Thomas, replaced him.[39] Ironically, a law school had rejected Justice Marshall because of his race, but he went on to become one of the nation's foremost civil rights attorneys.[40] Most notably, in *Brown v. Board of Education of Topeka* (1954), Marshall successfully urged the Supreme Court to overturn the separate-but-equal doctrine.[41] In 1967, President Lyndon Baines Johnson appointed Justice Marshall to the Supreme Court where he continued to advocate for civil rights.[42] Likewise, in 2009, Justice Sonia Sotomayor became the first Latina Justice to join the Court.[43]

Although it is easy to focus the lens of diversity exclusively on race and sex, doing so is overly simplistic since diversity encompasses far more. In this regard, the justices exhibit many other kinds of diversity as well. For instance, they represent a wealth of ethnic and ancestral backgrounds, including Irish, Puerto Rican, Russian, Czech, and German heritages. As of the summer of 2016, they ranged in age from 56 (Justice Kagan) to 83 (Justice Ginsburg). With regard to marital and parental status, most have children, but Justice Sotomayor and Justice Kagan do not. Nor has Justice Kagan ever married. Turning to prior work experience,[44] the justices had worked in private practice, served as judges, worked as law professors, and/or even served as senators or members of the U.S. Cabinet. [45] These distinct personal and professional experiences may significantly impact and inform their decision-making.

In other ways, however, the Supreme Court has remained unchanged. For example, as of February 2017, six of the current justices are white, and five are male. Nearly every member graduated from Harvard or Yale; Justice Ginsburg is an exception only because she transferred from Harvard to Columbia for personal reasons. Finally, as of September 2016, every justice self-identifies as Catholic or Jewish.

Federal Circuit Courts: At the federal circuit courts, a similar pattern emerges with one distinction. The vast majority of federal appellate judges are still white males, but most are Protestant and as of 2012, less than a third possessed Ivy League educations.[46] A sizeable minority enjoyed prior experience as a district court judge and/or in private practice before joining the bench.[47] They bring a wealth of varied experience to the bench, ranging from public service and private practice to law teaching and prior state or federal judgeships.[48]

Federal District Court Judges: Like their federal appellate counterparts, most federal district court judges are male, white, heterosexual, and over 40 when appointed.[49] Like their appellate counterparts, federal district court judges possess prior experience in public interest work, criminal law, private practice, etc. Many attended Ivy League schools or other private universities.[50]

State Judiciary: The majority of state court judges are white, male, heterosexual, and were appointed when over 40.[51] In fact, as of 2015, 18 state supreme courts were *all* white and two were *exclusively* male.[52] As of 2016, six state supreme courts included only one woman.[53] State court judges possess experience in the practice and on the bench.[54] Interestingly, "[a]bout three-fourths of all state jurists were born in the state in which they serve, and less than a third went out of state for their undergraduate degrees or for their law degrees. . . . [O]f those serving on the state supreme court bench, only 13 percent have any prior federal experience, whereas 93 percent have some type of prior state experience."[55]

E. DIVERSITY BEHIND THE BENCH

In some ways, diversity *behind* the bench can be as important as diversity *on* the bench. Perhaps for this reason, some judges intentionally select law clerks who will bring diverse perspectives to their Chambers and more fully inform the judge's decision-making. For instance, a male judge may insist on hiring at least one female clerk to have the benefit of her perspective, while a politically conservative judge may deliberately hire at least one moderate or liberal-leaning clerk to act as a sounding board in decision-making.

A National Judicial Clerkship Study released in February 2000 revealed that "15 percent of all judicial clerkships were held by minorities, despite the fact that minorities made up 30 percent of the general population and 20 percent of law students."[56] In 2009, 14% of federal judicial clerks and 18% of state court clerks self-identified as persons of color.[57] In 2012, the Administrative Office of the U.S. Courts shared statistics, demonstrating that the number of white federal appellate clerks had dropped from 81.8% to 78.9% between 2009 and 2010, African American clerks remained at 2.4%, Hispanic clerks rose from 1.5% to 2%, and Asian-American clerks dropped from 6.7% to 6.2%.[58] With regard to federal district court clerks, between 2009 and 2010, the number of white clerks decreased from 86% to 84.1%, African American clerks rose from 3.1% to 3.2%, Hispanic clerks remained steady at 3.3%, and Asian-American clerks inched from 4.5% to 4.6%.[59] "From 2009 to 2010, the number of males working as appellate court law clerks dropped from 57 to 55 percent."[60] "At the district level, the numbers of both men and women held steady, with males staying at 38.9% and women at 61.1%."[61]

Notably, these reports fail to reflect whether any clerks identified as Native American or Pacific Islander. Nor does the report examine whether clerks possess other equally important aspects of diversity that are often overlooked, such as distinct political or religious affiliations, differing socioeconomic, educational, ethnic, geographic, and work backgrounds, parental or marital status, disability, sexual orientation, age, etc. These aspects of diversity, albeit sometimes less visible, are equally important at enhancing diversity behind the bench. In sum, diversity comes in all shapes and sizes with both visible and less visible forms providing countless benefits to judicial decision-making.

Notably, the degree of diversity appears to vary by court. For instance, 80.7% of Ninth Circuit clerks in a 1999 study self-identified as white as compared to 92.2% of First Circuit clerks.[62] Likewise, a 1998 study of U.S. Supreme Court clerks found:

> [F]ewer than 2% of the 394 clerks . . . were African American, and even fewer were Hispanic. About 5% were Asian. Women . . . still amount to only one-fourth of the total. . . . Even though more than

40% of law school graduates now are women and nearly 20% are minorities, they largely have been bypassed for the most prestigious work a young lawyer could have.[63]

The noticeable dearth of diversity behind the bench has prompted calls for the judiciary to make concerted efforts to attract and hire more diverse candidates.[64] For example, the American Bar Association has urged prospective employers, including judges, to embrace diversity as "a core value that is integrated into . . . recruitment and retention."[65] In addition, clerkship placement programs aimed at increasing the diversity of law clerks have sprung up across America. One such program—*Just the Beginning* ("JTB")—places minority law students in judicial internships and clerkships.[66] In 2014, JTB's Summer Judicial Internship Diversity Program reportedly placed 88 minority law students into judicial externships.[67] Similarly, District Judge Gerald Bruce Lee (ED-VA) and five fellow judges created *Share the Wealth* in 2001, which places minority law graduates into clerkships with participating federal judges each year.[68] Other courts have commissioned studies to devise action plans to increase diversity behind the bench.[69] As noted above, some judges also consider aspects of diversity as plus factors or take diversity into account in less formal ways, such as asking applicants what diverse perspective they will bring to Chambers.

F. STRUCTURE OF THE JUDICIARY

The federal court system consists of Article III courts—those created pursuant to Article III of the Constitution, such as the U.S. Supreme Court and federal circuit courts—and Article I courts, which were created by statute pursuant to Article I. Article III judges enjoy a lifetime tenure to better insure their judicial independence. As explained earlier, the President appoints them, but they must also endure a rigorous Senate confirmation process; some judicial appointments are never confirmed. Due to their heavy caseload, Article III judges are usually permitted to hire up to four clerks per Chambers. By comparison, Article I judges, such as judges on the United States Court of Federal Claims, do not enjoy a lifetime tenure and may be permitted to hire only one or two clerks per Chambers. Their selection process is still quite rigorous, and there are no distinct differences between the knowledge and skills gained during an Article III or Article I clerkship. That being said, many prospective employers perceive Article III clerkships as more prestigious perhaps because they are usually more difficult to obtain.

As illustrated below, the judiciary can further be divided into the federal and state court systems, which usually mirror one another. U.S. Supreme Court clerkships are the most highly regarded in the federal system, while clerkships with the equivalent state court of last resort are the most competitive in state court systems. Both provide incredibly valuable learning experiences.

As explained above, the federal judiciary has three primary components: (1) the Supreme Court of the United States, which is the nation's highest court; (2) 13 United States Courts of Appeal (also known as *circuit courts*); and (3) 94 federal district courts. Each federal circuit court, except the United States Court of Appeals for the Federal Circuit, hears appeals arising from the district courts within the circuit. District courts function as trial courts, deciding cases in the first instance. They hold trials and hearings. Losing parties may appeal as of right, meaning that timely appeals are automatically accepted so long as the court has subject-matter jurisdiction. By way of illustration, the United States Court of Appeals for the Fourth Circuit ("Fourth Circuit") would hear an appeal arising from the Eastern District of Virginia because Virginia is one of several states located within the Fourth Circuit. Although Washington, D.C., is not a state, it possesses the United States District Court for the District of Columbia. The United States Court of Appeals for the D.C. Circuit hears appeals arising from the U.S. District Court for the District of Columbia and has resolved many noteworthy cases through the years. By statute, Congress also created the United States Court of Appeals for the Federal Circuit ("Federal Circuit"), which enjoys nationwide, statutorily vested jurisdiction over specific types of cases, such as those arising in patent law.

In addition, specialty courts, such as the United States Court of Federal Claims and United States Court of International Trade, exist as well as federal magistrate and bankruptcy courts. Specialty courts usually function as trial courts, but losing parties may appeal as of right to the appropriate appellate court, often the Federal Circuit. Some specialty courts also serve an appellate function. For instance, parties seeking money damages against the United States for breach of a government contract may seek a bench trial—one without a jury—in the United States Court of Federal Claims and appeal the decision to the Federal Circuit. However, petitioners alleging vaccine-related injuries file petitions with the Office of Special Masters, which decides the case in the first instance without a jury; a losing party may seek review from the U.S. Court of Federal Claims and then the Federal Circuit.

At every level, judges hire law clerks to assist them in resolving their cases. Law clerks are practicing attorneys who become integral members of a judge's personal staff. The number of law clerks varies by court with U.S. Supreme Court Justices and federal appellate judges hiring three to four per Chambers. By comparison, federal magistrate judges may generally only hire one law clerk and one judicial assistant per Chambers; some forego a judicial assistant and hire a second law clerk to serve a dual role as both clerk and judicial assistant.[70]

G. AN OVERVIEW OF THE COURTS

Supreme Court of the United States: The U.S. Supreme Court is America's highest court. To balance and complement the powers of the Executive and Legislative Branches, the framers of the Constitution drafted Section One of Article III, which provides that "[t]he judicial Power of the United States, shall be vested in one supreme Court, and in such inferior Courts as the Congress may from time to time ordain and establish." Subsequently, Congress enacted the Judiciary Act of 1789, which formalized the composition and procedures of the U.S. Supreme Court, articulated 13 judicial districts, and organized the districts into three federal circuits: Eastern, Middle, and Southern.[71] In February of 1790, the U.S. Supreme Court began meeting at the Merchants Exchange Building in New York City.[72] John Jay—the nation's first Chief Justice[73]— and his five Associate Justices also "rode circuit."[74] On August 3, 1791,[75] the Supreme Court issued its first opinion—*West v. Barnes*.[76] At the time, local newspapers reprinted full or excerpted versions of the opinion.[77]

Over time, the Supreme Court expanded; by 1869, it had increased from six to nine justices and remains at nine still today.[78] As of February 2017, the members of the Supreme Court included Chief Justice John Roberts, Jr., and Associate Justices Anthony Kennedy, Clarence Thomas, Ruth Bader Ginsburg, Stephen G. Breyer, Samuel A. Alito, Jr., Sonia Sotomayor, and Elena Kagan. As explained earlier, justices undergo a rigorous confirmation process. The President appoints justices to the Supreme Court subject to Senate approval. To better ensure judicial autonomy, justices enjoy lifetime tenure.[79] Even after they retire, they still retain a Chambers at the Court and may hire a law clerk.

Like its size, the Supreme Court also changed its location through the years, meeting in New York City until 1790 and then moving along with the Capital to Philadelphia. In 1800, the Supreme Court took up residence in the Capitol Building in Washington, D.C. Finally in 1929, Supreme Court Chief Justice and former President William Howard Taft convinced Congress to allocate funds to construct a separate Supreme Court building across the street from the Capital. Chief Justice Taft commissioned famous architect Cass Gilbert to design "a building of dignity and importance . . ." worthy of the judiciary.[80] Construction began in 1932, and the $9.7 million building was completed three years later, remarkably coming in $94,000 under budget.[81] The building's grandeur makes clear that the judiciary is a powerful and independent branch of the government. Its main entrance architrave reads "Equal Justice Under Law," and art and sculpture replete with symbolism adorn its interior and exterior.[82]

The Supreme Court hears hundreds of case each year on a diverse array of novel and complex legal issues. Section Two of Article III grants the Supreme Court jurisdiction over various matters, including cases that involve interpretation of the Constitution, federal laws, or treaties, "cases affecting Ambassadors, other public Ministers and Consuls," cases involving admiralty and maritime jurisdiction, and suits against the United States or between two or more states.[83] At its discretion, the Supreme Court also hears appeals from federal circuit courts.[84] A losing party at the circuit court must file a timely petition for certiorari with the Supreme Court, which the other party can oppose.[85] The Supreme Court currently receives between 7,000 and 8,000 petitions each year but annually grants certiorari in approximately 80.[86]

By statute, the Supreme Court term begins on the first Monday in October and continues through late June or early July, although the Court usually only issues opinions during the latter months. Each term includes intervals in which the Court *sits*, hearing cases and issuing opinions, and takes a *recess*, during which the Court writes opinions and handles other Court business. When the Court is sitting, it hears oral arguments from 10am to 3pm with a break.[87] At oral argument, each party is typically allotted thirty minutes to argue although exceptions exist.[88] There is no jury and no live witness testimony.

To handle this busy docket, each justice hires three to four law clerks, each for one year, to assist with the justice's caseload, while the Chief Justice may hire up to five law clerks.[89] Supreme Court clerkships are incredibly prestigious and competitive. Most Supreme Court clerks have attended well-regarded law schools and graduated at the top of the class. Most, if not all, also have prior practice experience, clerkship experience, or both.

The Supreme Court Fellows Program provides another valuable way to gain experience and exposure to the judiciary. Each year, the Supreme Court Fellows Commission selects four individuals to complete one-year fellowships at the Supreme Court, the Administrative Office of the United States Courts, the Federal Judicial Center, or the United States Sentencing Commission.[90] While some fellows have practice experience, others do not. Fellows gain unique insight into judicial administration, policy development, and education. Notably, the Commission "is particularly interested in applicants who are completing a judicial clerkship and are interested in broadening their understanding of the judicial system through exposure to federal court administration."[91] One fellow will work in the Office of the Counselor to the Chief Justice, and among other things, will brief foreign jurists, court administrators, and dignitaries on the Supreme Court's history and procedures.

Federal Circuit Courts: The United States is divided into twelve regional circuits, including the United States Court of Appeals for the District of Columbia. In addition, the Federal Circuit was established by statute in 1982 to achieve greater uniformity in specific areas of federal law, particularly patent law. Although the Federal Circuit sits in Washington, D.C., it possesses nationwide jurisdiction over appeals from any district court that involve a question of patent law. In addition, the Federal Circuit reviews appeals from the U.S. Court of International Trade, U.S. Court of Federal Claims, Merit Systems Protection Board, Board of Contract Appeals, U.S. Court of Appeals for Veterans Claims, and certain administrative decisions as well.

With regard to the twelve regional circuits, the number of judges on each court varies based upon both the number of states and districts within the circuit's corresponding geographical region. The largest—the Ninth Circuit—is comprised of roughly thirty judges at any given time, each of whom may hire up to four law clerks. The First Circuit is the smallest circuit court with only six active judges and four senior judges.[92] Interestingly, since retiring, former Supreme Court Associate Justice David Souter often sits by designation on the First Circuit. Notably, Congress established the Eleventh Circuit in 1981 to handle cases originating in Alabama, Florida, and Georgia—states that were formerly included in the Fifth Circuit.

Composition of the Regional Federal Circuits[93]

First Circuit (smallest)	Maine, Massachusetts, New Hampshire, Rhode Island, and Puerto Rico
Second Circuit	Connecticut, New York, and Vermont
Third Circuit	Delaware, New Jersey, Pennsylvania, and the U.S. Virgin Islands
Fourth Circuit	Maryland, North Carolina, South Carolina, Virginia, and West Virginia
Fifth Circuit	Louisiana, Mississippi, and Texas
Sixth Circuit	Kentucky, Michigan, Ohio, and Tennessee
Seventh Circuit	Illinois, Indiana, and Wisconsin
Eighth Circuit	Arkansas, Iowa, Minnesota, Missouri, Nebraska, North Dakota, and South Dakota
Ninth Circuit (largest)	Alaska, Arizona, California, Guam, Hawaii, Idaho, Montana, Nevada, Northern Mariana Islands, Oregon, and Washington
Tenth Circuit	Colorado, Kansas, New Mexico, Oklahoma, Utah, and Wyoming
Eleventh Circuit (newest)	Alabama, Florida, and Georgia
D.C. Circuit (feeder to the U.S. Supreme Court)	District of Columbia

As noted earlier, a losing party at the district court may appeal as of right, or automatically, to the appropriate circuit. So long as the appeal is timely and the circuit court has jurisdiction, the circuit court will docket the case for *Court Week*—a designated week each month during which the circuit hears oral argument in each case submitted for argument. The circuit court will also resolve cases that are submitted *on the briefs*, meaning that the case will be resolved without oral argument. Circuit court judges sit on three-judge panels and may issue a unanimous decision or a fractured decision that contains a concurrence[94], a dissent,[95] a dubitante opinion,[96] or even some combination thereof. A losing party may request that the panel review its decision and/or that the entire court hear the case en banc.[97] The court sitting en banc may overturn or affirm a prior panel decision from the court. As explained above, a losing party may also petition the Supreme Court for certiorari, and the Supreme Court will hear the case at its discretion. The Supreme Court is especially likely to grant certiorari when there is a circuit split on an important legal issue or when a circuit court sitting en banc produced a splintered decision. Each instance reflects that reasonable minds disagree about the issue. When the case presents a complex and novel issue likely to recur, the Supreme Court is also likely to grant certiorari to provide clarity to lower courts and to the public.

Notably, federal circuit courts engage in error correction; they do not hear witnesses or hold trials. As such, the workflow is typically more predictable than at the trial level, and clerks spend the vast majority of their time assisting their judges in preparing for oral argument and drafting opinions. Circuit judges are usually permitted to hire up to four clerks per Chambers, and these positions are highly competitive in part because circuit clerkships are so prestigious. In fact, some circuit courts, such as the D.C. Circuit Court, are considered "feeders" to the U.S. Supreme Court.[98] So-called "feeder" judges may also exist.[99] Applicants may take these factors into account when deciding where to clerk. For a full list of federal circuit court judges, please visit the website for the Administrative Office of the U.S. Courts.[100]

Federal District Courts: In addition to the circuit courts, the United States consists of 94 district courts. Each state contains at least one district court; no state contains more than four. The various districts are generally denoted as Eastern, Western, Southern, Northern, and Middle. Perhaps not surprisingly, the Southern District of New York and Central District of California are the largest districts in America, each boasting roughly 28 judges. The United States District Court of Puerto Rico consists of seven active judges and three senior judges.[101] The United States District Court for the District of Columbia is particularly renowned and has handled countless noteworthy cases through the years.

Each district court judge may hire one to two law clerks. District courts provide an incredible learning experience because they hear both civil and criminal cases and handle bench and jury trials as well as other litigation-related hearings. Although some prospective employers may perceive district court clerkships as less prestigious than their circuit counterparts, district court clerks gain unparalleled insight into every stage of the litigation process. As a result, their work is often varied, unpredictable, and fast-paced.

Each district court is paired with a federal bankruptcy court, which exclusively handles bankruptcy matters. Many district courts are also paired with federal magistrate judges who oversee certain aspects of litigation, such as discovery.[102] Both bankruptcy and magistrate judges hire law clerks, but they are typically limited to one law clerk per Chambers. For a full list of federal district judges, please visit the website for the Administrative Office of the U.S. Courts.[103]

Federal Territorial Courts: Guam, the United States Virgin Islands, and the Northern Mariana Islands each have one territorial court that enjoys the same jurisdiction as a federal district court within a state. Guam and the Northern Mariana Islands only have one judge apiece. Interestingly, territorial courts were created pursuant to Article IV, and as such, judges serve ten-year terms rather than enjoying a lifetime appointment. Territorial court judges generally hire one to two law clerks per Chambers.

Federal Specialty Courts: Through the years, Congress has also created specialty courts at both the trial and appellate levels. These Article I courts enjoy statutorily vested jurisdiction over a specific subset of cases. Some specialty courts like the Military Appeals Court and U.S. Court of Appeals for Veterans Claims serve an appellate function. Countless specialty trial courts also exist, including the U.S. Court of International Trade and U.S. Tax Court. Several of these courts are described in more detail in the chart below.

Federal Specialty Courts

Specialty Court	Location	Subject Matter Jurisdiction
Court of Appeals for the Armed Forces	Washington, D.C.	This is an Article I court that exercises worldwide appellate jurisdiction over members of the United States Armed Forces on active duty and other persons subject to the Uniform Code of Military Justice. It reviews the record in: "1) all cases in which the sentence, as affirmed by a Court of Criminal Appeals, extends to death; 2) all cases reviewed by a Court of Criminal Appeals which the Judge Advocate General orders sent to the Court of Appeals for the Armed Forces for review; and 3) all cases reviewed by a Court of Criminal Appeals in which, upon petition of the accused and on good cause shown, the Court of Appeals for the Armed Forces has granted."[104] This court includes five civilian judges appointed for 15-year terms. The court reviews decisions from the intermediate appellate courts of the services: the Army Court of Criminal Appeals, the Navy-Marine Corps Court of Criminal Appeals, the Coast Guard Court of Criminal Appeals, and the Air Force Court of Criminal Appeals.
U.S. Court of Appeals for Veterans Claims	Washington, D.C.	"The United States Court of Appeals for Veterans Claims is a national court of record, established under Article I . . . The Court has exclusive jurisdiction to provide judicial review of final decisions by the Board of Veterans' Appeals, an

		entity within the Department of Veterans Affairs. The Court provides veterans an impartial judicial forum for review of administrative decisions by the Board of Veterans' Appeals that are adverse to the veteran-appellant's claim of entitlement to benefits for service-connected disabilities, survivor benefits and other benefits such as education payments and waiver of indebtedness. In furtherance of its mission, the Court also seeks to help ensure that all veterans have equal access to the Court and to promote public trust and confidence in the Court."[105]
U.S. Court of International Trade	New York City	"The mission of the United States Court of International Trade is to resolve disputes by: Providing cost effective, courteous, and timely service to those affected by the judicial process; Providing independent, consistent, fair, and impartial interpretation and application of the customs and international trade laws; and Fostering improvements in customs and international trade law and practice and improvements in the administration of justice."[106]
U.S. Tax Court	Washington, D.C.	"The United States Tax Court is a court of record established by Congress under Article I of the U.S. Constitution. When the Commissioner of Internal Revenue has determined a tax deficiency, the taxpayer may dispute the deficiency in the Tax Court before paying any disputed amount. The Tax Court's jurisdiction also includes the authority to redetermine

		transferee liability, make certain types of declaratory judgments, adjust partnership items, order abatement of interest, award administrative and litigation costs, redetermine worker classification, determine relief from joint and several liability on a joint return, review certain collection actions, and review awards to whistleblowers who provide information to the Commissioner of Internal Revenue on or after December 20, 2006."[107]
U.S. Court of Federal Claims	Washington, D.C.	This court was created in 1982 to hear claims for money damages against the federal government arising under the Constitution, money-mandating federal statutes, executive regulations, or contracts, express or implied in fact, with the United States. Cases commonly include Fifth Amendment takings, civilian and military pay claims, intellectual property, and various statutory claims against the United States. It also serves an appellate function over Vaccine Act appeals from the Office of Special Masters.[108]
Office of Special Masters (within the U.S. Court of Federal Claims)	Washington, D.C.	"The National Vaccine Injury Compensation Program (Vaccine Program) comprises Part 2 of the National Childhood Vaccine Injury Act of 1986 (Vaccine Act). See Pub. L. No. 99–660, 100 Stat. 3755 (1986) (codified as amended at 42 U.S.C. §§ 300aa–1 to –34). The Vaccine Act became effective October 1, 1988. It establishes the Vaccine Program as a no-fault compensation program whereby

		petitions for monetary compensation may be brought by or on behalf of persons allegedly suffering injury or death as a result of the administration of certain compulsory childhood vaccines. Congress intended that the Vaccine Program provide individuals a swift, flexible, and less adversarial alternative to the often costly and lengthy civil arena of traditional tort litigation."[109]
Tribal Courts		"Tribal courts are courts of general jurisdiction which continue to have broad criminal jurisdiction. The general rule is that states have no jurisdiction over the activities of Indians and tribes in Indian country. Public Law 280 (PL 280) created an exception to this rule in certain states. The U.S. Congress gave these states criminal jurisdiction over all offenses involving Native Americans on tribal lands. Through PL 280, the federal government transferred to these states the federal government's criminal jurisdiction over Indian country, and it opened state courts up as forums for civil litigation that had previously only been able to be brought in tribal or federal courts. The effect of PL 280 is that in many areas state and tribal courts share jurisdiction."[110]

H. STATE COURTS

Most state court systems mirror the structure of the federal judiciary. They usually include trial courts, intermediate appellate courts, and a court of last resort, often called the State Supreme Court. However, exceptions exist. For example, Delaware, the District of Columbia, Maine, Montana, Nevada, New Hampshire, North Dakota, Rhode Island, South Dakota, Vermont, West Virginia, and Wyoming lack intermediate appellate courts. Similarly, New York's highest court is known as the New York Court of Appeals, rather than the New York Supreme Court. If applying for a state court clerkship, be sure to research the judicial structure for that state perhaps by visiting the website of the National Center for State Courts.[111]

As in the federal judiciary, state trial courts handle jury trials and litigation-related motions. Like the federal circuit courts, in most states losing parties at the trial level may appeal to state intermediate appellate courts. State appellate judges typically hear cases in three-judge panels. The panels do not fact-find or have trials; as noted earlier, they only engage in error correction. As with the U.S. Supreme Court, state courts of last resort usually decide which cases to hear and sit en banc, meaning that the entire court hears and decides each case. The court of last resort often decides complex and novel issues. Occasionally a federal court will certify a novel question of state law to the appropriate state court for resolution.

Because the structure of state courts varies, conduct independent research regarding the judicial structure of the state in which you plan to clerk.

Judges at every level of the state judiciary hire law clerks; judges on the court of last resort are usually permitted to hire two clerks per Chambers.[112] Although these clerkships are somewhat less competitive than federal clerkships, they provide invaluable learning experience. The work of state trial courts is often just as hectic, varied, and unpredictable as that of federal trial courts. By comparison, intermediate appellate courts and state courts of last resort offer clerks a chance to more deeply explore each legal issue. State court clerkships are especially beneficial for individuals who plan to practice in the court's home state after his or her clerkship concludes.

Finally, some states also include specialty courts, such as the North Carolina Business Court, and courts of limited jurisdiction, such as family or probate courts, which also provide additional clerkship opportunities. For example, an applicant interested in practicing family law would likely find a clerkship at a family court to be particularly valuable. For a full list of state court judges and their locations, visit the National Center for State Courts.[113]

I.   OTHER COURT-RELATED OPPORTUNITIES

Even if you are unable to obtain a judicial clerkship, other excellent court-related opportunities, both domestic and international, exist that will provide you significant exposure to the judicial system.[114] Below is a non-exhaustive list of such opportunities.

Administrative Agencies: Administrative law judges at many federal and state administrative agencies hire law clerks.[115]

Administrative Office of the United States Courts: The Administrative Office of the U.S. Courts ("AO") provides program management, legal counsel, legislative services, and administrative support to the federal courts and their policy-making body, the Judicial Conference.[116]

American Bar Association: The American Bar Association ("ABA") is a voluntary bar association for lawyers and law students that fosters their development and continuing education. The ABA Rule of Law Initiative ("ABA ROLI") "promotes greater independence, accountability and transparency in judicial systems; assists in drafting and implementing codes of judicial ethics; promotes judicial education and training; and helps to enhance court administration and efficiency."[117] The ABA ROLI has even created a tool known as the Judicial Reform Index ("JRI"), which evaluates judicial reform and autonomy.[118] Since 2001, the ABA ROLI has used the JRI to assess judicial systems in 20 countries.[119] Notably, the ABA also staffs a Standing Committee on the Federal Judiciary that evaluates the qualifications of potential nominees to federal courts.[120]

Federal Judicial Center: The Federal Judicial Center ("FJC") is the federal judiciary's education and research agency. It provides continuing education for federal judges and court staff on a diverse array of topics from practice skills to empirical data regarding judicial reform.

United States Sentencing Commission: The United States Sentencing Commission utilizes social science, legal, and policy research to analyze American approaches to crime and punishment and then develop and revise federal sentencing guidelines accordingly.

J. JUDICIAL PROCESS AND PROCEDURE

Law clerks must become intimately familiar with their court's process and procedure, which is governed by both general and local rules. Before your clerkship commences, learn the procedural rules that apply at your court.[121] By way of illustration, the Federal Rules of Civil Procedure and Federal Rules of Evidence govern proper procedure in federal civil cases. The Federal Rules of Criminal Procedure and Federal Sentencing Guidelines apply in federal criminal proceedings. The Federal Rules of Appellate Procedure govern federal appellate matters. Yet important distinctions exist. For example, federal district courts handle both criminal and civil matters, while other trial courts, such as the U.S. Court of International Trade, only handle civil cases. Some courts, such as the U.S. Court of Federal Claims, only provide trials without juries.

Notably, most courts promulgate *local* court rules that supplement the federal rules, and some judges even establish additional procedural rules specific to their Chambers. For example, the Office of Special Masters within the U.S. Court of Federal Claims has promulgated Vaccine Rules, which govern practice in that unique forum. These rules trump any conflicting rules that would otherwise be generally applicable. Local rules are usually available on the court's website. While an in-depth discussion of the various general and local rules and practices exceeds the scope of this chapter, the key takeaway point is that a law clerk must learn the relevant rules at the outset of the clerkship.

K. UNDERSTANDING COURT TERMINOLOGY

A distinct vocabulary exists that is specific to the judiciary, and law clerks must quickly become fluent in it. To assist in that regard, below is a non-exhaustive glossary of terms commonly used in Chambers.

Chief Judge: Each court has one *chief judge* who is responsible for resolving cases but also possesses a leadership and administrative role. The chief judge should always be referred to as "Chief Judge." The most senior judge on the court does not necessarily hold the Chief Judge position. For example, Chief Justice John Roberts, Jr., serves this function on the U.S. Supreme Court, but as of February 2017, Justice Anthony Kennedy was the most senior justice on the Court.[122]

Senior Judge: A *senior judge* is one who possesses senior status. Senior status is a form of semi-retirement for federal and some state judges. In the federal judiciary, a judge must be at least 65 years of age and have served in federal courts for 15 years to qualify, with one fewer year of service required for each additional year of age.[123]

Active Judge: An *active judge* is any working judge that has not yet taken senior status. Always refer to the judge as "Judge," never "Sir" or "Ma'am." On the U.S. Supreme Court, all justices aside from the Chief Justice are referred to as *associate justices*, but the same is not true of lower federal courts.

Judicial Assistant: A *judicial assistant* ("JA") is a judge's personal administrative assistant. A JA performs various administrative functions in Chambers and is generally not hired for a set term. A JA need not possess a law degree or any legal training; indeed, most do not. However, in some Chambers, a judge hires a law clerk to serve a dual role as clerk and JA. Always refer to the JA as "Mr." or "Ms." unless and until the JA permits you to use his or her first name.

Career Clerk: A *career clerk* is a lawyer who is a member of the judge's personal staff and who is not hired for a definite term. A career clerk often plays a supervising role in Chambers, overseeing the work of other clerks and even assigning them cases. A career clerk sometimes serves a dual role as the judge's administrative assistant. Not all judges hire career clerks, and some Chambers hire a single career clerk and additional term clerks.

Term Clerk: A *term,* or *elbow, clerk* is a lawyer who is a member of the judge's personal staff and who is hired for a defined term usually of one to two years.

Clerk of the Court: Each court has a *Clerk of the Court* who, in his or her capacity as an officer of the court, performs a vast array of roles, such as maintaining a record of the court, overseeing conflict checks, administering oaths, etc. The Clerk of the Court serves the entire court, rather than a single judge, and is not hired for a pre-defined term.

U.S. Marshals:[124] The *U.S. Marshals Service* is America's oldest federal law enforcement agency, serving since 1789. They protect federal judicial officials, including judges, law clerks, attorneys, and jurors. In particular, Court Security Officers ("CSOs") maintain courthouse security at courts across the country. Marshals also oversee courthouse construction projects to ensure the safety of judicial officials and employees.

Office of General Counsel: The *Office of General Counsel* ("OGC") is an office comprised of attorneys who serve the entire court, rather than a single judge. They are not hired for a set term and assist the court in various legal matters, such as managing court mediation programs and investigating potential ethics issues.

Staff Attorney: A *staff attorney* is hired for an indefinite term to assist the entire court with legal matters.

In conclusion, just as the judiciary is integral to the American legal system, law clerks are integral to the judiciary. A vast array of courts and court-related opportunities exist, each of which provides a distinct but valuable clerkship experience.

L. SUPPLEMENTAL RESOURCES

1. REBECCA A. COCHRAN, JUDICIAL EXTERNSHIPS: THE CLINIC INSIDE THE COURTHOUSE (4th ed. 2016).

2. CHRISTINE COUGHLIN, JOAN MALMUD ROCKLIN, & SANDY PATRICK, A LAWYER WRITES: A PRACTICAL GUIDE TO LEGAL ANALYSIS (2d ed. 2013).

3. MARY L. DUNNEWOLD, BETH A. HONETSCHLAGER, & BRENDA L. TOFTE, JUDICIAL CLERKSHIPS: A PRACTICAL GUIDE (2010).

4. DEBRA M. STRAUSS, BEHIND THE BENCH: THE GUIDE TO JUDICIAL CLERKSHIPS (2002).

Notes

[1] JAMES MACDOUGALD, UNSUSTAINABLE 15 (2010).

[2] Elizabeth Landau, *Researchers: Jamestown Settlers Resorted to Cannibalism*, CNN (May 2, 2013), http://www.cnn.com/2013/05/01/us/jamestown-cannibalism/index.html?eref=rss_top stories.

[3] JOHN R. VILE, THE CONSTITUTIONAL CONVENTION OF 1787: A COMPREHENSIVE ENCYCLOPEDIA OF AMERICA'S FOUNDING 188 (ABC-CLIO vol. 1 2005).

[4] THE NEW CAMBRIDGE MODERN HISTORY VOLUME VIII THE AMERICAN AND FRENCH REVOLUTIONS 1763–93 524 (A. Goodwin ed., Cambridge University Press, 1965).

[5] *The Articles of Confederation*, THE LIBRARY OF CONGRESS, https://www.loc.gov/rr/program/bib/ourdocs/articles.html.

[6] Johnathan Smith, *The Depression of 1785 and Daniel Shays' Rebellion*, 5 WILLIAM & MARY QUARTERLY 77, 78 (1948).

[7] *Id.*

[8] *U.S. Debt and Foreign Loans, 1775–1795*, OFFICE OF THE HISTORIAN, https://history.state.gov/milestones/1784-1800/loans.

[9] Notably, after winning the war, Washington simply retired to his estate, Mount Vernon, to live out his days as a farmer. In so doing, he proved he was neither king nor tyrant; rather, Washington had the nation's best interests at heart. STEVEN H. JAFFE, WHO WERE THE FOUNDING FATHERS? 20 (1996).

[10]   The first ten amendments to the Constitution constitute the Bill of Rights. Among other things, they protect freedom of the press, religion, and speech as well as a person's right to bear arms.

[11]   *Constitution Day*, U.S. SENATE, http://www.senate.gov/artandhistory/history/common /generic/ConstitutionDay.htm.

[12]   Letter from Lord Acton (John Emerich Edward Dalberg) to Archbishop Mandell Creighton (Apr. 5, 1887) (on file with the Online Library of Liberty).

[13]   James Madison, Speech at the Constitutional Convention (July 11, 1787).

[14]   THE FEDERALIST NO. 49 (James Madison).

[15]   Indeed, more than 13,000 executive orders have been issued since 1789, and all but two have survived constitutional challenges. President Franklin Delano Roosevelt issued 3,522 executive orders during his presidency, while President Barack Obama had issued only 168 as of January 2014. *Executive Orders Coming? Here's How They Work*, CNBC, http://www.cnbc.com/ 2014/01/28/executive-orders-what-they-are-and-how-they-work.html (last visited Sep. 2, 2016). For example, in July 2014, President Barack Obama signed an order that prohibited federal contractors from discriminating against employees or applicants on the basis of gender identity or sexual orientation. *President Obama Signs a New Executive Order to Protect LGBT Workers*, THE WHITE HOUSE, https://www.whitehouse.gov/blog/2014/07/21/president-obama-signs-new-executive-order-protect-lgbt-workers (last visited Sept. 2, 2016).

[16]   U.S. Const. art. III, § 1.

[17]   *Judiciary Act of 1789*, LIBRARY OF CONGRESS, http://www.loc.gov/rr/program/bib/ourdocs/ judiciary.html (last visited Oct. 10, 2016).

[18]   *The Court as an Institution*, SUPREME COURT OF THE U.S., https://www.supremecourt.gov/ about/institution.aspx (last visited Aug. 31, 2016).

[19]   *Id.*

[20]   *John Marshall*, BIOGRAPHY.COM (2016), http://www.biography.com/people/john-marshall-9400148.

[21]   *Marbury v. Madison*, 5 U.S. 137 (1803).

[22]   Keith E. Whittington, *The Least Activist Supreme Court in History? The Roberts Court and the Exercise of Judicial* Review, 89 N.D. L. REV. 2219, 2231, Fig. 3 (2014).

[23]   THE FEDERALIST NO. 47 (James Madison).

[24]   Article III judges serve on courts, such as the U.S. Supreme Court or federal circuit courts, that were created pursuant to Article III of the Constitution.

[25]   *Federal Judicial Nominations: 9 Steps from Vacancy to Confirmation*, CENTER FOR AMERICAN PROGRESS (2013), https://www.americanprogress.org/issues/general/news/2013/01/29/ 50996/federal-judicial-nominations-9-steps-from-vacancy-to-confirmation/.

[26]   *How the Confirmation Process Works*, JUDICIAL NOMINATIONS, http://judicialnominations .org/how-the-confirmation-process-works (last visited Aug. 31, 2016).

[27]   For a fictional depiction of this vetting process, see "The Supremes," Episode 17, Season Five of *The West Wing. The Supremes,* INT'L MOVIE DATABASE, http://www.imdb.com/title/tt074 5708/ (last visited Sept. 16, 2016) ("A Supreme Court Justice dies, forcing the administration's hand on picking a desirable replacement who can be confirmed by a hostile Congress.").

[28]   *Federal Judicial Nomination Process*, LEADERSHIP CONFERENCE ON CIVIL AND HUMAN RIGHTS, http://www.civilrights.org/judiciary/courts/nominations.html (last visited June 10, 2016).

[29]   Scott Bomboy, *How Does the Senate Handle a Supreme Court Nomination?,* CONSTITUTION DAILY (Mar. 16, 2016), http://blog.constitutioncenter.org/2016/03/how-does-the-senate-handle-a-supreme-court-nomination/.

[30]   For more information regarding the selection process of state judges, see REBECCA A. COCHRAN, JUDICIAL EXTERNSHIPS: THE CLINIC INSIDE THE COURTHOUSE (4th ed. 2016).

[31]   Indeed, whole books have been written on this subject. *See generally* JUDGE RICHARD POSNER, HOW JUDGES THINK (2008).

[32]   *See* King v. Burwell, 135 S. Ct. 2480, 2500 (2015) (in which Justice Scalia contends that the Supreme Court's decision involved "interpretive jiggery-pokery" rather than strict adherence to the Constitution).

[33]   *See* Grutter v. Bollinger, 539 U.S. 306, 123 (2003).

[34]   Daniel Selden, *Judge Reyna's 'Devotion to Justice' Earns Respect, Attention*, BLOOMBERG BNA (Sept. 2016), http://www.bna.com/judge-reynas-devotion-n73014447123/.

[35]   *Id.* (quoting Abigail Perdue).

[36]   *Members of the Supreme Court*, SUPREME COURT OF THE U.S., https://www.supremecourt.gov/about/members.aspx (last visited Aug. 31, 2016).

[37]   Bradwell v. State of Illinois, 83 U.S. 130 (1873).

[38]   *Thurgood Marshall Confirmed as Supreme Court Justice*, HISTORY.COM, http://www.history.com/this-day-in-history/thurgood-marshall-confirmed-as-supreme-court-justice (last visited Aug. 31, 2016).

[39]   *Thurgood Marshall,* BIOGRAPHY.COM (2014), http://www.biography.com/people/thurgood-marshall-9400241#related-video-gallery.

[40]   *Id.*

[41]   Brown v. Board of Ed. of Topeka, 347 U.S. 483 (1954).

[42]   *Thurgood Marshall, supra* note 53.

[43]   *Id.*

[44]   Mark Hurwitz & Drew Lanier, *Judicial Diversity in Federal Courts: A Historical and Empirical Exploration*, 96 JUDICATURE 76, 79 (2012).

[45]   *Id.*

[46]   Hurwitz & Lanier, *supra* note 58.

[47]   *Id.*

[48]   Hurwitz & Lanier, *supra* note 58, at 82.

[49]   *See, e.g.*, Sital Kalantry, *Women in Robes*, AMERICAS QUARTERLY (Summer 2012), http://www.americasquarterly.org/women-in-robes; Jacklyn Belczyk, *Most US Federal Court Judges Still Men, but Demographics Changing: Report*, JURIST (Aug. 18, 2009), http://www.jurist.org/paperchase/2009/08/federal-court-demographics-changing-to.php; Adam Serwer, *Obama Leaves his Mark on the Federal Bench*, MSNBC (June 11, 2014), http://www.msnbc.com/msnbc/obama-leaves-his-mark-the-federal-bench.

[50]   *Federal Judges*, IPP DIGITAL (May 14, 2008), http://iipdigital.usembassy.gov/st/english/publication/2008/05/20080522224217eaifas0.5669672.html#axzz4NIdstQCy.

[51]   *National Database on Judicial Diversity in State Courts*, AMERICAN BAR ASSOCIATION, https://apps.americanbar.org/abanet/jd/display/national.cfm (last visited Sept. 2, 2016); *Profile of General Population and Housing Characteristics*, U.S. CENSUS BUREAU, http://www.stats.indiana.edu/c2010/dp1/FactfinderINandUS.pdf (last visited Sept. 2, 2016).

[52]   *Number of Appellate Court Judges*, http://data.ncsc.org/QvAJAXZfc/opendoc.htm?document=PublicApp/SCO.qvw&host=QVS@qlikviewisa&anonymous=true&bookmark=Document*BM81 (last visited Sept. 29, 2016).

[53]   *Id.*

[54]   *Id.*

[55]   *Id.*

[56]   Debra Strauss, *Diversity Begins at Home: Supreme Court Clerkships and Affirmative Action*, JURIST (Apr. 4, 2003), http://www.jurist.org/forum/forumnew105.php.

[57]   Karen Sloan, *Judges Do Something about Dearth of Diverse Clerks*, NAT'L L. J., http://www.nativeamericanbar.org/wp-content/uploads/2014/01/Judges-Doing-Something-About-Dearth-of-Diverse-Clerks-_-National-Law-Journal.pdf (May 12, 2014); *see also* Tony Mauro, *Diversity and Supreme Court Law Clerks*, 98 MARQ. L. REV. 361, 361 (2014) ("In addition to the power and influence of the law clerks, I was struck by how few clerks were women or minorities . . . to an overwhelming degree, it was white males who were capturing this brass ring, winning this almost guaranteed ticket to the upper echelons of the legal profession.").

[58]   Maria Chutchian, *Statistics Show Little Change in Law Clerk Diversity*, LAW360 (May 3, 2012), http://www.law360.com/articles/336973/statistics-show-little-change-in-law-clerk-diversity.

[59]   *Id.*

[60]   *Id.*

[61]   *Id.*

[62]   *Courting Clerkships: The NALP Judicial Clerkship Study*, NAT'L ASS'N OF LAW PLACEMENT (2000), http://www.nalp.org/courtingclerkships.

[63]   *See also* Christopher R. Benson, *A Renewed Call for Diversity among Supreme Court Clerks: How a Diverse Body of Clerks Can Aid the High Court as an Institution*, 23 HARV. BLACKLETTER L.J. 23 (2007).

[64]   Tony Mauro, *Activists Protest Court's Lack of Minority Clerks*, USA TODAY, Oct. 6, 1998, at 10A.

[65]   Chutchian, *supra* note 75.

[66]   Sloan, *supra* note 74.

[67]   Chutchian, *supra* note 75.

[68]   http://jtb.org/share-the-wealth/.

[69]   *See, e.g., Promoting and Ensuring the Diversity of Judicial Staff Attorneys and Law Clerks within the Florida State Courts System, Committee Report and Recommendations*, FLA. COURTS, http://www.flcourts.org/core/fileparse.php/243/urlt/lawclerk_report.pdf (last visited Oct. 10, 2016).

[70]   DEBRA STRAUSS, BEHIND THE BENCH: THE GUIDE TO JUDICIAL CLERKSHIPS 55 (2002). [hereinafter BEHIND THE BENCH].

[71]   1 Stat. 73.

[72]   *The Court as an Institution, supra* note 31.

[73]   *Id.; see also Members of the Supreme Court of the United States*, SUPREME COURT OF THE UNITED STATES, https://www.supremecourt.gov/about/members_text.aspx (last visited Sept. 4, 2016).

[74]   *The Court as an Institution, supra* note 31.

[75]   *Id.*

[76]   West v. Barnes, 2 U.S. 401 (1791). The case involved William West, a farmer, Revolutionary War general, and judge. West owed a mortgage and sought permission from the state of Rhode Island to conduct a lottery to pay off the remainder of the mortgage after the war. Most of the proceeds from the lottery were paid in paper currency. David Leonard Barnes, an attorney and later a judge, sued, alleging that a Rhode Island statute about lodging payment required West to pay the debt in gold or silver. The Supreme Court ruled for Barnes on procedural grounds and declined to decide whether it had authority to overturn the Rhode Island statute at issue in the case.

[77]   THE DOCUMENTARY HISTORY OF THE SUPREME COURT OF THE UNITED STATES, 1789–1800, at 11 (Maeva Marcus ed., 1998).

[78]   The number of Supreme Court Justices has changed six times since the Court's creation. Yet there have been only 17 Chief Justices and 100 Associate Justices, with Justices serving for an average of 16 years. *The Court as an Institution, supra* note 31.

[79]   Power to nominate the Justices is vested in the President of the United States, and appointments are made with the advice and consent of the Senate. Article III, § 1, of the Constitution further provides that "[t]he Judges, both of the supreme and inferior Courts, shall hold their Offices during good Behaviour, and shall, at stated Times, receive for their Services, a Compensation, which shall not be diminished during their Continuance in Office."

[80]   *The Supreme Court Building*, SUPREME COURT OF THE U.S., http://www.supremecourt.gov/about/courtbuilding.aspx (last visited Sept. 6, 2016).

[81]   *Id.*

[82]   *Id.*

[83]   U.S. Const. art. III § 2, cl. 1.

[84]   *Landmark Judicial Legislation*, FED. JUDICIAL CTR., http://www.fjc.gov/history/home.nsf/page/landmark_12.html (last visited Sept. 6, 2016).

[85]   Chief Justice Taft also convinced Congress to enact a law codifying the certiorari process so that the Court has discretion to select which cases to hear. Saul Brenner, *Granting Certiorari by the United States Supreme Court: An Overview of the Social Science Studies*, 92 Law Libr. J. 193 (2000).

[86]   *Frequently Asked Questions*, SUPREME COURT OF THE U.S., https://www.supremecourt.gov/faq.aspx#faqgi9 (last visited Sept. 6, 2016).

[87]   *Supreme Court Procedures*, U.S. COURTS, http://www.uscourts.gov/about-federal-courts/educational-resources/about-educational-outreach/activity-resources/supreme-1 (last visited Oct. 15, 2016).

[88]   The Court permitted two and a half hours of oral argument in *Obergefell v. Hodges*, 135 S. Ct. 2584 (2015), which involved whether same-sex couples had a constitutional right under the Fourteenth Amendment to marry.

[89]   BEHIND THE BENCH, *supra* note 87, at 56.

[90]   *Fellowship Placements*, SUPREME COURT OF THE U.S., https://www.supremecourt.gov/ fellows/fellowships.aspx (last visited Sept. 6, 2016).

[91]   *Id.*

[92]   *First Circuit U.S. Court of Appeals Case Law*, JUSTIA, http://law.justia.com/cases/federal/ appellate-courts/ca1/ (last visited Oct. 15, 2016).

[93]   The United States Court of Appeals for the Federal Circuit is not listed here because its jurisdiction is statutorily vested.

[94]   A *concurring opinion* is one in which the author agrees with the outcome but not the reasoning of the majority opinion. A concurring opinion lacks precedential authority.

[95]   A *dissenting opinion* is one in which the author would have decided the case differently than the majority. A dissent lacks precedential authority.

[96]   A *dubitante opinion* is one in which the author is dubious about the majority's reasoning and outcome but not so much that he or she drafts a concurrence or dissent. Dubitante opinions are highly rare.

[97]   An *en banc decision* is one in which all active judges hear and decide the case, rather than a three-judge panel. One exception is the Ninth Circuit, which does not require all judges to sit for each en banc case.

[98]   Lawrence Baum & Corey Ditslear, *Supreme Court Clerkships and "Feeder Judges,"* 31 THE JUSTICE SYSTEM J. 1 (2010).

[99]   *Id.*

[100]   *Administrative Office of the U.S. Courts*, UNITED STATES COURTS, http://www.uscourts .gov/topics/administrative-office-us-courts (last visited Sept. 13, 2016).

[101]   A *senior judge* is a judge who has taken senior status. Senior status is a form of semi-retirement for United States federal judges and judges in some state court systems.

[102]   *The Role of Magistrates in Federal District Courts*, THE FEDERAL JUDICIAL CENTER, http:// www.fjc.gov/public/pdf.nsf/lookup/magroles.pdf/$file/magroles.pdf (last visited Sep. 14, 2016).

[103]   *Administrative Office of the U.S. Courts*, *supra* note 117.

[104]   10 U.S.C. § 867.

[105]   *United States Court of Appeals For Veteran Claims*, U.S. COURTS, http://www.uscourts .cavc.gov/ (last visited Sept. 14, 2016).

[106]   *Id.*

[107]   *About the Court*, U.S. TAX COURT, https://www.ustaxcourt.gov/about.htm (last visited Oct. 15, 2016).

[108]   *About the Court*, U.S. COURT OF FEDERAL CLAIMS, http://www.uscfc.uscourts.gov/about-court# (last visited Oct. 15, 2016).

[109]   *Vaccine Claims/Office of Special Maters*, U.S. COURT OF FEDERAL CLAIMS, http://www. uscfc.uscourts.gov/vaccine-programoffice-special-masters (last visited Oct. 15, 2016).

[110]   *Trial Courts Resource Guide*, NATIONAL CENTER FOR STATE COURTS, http://www.ncsc.org/ Topics/Special-Jurisdiction/Tribal-Courts/Resource-Guide.aspx (last visited Oct. 15, 2016).

[111]   *Id.*

[112]   Given the similarities between state and federal courts, the same general advice regarding federal clerkships often applies with equal force to state court clerkships. Where a notable distinction does exist, the book will usually note this.

[113]   *Id.*

[114]   Although a discussion of international courts exceeds the scope of this book, it should be noted that clerkships at such courts do exist and provide an unparalleled experience for attorneys who plan to pursue careers in international or comparative law. For more information, see BEHIND THE BENCH, *supra* note 87, at 70.

[115]   *Agencies Employing Administrative Law Judges*, ASSOCIATION OF ADMINISTRATIVE LAW JUDGES, https://aalj.org/agencies-employing-administrative-law-judges; *see also* BEHIND THE BENCH, *supra* note 87, at 68–69.

[116]   By statute, Congress has vested the U.S. Supreme Court with the power to prescribe rules of procedure for the lower federal courts. *See* 28 U.S.C. § 2071 et seq.

[117]   *Judicial Reform*, AM. BAR ASS'N, http://www.americanbar.org/advocacy/rule_of_law/ thematic_areas/judicial_reform.html (last visited Sept. 16, 2016).

[118]   *Id.*

[119] *Id.*

[120] *Standing Committee on the Federal Judiciary*, AM. BAR ASS'N, http://www.american bar.org/groups/committees/federal_judiciary.html (last visited Sept. 14, 2016).

[121] *See, e.g., Internal Operating Procedures*, U.S. COURT OF APPEALS FOR THE FEDERAL CIRCUIT (2016), http://www.cafc.uscourts.gov/rules-of-practice/internal-operating-procedures.

[122] This statement is current as of July 2016.

[123] Milton J. Valencia, *Senior Status Lets Judges Keep Working—For Free*, BOS. GLOBE (Dec. 12, 2014), https://www.bostonglobe.com/metro/2014/12/11/senior-status-lets-federal-judges-keep-working-for-free/SWLnor4WeryHTKmN1vmckN/story.html.

[124] *Major Responsibilities of the U.S. Marshals Service*, U.S. MARSHALS SERVICE, https://www.usmarshals.gov/duties/.

CHAPTER 3

PREPARING TO CLERK

■ ■ ■

Every clerkship is unique. Thus, there is no one right way to prepare for a clerkship. That being said, all clerks must be effective legal analysts, writers, editors, researchers, and communicators. They must be able to manage time and stress effectively. Finally, they should exemplify ethics and professionalism. Keeping these considerations in mind, this chapter provides a brief overview regarding how you can best prepare for a clerkship. In addition to reviewing this chapter, you should, upon accepting an offer to clerk, ask your judge what he or she recommends that you do to prepare yourself to immediately add value to Chambers once your clerkship commences. The judge's outgoing clerks will also be able to provide you with invaluable advice.

A. PLANNING YOUR COURSE OF STUDY

Judges value law clerks who are strong researchers and writers. Thus, performing well in relevant courses that engender the skills and knowledge necessary to succeed as a law clerk will certainly enhance your chance of selection. While not required of judicial clerkship or externship applicants, completion of these courses will ensure that you are better positioned to obtain a clerkship or externship and are prepared to perform well in that position.

Complete Courses that Relate to Judicial Drafting, Process, and Procedure: Select courses that will hone your research, writing, and analytical skills as well as courses that will enhance your knowledge of the subject matter within the court's jurisdiction, particularly civil procedure. For example, at Wake Forest University School of Law, I advise prospective law clerks to take courses, such as *Advanced Legal Research, Complex Civil Litigation, Federal Jurisdiction* (if the individual seeks a federal clerkship or externship), *State-Specific Practice and Procedure* (if the student seeks a state court clerkship and such a course is offered), *Trial Practice, Advanced Civil Procedure, Advanced Trial Practice, Equitable and Legal Remedies, Litigation Drafting, Pre-Trial Practice and Procedure*, and *Appellate Advocacy*. Courses like *Pre-Trial Practice and Procedure, Trial Practice*, and *Advanced Trial Practice* are particularly helpful if you seek a trial court clerkship, while *Appellate Advocacy* will be incredibly useful if you secure an appellate clerkship. Courses with a strong, legal writing component, such as *Litigation Drafting* and *Appellate Advocacy*, will hone your legal writing skills.

Increasingly, law schools offer upper level judicial writing courses, such as *Legal Writing for Judicial Chambers* or *Judicial Clerking*. Such courses are tremendously beneficial. In addition, take any course that will enable you to read and study the most impactful and well-written judicial opinions of our time. For example, Wake Forest currently offers a *Great Jurists* seminar. If your school offers such a course, take it since you can only become a great legal writer if you read, study, and learn from great legal writing. Such courses also offer an opportunity to produce a strong writing sample, which all or most judges require.

Take Courses Relevant to the Court's Jurisdiction: Courses tailored to the specific jurisdiction of the court may also be helpful. For example, if you plan to apply for a clerkship at the United States Court of Appeals for the Federal Circuit, courses in international trade, government contracts, intellectual property, and federal income tax may be particularly helpful. Likewise, a bankruptcy court may prefer that you have taken *Bankruptcy*, and a Tax Court will prefer that you have completed tax courses. A district court will expect you to have taken civil law courses as well as criminal law and criminal procedure. Where such courses do not exist, work with your administration to design an independent study, practicum, or externship to gain the substantive knowledge relevant to your clerkship. In exceptional instances, it may be helpful to take an online or summer course at another law school, which does offer that subject matter, or to obtain a subject-specific LLM degree, perhaps in tax law or government contracts law, before applying to clerk.

As noted above, research courses, particularly those tailored to your court's jurisdiction, are also incredibly beneficial. For example, research techniques most useful in tax law may be quite distinct from those that are useful when researching criminal law. If your school does not offer such a subject-specific research course, speak with your Academic Dean about designing an independent study in the semester before you will apply for a clerkship or commence your clerkship. For more information regarding how to perform legal research during a clerkship, please see Chapter 10.

Acquire Relevant Work Experience: Judges may also prefer applicants who possess pertinent work experience either as an attorney or law clerk. For this reason, waiting to apply for a clerkship until you have gained some experience in a law firm or other practice setting may significantly enhance your chance of success. Indeed, some judges will not hire law clerks unless the clerk has either practiced law for at least a year or completed another clerkship. If you are applying for a clerkship during law school, completing a judicial externship or participating in a legal clinic may provide you with relevant experience that will strengthen your application. Many law schools permit students to complete an unpaid judicial or legal externship during the school year for academic credit. Work with your Office of Career and Professional Development to secure and complete such an opportunity as the skills and experience you gain will increase your ability to secure a clerkship upon graduation. Peruse reading on that subject matter on your own or serve as a research assistant to a professor who writes in the area of the court's jurisdiction. Do whatever you can to obtain a mastery of the knowledge and skills necessary to hit the ground running when your clerkship commences.

Participate in a Judicial Externship Program: In addition, some law schools also provide special programs that enable students to complete judicial or legal externships, paid or unpaid, during the summers after the first and second year of law school. Take full advantage of such programs and make your externship experience count. For example, at Wake Forest, the Washington, D.C. Summer Judicial Externship Program places select rising second-year and third-year law students into unpaid summer judicial externships at participating federal courts. Program externs meet weekly to take a course tailored to judicial clerking. The course thoroughly explores topics such as judicial ethics, confidentiality, professionalism, and judicial drafting. Guest speakers, including law firm partners, former law clerks, in-house counsel, and federal judges, speak to the students on various topics. Students draft 11-day memos, portions of a bench memo and judicial opinion, and a scholarly paper relating to the judiciary. Students attend oral argument at the United States Court of Appeals for the Federal Circuit and tour the U.S. Supreme Court. The course and reading assignments enrich the externship experience and aim to improve the externs' performance, particularly their research and writing skills. As such, it offers tremendous advantages to participants. Participating in similar programs, to the extent your law school offers them, will greatly enhance your chance of obtaining a clerkship and increase your ability to perform well during the clerkship. Wherever you extern, make the most of the experience by finding a good mentor, developing lasting relationships, exemplifying professionalism and a strong work ethic, and learning all you can from your supervisors. In addition, advise your supervisor at the outset of the externship that you hope to obtain a writing sample and/or a reference/recommender during the externship. This is yet another lasting benefit of completing a judicial externship.

Take a Judicial Clerking Course: Even if you do not participate in an externship program, take a judicial clerking course to the extent your law school offers one. For example, as noted earlier, Wake Forest currently offers two judicial drafting courses. *Judicial Opinion Drafting for Chambers* is offered during the spring semester each year, while *Judicial Clerking* is offered each summer in conjunction with the D.C. Summer Judicial Externship Program. Students in the latter course complete a judicial externship during the day and take a comprehensive course on judicial clerking one evening per week, which covers everything from judicial ethics and confidentiality to judicial drafting. If your law school lacks such offerings, encourage your school to create one. If it cannot, then determine whether you can take such a course at a different school during the semester or in an online format. Such courses will better prepare for you a vast array of clerkship duties from judicial opinion drafting to docket management—topics that are not likely covered in first-year legal writing. Such courses will also provide an opportunity for you to receive instruction and feedback on such assignments so that you do not repeat any errors during your externship or clerkship. They will also greatly enhance the strength of your clerkship application, particularly if you receive a high grade in the course and a strong recommendation from its professor.

Participate in a Clinic: Clinics also provide pertinent and beneficial legal work experience that may enhance your chance of obtaining a judicial externship or clerkship. At Wake Forest, we encourage students seeking appellate clerkships to participate in the *Appellate Advocacy Clinic.* Students in that clinic have participated in cases appearing before various appellate courts and even the U.S. Supreme Court, so it is an incredibly enriching experience. Many law schools offer similar clinics devoted to appellate work. We encourage students seeking a trial court clerkship to participate in our *Litigation Clinic*, which handles a vast array of litigation in federal courts. Participating in a clinic will enhance the analytical, research, writing, and practical skills necessary to exceed expectations during your ensuing clerkship or externship.

Choosing proper courses and experiential opportunities is only half the battle; more importantly, you must perform very well in the courses and experiential opportunities you choose, particularly those that involve research and writing. Good grades and high class rank are important considerations for most judges when selecting a law clerk.[1] Yet some judges afford heightened consideration to an applicant's performance in clinics and experiential courses since those courses most directly involve the analytical, writing, and research skills that law clerks will be using daily. In addition, some judges give greater weight to the recommendations of clinical professors since those professors have closely assessed the applicant's professionalism, written work product, and research skills. Thus, it is incredibly important to perform well in your experiential courses and develop positive, meaningful relationships with your professors.

Planning Your Course of Study—Judicial Clerkships and Externships

Judges value law clerks who are strong researchers and writers. While not required of judicial clerkship or externship applicants, completion of these or similar courses will ensure that you are well positioned to obtain a clerkship or externship offer and are prepared to perform well in that position.

Basic Courses for Judicial Clerkships and Externships

- Judicial Clerking *(offered each summer)*
- Legal Writing for Judicial Chambers
- Advanced Legal Research
- Complex Civil Litigation
- Federal Jurisdiction *(if you seek a federal clerkship or externship)*
- Trial Practice *(if you seek a trial court clerkship)*

Related Courses for Judicial Clerkships and Externships

- Advanced Civil Procedure
- Advanced Trial Practice
- Equitable and Legal Remedies
- Great Jurists Seminar
- Pre-Trial Practice and Procedure
- Any upper level writing or skills course

Courses tailored to the specific jurisdiction of the court are also important. For example, if you plan to apply for a clerkship at the United States Court of Appeals for the Federal Circuit, courses such as *International Trade, Intellectual Property, Patent Law, Trademark Law, Federal Income Tax, Government Contracts*, and *Vaccine Law* may be particularly helpful. Likewise, a bankruptcy court may prefer that you have taken *Bankruptcy*, and a Tax Court will prefer that you have completed tax courses. Research courses tailored to your court's jurisdiction may also be beneficial.

Judges may also prefer applicants who possess pertinent legal work experience. Completing a judicial externship or participating in a legal clinic will provide you with relevant experience that will strengthen your application.

Clinics

- Appellate Advocacy Clinic
- Innocence and Justice Clinic
- Litigation Clinic

In addition to the litigation-centered clinics listed above, other clinics also provide pertinent and beneficial legal work experience.

B. CHOOSING YOUR EXTRACURRICULAR ACTIVITIES

In addition to selecting appropriate courses and experiential learning opportunities, it is important to be intentional when choosing extracurricular activities and assuming leadership roles. Some judges will use an applicant's law school involvement as a proxy to assess whether the applicant takes initiative and how he or she manages time and stress. Other activities, such as journal experience, may demonstrate that an applicant possesses a particular skill set and has enjoyed significant opportunities to refine those skills. Below is a non-exhaustive list of extracurricular activities that may enhance your clerkship or externship application.

Join a Journal: Many judges prefer journal membership; some require it. Judges are especially impressed with students who take leadership roles on a journal, particularly Law Review. Journal membership reflects a strong academic background since many journals only accept students in the top percentage of the law school class. Students who "write on" to a journal instead of "grading on" obviously possess excellent writing, editing, and citation skills, which are essential to success as a law clerk. In addition, journal responsibilities provide students with additional opportunities to hone their writing, research, and editing skills, which will enable them to hit the ground running once in Chambers. Judges are particularly impressed with applicants who have written or published a note with the journal. Note, however, that many judges will consider applicants who are members of *any* journal, not just Law Review, although the latter is certainly the most prestigious.[2]

Participate in Moot Court: Many judges value Moot Court membership, especially students who assume leadership roles. Typically, only the most gifted advocates are selected for Moot Court, so membership signals that the student is a strong writer and oralist—skills that are critical to being a successful law clerk. In addition, as with journal experience, participation in Moot Court competitions will help Moot Court members to further improve their oral and written advocacy skills.

Extracurricular Activities and Community Service: Many judges value participation in extracurricular activities or community service, particularly if an applicant assumes a leadership role or founds an organization. Such participation not only shows that the applicant is well rounded but also displays the applicant's ability to work well with others, to be an integral member of a team to produce a joint product, to manage his or her time wisely, and to maintain a healthy work/life balance.

Community service is especially impressive since it exemplifies the applicant's commitment to serving others for the common good, which is one of the primary goals of the judiciary. Some judges will only hire law clerks who have exhibited a spirit of service.

In choosing your activities, however, be careful not to overextend yourself, particularly during your first year of law school. A strong academic foundation is typically a judge's primary concern; thus, an applicant cannot overshadow poor grades with excessive involvement in various activities. Your application and interview should highlight how your participation in the activity has helped you to develop skills transferable to a clerkship.

TA or RA Experience: Many judges strongly prefer applicants who have served as a teaching assistant ("TA"), research assistant ("RA"), or both. A professor will only select a student as a TA or RA if the student exemplifies a strong work ethic, intellect, integrity, professionalism, and trustworthiness. Furthermore, most professors require review of a student's written work before hiring the student as a TA or RA to ensure that he or she is a strong researcher, writer, and editor. Finally, the TA or RA must be an effective communicator capable of explaining his or her ideas, meeting deadlines, and working well with others. Judges look for these same skills during the hiring process, so selection as a TA or RA signals to the judge that at least one professor observed those characteristics in the applicant. In addition, TA and RA duties enable the student to further hone those skills, becoming a better thinker, writer, editor, researcher, and communicator.[3]

Clinics or Judicial Externships: As mentioned earlier, many judges prefer or require clinical or externship experience since both opportunities allow students to apply their substantive legal knowledge in practical ways and in real-world settings. In addition, judicial externs have prior experience with judicial drafting, judicial ethics, courtroom decorum, docket management, and the Chambers atmosphere so that they are far better equipped to add value to Chambers once the clerkship or externship commences.

Judicial externships and internships are particularly attractive to judges because they reveal experience working in a collaborative environment, managing a busy docket, drafting judicial documents, as well as a practical understanding the scope and contours of judicial ethics and Chambers confidentiality. Furthermore, if you plan to seek a clerkship, disclose this to your supervising clerk at the outset of your judicial externship. Discuss the possibility of producing a writing sample during your externship that you may include in your clerkship application. Ask your supervising clerk to expose you to experiences that will prepare you both to obtain a clerkship, such as shadowing a clerkship interview. Make an effort to meet clerks and externs from other Chambers as well. As your externship comes to an end, ask your supervising clerk or judge to serve as a reference for you or, if the relationship is particularly close, to write a letter of recommendation on your behalf. Before your externship concludes, ask your supervising clerk to review your resume and if possible, conduct a mock interview. With your judge's permission, keep a conflicts list from your externship to avoid potential conflicts of interest during subsequent positions, including a post-graduate clerkship. Send a handwritten thank you note to your judge and each member of Chambers, including the judicial assistant, at the conclusion of your externship to express your gratitude for their mentorship and kindness. In post-externship interviews, emphasize the lessons learned from your externship in your cover letter and other application materials. Yet always maintain Chambers confidentiality. After your externship concludes, make a concerted effort to maintain good relationships with Chambers, through sending occasional emails when a case you worked on is issued or affirmed, mailing holiday or birthday cards, and scheduling visits or coffees with your supervising clerk or judge when and if you are in town. Never let the relationships grow stale and alert your Chambers of professional accomplishments and developments, particularly if you have begun applying for post-graduate clerkships.

Work Experience: Finally, many judges prefer students who possess relevant work experience, either before, during, or after law school and preferably in the areas of law within the court's jurisdiction. Chambers typically have little time and few resources, financial and otherwise, to train new law clerks, so it is helpful when new clerks receive such training *before* the clerkship begins. Law firms and agencies provide such training. Work experience also increases the maturity of one's writing and enriches his or her understanding of professionalism. For these reasons, some Chambers will only consider applicants with relevant work experience; some will only accept applications from practicing attorneys or current clerks, not law students.

C. DEVELOPING AND MAINTAINING MEANINGFUL RELATIONSHIPS

Establishing meaningful relationships is essential for any prospective clerk. All judges require applicants to submit at least one letter of recommendation, often two or three. While some judges prefer a letter from a former employer, others require or prefer letters from a former employer and a professor, preferably a person with whom you have worked closely and who has assessed your written work product. As a result, develop and maintain positive relationships with your professors and employers. Exemplify professionalism and a positive attitude. Be punctual and meet deadlines. Do not request extensions unless absolutely necessary. Do your best work. Be courteous and sincere. Never plagiarize or do anything that reflects negatively on your trustworthiness. Get to know your professors before you need to ask them to serve as a reference, write a recommendation letter, or call a judge. Say thank you when your professor or employer takes time to conference with you over a draft or give you guidance. Provide a thoughtful handwritten thank you note. Develop a meaningful relationship so that when your professor and/or employer is called upon to serve as a reference for you, he or she will be well equipped to describe the kind of person you are inside and outside the classroom or office. Even after the class or term of employment ends, work to maintain the relationship by sending occasional emails or notes or scheduling opportunities to catch up over coffee or lunch. Send holiday or birthday cards or messages, as appropriate. It is a good rule of thumb to also apply these same principles to other points of contact besides professors and employers, such as former fellow members of Greek organizations or alumni organizations.

Finally, if you are considering clerking, notify your Clerkship Advisor and Faculty Advisor early in the process so that they can offer additional guidance. Speak with a member of your law school's Clerkship Committee or to its Director of Clerkships, if one exists. Contact those individuals early so that they can not only ensure that you are staying on the right track to obtaining a clerkship but can also send critical opportunities your way, such as clerkship or externship openings. Attend your law school's sessions on obtaining clerkships and talk to professors who have clerked for the judge for whom you hope to clerk. Also speak to other students who have performed judicial externships or to alumni who are current or former clerks at courts of interest. To the extent possible, expand your search beyond your law school and include individuals from your undergraduate institution as well. Once you have developed a meaningful personal connection, ask permission to add the individual as a contact on *LinkedIn* but work to maintain a more personal connection through emails, telephone calls, coffees, lunches, etc. Stay current on well publicized, important decisions pending or recently issued at your court(s) of interest and keep abreast of potential clerkship openings at them as well.

Below is a non-exhaustive checklist you can use to determine if you are taking proper steps now to secure a clerkship later.

Law Student Checklist

1. Am I developing meaningful relationships with my professors, employers, and classmates? ☐

2. Am I performing very well in my courses, especially those that involve research and writing? ☐

3. Am I continuously improving my research, writing, editing, oral communication, and analytical skills? ☐

4. Am I a journal or Moot Court member? ☐

5. Am I taking coursework relevant to the court's jurisdiction and performing well in those courses? ☐

6. Am I developing a good writing sample or writing a note for my journal? ☐

7. Am I participating in extracurricular activities or community service that will help me to develop skills necessary to perform well as a clerk? ☐

8. Am I taking on leadership roles in at least some of my activities? ☐

9. Am I serving as a TA or RA? ☐

10. Am I completing a clinic or judicial externship during the school year or summer? ☐

11. Am I completing a relevant legal externship during the school year or summer? ☐

12. Am I reaching out to relevant points of contact, such as members of the Clerkship Committee or alumni now clerking for courts of interest, and maintaining those relationships? ☐

13. Am I staying current on the important pending cases and clerkship opportunities at my court(s) of interest? ☐

For more information on preparing to clerk, see Appendix A.

D. SUPPLEMENTAL RESOURCES

1. MARY L. DUNNEWOLD, BETH A. HONETSCHLAGER, & BRENDA L. TOFTE, JUDICIAL CLERKSHIPS: A PRACTICAL GUIDE (2010).

2. DEBRA M. STRAUSS, BEHIND THE BENCH: THE GUIDE TO JUDICIAL CLERKSHIPS (2002).

Notes

---

[1]   *Courting Clerkships: The NALP Judicial Clerkship Study*, NAT'L ASS'N FOR LAW PLACEMENT, INC., (Oct. 2000), http://www.nalp.org/clrktb27_45#29.

[2]   *Id.*

[3]   *Id.*

CHAPTER 4

APPLYING TO CLERK

■ ■ ■

Judicial clerkships are highly coveted due to the lasting benefits they confer and the professional opportunities to which they may give rise.[1] As such, clerkships are extremely competitive and often difficult to obtain. Indeed, a single judge might receive hundreds of applications from across America for a single clerkship opening. Because most judges may hire only one to four law clerks, scores of qualified applicants compete for each slot. For this reason, it is incredibly important to set yourself apart during the application process. This chapter provides some non-exhaustive guidance to help you do just that.

A. QUALITIES THAT JUDGES SEEK IN CLERKSHIP APPLICANTS

To set yourself apart during the application process, you must first fully understand what a clerkship entails and which qualities your prospective judge desires in a law clerk. Only then can you highlight and emphasize these qualities during the application process. This book illuminates the responsibilities of a clerk as well as the attributes that most judges seek in applicants, but note that such preferences may vary judge to judge. Thus, it is always a good idea to speak to a member of your law school's Clerkship Committee, former law clerks who served the judge(s) to whom you have applied, a representative from your Office of Career and Professional Development, and other sources to gain additional insight.

It is also helpful to understand what judges do *not* require. Through the years, I have heard countless students opine, "Unless I am in the top of my class or on Law Review, I have no chance of obtaining a clerkship." This is a myth. Many judges peruse applicants holistically and consider a vast array of factors when selecting a law clerk. While having top grades or journal membership certainly bolsters an application, the absence of these factors will not necessarily preclude an individual from obtaining a clerkship. To the contrary, judges consider each applicant's grades, rank, coursework, letters of recommendation, work experience, leadership roles, community involvement, extracurricular activities, writing, research, and communication skills, character, and personality among other things. Some judges will weigh one factor more heavily than another, and this varies from one judge to another.

In general, judges typically prefer a candidate with good grades and a high class rank at a well respected law school. However, this is not a hard and fast rule. For example, a judge might consider a student with slightly lower grades or rank at a more competitive law school, especially if the student is heavily engaged in the law school community, had earned high grades in writing-intensive courses, or had completed relevant externships and clinics.

As explained below, judges also value strong research, writing, editing, and oral communication skills. After all, law clerks will spend the vast majority of their time engaged in these activities. Thus, they must be able to write effectively and clearly communicate their findings to the judge in meetings and discussions. While the attorneys filing the briefs should ideally have completed all of the relevant research for the court, law clerks sometimes discover that briefs omit or misstate seminal cases, fail to discuss relevant case history, or overlook threshold legal issues, such as jurisdiction or timeliness. In fact, the court may raise lack of jurisdiction *sua sponte*, or on its own motion.

Thus, it is important to showcase your research, writing, and oral communication skills in your application materials and interview. To strengthen your application, achieve high grades, particularly in your legal research and writing courses, and make an effort to take at least one writing or skills course, clinic, or externship in each semester of law school. Take *Judicial Clerking* or *Judicial Drafting* to the extent your school offers those courses and seek permission to take them elsewhere for credit if it does not. Participate in experiential learning opportunities, such as judicial externships, clinics, and practicums, whenever possible. Take *Advanced Legal Research* to refine your research abilities. Provide recommendations from research and writing professors or list them as references. Highlight experiential courses on your resume, serve on a journal or on Moot Court, work as a research assistant or teaching assistant during law school, and provide an impeccable resume and cover letter.

Law clerks must also possess exceptional editing skills. A law clerk must frequently edit his or her work and that of others, such as a peer's draft opinion. A law clerk who submits an opinion that contains typographical, grammatical, citation, or formatting errors risks losing credibility; issuing an opinion with such errors could mar the judge's reputation and undermine public trust in the court. Worse yet are substantive errors as when an opinion misstates a key controlling case or overlooks a material fact. Thus, a law clerk must be a strong editor who understands how to effectively give and receive constructive criticism.

Judges also prefer applicants who have performed well in coursework relevant to the court's jurisdiction or procedure. All applicants should aim to do well in generally applicable courses, such as *Evidence, Professional*

Responsibility, and *Civil Procedure.* In addition, applicants who wish to obtain a clerkship at a Bankruptcy Court should take and perform well in *Bankruptcy*, while students who wish to work at the Office of Special Masters would perhaps enhance their chance of selection by participating in a Vaccine Law Clinic or taking *Law and Medicine.* Students interested in clerking at the United States Court of Appeals for the Federal Circuit should study intellectual property, particularly patent law, as well as courses in international trade, government contracts, federal income tax, and other areas within the court's jurisdiction. Such courses evince an interest in and substantive familiarity with the court's subject matter and relatedly, demonstrate greater preparedness for the clerkship. In selecting which courses will best enhance your application, consult the court's website to determine the court's subject matter jurisdiction. Also review Chapter 3 of this book and explore your law school's website to determine if it contains additional resources regarding how to best plan your course of study if you plan to clerk. Speak with a member of your law school's Clerkship Committee or with the Director of Clerkships, if one exists. Consult your faculty advisor or your assigned Career Counselor. Each of these resources will help you tailor a course of study that will enhance your application and better prepare you to clerk. Notably, however, relevant coursework will strengthen your application, but the absence thereof will not sink it. For example, a government contracts practitioner who never took *Federal Income Tax* may still obtain a clerkship at the United States Court of Federal Claims, even though that court handles certain tax lawsuits brought against the federal government. This is because clerks can usually teach themselves areas of law with which they are unfamiliar.

Aside from these qualities, judges also often strongly prefer, if not require, applicants with journal and/or Moot Court membership, relevant work experience, relevant undergraduate coursework, strong undergraduate grades, extracurricular activities, leadership roles, community service and involvement, experience as a teaching assistant and/or research assistant, and clinical or judicial externship experience. Each credential evidences attributes salient to effective clerking. For example, a law clerk must be able to clearly explain a new concept, whether legal or factual, in a bench memo to his or her judge; selection as a teaching assistant not only shows that a professor trusts the student to take on this important role but also provides the student with an opportunity to hone the ability to explain complex concepts to others in a way that is easy to understand. Likewise, journal members spend countless hours reviewing and editing others' work, which requires discernment and strong editing skills, both of which are essential to effective clerking. Moot Court membership is a proxy for strong writing, research, and oral advocacy skills, as well as the ability to think quickly on one's feet. Relevant work experience may indicate professionalism, maturity, dependability, and discernment. Relevant undergraduate coursework may suggest a deeper understanding of issues commonly before the court; for instance, a Federal Circuit judge may prefer applicants who possess a hard science degree given the prevalence of patent cases on the court's busy docket. In each instance, the credential serves as a proxy for other predictors of success.

Because Chambers is a close-knit environment, interpersonal qualities are often just as important as academic qualifications to being a successful clerk. For example, a law clerk must be humble enough to understand his or her place in Chambers and not overstep boundaries. Put differently, there is no room for big egos in the small, collegial environment of Chambers. In this regard, judges seek individuals who are trustworthy, intelligent, helpful, self-motivated, team-oriented, positive, resilient, courteous, hardworking, diplomatic, dependable, thoughtful, well rounded, and discerning.

On the other hand, a law clerk must also possess enough confidence and diplomacy to advise the judge, albeit respectfully, if the judge appears to misunderstand a factual or legal issue in a case. Indeed, the law clerk's role is to help the judge formulate the right position; in so doing, the law clerk may need to occasionally explain that a controlling legal authority or a material fact may undermine the course of action that the judge initially wishes to take. It is critically important that the law clerk provide the judge with the entire landscape of relevant information, in support or in opposition, so that the judge can make a well reasoned and well informed decision that will deter or withstand an appeal.

Because the law clerk must provide the judge with the full legal landscape, the law clerk must also possess good judgment and discernment. The law clerk will be reading countless briefs and pleadings and perusing voluminous records and lengthy cases. Yet through it all, the law clerk cannot miss a material fact or key issue in a controlling case. Doing so could result in a reversible error and potentially tarnish the judge's credibility and reputation. Thus, it is essential that law clerks are detail-oriented and fastidious in their review of materials no matter how voluminous. As will be discussed in more detail below, judges will depend most heavily upon an applicant's recommendations, references, and interview to assess whether the applicant possesses the aforementioned qualities.

Judges also seek intelligent, thoughtful law clerks who will spot issues that others may have missed and perceive issues from every angle. They value clerks who manage their time effectively and are able to set and meet reasonable deadlines. They desire clerks who manage stress well since clerks will also often have to produce high quality, thorough work under tight time constraints and other pressures. Because judges do not have time to micromanage staff, law clerks must also be self-motivated project managers who take initiative. Clerks must be dependable and equally capable of working alone or on teams. This is important since some tasks, such as opinion drafting, are primarily solitary endeavors, while others, such as editing a co-clerk's opinion, require collaboration. Chambers is a small environment suitable only for team players who will step up to assist the judge as necessary and go the extra mile to accomplish Chambers' goals, even if that means volunteering to stay late, cancelling plans, or working over a weekend or holiday. Such sacrifices should be made cheerfully, not begrudgingly.

A positive attitude and passion for excellence are must-haves for any successful law clerk. For this reason, it is important for law clerks to be helpful and encouraging team players with strong work ethics. A good law clerk cannot simply submit an opinion because the clock strikes 6:00 pm; each law clerk must be fully committed to producing his or her best work no matter how long it takes. Finally, a law clerk must be committed to serving others, not simply to self-advancement. After all, the clerk must give 100% to produce an opinion that will never bear his or her name or be attributed to him or her. The clerk must also be resilient enough to maintain a positive attitude in the face of intense time pressure, stress, a heavy workload, and criticism.

In addition to the aforementioned character traits, some judges may also, for personal or professional reasons, place great emphasis upon hiring law clerks from their alma maters or from organizations to which they belong, such as a bar association. Others prefer individuals who share community ties or common interests. For example, a judge from West Virginia might prefer to hire West Virginia natives, while a graduate of Washington and Lee University School of Law ("W&L") might give heightened consideration to other W&L alumni. Such personal preferences are not uncommon but vary from one judge to another.

The key to success is knowing, to the extent possible, what your prospective judge seeks. Although this book provides much insight in that regard, there is significant variance in law clerk functions and responsibilities. Visit the court's website and read the judge's biography contained there. If possible, confer with individuals who have actually clerked for the judge or court to which you are applying. Nothing is more insightful than speaking with the judge's former clerks who know him or her on a personal level. Always bear in mind, however, that the information you receive is only as reliable as the giver. If a law clerk performed poorly and as a result, had a less-than-ideal relationship with his or her judge, the law clerk may review the judge poorly while omitting the critical fact that poor performance was the real reason for the unproductive relationship. Thus, seek wise counsel from persons of good repute whom you trust, respect, and admire, and if possible, speak to more than one former clerk of your prospective judge to obtain a wider, more complete range of perspectives.

But how do you track down these former clerks or externs? Some judges freely provide a list of former clerks with whom you can speak. Others will provide names upon request, although it is probably ill-advised to request such a list as it may signal to your judge that you are not 100% committed to clerk for him or her. Your law school's Office of Career and Professional Development or Office of Alumni Affairs may keep a running list of faculty, staff, and graduates from your law school who have clerked for various judges. This is a great resource because individuals within your law school community are likelier to provide you with candid advice upon which you can rely. A judge's former colleagues or professors may also provide probative insights into which qualities particularly resonate with the judge. However, even if you are unable to speak to any former clerks or colleagues, the qualities that your judge values most will often inform his or her judicial opinions. So read the judge's recent or seminal opinions to discern which qualities likely matter most to him or her.

After you have researched what your prospective judge seeks in a law clerk, brand yourself accordingly. Tailor your cover letter, resume, and interview talking points to demonstrate that you are well suited for the position. Put differently, emphasize points of connection, attributes, and experience that reflect your suitability for clerking. For your top judges, consider submitting a paper application customized to each judge; it should highlight specific points of connection with those judges, such as community ties, a common alma mater, etc. This attention to detail will show your enthusiasm and interest and set you apart from other applicants. Below is a non-exhaustive chart listing various criteria that will set you apart during the application process.

Attributes That Will Set You Apart

Usually Required	Preferred* (some judges may require any or all of these attributes)	A Plus Factor
Good grades/ High class rank	Prestigious law school	Graduate of judge's alma mater(s)
Strong research, analytical, writing, and editing skills	Journal experience and/or Moot Court membership	Member of organization with which judge is affiliated (*e.g.,* Hispanic Bar Association, Pi Beta Phi, Phi Delta Phi)
Good character and interpersonal skills	Relevant work experience, preferably legal	Common interests or practice area
Relevant coursework	Leadership or extracurricular involvement	Community ties and connections (some judges prefer to hire clerks who have lived or practiced in the area where the court is located)
Strong recommendations	Community service/volunteering/spirit of service	Plans to practice in the area after completing the clerkship
Strong writing sample(s)	TA and/or RA experience	Publications
	Clinic and/or judicial externship	Awards (*e.g.,* Best Brief Award)

Now that we have established what judges *typically* seek in applicants, it is important to dispel some common myths surrounding clerkships. First, as noted above, an applicant need not have a pre-existing connection with a judge, court, or geographical area to obtain the position.[2] In fact, to quash any perception of nepotism, some judges will not even accept applications from persons who could be perceived as having a special connection with the judge, such as relatives. Of those clerks who do report having enjoyed a "special connection," many may have simply served as judicial externs with the judge during law school.

B. FORMULATING AN EFFECTIVE CLERKSHIP-SEEKING STRATEGY

A successful clerkship-seeking strategy has three primary steps: self-assess, apply, and manage. First, self-assess to decide which clerkship will be the best fit for you. Next, apply for a clerkship at the proper time and in the proper way. Include the correct documents and make sure they are well edited. Cast a wide net but never apply to a job you would not accept. Be realistic in your expectations and flexible in your location; you increase your chance of obtaining a clerkship if you are not wedded to a single judge, particular court, or specific city or state. Explain any gaps in your application, such as a low grade in a relevant course or a year of unemployment. Consider ways to offset this "gap," such as waiting to apply until you have obtained practice experience. After reviewing this chapter, speak to your Faculty Advisor and a member of your law school's Office of Career and Professional Development to determine where you should apply and how to prepare your applications.

In deciding where to apply, be creative. Use your relationships, communities, and social networks to enhance your ability of obtaining a clerkship. Although most clerks do not obtain clerkships through connections, they can sometimes help you to at least get a foot in the door. Utilize former co-workers, college, and law school alumni networks, Greek organizations, friends and family, social media platforms, law school resources like the Office of Career and Professional Development and the Alumni Office, and Internet job sites. Ask an alumni connection to conduct a purely informational interview with you that will shed light on his or her former clerkship or simply provide you with feedback regarding how to improve your interviewing skills. If impressed, the interviewer might, on his or her own initiative, recommend you to his or her former judge.

Finally, once you have submitted your applications, manage them effectively. Stay organized. Maintain a spreadsheet or similar table to track where you have submitted applications, when you have received a response, additional materials you must provide, etc. Promptly send handwritten thank you notes to your recommenders and interviewers. Set calendar alerts to remind you when to follow up with Chambers regarding the status of your applications. Although this is a quick overview, the sections that follow will further unpack each step in this clerkship-seeking strategy.

1. STEP ONE: SELF-ASSESS

How do I decide where to apply?

The first step is to determine *where* to apply. Chambers is a small, familial atmosphere, so it is vital that your personality is a good fit with Chambers. When deciding whether to apply for a judge, speak to the judge's former clerks or persons familiar with the judge, if possible, to assess whether you would be a good cultural fit. As noted above, in many instances, your law school's Office of Career and Professional Development or Alumni Office will maintain a list of law school alumni who have clerked for judges. This is a great way to learn more about a judge.

Keep an open mind. There are various types of judicial clerkships at the federal, state, and local level. At the federal level, there are Article III and Article I courts. Article III of the United States Constitution vests Congress with the right to enact legislation to create federal courts in addition to the Supreme Court of the United States.[3] Via such legislation, Congress has created over 100 Article III courts, including 94 federal district courts, 13 federal circuit courts, and the United States Court of International Trade.[4]

In addition, visit each court's website to learn about its subject-matter jurisdiction. Ask yourself whether the areas of law that the court handles interest you and will provide a good foundation for your long-term professional goals. Most Article III courts hear civil and criminal cases arising from their respective geographic jurisdictions. For example, the United States Court of Appeals for the Fourth Circuit hears appeals from district courts in states within that circuit, including district courts in North Carolina, West Virginia, and Virginia. However, the United States Court of Appeals for the Federal Circuit sits in Washington, D.C., and enjoys statutorily vested jurisdiction over cases from any district that involve a question of patent law as well as appeals from certain specialty courts like the United States Court of Federal Claims and U.S. Court of International Trade. Thus, courts vary in their subject matter coverage with district and circuit courts hearing a diverse array of civil and criminal cases, while more specialized courts, such as the U.S. Court of International Trade, may handle only one area of law. Thus, you must decide whether you prefer to become a subject matter expert in a single practice area or be a generalist who learns a little about many different areas. If you wish to practice criminal law in the long-term, it may be ill-advised for you to clerk for courts that do not handle criminal matters. Instead, a district court clerkship might be more suitable. That being said, any clerkship will enhance your writing, research, editing, and analytical abilities, and those skills are transferable to any post-clerkship position.

Courts vary not only in jurisdiction but also in prestige. Supreme Court and federal appellate clerkships are usually considered the most prestigious and accordingly, are often the most difficult to obtain. Justices and appellate judges typically only hire applicants with prior work and clerkship experience as well as top grades from competitive law schools. However, there are exceptions to every rule, and there is no harm in applying for these positions, especially if you possess other salient qualities, such as work experience prior to law school, a notable publication, or judicial externship experience.

Applicants who apply to lesser known courts may increase their chance of obtaining a clerkship. For example, many Article I courts exist across the country, such as the U.S. Territorial Courts in Guam, the Virgin Islands, and other territories, the U.S. Bankruptcy Courts, U.S. Tax Court, U.S. Court of Federal Claims, U.S. Magistrate Courts, and the Office of Special Masters within the U.S. Court of Federal Claims. While these positions are quite competitive, the applicant pool is somewhat smaller simply because many people do not realize that these courts accept law clerks. Because fewer people apply, there is a greater chance of obtaining a clerkship even if you lack prior clerkship or work experience. Most importantly, the clerkship experience at these courts is no less valuable. As one former clerk at the U.S. Court of Federal Claims observed, "clerking is the Swiss Army Knife of the legal profession" because it prepares you for virtually any subsequent legal position.

The same is true of state court clerkships, which provide excellent learning opportunities. Each state will typically have trial courts and a state court of last resort as well as specialty courts such as family courts. Most states also possess intermediate appellate courts of general jurisdiction. Clerkships at state and local courts may be perceived as less prestigious, but they are no less beneficial than a federal clerkship. This is especially true if your long-term plan is to litigate cases within the state in which you clerked. In this regard, a state or local clerkship not only enables you to become familiar with local law and procedure, but it also provides an invaluable opportunity to form meaningful ties and connections in the community where you plan to practice. For these reasons, a state clerkship can sometimes be equally, if not more, beneficial than a federal clerkship, depending on your long-term professional goals. In addition, a state clerkship may also make you more attractive to a federal judge; it is not uncommon for a state court clerk to complete a second clerkship at the federal level.

As noted above, to enhance your chance of obtaining a clerkship, cast a reasonably wide net, but never apply for a clerkship that you would not ultimately accept; this wastes the judge's resources and time. In addition, the Online System for Clerkship Application and Review ("OSCAR")—a centralized resource for applying to federal clerkships that is discussed in more detail below—limits applicants to approximately 100 pending applications. Even so, the wider the net, the likelier you are to secure a position. Always confer with your Career Counselor, Faculty Advisor, or Director of Clerkships to determine whether you should apply, to where, by when, and anything you should do to explain or offset deficiencies in your application. If your school does not have a Director of Clerkships, then seek out a member of the Clerkship Committee to the extent one exists or talk to a trusted professor who formerly clerked.

Do not hesitate to apply to a clerkship located in a city with which you have no existing connection. Because federal clerkships are generally last only one to two years, most federal judges do not require an applicant to have existing ties to the locality in which the court resides or plan to practice there after the clerkship concludes. Most judges simply seek applicants who possess the qualities necessary to add immediate value to Chambers. As such, you may apply to clerkships across the country or even abroad.[5] However, this prevailing wisdom is perhaps less true of older judges and with judges at state and local courts who may still tend to prefer individuals who plan to reside and practice in the community after the clerkship concludes.

Location is another relevant consideration. It is unwise to apply to a court in a city you have never visited. It is important to know beyond a doubt that you could reside happily in the community during the clerkship term as dissatisfaction with one's personal environment could impede professional performance and enjoyment of the clerkship. That being said, you are not required to ultimately practice or even be barred in the state in which you clerk. Because judges usually hire clerks for a short term, some attorneys use the clerkship to experience a new city or to transition to a new locality. There is no requirement that you have ties to the clerkship location, although in some instances those connections might strengthen your application. Choose a location in which you will be happy outside of work as contentment in your personal life usually translates into better work product in your professional life.

On a related note, consider the cost of living, particularly if you are clerking immediately after law school. As noted earlier, law clerks are not paid as generously as other entry-level legal positions, such as first-year associates at law firms. Thus, a clerkship in New York City where cost of living is quite high might be less desirable from an economic perspective than clerking in a smaller town or mid-sized city. That being said, a New York City clerkship might offer extremely interesting and sophisticated work as well as high profile cases.

Moreover, choose a clerkship that will best suit your long-term goals. For example, if you plan to practice bankruptcy, it may be most beneficial for you to clerk in a bankruptcy court. As appropriate, limit your "net" to bankruptcy courts. However, if you simply wish to practice general litigation, then clerking at virtually any court in any locality will be incredibly beneficial because the knowledge gained and skills honed during the clerkship are transferable to any practice area or workplace setting.

In sum, deciding where to clerk is a personal decision that you should thoughtfully consider. No one can make the decision for you because no one knows you as well as you know yourself. And in the end, you are the one who must ultimately live with the decision. So choose wisely, taking into account your judge, your potential co-clerks, your location, etc. Talk to your spouse or significant other. Do all of this *before* you apply so that you do not waste your time or that of Chambers. Never apply and certainly never interview for a position that you know you would not accept. Once you have received a clerkship interview, the judge will likely expect you to know on the day of the interview whether or not you would accept the offer should one be extended. These kinds of "exploding offers" are not unusual, so be prepared. To assist you in researching with whom you should apply, the section below outlines helpful tools to research judges and courts.

How do I effectively research my prospective judge and court?[6]

Conducting thorough and thoughtful research on your prospective judge and court is essential to determining whether to apply. It will also prove useful as you prepare for the interview should an offer to interview be extended. Countless tools for performing judicial research exist, so the resources discussed herein are by no means exhaustive. Confer with your law school librarian as necessary for additional research tips and tools.

Court websites and legal directories, such as the *Biographical Directory of Federal Judges*,[7] will provide basic information about your prospective judge. The Directory includes the biographies of judges who have served since 1789 on the U.S. Supreme Court, U.S. district courts, current and former appellate courts, the U.S. Court of International Trade, and the U.S. Court of Federal Claims. It even permits you to search via various attributes, such as race and sex. Similarly, the *Biographical Directory of the Federal Judiciary* goes a step further by sharing interesting statistics, such as the first women judges, judges who have been impeached, etc.[8] The judicial profiles included in the *Almanac of the Federal Judiciary* detail each judge's academic and professional background, notable rulings, etc., and sometimes provide commentary from attorneys regarding their experience with the judge.[9] In addition, each court website includes a short biography of each sitting judge.[10]

Electronic databases like Westlaw will also be incredibly helpful. Westlaw's Profiler Section contains a comprehensive resource—*Profiles of*

Attorneys and Judges—that contains more than a million profiles of law firms, courts, judges, and lawyers from all 50 states, Puerto Rico, the Virgin Islands, the District of Columbia, Canada, England, and Europe; coverage begins in 1990. The Profiler Section also includes *Profiles of Patent Judges* and *Profiles of Trademark Judges* as well as reports of litigation history and even records of judicial reversal. To search for judges in Westlaw, choose *Search Cases*; then select *Advanced Search*. Select the *Judges* field from the Advanced Search options and input the judge's name. To access judge information in Lexis Advance, select the *Litigation Profile* suite from the upper-left drop down menu on Lexis Advance. Select *Judge* as your category and then enter the name of the judge in the search box. There are also selected state judicial directories that can be accessed from the Lexis Advance home page by choosing *Directories*, then *Judge Directories*. To search for judges using docket information in Bloomberg Law, go to *Dockets* and input a judge's name in the *Judge* field. Bloomberg Law also provides the ability to search for people from the Bloomberg Law home page by clicking on *Search & Browse* and then choosing *People*. This source provides career information, educational history, awards, and other information including current news stories about the judge. In addition to Bloomberg, you can also find news about your judge by searching Google or using the News databases in Westlaw or LexisAdvance. In addition, Ravel Law now offers a helpful *Judge Analytics* tool.[11] Confer with your law librarian to see if your law school has access to these databases or to obtain more information regarding how to most effectively use them.

Applicants seeking Supreme Court clerkships should review the *Guide to the U.S. Supreme Court*, which among other things, discusses the Supreme Court's history and procedures. It also provides biographical information regarding current and former Supreme Court justices.[12] Other useful sources on the Supreme Court include *The Supreme Court Justices: A Biographical Dictionary*,[13] *The Supreme Court Justices: Illustrated Biographies 1789–2012*,[14] and *Out of Order: Stories from the History of the Supreme Court*.[15]

Other helpful clerkship resources include BNA's *Directory of State and Federal Courts, Judges, and Clerks*,[16] which contains contact information for judges and clerks as well as information regarding judicial nominees. For applicants interested in judicial diversity, the *Directory of Minority Judges of the United States*[17] compiles information regarding judges who self-identify as persons of color or who work as Tribal Court Judges. It also includes a chart detailing the number of minority judges within each state. Individuals seeking state court clerkships may consult the *Directory of State Court Clerks & County Courthouses*,[18] which provides contact information for state appellate, trial, and county clerkships as well as statistics and trends involving state court litigation.

Finally, one way to obtain a federal clerkship is to track the list of federal judicial nominations and to apply as soon as a new judge is confirmed. A new judge may be unfamiliar with OSCAR and thus, less likely to advertise there. In addition, the new judge will have several spots available, and fewer applicants will likely apply simply because they are unaware that the new judge has just been confirmed. Taken together, these factors and your sincere interest in this judge may enhance your chance of securing a clerkship. To track judicial nominations, visit the Judicial Nominations Database[19] or Thomas.gov.[20] The United States Courts website also provides a list of federal judicial confirmations.[21]

In conclusion, countless resources exist to research your prospective judge and court. Use them judiciously when deciding whether to apply, when crafting your application materials, and when preparing for clerkship interviews. Confer with your Office of Career and Professional Development and/or your law librarian for additional information. Most importantly, as noted earlier, talk to former clerks who served the judge if possible. To locate former clerks, use your law school's alumni database to investigate whether any alumni clerked for the judge. Your Clerkship Committee may track whether faculty members know or clerked for judges. Use these resources to your advantage. No matter how much research you do, there is simply no substitute for speaking with someone who has actually served your prospective judge.

When should I apply?

Once you have selected the judges to whom you will apply, you must decide *when* to apply. As with everything else, good timing is key. Until quite recently, a federal hiring plan imposed a rigid timeline upon participating federal judges and third-year law students applying for federal clerkships. Under that plan, law students were not permitted to apply for clerkships until the summer preceding their third year of law school, participants received all clerkship applications on the same date, and judges did not interview law student applicants until the fall of that same year. This plan proved problematic because judges increasingly opted out of the plan, and applicants who were not in law school, such as practicing attorneys, were not confined to the same timeline. They could apply and interview whenever they chose, often securing positions before judges even received applications from law student competitors. Perhaps as a result, these limitations were removed. Now applicants, whether law students or practitioners, may apply whenever they choose, and judges interview and hire applicants year-round.

Although federal judges are no longer constrained by the hiring plan, many still seem to prefer applicants who have completed at least three semesters of law school. In light of this, law students who seek post-graduate clerkships should ideally research positions in the spring of their second year, build a list of judges to which they wish to apply, and review and perfect their writing sample, resume, and cover letter. By April 1, they should request recommendations and submit their final materials to OSCAR no later than July 1. Notably, this is only a suggested timeline. Specialty courts, magistrate judges, and state courts appear to hire later than federal appellate and district court judges, so a different timeline may work well for those positions. In addition, a different timeline may be advisable so that you can present your most attractive resume. For example, if you apply in the spring of your second year, you may be unable to include the judicial externship you are completing during your 2L summer or the high grades you will obtain in the relevant coursework you are taking during the spring semester. You can always supplement your application, but there is a chance that it will already have been discarded before you have an opportunity to do so. On the other hand, the early bird often gets the worm. Bear these competing concerns in mind as you determine your application timeline.

Significantly, there is no hard and fast rule requiring a person to clerk immediately after law school. To the contrary, many attorneys practice for several years or complete a fellowship before applying to clerk. There are many advantages to choosing a less traditional clerkship trajectory. Doing so may enhance your chance of obtaining a more prestigious clerkship, while your practice experience will likely help you be a more capable clerk. In fact, some judges only hire clerks who have post-graduate practice experience. Preferences vary by Chambers.

Waiting may also help you offset any gaps or deficits in your application materials. For instance, if you are not in the top 25% of your class, it may be beneficial for you to work for a few years after law school before applying. Applying after graduation may not only enhance your ability to obtain a clerkship but also may improve your chance of securing one at a more prestigious court. Increasingly, federal judges, especially at the appellate level, only hire clerks with post-graduate practice experience. Such practical experience often enables a clerk to make a more meaningful contribution to Chambers and to be better prepared to hit the ground running. Indeed, this emerging trend may be a by-product of the recent recession during which many law firms laid off capable, young associates purely for budgetary reasons; these associates flocked in great numbers to clerkship positions. As a result, judges who had previously hired law students noticed more experienced attorneys in the applicant pool. Judges who hired those attorneys likely noticed a palpable difference in the quality of their work, maturity, and professionalism. As a result, some judges who had previously primarily hired law students may have shifted their preference to attorneys with practical experience. Other judges might hire law students but only for a clerkship term several years in the future, requiring the law student to gain some post-graduate work experience before joining Chambers. This trend is especially noticeable in federal circuit courts. Again, however, exceptions exist to every rule, and a Chambers may relax these requirements for applicants with relevant judicial externship or clinical experience or for applicants with significant, relevant work experience *prior* to law school.

After you have completed a thoughtful self-assessment regarding where and when to apply, begin building your application.

2. STEP TWO: APPLY

What is OSCAR, and how do I use it?[22]

The Online System for Clerkship Application and Review ("OSCAR") is the online centralized application system typically used to apply for federal judicial clerkships. To use OSCAR, visit https://oscar.uscourts.gov/ and create an account. Click *Register* and then in the next window, *Are you applying?* In the Applicant Registrant window, you will provide general information about yourself, set email notifications, discuss your academic background and bar membership (as applicable), prior work experience, and list any professional organizations to which you belong, such as the American Bar Association. Be thorough and honest as you complete your profile as it will be available to prospective judges. When this process concludes, you will be asked to verify that the information provided is true and accurate. Note that judges seek clerks who are trustworthy, so any inaccuracies or misrepresentations in the information provided could adversely impact your candidacy.

Next, OSCAR will ask you to build your application by uploading a cover letter, resume, and other documents. When applying, provide all of your application materials to the Chambers unless doing so is expressly forbidden. For example, provide all three of your recommendation letters to a judge that does not specify how many he or she will consider or that does not require them at all; however, if the judge limits you to two recommendations or prohibits a writing sample, be sure to follow those instructions.

Application Materials

The chart below discusses the application materials that Chambers typically prefer or require.

Definitely Submit	Consider Submitting	Additional Considerations
Cover Letter		
Resume	Rider *(attach this to your transcript or any other document in which you need to explain content that might reflect adversely upon you, such as a temporary withdrawal from law school)*	
Law School Transcript	Undergraduate Transcript *(attach this if it shows additional relevant coursework, if you graduated from a prestigious school or completed a difficult major, to show a trend of improvement each year during college, etc.)*	An undergraduate transcript can be especially helpful for certain positions. For example, applicants to the Office of Special Masters or United States Court of Appeals for the Federal Circuit may wish to provide a college transcript reflecting their science-related coursework, particularly if they did not major in a hard science.
Writing Sample	Second or Third Writing Sample *(attach this to showcase your writing range, such as your ability to write a persuasive brief, an objective memo, and a*	Some Chambers require an original writing sample that only the applicant has reviewed.

	judicial opinion or bench memo)	
Two Recommendation Letters or a List of References	Third Recommendation *(if possible, include a third recommendation from a former employer to showcase your performance in the workplace as well as in class)*	An employer recommendation is strongly encouraged for applicants who have practice experience. Likewise, law student applicants should seek recommendations from attorneys who supervised them during their law school externships or clinic(s).

Click on the *Add new* button to begin uploading documents. All documents must be in PDF format and less than 300KB. As noted above, most judges will require the following materials to apply: (1) a cover letter; (2) a resume; (3) a writing sample; (4) a law school transcript; and (5) two to three letters of recommendation or a list of references. Some judges require additional or different materials than others. For example, one judge might require multiple writing samples of varying lengths, while another might limit applicants to a single writing sample of no more than ten pages. Be sure to review the application instructions carefully regarding which materials are required, by which date, and in which format.

Furthermore, some federal judges require submission via OSCAR only; others permit only paper applications. However, many judges still accept submissions via both formats, but such judges typically advise against an applicant submitting in both formats. Before submitting, verify that your documents are well edited; a judge may deny your application simply because of a single typo in a cover letter. So edit carefully.

As will be discussed below, OSCAR then performs a mail merge, sending your materials to all judges to whom you apply. Thus, keep this in mind as you create each document. Make them more generic, addressing them to "Dear Judge," etc. However, for the judges in which you are most interested, it is preferable to draft a tailored cover letter and to ask your recommenders to do the same, perhaps including details specific only to that judge. You may also wish to apply on OSCAR and to email a paper application directly to Chambers, unless doing so is discouraged. This will be addressed in more detail below.

After you have uploaded your application documents, identify your recommenders. Unless you do this, the application letters that your recommenders upload will not be associated with your application packet and thus, will not be provided to your prospective judges. Faculty members from your current law school will likely be automatically listed as potential recommenders, but if you wish to have a non-faculty member recommend you, such as a former supervisor, call OSCAR's support line or consult a representative from your law school's Office of Career and Professional Development for assistance. Once you create your draft application, OSCAR will email each recommender and request that he or she upload your recommendation letter. OSCAR will associate this letter with your application and include it in the mail merge so that your recommender is not required to mail multiple letters to the various judges to whom you apply.

After you have created your draft application, select the law clerk and staff attorney positions for which you wish to apply. Judges are organized alphabetically by last name. Staff attorney positions are listed separately by court because they do not serve individual judges; they are court employees rather than members of a judge's personal staff. For ease and convenience, you can search for open positions by court or by type of judge. A position that is no longer available is usually grayed out, while open positions typically include a box with a checkmark that says *Apply online*. Pay close attention to the term for which the judge is advertising. Many judges hire clerks years in advance, so even if it is only the summer of 2017, the judge may already be recruiting clerks for the 2020–2021 judicial term. Be sure to only apply for clerkships for which you will be available. It is also important to periodically check OSCAR as new positions come available every day, and you can continuously apply to new positions. Cast a wide net, but as noted above, never apply for a position that you would not ultimately accept. That being said, OSCAR does limit applicants to 100 open applications at any given time, and you can determine how many applications you have submitted by viewing *Total Finalized Applications* on the right hand side of OSCAR's home page.

After selecting a position for which to apply, click on the judge's name, click the position tab, and then select *View and Apply*. Peruse the judge's application criteria carefully. As earlier observed, some judges only accept individuals with journal membership or Moot Court experience; others require multiple writing samples, while some request only one. Some positions advertised on OSCAR instruct applicants to send paper applications although this is rare. Whatever the case may be, follow the judge's instructions carefully. An applicant who cannot follow the application instructions demonstrates a failure to pay attention to detail or a deliberate disregard for the judge's instructions both of which reflect adversely on the applicant's suitability for the position. Judges receive hundreds of applications for each position; a failure to follow instructions is an easy way to filter out applicants.

After you have read the judge's instructions carefully, select the proper documents from the drop down menu. Change your recommenders as appropriate; for example, you may have three recommenders, but the judge to whom you are applying only permits two recommendation letters. After selecting the necessary documents and recommenders, choose *Create Draft Application* and then *Finalize Application*. Please note that after you select the latter option, you can no longer revise your application, except that you will be able to supplement your transcript. Furthermore, as soon as your application is finalized, the judges to whom you have applied are able to view it.

Should technical issues arise while you are building your application, contact a member of your law school's Office of Career Services and Professional Development or email oscar-support@ao.uscourts.gov. The OSCAR Support Team can also be reached via telephone toll-free at 866-666-2120 from 8am to 5pm Monday through Friday. For this reason, if you are unfamiliar with OSCAR, it is advisable to build your application during regular business hours when you have access to assistance from these sources.

Although most federal judges employ OSCAR, some do not. Likewise, some states like Minnesota have created more centralized online judicial clerkship application systems,[23] but other state judges require applicants to either mail paper applications or email an application packet directly to Chambers. They often post applications on law school job posting sites or advertise openings by word-of-mouth. Work closely with your law school's clerkship resources to determine how to research open positions that are not advertised on OSCAR. To the extent you apply to such positions, tailor each application to the specific Chambers. The same holds true for state court and local clerkship positions many of which are only advertised by other means, such as postings on law school job sites or by word-of-mouth.

How do I draft an appropriate cover letter?

Your cover letter is your first impression, so make it count. Use a proper address and salutation. In the first paragraph, state your class year and school. Specify the judicial term in which you wish to clerk. Explain succinctly why you would make a valuable contribution to Chambers as opposed to why clerking would benefit you. Do not use the same generic cover letter that you used for law firm and other positions, etc. Instead, tailor your cover letter to the clerkship position.

In the next paragraph, discuss your academic qualifications and relevant work experience. Again, consider your clerkship responsibilities and highlight aspects of your credentials that demonstrate why you are well suited for the position. For instance, writing and research are critical to any clerkship, so spotlight your strong writing skills or high grades in coursework relevant to the court's jurisdiction. Also emphasize relevant practical experience, such as judicial externships or clinics. Omit irrelevant details and summarize highlights from your transcript; do not recite it.

Interpersonal qualities are often as predictive of success as academic qualifications and work experience. As such, in the next paragraph consider the qualities that judges seek in law clerks, such as trustworthiness, a strong work ethic, and dependability. Highlight these interpersonal qualities and explain why you would be a good personality fit for Chambers.

In the final short paragraph, indicate your availability for an interview. Thank the judge for considering you and state that you look forward to hearing from the judge. Conclude with an appropriately formal closing, such as "Regards" or "Sincerely." Sign and then type your full name. If you are enclosing other materials in a paper application, add the word "Enclosures" two to three lines below the signature line on the left-hand margin of the letter.

Edit your cover letter carefully. Your prospective judge will review the cover letter to assess your writing skills, editing abilities, precision, clarity, brevity, and attention to detail. If you produce a poorly written cover letter, potential employers will likely deny your application.

Below is a sample cover letter.

The Honorable Mary Lycans
United States District Court for the Southern District of West Virginia
123 Asbury Road
Huntington, West Virginia 25701

December 7, 2017

Dear Judge Lycans,

I am a rising second-year law student at Lake Forest School of Law. I write to apply for a clerkship in your Chambers for the 2018–2019 judicial term. Given my strong writing skills, relevant work experience, and excellent interpersonal skills, I know I can make a meaningful contribution to your Chambers.

I am particularly well suited to clerk in your Chambers because of my strong research, writing, editing, and analytical skills. To hone my writing abilities, I have taken many experiential courses, including *Legal Writing I* and *II, Judicial Drafting, Advanced Legal Research,* and *Appellate Advocacy.* I have also participated in Lake Forest's *Elder Law Clinic.* I performed well in each course and even received a CALI Award for obtaining the highest grade in *Appellate Advocacy.* Through this coursework, I have conducted discrete legal research, interacted with clients and counsel, worked collaboratively with other law students, drafted bench memoranda and judicial opinions, strengthened my analytical abilities, and honed my editing skills.

I am also well equipped to hit the ground running in your Chambers due to my relevant work experience. Prior to law school, I worked for one year as a paralegal at Miller & Ropes, LLP, in Providence, Rhode Island. Among other things, this rewarding experience taught me how to effectively manage my time, work well under pressure, maintain client confidentiality, and handle constructive criticism.

In addition to my strong academic qualifications and relevant work experience, I also have strong interpersonal skills that set me apart from my peers. I am a quick learner who is hardworking, self-motivated, dependable, trustworthy, sincere, helpful, and creative. I work equally well alone or with others.

Enclosed herein for your review are my resume, writing sample, transcript, and two letters of recommendation. Please feel free to contact me should you have any questions or require additional information. I am available to interview at your convenience. Thank you for considering me. I look forward to hearing from you.

Sincerely,

Janet Lynn Asbury

How do I draft an appropriate resume?

A resume is a marketing tool used to summarize your credentials for your prospective employer. An accurate, well edited resume is essential to obtaining a clerkship. Before drafting your resume, thoughtfully examine the roles and responsibilities of law clerks.

Once you have a good understanding of what the position entails, tailor your resume to highlight the credentials that best demonstrate that you possess those qualities. Use active verbs and key words like "writing" and "research" that you know are essential to effective clerking. Be succinct since judges appreciate brevity and edit carefully. After all, your prospective judge will use your resume to assess whether you are detail-oriented and a strong writer. If your resume contains typographical or other errors, the prospective judge is unlikely to consider you. Organize your materials in reverse chronological order from most recent to least recent. Remove irrelevant work experience. Consider separating legal from relevant non-legal work experience; designate the latter with a subheading that states "other relevant work experience." Omit any irrelevant work experience.

Do not remove relevant information just to squeeze your resume onto one page, particularly if you worked prior to law school or are applying to clerk after a post-graduate position. An interested reader will take the time to read a second page, but do not exceed two pages. However, do use font, formatting, and margins to try to get onto one page if you extend only a few lines onto the second page. Include your academic qualifications, relevant work experience, publications, bar admissions or licensure, community service or extracurricular activities, leadership positions, honors or awards, language skills, interests, or other skills relevant to clerking. Include bullet point details under each job listing to succinctly explain the tasks performed there, which would prepare you to perform well as a clerk. In explaining job duties, use active verbs and sentence fragments that do not include periods. Use elegant variation, alternating the active verbs that you use to describe your various roles. Be completely accurate in everything listed on the resume; never overstate or misrepresent. Doing so reflects negatively on your veracity for truthfulness, but trustworthiness is essential to a successful clerk, particularly since your judge must trust you to maintain Chambers confidentiality.

Below is an annotated resume for your review. Consult with your Office of Career and Professional Development for additional information on resume writing and seek review from your Career Advisor, Faculty Advisor, or other respected mentors.

Violet Sofia

123 Main Street
Arlington, Virginia 22203
(304) 212-3456
violetsofia@gmail.com

EDUCATION

University of Michigan School of Law, Ann Arbor, MI   May 2014
J. D., *magna cum laude*
Honors: Order of the Coif
                 Michigan Journal of Social Policy and the Law
                 CALI Award for highest grade obtained in *Appellate Advocacy*
Leadership: Phi Alpha Delta, Clerk-Secretary
               Michigan Student Animal Legal Defense Fund, President

University of Richmond, Richmond, VA   May 2011
B. A. (English and Philosophy), *summa cum laude*
Honors: Phi Beta Kappa
         The Jameson Award (conferred upon the B.A. graduate
               who obtains the highest record)
               Dean's List
Leadership: Pi Beta Phi, Social Chair
               Resident Advisor

EXPERIENCE

Morgan Rose, LLP, Philadelphia, PA   Aug. 2014–Present
Employment Attorney
- Conducted discrete research on various tax issues
- Drafted memos, client letters, discovery requests, deposition outlines, and other legal documents
- Led client meetings
- Deposed expert witnesses and defended depositions
- Served as second chair at hearings, oral arguments, and trials

PUBLICATION

- Violet Sofia, *For Love or Money: Examining Marital Status Discrimination in the Context of the U.S. Tax Code*, Michigan Journal of Social Policy and Law, Fall 2016

LANGUAGE PROFICIENCY

- Conversational in Spanish

INTERESTS

- Travel, volunteering at the SPCA, soccer, reading, historical documentaries, and photography

How do I select a good writing sample?

Because effective writing and editing are key criteria in the clerkship selection process, it is essential that you provide one or more strong writing samples that accurately reflect your writing, analytical, research, and editing abilities. To many judges, an applicant's writing sample and writing grades are the most important criteria for selection and may thus be afforded greater weight than other grades, class rank, or journal membership.

The first step is to select the best writing sample. Typically, students select a recent writing assignment on which they received a very high grade. Practitioners may select a work product that received minimal revisions.[24] These may or may not be the best strategies. In choosing a writing sample, take into account the court and judge's jurisdiction. Selecting a writing sample that relates to the court's subject matter jurisdiction demonstrates substantive familiarity with knowledge of the material often pending before the court, which simultaneously evinces an interest in and preparedness for the clerkship. The risk of this approach, however, is that the court will know the substantive area inside and out and thus, may subject the sample to greater scrutiny than a writing sample on a topic with which the Chambers is somewhat less familiar. Second, simply choosing the assignment on which you received the highest grade may not be the best approach, particularly if the assignment was not sufficiently complex to demonstrate your ability to synthesize difficult material. One approach is to provide two writing samples—one that showcases objective writing and another that highlights your ability to write persuasively. Often the objective writing example, usually a research email, short memo, or client letter, will be shorter, no more than six pages, while the persuasive writing sample, usually a brief or excerpt of a brief, will be longer, but still no more than ten to twelve pages. If you have drafted a bench memo or judicial opinion in a course, clinic, or externship, these may be excellent writing samples since they illustrate prior experience with judicial drafting. Thus, such samples may be preferable even if you received a lower grade than on a much less complex objective memo. In making these decisions, confer with your writing professor, Career Counselor, Director of Clerkships, or Clerkship Committee.

Start this selection process very early, at least two to three months before you plan to submit your materials. This will enable you to seek additional review and feedback from your law school's writing center, teaching assistant, and/or writing professor and to incorporate that feedback into your writing sample.

Once you have selected your writing sample, work diligently to perfect it. First, incorporate the suggested edits that your reviewer professor or supervisor has made on the final graded version. Meet with or email your

TA or professor to the extent you have any questions relating to the edits. Confer with your TA and/or professor to ask him or her to provide additional review of the writing sample so that you can convert it into a writing sample. If your professor and/or TA are unavailable to assist, confer with the writing center and/or seek peer review from a peer who is a strong writer and editor. To the extent you seek outside review, be mindful of the timing of your request. Allow additional time if you make the request around the holidays, final exams, or over the summer. During these times, professors' schedules are especially hectic and often require travel, which may make them unavailable for lengthy periods of time. When you provide the writing sample, provide the professor with a reasonable deadline by which you would like to receive the edits to the extent possible. Be considerate of the professor's schedule as well and work to select a mutually convenient deadline that will give you sufficient time to carefully incorporate the feedback. Always provide the reviewer with a handwritten thank you note to show gratitude for the help proffered.

Note that you may tweak the writing sample as appropriate. For example, if your brief is 20 pages long, you may tweak it to only include the excerpts that relate to issue one. However, if you do tweak a writing sample, include an italicized introductory description that explains the nature and purpose of the assignment and clarifies that you have provided only an excerpt. You may also change the assignment format. For example, if Moot Court required you to use 14-point font, you can change the font of your brief to 12-point font so that it is a more appropriate length for use as a writing sample. Generally you need not discuss such minor formatting changes in your descriptive introduction of the sample.

To ensure that your writing sample reflects your independent work, judges typically do not permit writing samples that resulted from collaborative projects. Some even require submission of an original writing sample, meaning a sample on which no one, not even a TA or professor, has provided feedback. One way to provide an original writing sample is to maintain copies of your original drafts of assignments so that you can hone these drafts on your own into an original writing sample.

Another emerging trend is a timed writing exercise. Increasingly, judges require applicants to complete a short, timed writing assignment *during* the interview. This new measure addresses concerns that applicants do not write well under the tight time constraints often imposed in Chambers and that writing samples are often a product of so much peer review and feedback that the writing sample no longer accurately reflects an applicant's independent writing and editing ability. Thus, courts and other employers, including law firms and government agencies, are more frequently incorporating these components into their selection process. In response, some writing professors are incorporating timed writing assignments into their courses to prepare students for such timed writing components. Even if your courses do not include a timed writing exercise, you can prepare yourself for a timed writing assignment by using a practice essay from a commercial outline and timing yourself as you craft the response. Then compare your response to the model answer. Another option is to use the legal analysis exercises in *Legal Analysis: 100 Exercises for Mastery*.[25] Give yourself approximately 45 minutes to an hour for each exercise and do your best work. Then compare your response to the model answer in the back of the book. Your TA or writing professor may be willing to create timed exercises for you to complete or at least review the assignments that you have assigned yourself. Practice makes perfect. Also be aware that Chambers may or may not warn you in advance of the interview that timed writing will be a component of the selection process. However, you can often discover this information by speaking to other individuals who have interviewed with that judge in advance of the interview.

Your writing sample must be perfect, so edit carefully. Revise with purpose. Edit the sample once just for proper citation and a second time just for typographical errors. Each time edit with a different purpose in mind. Read it aloud. Read paragraphs out of order. Edit paragraph by paragraph, sentence by sentence, and word by word. Use Spellcheck but do not rely on it exclusively. Print out a hard copy and edit it page by page, inputting the edits into the computer version after you complete each page of hard copy editing. Seek peer review, TA review, professor review, etc. Your writing sample should be your very best work. Be sure that track changes are turned off, and then save the sample as a PDF. Properly label your writing sample with your first and last name and "Writing Sample." For example, the label might say "Nicole Rhoads Writing Sample." Your label should not list the class for which it was submitted or the version number or date of the document. For example, a writing sample labeled "Nicole Rhoads Writing Sample Version 8" shows the Chambers that you have certainly taken time to perfect the writing sample. However, it also illustrates that it took the writer eight versions to produce high quality work, and in a Chambers requiring fast turnaround of thorough writing, this information may not necessarily enhance your chance of obtaining a clerkship.

Do not just prepare a single writing sample even if that is all that the judge requires. Always have a backup on hand as it is not uncommon for a judge to require an additional writing sample from an applicant once he or she is selected for an interview. In such a case, you will not have much time to submit the additional writing sample, and it will exemplify preparedness and professionalism if you already have a second writing sample available. In addition, many Chambers require multiple writing samples from the start. Thus, for ease and convenience, be prepared.

How do I choose a recommender or reference?

Effective recommendation letters or references play a crucial role in clerkship selection. Judges often afford great weight to the insights of professors and employers who know the applicant personally and professionally. But the value of the recommendation hinges upon the nature of the relationship between the recommender and the applicant. So only choose a recommender who knows you quite well both inside and outside the classroom or the office—a person who can attest not only to your professionalism and work product but also to your character and personality.

In this regard, students should strive to develop close relationships with their professors and employers early on in their careers. A professor may have a class of 40 students, so it is the student's burden to make the extra effort to visit the professor during office hours or invite him or her to coffee to form and maintain a good relationship. It is also important to do this sincerely, not strategically. A professor or employer may resent an applicant who makes no attempt to form or maintain a relationship until after the student needs a recommendation. In such cases, formation of the relationship is overtly strategic, and this reality may poison the relationship. A far better approach is to sincerely form positive relationships with peers, professors, TAs, and supervisors from the outset of the relationship and make a concerted effort to maintain that relationship in small, intentional ways whether through occasional emails and correspondence, visits to office hours, or invites to lunch or coffee. Meet with your professors throughout the semester as questions arise. Develop these relationships before any need for a reference arises and always reciprocate. Indeed, in some instances, you may be able to assist a peer or professor in some way and never ask that person to recommend you. Put differently, relationships cannot be created solely on a quid pro quo basis. Instead, be real and sincere. Sincerity will facilitate the development of strong relationships that have lasting benefits for all involved.

In selecting a recommender or reference, most applicants typically include at least one professor. Do not simply choose the professor in whose class you obtained your highest grade. Instead, choose a professor with whom you have a close relationship and who can also attest to your writing, research, and editing skills. For example, ask your writing or research professor or a professor for whom you wrote a lengthy paper in a small seminar class. Choose a professor for whom you served as a RA or TA or a person who advised you on your journal note. Choose your independent study, clinic, or practicum advisor. It is important that you earned a high grade in the class, but it is more important that the professor can attest to your personal attributes as well as your writing and research abilities. Otherwise, the professor will only be able to provide a form recommendation letter that simply regurgitates information already available on the transcript. Such a letter might say, "Out of a civil procedure class of 63 students, Mr. Alexander earned the third highest grade on the exam—a 94—and earned an A in the course. Based on his performance in my course, I feel confident that he would perform well as a law clerk in your Chambers." Chambers receive hundreds of these formulaic letters, and they are not very helpful. After all, they typically do not expound upon the nature of the exam, the applicant's personal character or professionalism, or the applicant's ability to write, research, and edit effectively. As such, these recommendations will not set an applicant apart in the way that a customized letter discussing facets of the applicant not apparent from the law school transcript might. If you have had a professor in a writing course or clinic in which you performed well, then the professor may be an excellent choice for a recommender. If not, you may wish to consult the professor to determine if you could perform a writing and research assignment so that the professor might be willing and able to attest to your writing, research, and editing abilities as well as your ability to meet deadlines and handle constructive criticism. In sum, choose your recommender wisely, and select a professor who will take the time to draft a comprehensive, thoughtful letter that reflects who you are as a person.

Judges may afford special weight to the recommendation of a former law clerk, colleague, or friend. Early in the process of selecting recommenders, confer with your Career Counselor and Alumni Office to determine if any professors have clerked for the Chambers to which you are applying. Many judges also assign great value to recommendations from a former supervisor who can attest to your work ethic, maturity, and professionalism. This is primarily helpful if the supervisor worked with you for a reasonable length of time, such as one year. If permissible, submit recommendations from a combination of individuals, including a former supervisor and a professor. Applicants who have practical experience should definitely include a recommendation from a current or former supervisor; failure to do so will likely reflect adversely on your clerkship application.

In conclusion, when selecting a recommender, always keep in mind the qualities salient to a successful law clerk. Choose a recommender who can speak meaningfully and intelligently about your dependability, trustworthiness, professionalism, integrity, and interpersonal skills.

When you request a recommendation, make the recommendation process as easy and convenient as possible for the recommender. Provide the recommender with all of your application materials, such as your cover letter, transcript, and resume. Also provide any submission information that he or she may require up to and including stamped and addressed envelopes for each Chambers. Make the recommender's job as easy as possible. Also, provide the recommender with a reasonable deadline by which the recommendation must be mailed. In selecting the deadline, take into account the recommender's schedule and obligations. Build in extra time for contingencies. Email the recommender two weeks before the recommendation is due to determine if the recommender requires any additional information or has any questions. Gently remind the recommender of the upcoming deadline. Thank the recommender for taking the time to draft the letter. Ask the recommender to notify you when the letter is submitted. After the letter has been submitted, send the recommender a thoughtful, handwritten thank you note. Bear in mind that writing a thoughtful recommendation takes time and is non-compensable work that exceeds the scope of the recommender's duties and obligations. Thus, always be patient, gracious, and grateful for the recommender's efforts regardless of the outcome.

Some judges require recommendation letters. Others require only a list of references. If given the choice, recommendation letters are always more helpful than references because if your application is on the cusp, a thoughtful, glowing recommendation letter can you set you apart, and Chambers may not take the time to contact your references.

If you are limited to a list of references, choose wisely. Always ask an individual before you list him or her as a reference. If he or she agrees, provide the reference with information about the position as well as your application materials. Notify the reference of the estimated time frame in which he or she may be contacted and by whom. Send the reference a timely thank you note for taking time to serve as a reference. In selecting a reference, the same basic principles outlined above apply with equal force.

Furthermore, in selecting a recommender, it is helpful to select individuals who can attest to your performance in different capacities. For example, you might choose a writing professor who also served as your faculty advisor or for whom you served as a TA. You might also select a former employer for whom you worked prior to, during, or after law school who can attest to your professionalism and work product in the capacity of a paid employee rather than a student. As your final recommender, you might select your clinical professor who could attest both to your performance as a student as well as to your work with the clinic's clients.

Recommenders can enter a single generic recommendation letter addressed to "Dear Judge" that will append automatically to a clerkship application. It is unreasonable to ask a recommender to send a customized recommendation letter to each judge, but a recommender might be willing to do so for your top five choices.

In addition to a letter, some recommenders may be willing to telephone a Chambers to provide additional support for a candidate. Again, it is unreasonable and inappropriate to ask a recommender to telephone multiple judges, but a recommender might be willing to telephone your top three to five choices. In the alternative, it may be a best practice to simply notify the recommender when you receive a request for an interview and ask the recommender to call the Chambers if available. Be aware, however, that telephoning Chambers may or may not be helpful to your application. While some Chambers welcome the additional information, other Chambers may find it overly assertive or even pushy, particularly if the applicant has not been asked to interview. In this regard, use your judgment and confer with your Career Counselor, former clerks or colleagues of the judge, or your Clerkship Director.

Finally, show gratitude. Send a prompt handwritten thank you note to each recommender thanking them for taking time out of their busy schedules to assist you in the application process. Feel free to follow up with the recommender a few weeks after the request is made to determine if he or she requires additional information. However, avoid being pushy.

In addition to building a strong application, what other measures should I take before I submit my clerkship application?

Before you submit your application, peruse, protect, and preserve your personal brand. Doing so requires you to investigate your social media presence and alter it as necessary. To do this, search for yourself using search engines as well as social media platforms. Your prospective judges may investigate your Internet presence to gain insight into your personal character. Thus, before applying, remove inappropriate photographs, tweets, or other posts from your various social media accounts. Edit your profiles accordingly. Consider changing your profile names to a nickname or code name rather than a name that is easily identifiable. Tailor your privacy settings to make it more difficult for a prospective judge to see your profile or posts; make your settings as restrictive as possible. Yet be aware that no matter how restrictive your privacy settings are, they are not foolproof. For this reason, never post anything on social media that you would not want an employer, friend, or family member to see. Being social media savvy is the only way to protect your brand. That brand is important because a clerk must do nothing in his or her professional or personal life to diminish the integrity and dignity of the judge he or she serves. Similarly, never add prospective judges or their law clerks as "friends" on social media or follow their profiles before or during a clerkship. Maintain a healthy separation between your personal and professional life.

3.   STEP THREE: MANAGE

Now that you have submitted your applications, manage them effectively. Hopefully, you will receive an offer to interview; if you do not, do not be discouraged. There is no rule against reapplying, and it would be highly rare for a past rejection to adversely impact a second attempt to obtain a clerkship. To the contrary, reapplying shows perseverance, determination, and sincere interest in a judge. If you decide to withdraw from the process, use OSCAR to notify the judges with whom you have applied so that you do not waste their time and resources. If you do receive an offer to interview, the section that follows will assist you in preparing.

C. INTERVIEWING FOR A CLERKSHIP

Clerkships are highly competitive. Thus, even the most impressive application will not yield countless offers to interview. However, if you do receive an offer to interview, then the Chambers likely wishes to offer you the position so long as you are competent, authentic, personable, and otherwise a good cultural fit. The section that follows will discuss the format for a typical clerkship interview, how to prepare for an interview, and ways to positively stand out during an interview.

What is the standard format for a clerkship interview?

There is no standard format for a clerkship interview. To the contrary, interview protocol varies by Chambers. Typically, a law clerk or judicial assistant will telephone an applicant to schedule an interview in person, by telephone, or via videoconferencing technology. The latter is increasingly common. In some Chambers, a law clerk will conduct a preliminary phone interview before inviting you to Chambers for an interview. During the interview, you may meet with each law clerk individually or meet with all of the law clerks at once in a conference room in Chambers. Usually you will only meet with the judge if you pass muster during this screening process. In other Chambers, however, the judge may wish to meet with you first and then have you speak to each law clerk. There is significant variance in the protocol, but speaking to former law clerks for the judge may provide insight into what kind of interview you can expect. Although interview formats vary by judge, below are some general interview tips that may prove helpful.

General Interview Tips

1.	Research your court, judge, and interviewers; note points of connection
2.	Get a good night's sleep
3.	Lay out your outfit, bag, and accessories the evening before the interview
4.	Plan and try out your route to the interview location the day before (*e.g.*, check the metro or bus schedule, confirm there is money on your metro card, etc.)
5.	Eat a good breakfast *before* you dress to avoid staining your suit
6.	Exercise, meditate, or do another activity to de-stress
7.	Plan for contingencies
8.	Draft your talking points on a summary sheet or index cards and review them
9.	Dress to impress but be conservative and comfortable
10.	Eat a breath mint fifteen minutes before the interview
11.	Arrive ten to fifteen minutes early
12.	Bring extra copies of your application materials; invest in a nice bag and/or leather portfolio
13.	Dry and lotion hands before the interview

How should I prepare for the clerkship interview?

Research and practice are the two ingredients that will result in an effective clerkship interview. Prior to the interview, consult your Career Counselor or Clerkship Director to receive tips and information regarding how to prepare for the interview. Use the research tools outlined above to review the judge's biographical information and to discern important points of connection. For additional insight, confer with faculty members, alumni, former clerks, or peers who clerked or externed for the judge. Review the court's website to learn about the court's jurisdiction, location, etc. For example, the United States Court of Appeals for the Federal Circuit sits in Washington, D.C., and has statutorily vested jurisdiction that is nationwide. You should be fully aware of this information preferably before applying for the position but most definitely before interviewing. Otherwise, it will become abundantly clear to Chambers that you are not really interested in *this* court and *this* judge. In addition, review the judge's notable recent decisions. Be able to speak intelligently about the court's seminal cases and to answer questions regarding whether any recent decisions of the court particularly interest you. Obtain a list of potential interview questions from your Career Counselor or advisor and prepare talking points for each question. If no such list exists, then brainstorm and create your own. Ask the former clerks and professors that you consult about the types of questions you should expect to receive; note, however, that due to confidentiality reasons, they may be unable or unwilling to share specific questions. Prepare three talking points for each question and edit them carefully so that they are concise. Order your points from strongest to weakest, placing your strongest point first, your second strongest point second, and so on. Keep your answers to three to five sentences where possible. Brevity, precision and clarity (as well as other hallmarks of oral advocacy) apply with equal force in interviews.

Aside from thorough research, practice makes perfect. After conducting your research and preparing adequate talking points, ask a trusted advisor, such as your career counselor, to conduct a mock interview with you. The interview should closely mirror the format and time of the actual interview. For example, if the interview will occur via videoconferencing technology or over the telephone, use that format for the mock interview. If the actual interview will last only 30 minutes, then limit the mock interview to 30 minutes. Ask the interviewer to provide feedback regarding your interview skills and incorporate that feedback. Practice multiple times. Record yourself if possible and view the recording. This will enable you to discern bad habits, such as distracting hand gestures or facial expressions, of which you are unaware. For more information on successful interviewing, consult your Career Counselor.

How should I dress for the clerkship interview?

To make a good impression at the clerkship interview, dress to impress. Wear conservative business professional attire. Wear closed-toed shoes and avoid any accessory or item of clothing that is too loud, noisy, low-cut, tight, or short. Avoid accessorizing to excess; wear minimal jewelry and makeup. Be conservative but comfortable. Groom yourself appropriately, keeping your hair out of your face. For more tips, review the chart below. Note, however, that the suggestions below are not one-size-fits-all. Rather, use your judgment regarding how you will appear the most professional, confident, and comfortable during the interview.

Dress to Impress

1.	Aim for business professional, not business casual.
2.	Be remembered for what you say, not how you look.
3.	Plan your outfit a few days before in case you need to purchase an item, take something to the dry cleaners, etc.
4.	Lay out your entire outfit, including shoes and accessories, the evening before; steam it, etc.
5.	Dress conservatively.
6.	Dress comfortably. Do not wear shoes or other items for the first time on the day of the interview. Test them out the day before the interview.
7.	Keep hair out of your face. Groom as necessary to present your best self.
8.	Avoid non-conservative nail polish and nail art; as a best practice, stick with a French manicure or clear nail polish.
9.	Avoid noisy shoes, watches, or other distracting accessories.
10.	If you wear cologne or perfume, wear a minimal amount. Note that some interviewers may be allergic or highly sensitive to these chemicals.
11.	For some Chambers, women should consider wearing panty hose and low heels.
12.	Turn off or remove electronic devices, such as smartphones or noisy digital watches.
13.	To set yourself apart, consider choosing one memorable item or tasteful conversation piece, such as a class ring, sorority pin, interesting broach, or a colored blouse or scarf.

What should I bring with me to the interview?

Invest in a nice, well-kept messenger bag or satchel to carry to your interview. Women may wish to only carry a purse. Inside bring your portfolio. Include extra copies of all of your application materials. Some interviewers will ask you for a copy simply to test your preparedness; others will print their own copies. Bring a bottle of water and/or dry snack if you fear you might get hungry before the interview, but put them away before the interview commences. Have your photo identification available for admission to the court. Bring your phone in case you are running late or get lost, but be sure it is turned off before the interview begins. Do not just silence it as the vibration noises may be distracting to your interviewers.

In addition, consider packing a small "emergency kit" tailored to your needs. Such a kit may be helpful because it enables you to minimize interview anxiety by controlling the things that you can control. Some retail stores sell "bridal emergency kits" and "groom emergency kits" for use on a wedding day. These kits are good starting points, but it is still important to tailor the kit to your personal needs. A kit might include any or all of the following: (1) a breath mint (take this 15 minutes before the interview so it has time to fully dissolve); (2) a safety pin or fashion tape; (3) a comb; (4) bandages; (5) headache medicine; (6) an antacid; (7) a toothpick or dental floss; (8) nail clippers or a nail file; (9) contact lenses, contact solution, or eyeglasses; (10) tissues; (11) a hair band or bobby pin; (12) feminine hygiene products; and an (13) Epipen or other medication. What items might you include in your kit?

What are the most common mistakes that applicants make during interviews?

If you receive an offer to interview, the judge probably wants to hire you. Your paper credentials have clearly impressed Chambers, so the goal of the interview is to determine if you will otherwise be a good fit. Are you likeable and interesting? Are you articulate and well spoken? Do you possess strong interpersonal skills? Will you be a contributing member of the Chambers family? Can you carry on a lively conversation? For this reason, the most common complaints about interviewees relate to their inability to articulate clear, succinct, and accurate responses to questions or their inability to carry on a conversation with the interviewers. Furthermore, people often assume that a person writes the way he or she speaks. Thus, if your oral communication skills are poor, an interviewer is likely to assume that you are also an ineffective written communicator. Less often, applicants evidence a lack of trustworthiness or other character attributes necessary to being a successful clerk. Below is a chart detailing common complaints about interviewees.

Common Complaints About Applicants

Unprepared; did not research job, judge, or court
Inaccurate responses to questions
Unable to communicate clearly/inarticulate
Unclear, disorganized, and/or long-winded responses
Lacked passion and enthusiasm
Boring or appeared to be bored
Not a team player
Poor interpersonal skills
Disingenuous/Answered questions in a manner inconsistent with information provided to other interviewers or on the resume
Too nervous/fidgety (denotes a lack of trustworthiness and confidence)
Too casual/informal/arrogant
Talked too much or too quickly (a wordy speaker is likely to be a wordy writer, and judges prize brevity)
Did not listen to the question
Tardy to the interview without an excuse
Impolite
Bad attitude/hostile/defensive when answering questions
Not a good personality fit with Chambers for other reasons

How can I craft effective answers to questions during the interview?

Below are some tips that will help you develop strong answers to typical interview questions.

1.   Implement the hallmarks of persuasive oral advocacy that you learned in your *Legal Writing II* and *Appellate Advocacy* courses.

2.   Listen carefully to the question asked.

3.   Think before you speak, crafting an articulate response.

4.   Answer the call of the question. On occasion, use the end of the question to begin your answer; doing so narrows the scope of the answer and prevents you from going off on an unhelpful tangent. It also affords you a few more seconds to consider your response before you communicate it.

5.   Organize your response so that you state your most important talking point first.

6. Be brief. Limit each response to three to five sentences.

7. Be precise. Choose your words wisely.

8. Avoid grammatical errors. Edit out fillers, such as "like" or "umm." Interviewers will draw conclusions about your writing and editing abilities based on your oral communication skills.

9. Use transitional words and phrases as well as elegant variation in your word choice.

10. Be honest and sincere but avoid oversharing. Exercise good judgment in formulating the content of your response always considering whether it may raise any red flag for the listener.

11. Speak slowly and articulate your words. Speak loudly enough for the other listener to hear, especially during a phone interview. Avoid an inflection at the end of a sentence that makes it sound more like a question than a response. Some interviewers may construe this as demonstrating a lack of confidence.

12. For a live interview, avoid distracting hand gestures and facial expressions; hold a pen or your portfolio as necessary.

13. If you do not understand a question, politely say, "I'm not sure I understand your question. Are you asking . . ."

14. If you do not hear a question, ask the interviewer to please repeat it.

15. Be gracious and friendly. Say "please" and "thank you." Never interrupt the interviewer and apologize promptly if you do.

16. Exhibit appropriate emotional responses. Feel free to smile when speaking about light-hearted topics or things about which you are passionate; do not smile or laugh, however, when discussing something more serious, such as a vaccine case in which a petitioner died. The latter can be difficult for individuals who laugh or smile unintentionally whenever nervous, but recording yourself during a mock interview will make you aware of whether you fall into that category so you can preempt that kind of unintentional reaction.

17. Allocate your gaze to all of your interviewers if there are multiple clerks participating. Start and end your gaze with the person who asked the question, moving your head slowly only while answering the question.

18. Be polite. Thank the interviewers for offering you an opportunity to meet with them.

19. Sit up straight during the interview; do not slump back in the chair. Poor posture denotes a lack of confidence, while appearing too comfortable in the chair indicates overconfidence or that the applicant does not appreciate the gravity of the clerkship role.

20. Maintain eye contact while answering questions; looking down, up, or away suggests a lack of confidence or veracity. Looking around the room while the interviewer is speaking suggests that the applicant is bored or disengaged from the conversation.

To further assist you in preparing for a clerkship interview, here is a list of potential questions as well as an example of an effective and less effective response to each with accompanying commentary.

1.　Tell me something about yourself that is not on your resume.

Effective Response: I have traveled to 23 countries and am always planning my next trip. I really enjoy experiencing different cultures and meeting new people. My most illuminating travel experience was when I traveled solo to Croatia and sailed around the Dalmatian Coast on a small yacht with 15 strangers. It challenged me to get outside my comfort zone and overcome my fears, but I learned a tremendous amount about myself and made 15 new friends in the process. Through my travels, I've enjoyed amazing opportunities to stretch myself and grow whether the adventure has involved snorkeling with sharks, swimming with a special needs sea lion, ziplining over a rainforest, or whitewater rafting through a jungle river. Through it all, I've pushed myself, overcome obstacles, and really grown as a result.

Comments: This response does not regurgitate information on the resume. Even if the resume indicates an interest in traveling, it probably does not contain these specific details. A listener might glean from this response that the individual takes initiative, works well alone or with others ("the new friends on the yacht"), is independent, and rises to the challenge. The response also demonstrates global-mindedness and intellectual curiosity, all qualities that would likely intrigue the interviewer. It is also an interesting and sincere response that would spur further conversation. And it is a memorable, unique response that an interviewer will not soon forget. There is nothing generic about it, and it provides real insight into the applicant's personality. On the other hand, it includes only one major talking point, rather than three. It is also bit long.

Less Effective Response: I am currently going through a very messy divorce from my husband of five years. I hope that relocating to a new city and devoting myself to a new job will be the fresh start that I need at this point in my life.

Comments: This response is real and personal. The applicant listened to the question and did not simply regurgitate information on the resume, which is a common mistake. However, this response likely goes too far. It is too personal and exemplifies oversharing. In addition, it undermines the applicant's suitability for the position since it appears that the applicant is primarily applying for the job, not to make a meaningful contribution to Chambers, but instead to get a fresh start. The response may also raise concerns that personal issues may undermine the applicant's work product. The applicant has not applied for the job for the right reasons.

Takeaway Point: Listen to the question. Do not rehash information on the resume, such as prior work experience or academic qualifications. Be personal but keep it positive. The response should provide insight into who you are as a person and demonstrate, not undermine, your suitability for the position.

2. Why are you interested in clerking?

Effective Response: I'm interested in clerking because I really enjoy research and writing and want to use those skills to make a meaningful contribution to your Chambers. Clerking would also give me an opportunity to serve the public by assisting Chambers in efficiently and effectively resolving cases. Finally, I also hope to gain a behind-the-scenes view of judicial decision-making. I know that I would learn so much from you given the quality of your opinions and your ten years of experience on the bench.

Less Effective Response: I want to clerk because I want to be a litigator here, and I know that clerking will help me hone my skills and one day fulfill that goal.

Comments: The former response focuses on what the applicant will do to help effectuate the goals of Chambers. I refer to this as the *JFK Principle.* President John F. Kennedy famously encouraged Americans to "ask not what your country can do for you but what you can do for your country." Likewise, an effective response to this question will explain what you can do for your judge, not what your judge can do for you. Put differently, it should emphasize what value you will add to Chambers rather than how clerking will enhance your resume. By contrast, the latter response demonstrates what I call the *stepping stone mentality.* It makes very clear that the applicant is really primarily interested in what he or she will *gain* from the clerkship, not what he or she can *contribute* to Chambers. In addition, use of the phrase "hone my skills" may suggest that those skills are not already strong and that the applicant aims to use the clerkship as a training ground to correct deficiencies in his or her writing, research, and editing skills—deficiencies that may make the applicant unsuitable for the position.

Takeaway Point: Focus your response on the contribution you will make to Chambers, not on what clerking will do for you. Choose your words wisely, never framing your goals or qualifications in a way that paints you as unfit for the clerkship. To tailor your response, begin your response with the end of the question.

3. What specifically interests you about this court? *(For our purposes, let's pretend that this question is asking about interest in the Office of Special Masters.)*

Effective Response: I am interested in the Office of Special Masters because I really enjoy vaccine law, particularly because I majored in biology in college. It's so interesting to see the intersection of law and medicine in vaccine cases, and I found my related coursework, such as *Bioethics* and *Torts* fascinating. In addition, my two friends, Joey and Elizabeth, both externed at OSM during law school and spoke so highly of their experiences. Based on their recommendations, I know that Chambers is incredibly collegial and that it would be a great fit for me both personally and professionally.

Comments: The response is well organized with the strongest point first. It is succinct but warm. It is real and sincere. It also demonstrates awareness of the OSM's specialized subject matter jurisdiction and shows that the applicant has spoken with former OSM externs to garner information about whether OSM would be a good fit. This indicates sincere enthusiasm in the position as well as preparedness for the interview.

Less Effective Response: I want to clerk here because it will give me a chance to put my research and writing into practice and to work hand in hand with some of the sharpest judges and law clerks in America.

Comments: This is a very generic, standard response. Thus, it is too vague to be helpful. Because it reveals nothing specific about this court that interests the applicant, it does not effectively answer the question. In fact, this response would apply with equal force to *any* court in America. Furthermore, to the extent this response is about OSM, it is inaccurate because the decision-makers at OSM are known as special masters, not judges. Thus, it also shows a lack of preparedness for the interview.

Takeaway Point: Listen to the question. If it calls for specific details, provide them. Research the position and prepare accurate responses.

4. *Why are you interested in our judge specifically?*

Effective Response: I am interested in Judge Wyatt specifically because he has consistently stood up for the rights of animals and taken a hard line against animal abusers. Preventing animal cruelty is an area about which I am incredibly passionate, and I appreciate his conviction and consistency in these cases, which are not always taken seriously. In addition, his opinions are incredibly well written, and he is highly well regarded in the legal community. He has been a sitting judge for over 15 years, and I would welcome a chance to learn from such a seasoned, experienced judge. Finally, my former teaching assistant, Heath Brecklin, externed for Judge Wyatt last year and encouraged me to apply. Heath couldn't say enough wonderful things about Judge Wyatt, so I know he would be a great professional and personal role model. For all of these reasons, I am incredibly interested in clerking for Judge Wyatt.

Comments: Although the organization of the response could perhaps be tweaked, it is honest, sincere, and provides concrete details about Judge Wyatt. It also shows that the applicant has done his or her due diligence before interviewing, and that a former extern believes the applicant would be a good fit.

Less Effective Response: I am interested in clerking for Judge Wyatt because he is an insightful judge with a wealth of experience from whom I could learn so much.

Comments: This response is too concise and too vague. One could simply insert another judge's name in place of Judge Wyatt and repeat this "line" at other interviews. It is too impersonal and scripted.

Takeaway Point: Be personal and sincere. Provide concrete details. Tailor your response to your prospective judge.

5. What, if any, ties do you have with this city?

Effective Response: I have significant ties to the city. My aunt and uncle lived and worked here throughout my childhood, so I visited them often and would enjoy living near them while clerking. In addition, I externed here during the summer after my first year of law school and know it would be an excellent personal fit for me. I also have several friends from college and law school who reside here.

Comments: This response answers the question but shifts the focus on why the personal fit and support network would enable the clerk to perform the position well, even during stressful times. It is clear, succinct, and well organized.

Less Effective Response: I would love to live here because it's so much fun to go out in the city. Even though I've never lived or worked here, I've spent two different spring break vacations here, and there are so many fun things to see and do. It's such an exciting place.

Comments: This response suggests that the clerk has applied for the position for the wrong reasons—to "tour" the city. In fact, the applicant offers up adverse information by conceding that he or she has "never lived or worked here." Furthermore, the applicant's only connections to the city have been during brief visits, and the applicant has not indicated any personal support network that would facilitate good performance during the clerkship. It sounds as if the applicant is merely using the clerkship as an excuse for an extended vacation in the city, which might undermine the applicant's dedication to the job, especially if weekend, late night, or holiday hours become necessary as is sometimes the case.

Takeaway Point: Phrase your answers in a way that enhances your qualifications, not in a way that inadvertently undermines them. Focus on why your connections to the city would enhance your performance, not on why you love the city itself. Do not emphasize facts that undermine your suitability for the position.

6.   *How do you handle time management?*

Effective Response: I manage my time effectively. For example, when I receive an assignment in law school, I immediately create a timeline, establishing mini-deadlines for myself to complete each task subsumed within the assignment, such as finalizing my research log, outlining my argument, finishing my case chart, etc. Then I hold myself to these deadlines and set up a TA review session to keep myself accountable. As a result, so far in law school, I have never had to request an extension for any assignment, even a draft, and I have never missed a deadline.

Comments: The response answers the question and supports the answer with a tangible illustration.

Less Effective Response: Yes, I'm very effective at managing my time.

Comments: The answer rests upon an unsupported conclusory assertion. As such, it is not very probative or helpful. If you make an assertion, support it with at least one specific example.

Takeaway Point: Support each assertion with a concrete illustration.

In addition to the tips above, be precise in your responses. Use accurate wording. Limit each response to no more than three main talking points or alternatively, three to five minutes. List out anticipated questions and draft three talking points for each. List them in order of strongest to weakest. Provide accompanying concrete examples for each as necessary. Tailor your response by beginning it with the end of the question. This also buys you time to formulate your response. Think before you speak. It is better to pause and speak slowly than to hurriedly respond in an inarticulate manner. Edit out phrases like "I think" and "I believe," which may evince a lack of self-confidence. Also omit fillers, such as "umm" and "like." Maintain an easy pace and friendly tone. Be honest and accurate. Listen to the question and only answer the question asked. Do not go off on a tangent. Begin the response with a yes or no as appropriate. Many of the same principles taught in your oral advocacy courses apply with equal force to an interview.

Below are some additional questions that you may receive:

1.	How might your relevant work experience make you well suited for this position?
2.	Why did you attend law school?
3.	Why did you choose your law school? How did you like it?
4.	What was your favorite course and why?
5.	What was your least favorite course and why?
6.	What is your biggest strength as a writer? Your biggest weakness?
7.	What sets you apart from other applicants?
8.	How do handle constructive criticism?
9.	Do you manage your time wisely?
10.	Do you work well under pressure or tight time constraints?
11.	How would you handle it if the judge disagreed with one of your recommendations?
12.	What do you do for fun?
13.	What are your long-term professional goals?
14.	Why are you deciding to apply for a clerkship now rather than at a different time in your professional career?
15.	Why should we hire you instead of an attorney with practice experience?
16.	Why are you leaving the practice to clerk?
17.	What relevant coursework did you complete that will prepare you for this position?
18.	Do you work better alone or on teams?
19.	What is your favorite aspect of law school?
20.	I noticed that you received a low grade in your writing course. Can you explain why?

How and when should I check on the status of my application?

Chambers differ significantly in the amount of time they take to respond to an applicant. While some Chambers interview applicants on a rolling basis, others accept applications through a set date and only review the applications after that deadline passes so they can view the applicant pool as a whole. Likewise, some judges extend exploding offers to applicants, meaning that the judge offers the position to the clerk over the phone or at the interview and expects an immediate yes or no. Other judges reach out to the applicant by phone or email after the interview to offer a position; this can occur immediately after the interview concludes or even days or weeks later. Speaking to your Career Counselor, Clerkship

Committee, or former law clerks, externs, or colleague of the judge is the best way to determine the judge's typical practice and timing regarding the interview. If you are unable to ascertain this information prior to the interview, you can typically ask this question of one of the law clerks during the interview.

As a best practice, be prepared for an exploding offer and never accept an interview with a judge if you know you would not accept the position. As soon as you determine you would not accept a position, perhaps due to an intervening change of circumstances that arose after you had applied, withdraw your application or graciously cancel the interview. The exception to this rule is if the intervening circumstance arises on the day before or day of the interview, when it would be incredibly rude to cancel. For example, if you are extended an offer that you plan to accept the morning of a clerkship interview, it may be acceptable to go through with the interview and alert Chambers of the changed circumstance if and only if an exploding offer is extended. This is an exceptional circumstance. Alert the Chambers as soon as possible thereafter, such as early on the next business day, to withdraw your application, briefly explain the reason why, and thank them for interviewing you.

If a judge does not extend an exploding offer to you, do not be discouraged. Anecdotal evidence suggests that fewer judges engage in this practice than in the past; some recent judicial appointments have likewise rejected it. Instead, many judges now give applicants several days to consider the position or require the applicant to undergo multiple interviews before extending an offer. However, exploding offers remain commonplace with more senior judges, and failure to provide an immediate yes on the spot may result in rescission of the offer. Such judges assume that if the applicant accepts the interview, he or she is prepared to accept an offer. The key is to know how to respond if and when you receive an exploding offer and to understand that by requesting more time to consider the position, you may forfeit it. This is not always the case. Some judges are perfectly willing to permit an applicant a day or even several days to consider a position and draw no adverse inference from the applicant taking that time. Some Chambers even prospectively offer that time without the applicant even having to awkwardly request it. But as mentioned above, these practices vary by Chambers.

If you do not receive an exploding offer, then you may wish to ask a law clerk at the conclusion of the interview when you might expect to hear about your application. Based on that response, determine when it is appropriate to follow up with Chambers. Typically, it is permissible to follow up if you have not heard anything within approximately two weeks. A status check sooner than that may be viewed as being overzealous or worse yet, pushy. In addition, an applicant can always supplement or update an application as a backhanded way of doing a status check without explicitly referring to it as such. This is appropriate when you have earned an award or accolade not on the resume, such as winning a Moot Court competition, publishing a note or article, or if you have received another round of grades that will enhance your application. Finally, you should always update Chambers if you receive another offer to interview or accept another offer, rendering you unavailable for the clerkship. This is professional and courteous. In the former instance, notification will also give the Chambers an opportunity to interview you before you are no longer available. The law clerk or judicial assistant will advise you regarding the easiest way to apprise Chambers of updates whether by phone or email; follow those instructions. Limit your status checks to one check two to three weeks out and then no more checks unless you have an update or competing opportunity.

Should I send a thank you note even if I do not obtain the position?

Absolutely. Two simple words can make all the difference in a clerkship interview: Thank you. Clerkship positions are highly coveted and extremely competitive. If a Chambers contacts you to schedule an interview, use the same format to contact Chambers as soon as possible and no later than the same business day. For example, if Chambers telephones you, return the call; do not send an email. And even if you are no longer available to interview, still return the call and thank the Chambers for considering you. Withdraw your application as soon as you become unavailable rather than wasting Chambers' time reviewing materials for a person who is no longer interested in the position. This is both professional and polite. If you are offered an interview that you do not accept, after returning the call or email, send a follow-up email thanking Chambers for considering you and extending you this wonderful opportunity. Be gracious. If you do interview, send a thank you email within a few hours of the interview and mail a handwritten thank you note the same day. If you do not, the Chambers may believe you do not plan to do so, and this lack of courtesy and gratitude could cut against you in the ensuing selection process. Even if you do not receive the position after interviewing, it is still important to send a thank you note expressing gratitude for taking time to speak with you. It is equally important to thank the other members of Chambers, including the law clerks and judicial assistant, responsible for establishing and participating in the interview. The judge will likely weigh their perceptions of applicants quite heavily in the selection process, so be gracious to everyone from the U.S. Marshal that greets you in the lobby to the judicial assistant who takes you to Chambers. Treat everyone with the respect and courtesy they each deserve.[26]

How do I craft a proper thank you note?

To be timely, it is permissible to send a short thank you email the same day as the interview. However, do promptly follow up with a lengthier, more personal handwritten thank you note. As noted above, it is preferable to mail it the same day as the interview, if possible, or at latest, the next day.

To craft an appropriate thank you note, invest in professional, conservative stationery. Write legibly, printing if your cursive handwriting is difficult to read. Use a ruler or another card to ensure that each line of the card is straight. Include a proper salutation, such as "Dear Judge Herbert" or "Dear David," if writing to a clerk. Thank the interviewer for taking time to meet with you. Recount meaningful details from the interview. Avoid writing a generic message. Edit carefully. Use sophisticated language and a formal tone. Include a proper closing, such as "Regards."

Here is a sample thank you note to a law clerk.

Dear Rachel,

    Thank you for taking time out of your hectic schedule to meet with me last week. I enjoyed learning about the Court's recent cybersecurity cases and hearing about your experience clerking for Judge David. Your thoughts on *Trinity* were especially insightful. Our meeting further confirmed that Chambers would be a perfect fit for me.

    Please do not hesitate to contact me if you require additional information or have any other questions. I look forward to hearing from you.

Regards,

Wyatt Easton

Below is a sample thank you note to a judge.

Dear Judge Asbury,

   Thank you so much for taking time out of your hectic schedule to interview me. It was such a pleasure to meet you, your law clerks, and your judicial assistant. I especially enjoyed hearing about your work as a U.S. Attorney in Huntington. It is so interesting how that experience continues to inform your judicial decision-making. Although I was incredibly excited about the prospect of clerking for you before our interview, meeting you only confirmed what an amazing opportunity and great fit it would be. Thank you so much for considering me, and I look forward to hearing from you. It would be an honor to work with you.

Sincerely,

Heath Brecklin

D. KEY TAKEAWAY POINTS

What mistakes made during the application process commonly prevent an applicant from obtaining a clerkship?

1. ***Typographical and grammatical errors in the application materials:*** Editing is one of the most important tasks of a law clerk, and your application is supposed to be your best effort. Thus, if you lack the attention to detail and editing skills necessary to produce a perfect cover letter, the judge has no reason to believe you will be able to produce a well edited draft opinion, especially if crafted under tight time constraints.

2. ***Including an incorrect salutation or mailing address:*** Many applicants cast a wide net, applying to judges across America. As such, they often draft a somewhat generic cover letter that they can use for multiple applications, such as a single cover letter tailored to a federal district court, which can be used for most of the federal district courts to which they apply, and another generic cover letter tailored to state supreme courts. However, if you convert your cover letter into a customized one tailored to a specific judge, be very careful not to send that same letter to any other judge, particularly if you have not properly altered the salutation and mailing address. This is incredibly off-putting to a Chambers, even one that understands the reality of clerkship applications. It also denotes carelessness and a lack of reverence for the judge and the position.

3.   *Failure to follow the judge's instructions with regard to what to submit or in what format:* If you do not take the time to review and follow the judge's instructions regarding something as mundane as the method or content of your application, the judge has no reason to believe that you will follow more complex instructions within Chambers when the instructions really count.

4.   *Failure to research the judge prior to the interview:* While most judges understand that applicants apply to numerous positions, they will expect applicants to be quite familiar with their court and Chambers before applying and certainly prior to the interview. For example, you should never need to ask "What kind of cases does this court handle?" during an interview. You should already understand the court's jurisdiction, location, and basic function. You should also be familiar with the judge's background and have read several of his or her seminal and/or recent opinions. Failure to adequately prepare for the interview evinces a lack of interest in the position and dedication to securing it.

5.   *Arriving late to the interview:* Judges depend on their law clerks to represent them. A person who arrives late to an interview without notice or a reasonable excuse has not only demonstrated a lack of professionalism but also has shown blatant disregard for the judge's hectic schedule. To avoid tardiness, map out the route to the court the day before the interview and actually time your travel there. Know exactly how to get there and how long it will take. Account for traffic and metro delays as well as weather. Then if the estimated time to arrive is 20 minutes, always tack on additional time to account for any unexpected contingency. Give yourself wiggle room. Aim to arrive at least ten minutes early to the interview; arriving much earlier than that can be perceived as rude, especially since the judge may be in the middle of another meeting or interview, and it can be awkward for an applicant to wait in the lobby for an excessive amount of time. If you arrive more than ten minutes early, wait downstairs or outside the court before heading to Chambers. When you schedule the interview, obtain the contact information for the person you should call or email should you be unavoidably late. If you are cutting it close, email or call just in case to say that you might be a few minutes late and apologize for your tardiness. Always offer to reschedule the interview if your late timing makes it inconvenient for Chambers. Aim to avoid

this through proper planning and preparation. After all, punctuality demonstrates professionalism and courtesy.

6. ***Being non-responsive or unappreciative:*** Clerkship positions are highly coveted and extremely competitive. If a judge contacts you to schedule an interview, use the same format to contact the judge as soon as possible and no later than the next business day. For example, if Chambers telephones you, return the call; do not send an email. And even if you are no longer available to interview, still return the call and thank the Chambers for considering you. Withdraw your application as soon as you become unavailable. This is both professional and polite. If you are offered an interview that you do not accept, after returning the call or email, send an email thanking Chambers for considering you and extending you this wonderful opportunity. Be gracious. If you do interview, send a thank you email within a few hours of the interview and mail a handwritten thank you note the same day. If you do not, the Chambers may believe you do not plan to do so, and this lack of courtesy and gratitude could cut against you in the ensuing selection process. Even if you do not receive the position after interviewing, it is still important to send a thank you note expressing gratitude for taking time to speak with you.

7. ***Excessive nervousness during an interview:*** Everyone gets nervous, and interviews are especially prone to create anxiety. However, manifestations of nervousness whether in the form of excessive sweating, shaky hands, distracting facial or hand gestures, nervous laughter, or stammering, can undermine your interview and make you appear less confident and competent than you actually are. To overcome such anxiety, complete mock interviews as often as possible, particularly with individuals whom you do not know well. Record the interviews if possible so you can diagnose and correct any problems.

For additional information, pay attention to the clerkship listserv. Review your law school's clerkship handbook as well as the supplemental resources listed below. Vermont Law School also provides a particularly helpful guide.[27] In addition, your law school's Office of Career and Professional Development and Clerkship Committee will likely host helpful information sessions throughout the year on clerking. Former law clerks and judicial externs are also excellent resources. Please also consult *Courting Clerkships: The NALP Judicial Clerkship Study* from October 2000, a portion of which has been reprinted in the Appendix of this book with the permission of the National Association for Law Placement.

E. SUPPLEMENTAL RESOURCES

1.   Federal Administrative Law Judges Conference, www.faljc.org.

2.   Federal Judicial Center, http://www.fjc.gov/public/home.nsf.

3.   National Association of Law Placement, http://www.nalp.org/ directories.

4.   National Center for State Courts, http://www.ncsc.org/.

5.   DEBRA M. STRAUSS, BEHIND THE BENCH: THE GUIDE TO JUDICIAL CLERKSHIPS (2002).

Notes

---

[1]   In general, the advice obtained herein is equally applicable to obtaining a judicial externship position, career clerkship, or staff attorney position at a federal, state, or local court.

[2]   *Courting Clerkships: The NALP Judicial Clerkship Study*, NAT'L ASS'N FOR LAW PLACEMENT (Oct. 2000), http://www.nalp.org/clrktb27_45#36 (only 8% of respondents who obtained clerkships reported having a pre-existing special connection with their judge).

[3]   U.S. CONST. Art. III.

[4]   *Court Role and Structure*, UNITED STATES COURTS, http://www.uscourts.gov/about-federal -courts/court-role-and-structure (last visited June 23, 2016).

[5]   For a discussion of clerkship opportunities at international courts, see DEBRA M. STRAUSS, BEHIND THE BENCH: THE GUIDE TO JUDICIAL CLERKSHIPS 70–72 (2002).

[6]   I wish to thank my colleague Sally Irvin, a dedicated law librarian and research professor at Wake Forest University School of Law, for her invaluable feedback regarding this portion of the chapter.

[7]   This resource is available for free online at http://www.fjc.gov/history/home.nsf/page/ judges.html.

[8]   FEDERAL JUDICIAL CENTER, BIOGRAPHICAL DIRECTORY OF THE FEDERAL JUDICIARY, 1789– 2000 (2001).

[9]   For additional attorney assessments of sitting judges, visit http://www.therobing room.com.

[10]   *See, e.g., Judges,* U.S. DISTRICT COURT FOR THE DISTRICT OF COLUMBIA, http://www.dcd. uscourts.gov/judges (last visited June 24, 2016).

[11]   http://www.lawsitesblog.com/2016/02/ravel-law-enhances-its-judge-analytics-tool.html (last visited Oct. 25, 2016).

[12]   DAVID G. SAVAGE, GUIDE TO THE US SUPREME COURT (5th ed. 2010).

[13]   MELVIN I. UROFSKY, THE SUPREME COURT JUSTICES: A BIOGRAPHICAL DICTIONARY (2014).

[14]   CLARE CUSHMAN, THE SUPREME COURT JUSTICES: ILLUSTRATED BIOGRAPHIES 1789–2012 (3d ed. 2013).

[15]   SANDRA DAY O'CONNOR, OUT OF ORDER: STORIES FROM THE HISTORY OF THE SUPREME COURT (2013).

[16]   "This Directory helps you quickly find contact information for courts around the country with listings for 2,147 state courts, 216 federal courts, and nearly 21,000 court personnel in the 50 states, the District of Columbia, and U.S. territories." http://www.bna.com/bnas-directory-state- p17179895046/ (last visited Oct. 25, 2016).

[17]   AM. BAR ASS'N, http://www.americanbar.org/groups/judicial/resources/diversity.html (last visited June 24, 2016); AM. BAR ASS'N, http://apps.americanbar.org/abanet/jd/display/national.cfm (last visited June 25, 2016).

[18]   LEADERSHIP DIRECTORIES, INC., DIRECTORY OF STATE COURT CLERKS AND COUNTY COURTHOUSES (2015).

19   *Judicial Clerkship Database,* UNIV. OF MICHIGAN LAW SCHOOL, https://www.law.umich .edu/careers/clerkships/Pages/JudicialDatabase.aspx (last visited June 24, 2016).

20   *Nomination by U.S. President,* Congress.gov, https://www.congress.gov/nominations (last visited June 24, 2016).

21   *Confirmation Listing,* UNITED STATES COURTS, http://www.uscourts.gov/Judgesand Judgeships/JudicialVacancies/ConfirmationListing.aspx (last visited June 24, 2016).

22   I wish to thank my colleagues, Kim Fields and Francie Scott, for their valuable input regarding this portion of the chapter.

23   *See, e.g.,* http://www.judiciary.state.nj.us/lawclerks/; http://agency.governmentjobs.com/ mncourts/default.cfm.

24   A practitioner may not use a writing sample absent client and partner permission. Even then, it must be redacted to remove identifying information, such as party names and the docket number.

25   CASSANDRA L. HILL & KATHERINE T. VUKADIN, LEGAL ANALYSIS: 100 EXERCISES FOR MASTERY, PRACTICE FOR EVERY LAW STUDENT (2012).

26   For more information regarding the importance of showing gratitude, read JENNIFER RICHWINE, WITH GRATITUDE: THE POWER OF A THANK YOU NOTE (2014).

27   To order the Vermont Law School Guide, visit http://www.vermontlaw.edu/careers/ judicial-clerkship-guide (last visited July 27, 2016).

CHAPTER 5

KNOWING YOUR ROLE

■ ■ ■

A law clerk plays a pivotal role in Chambers. Trial court clerks do a little bit of everything from managing the docket to drafting opinions. Among other things, they often handle attorneys' calls, draft letters, speeches, jury instructions, orders, and opinions, input minute entries, prepare the judge for status conferences, hearings, trials, and oral arguments, file opinions, review and edit opinions drafted by other clerks, conduct discrete legal research, schedule status conferences and other hearings, and even perform purely administrative tasks. In sum, a trial court clerk must do a vast array of things in a diverse array of cases and must do all of them well. The trial court clerk's days are typically very fast-paced, requiring him or her to move quickly and strategically from one task to another. For this reason, trial court clerks must have excellent time management, stress management, and organizational skills. They must also work well under pressure. Yet they play an essential part in the smooth functioning of Chambers.

An appellate court clerk plays an equally important, albeit markedly different, role in Chambers. Appellate court clerks generally do not speak with attorneys, schedule hearings, or get involved in the day-to-day management of the docket. Nor do they perform administrative tasks. For the most part, appellate clerks spend their days reviewing pending appeals, drafting bench memoranda to prepare the judge for upcoming oral arguments, meeting with law clerks or the judge about pending cases, editing other clerks' work product, and drafting opinions. While time management is incredibly important, appellate clerks tend to spend their days going narrow and deep into a case rather than jumping from one short, time-sensitive task to another. For example, it would not be unusual for an appellate clerk to spend eight consecutive hours doing nothing but drafting and revising a single opinion. For this reason, their hours and daily schedules are usually more predictable and often involve hours upon hours of in-depth research, writing, analysis, and editing.

Term clerks serve a judge for a set term. Terms vary by judge and court, but a term is typically one to two years. Many judges with multiple clerks establish terms so that only one clerk exits at a time; this better ensures that a new clerk will have at least one experienced clerk to orient him or her to Chambers. A career clerk serves a judge indefinitely and often plays a dual role of clerk and judicial assistant. Career clerks appear more common for senior than junior judges and are far less common than term clerks. In some Chambers, a judge has only a single career clerk, while in others the judge may have a career clerk who oversees one to three term clerks. Other courts retain staff attorneys who are not assigned to a particular judge or have clerks that are shared between multiple Chambers.

Law clerks play a critical role in the efficient function of Chambers. A law clerk's sole purpose is to support the judge and in doing so, to effectuate the judiciary's noble goal of promoting justice. You are your judge's first line of defense against error. Because your judge has so many cases on his or her docket, it is your duty to become a subject matter expert on a small subset of those cases and to give your judge wise, well-supported, and thoughtful counsel on the case, whether to place a hold on the opinion, or whether to grant en banc review.

Yet as important as that role of the law clerk is, it is always played behind the scenes. In your supporting role of law clerk, you never author an opinion. You never issue a ruling or decide a case. In fact, your name is never listed anywhere in any issued opinion, not even in a footnote acknowledging your contribution no matter how significant. Your judge is the author of the opinion. Your judge writes the opinion, and you merely provide a draft.

Understanding your role and staying in it is incredibly important. Any claims of "writing," authorship, or "deciding" a case on your resume, on social media, in interviews, etc., will not only breach Chambers confidentiality but will also seriously mischaracterize the scope of your role and duties. Such misstatements will likely prevent you from obtaining a future clerkship or other employment. It could also seriously damage your relationship with your judge and fellow clerks.

A. EXPECTATIONS OF A LAW CLERK

The expectations of a clerk may vary widely by judge. However, given the nature, scope, and importance of a clerk's duties, a clerk who meets or exceeds his or her judge's expectations will likely exemplify each of the following: (1) substantive knowledge of the law; (2) wisdom and intellectual curiosity; (3) strong writing, research, editing, and analytical skills; (4) the ability to think creatively and problem solve; (5) attention to detail; (6) good interpersonal skills; (7) a strong work ethic; (8) passion and enthusiasm for the law and for public service; (9) thoughtfulness and sensitivity to social context; (10) the ability to manage stress and time wisely and to maintain a good work/life balance; (11) the ability to give and receive constructive criticism effectively; (12) strong oral communication skills; (13) persuasiveness and diplomacy; (14) a strong sense of justice and fairness;

(15) integrity; (16) punctuality; (17) professionalism; (18) maturity; (19) depth; (20) dependability; (21) trustworthiness and loyalty; (22) sincerity; (23) well-roundedness; (24) compassion; (25) flexibility (intellectual and otherwise); (26) self-motivation and initiative; (27) strong organizational skills; (28) tempered conviction; (29) a strong moral compass; and (30) the ability to separate personal beliefs and bias from judicial decision-making. In addition, judges seek exceptional individuals who are fun, kind, and will make welcome additions to the unique Chambers family. Think of Chambers as a ship that will veer off course, never reaching its destination, if any member of the crew from the captain to the deckhand fails to satisfactorily play his or her part.

B. SPEAKING IN YOUR JUDGE'S VOICE

Every judge possesses a unique voice. As a law clerk, you must adopt that voice, too. To do this, read your judge's most well-known opinions before you commence the clerkship. Read the judge's articles, books, speeches, and the biography about him or her on the court's website. To understand the judge's voice, you must understand where the judge comes from, geographically but also experientially. Speak with former clerks to learn more about your judge and to discern the judge's judicial philosophy. Once you commence your clerkship, speak with the judicial assistant and the other clerks. Spend time with your judge over lunches or coffee. Get to know your judge as a person, not just as a judge. Ask your judge about his or her judicial philosophy and of which opinions he or she is most proud. Read those opinions carefully. Contemplate their rationale, word choice, tone, style, and thoughtfulness. Discuss those opinions with your judge or co-clerks and explore why they believe the opinion(s) were strong. Throughout the collaborative editing process with your judge, meetings with him or her to discuss cases, and observing the judge at oral argument, you will begin to better understand your judge's voice. Over time, speaking in your judge's voice will become second nature. Indeed, echoes of your judge's voice will likely resonate in every word you speak and write throughout your lifetime.

Throughout this intellectual exploration, you will likely not only discern your judge's voice, tone, and style or the preferred phrases that your judge likes to use, but more importantly, you will discern who your judge is as a judge and as a person. You will understand the mind and heart of the man or woman beneath the robe and the brilliant thinker behind the bench. The ability to interact with a phenomenal jurist face-to-face on a nearly daily basis is one of the most rewarding aspects of clerking. It is an incredible, once-in-a-lifetime opportunity that will benefit you for a lifetime, personally and professionally. You will learn not only how to be a better legal writer, thinker, researcher, and analyst, but more importantly, how to be a better human being.

How can I be sure to fully understand the scope and purpose of each assignment?

As shown below, an assignment memo typically addresses the following: (1) the scope and purpose of the assignment; (2) the preferred format and length: (3) the deadline; (4) the nature of the issue(s); (5) suggested places to look; (6) any strong samples of this type of assignment to review; (7) method of submission; (8) the audience and chain of readership; and (9) any other important considerations, facts, cases, reading, etc., that the drafter should be aware of before proceeding.

Understanding the Scope and Nature of the Assignment

- What is the case name? Parties? Panel members? (if you know)
- Who else is assigned to the case? (litigation team, other law clerks)
- What is the issue(s)? If there are multiple issues and one is dispositive, should I still address the rest or stop to consult with you?
- Who is the audience?
- Nature of the assignment (full memo, just send cases, just meet to discuss, etc.) (any good samples I should peruse)
- Relevant law (statute, regulation, key case)
- Any key facts/factual discrepancies
- Deadline (hard or flexible)
- Expected format (length, double-spaced, etc.)
- Where should I focus my research? (all feds, etc.) Any recommended research terms or strategies? Any recommended secondary sources to quickly familiarize myself with the relevant law? (only ask this if you are unfamiliar with the area of law)
- How much time should I spend before I consult with you?
- Preferred method of submission (draft by email, hard copy/highlighted cases attached)
- May I discuss this with other clerks in Chambers? Outside Chambers?
- Has anyone else examined this issue?
- Purpose: How will this be used?
- Anything else I should know?

Once you have fully prepared, attend the meeting with your judge or supervising law clerk. Be punctual to the meeting. Take a hard copy of your memo with you so that you can complete the remaining questions during the meeting. Bring hard copies of the other assignment-related materials as well. A hard copy is preferable since use of a laptop or iPad during a meeting, albeit far more common than in the past, may be off-putting to some judges and law clerks and is also a noisy distraction during the meeting. Use of the memo will exemplify professionalism and preparedness while also better ensuring that your meeting is maximally productive and efficient. In addition, use of the memo also better guarantees that you produce the product in the desired format, scope, and time frame, satisfying or even exceeding expectations. Finally, use of the memo to prepare for the meeting further indicates your respect for your judge and/or supervising clerk's valuable time; he or she has carved time out of what is certainly a very busy schedule to meet with you and answer your questions. As such, conclude each meeting by thanking your judge or law clerk for taking the time to meet with you.

C. MANAGING YOUR WORKLOAD

To effectively manage assignments, it is important to request assignments in advance so that you do not have gaps in your work unless assignments will naturally be assigned to you. This is particularly true for externs and less applicable to full-time law clerks. For example, in some Chambers, a rotating assignment wheel exists, which automatically doles out 11-Days, PFRs, and other incoming case assignments to whichever law clerk is at the top of the wheel when the case is assigned to Chambers. In other Chambers, a career clerk or judicial assistant assigns cases or tasks. In some Chambers, law clerks choose which cases they will handle. On the other hand, judicial externs nearly always receive assignments from supervising law clerks and less commonly, from the judge directly. For them, it is incredibly important to request assignments in advance to avoid lengthy gaps between assignments.

Do not overextend yourself or establish unreasonable deadlines. In some Chambers, the supervising clerk or judge may not always know what else is on your docket. You know your schedule and other commitments; thus, it is up to you to suggest reasonable deadlines and to courteously and gently alert the judge or law clerk if the suggested timeline is unworkable. Quality matters far more than being a person who says "yes" to every assignment but who, as a result, is unable to meet deadlines or produce high quality work. It is far better to establish a reasonable deadline at the outset and then produce good work within that deadline.

Do not request an extension absent exceptional circumstances. As a good rule of thumb, never request an extension for an assignment unless you believe a court would grant a filing extension for good cause shown. Good cause includes, *inter alia*, a death in the family or serious illness. It does not include a minor illness, such as a head cold or the mere fact that you underestimated how much time a specific assignment may take.

Although being a law clerk may typically have more predictable hours than working at a law firm, it is not always a 9 to 5 job. As a professional, you must stay late and work weekends or holidays as necessary to fully support your judge. Good time management will often preempt the need for such things, but rare instances may arise when you must make personal sacrifices to do your job well. Rise to the occasion. Your judge will expect you to possess the ability to juggle various assignments and manage your time wisely.

As a judicial extern, when you receive an assignment, schedule a short meeting with the assigning clerk or with your judge, depending on the circumstances. To ensure that you understand the scope and purpose of each assignment, use the sample assignment memo above as a starting point when preparing to meet with your supervising clerk or judge. Save it as a new document that reflects the case name and assignment on which you will work. Review all of the materials that have been provided to you in preparation for the meeting and use those materials to answer as many questions as possible from the memo. In this way, you will maximize the productivity of the meeting and not waste your supervisor's time asking questions to which you already know the answer. However, if you are uncertain, attempt to answer the question but confirm the answer at your upcoming meeting. As you review the materials, tweak the assignment memo, adding questions specific to the assignment but not answered in the materials. For more information on effective time management, see Chapter 7.

D. SUPPLEMENTAL RESOURCES

1. CALVERT G. CHIPCHASE, FEDERAL DISTRICT COURT LAW CLERK HANDBOOK (2007).

2. MARY DUNNEWOLD, BETH A. HONETSCHLAGER, & BRENDA L. TOFTE, JUDICIAL CLERKSHIPS: A PRACTICAL GUIDE (2010).

3. Gerald Lebovits, *Judges' Clerks Play Varied Roles in the Opinion Drafting Process*, 76 N.Y. ST. B.J. 34 (2004).

4. JOSEPH L. LEMON, JR., FEDERAL APPELLATE COURT LAW CLERK HANDBOOK (2007).

5. JENNIFER L. SHEPPARD, IN CHAMBERS: A GUIDE FOR JUDICIAL CLERKS AND EXTERNS (2012).

CHAPTER 6

JUDICIAL ETHICS AND CONFIDENTIALITY

■ ■ ■

Rules governing judicial ethics aim to ensure judicial independence, integrity, and legitimacy. In fact, Supreme Court justices[1] and other federal judges appointed pursuant to Article III of the U.S. Constitution enjoy lifetime appointments[2] to better ensure judicial autonomy and thus, the integrity of our courts. When judges or judicial employees engage in unethical conduct, the public loses trust in the judicial system. Without that trust, the system will eventually collapse as has occurred in other nations around the world. For this reason, Congress and other entities like the Committee on Codes of Conduct have promulgated ethical guidance for judges and judicial employees. These rules safeguard the judiciary's legitimacy. Because the judiciary is comprised of individuals, its integrity will be preserved only if each member of the judicial system acts with integrity. On the other hand, a single judicial employee's unethical conduct tarnishes the reputation of the entire judiciary. For this reason, it is essential that law clerks uphold the highest ethical standards throughout their clerkships and ideally, their careers.

Doing so is not always easy. Although many ethics questions can be identified and resolved using basic common sense, others prove more complicated. As a starting point, clerks should draw upon the general rules of professional responsibility they learned in law school and which are tested on the Multistate Professional Responsibility Exam ("MPRE"). Sometimes, however, different and generally more restrictive ethical rules apply to law clerks due to the special relationships they enjoy with judges; thus, what is permissible for a practitioner may be impermissible for a clerk.

This chapter provides a non-exhaustive overview of the ethical issues that law clerks commonly encounter. It is critical that clerks understand ethical guidelines and dutifully comply with them. As in the practice, it can be quite difficult for a clerk to establish a strong reputation in Chambers and at his or her court. However, a good reputation, once built, can be easily diminished, even destroyed, by a single ethical violation.

A. CLERKSHIP ETHICS

Various sources provide guidance regarding judicial ethics. In addition to these sources, your Chambers or court may have their own local or

Chambers-specific rules. Consult your judge at the outset of your clerkship to determine the scope of the ethical rules with which you must comply. As explained below, you should also review the most recent versions of the *Code of Conduct for Judicial Employees* and *Maintaining the Public Trust: Ethics for Federal Judicial Law Clerks*. You should carefully read The Ethics Reform Act of 1989 and other relevant statutes and regulations. Peruse the *Guide to Judiciary Policies and Procedures*. When determining whether a course of conduct is ethical, take an expansive view of the available ethics resources since conduct that may be permissible under one source may be prohibited by another more specific authority.

Which resources provide the most helpful guidance on clerkship ethics?

The Ethics Reform Act of 1989: President George H.W. Bush signed the Ethics Reform Act of 1989 into law on November 30, 1989.[3] This sweeping legislation amended earlier ethics laws and provided greater ethical oversight and guidance to all branches of the government. In particular, it banned most federal employees, including law clerks, from receiving honoraria and placed limitations on outside paid employment as well as the receipt of gifts.[4]

Criminal Statutes: Certain criminal statutes also govern clerk conduct. Although an exhaustive summary of these statutes exceeds the scope of the chapter, various conduct, such as bribery,[5] embezzlement, conversion of public money, records, or property,[6] making a false or fraudulent claim against the government,[7] concealing, removing or mutilating a public record,[8] or misusing a government vehicle[9] are unlawful. It is unlikely that a law clerk would be in a position to commit such violations, intentionally or otherwise, given the typical nature of clerkship duties. However, bribery is one exception, since it is conceivable that a party to a litigation could attempt to bribe a clerk or judge to secure a favorable outcome, particularly in a precedential matter with far-reaching implications, economic or otherwise, for the party.

Code of Conduct for Judicial Employees: The clearest and most commonly used ethics resource is the *Code of Conduct for Judicial Employees* ("Code"), which is produced by the Office of the General Counsel for the Administrative Office of the United States Courts ("AO") in conjunction with the Committee on Codes of Conduct.[10] All federal judicial employees must comply with the Code, except for clerks who serve U.S. Supreme Court Justices; the justices establish separate ethical guidelines for their clerks.[11] State courts also promulgate their own policies, many of which mirror federal guidelines.[12]

The Code succinctly explains five overarching ethical canons that govern federal judicial employees, including law clerks.[13] Canon 1 requires judicial employees to maintain the judiciary's independence and integrity, while Canon 2 prohibits impropriety or the appearance thereof. Canon 3 outlines performance standards, such as avoiding illegal activity, conflicts of interest, nepotism, or breaches of confidentiality. Canon 4 discusses a judicial employee's engagement in outside activity, such as pro bono legal work, while Canon 5 states that judicial employees should refrain from improper political activity, such as running for office or contributing funds to a partisan political organization or candidate. These canons will be discussed in more detail later in the chapter. Although unpaid judicial externs and interns do not technically fall within the definition of a "judicial employee," they are generally expected to adhere to the Code since they are temporarily members of a judge's personal staff.

Judicial Conference Regulations: In 1922, Congress enacted a statute that permitted the Judicial Conference to replace the body previously known as the Conference of Senior Circuit Judges.[14] The Judicial Conference continues to play a vital role in the administrative decision-making processes of the federal courts. It continuously studies the business operations of the federal courts in order to improve their efficiency.[15] After studying the conditions surrounding the general operations and procedures of the federal courts, the Judicial Conference submits suggestions to different courts in order to promote uniformity.[16]

The Chief Justice of the United States acts as the presiding officer of the Judicial Conference.[17] The rest of the Conference is comprised of the chief judge of each judicial circuit, the Chief Judge of the U.S. Court of International Trade, and a district judge from each judicial circuit.[18] The circuit chief judges' terms on the Judicial Conference are concurrent with each of their respective terms as chief judge in their individual circuit.[19] On the other hand, the district judge representatives are elected for terms that vary from three to five years as established by a majority vote of all the circuit and district judges within the respective circuit.[20]

Maintaining the Public Trust: In 2002, the Federal Judicial Center, which is the official education and research agency for the federal courts,[21] issued a helpful new resource—*Maintaining the Public Trust: Ethics for Federal Judicial Law Clerks* ("MPT") that is available for free online.[22] MPT provides a brief overview of key ethical issues that judicial employees may encounter, summarizes key ethics resources, and then explores ethics guidelines through a series of hypotheticals. It concludes with a helpful Ethics Checklist. Because MPT is so comprehensive and clear, many judges require their law clerks and externs to read it prior to commencing their work in Chambers; some even require externs and clerks to sign an acknowledgement form noting that they have read and understood MPT and agree to comply with it.

After reading this chapter, will I know all that is necessary about clerkship ethics?

No. As noted above, this chapter is by no means exhaustive. However, it will enable you to spot potential ethical issues and know how to effectively resolve them. The moment you suspect a potential ethics issue, research local rules and all other relevant canons, statutes, and sources.[23] If the answer remains unclear, escalate your question to your supervising clerk or judge. If the ethical matter is unusually complex or constitutes an issue of first impression, your judge may escalate the question to his or her court's designated ethics expert, ask you to seek guidance from the General Counsel's Office at the AO, or invite you to confidentially seek a formal advisory opinion from the Committee on Codes of Conduct.[24] Although such instances are rare, new and difficult ethical questions continually arise, particularly with the advent and implementation of technological advances that often outpace current guidance. For example, the Ethics Reform Act predated social media sites, which are commonplace today, and thus, its guidance did not contemplate them.

Why are clerks often subject to more restrictive ethical rules than practicing attorneys?

As noted above, some ethical restrictions are more stringent for law clerks than practitioners due to each clerk's special relationship with his or her judge. According to Advisory Opinion 51: "Among judicial employees, law clerks are in a unique position since their work may have direct input into a judicial decision. Even if this is not true in all judicial chambers, the legal community perceives that this is the case based upon the confidential and close nature of the relationship between [the] clerk and judge."[25]

Must unpaid judicial externs and interns comply with ethical rules?

Yes. Because judicial externs and interns, whether paid or unpaid, are members of the judge's personal staff and may enjoy (or be perceived as enjoying) a close relationship with the judge, they should operate under the assumption that the same ethical rules that govern law clerks likewise govern them. Although they may not technically constitute court employees, they do possess a special relationship with the judge and an ability to impact judicial decision-making via their research and contributions; this remains true even when the supervising clerk acts as an intermediary since his or her work likely relies, at least in part, upon the externs' and interns' research and contributions.

Do the guidelines only prohibit <u>actual</u> ethical violations?

No. Clerks must avoid actual ethical violations as well as conduct that could create an *appearance* of impropriety. Put differently, a clerk must avoid doing anything that might cause someone to believe that an ethical violation has occurred, even if one has not. This distinction is critical since a clerk can be dismissed simply for giving the impression of wrongdoing. Imagine a situation in which you are clerking for a judge. After you are assigned to a case, you discover that your boyfriend is an attorney working on the case. Although you know that you would never allow that relationship to improperly impact your analysis, that fact might not be readily apparent to the parties or to the public. As a result, you should immediately stop work and alert your judge that your continued participation in the case could give rise to the appearance of impropriety. Your judge will then decide whether to remove you from the case or permit you to continue working on it.

What, if anything, do the guidelines say about a law clerk's conduct?

A law clerk's conduct must always reflect positively on the judiciary. According to Canon 3C, a clerk should "be patient, dignified, respectful, and courteous to all persons ... and diligently discharge the responsibilities of the office in a prompt, efficient, nondiscriminatory, fair, and professional manner."[26] Never attempt to improperly influence cases, perform your duties in a way that "improperly favors" one party over another, or imply that you have the power to do either.[27] Avoid unlawful nepotism.[28] This is especially true in case assessment and judicial drafting. For example, a clerk must thoroughly and impartially assess each party's arguments and render a bias-free, thoughtful recommendation.[29]

What constitutes a conflict of interest, and how can a law clerk avoid one?

A *conflict of interest* refers to a situation in which an individual's personal interests may undermine or conflict with his or her professional responsibilities or interests or vice-versa. Judges recuse themselves to avoid conflicts of interest, and while a clerk lacks the authority to do the same, it is the clerk's ethical duty to at least alert his or her judge of any potential conflict so that the judge can remove the clerk from the matter as necessary. According to Canon 3F, a clerk "should avoid conflicts of interest in the performance of official duties."[30] In most Chambers, this prohibition embraces both *actual* conflicts of interests as well as the appearance of such a conflict. Imagine that a clerk's parent currently works for a party to the litigation pending before the judge. Even if the clerk would never allow that circumstance to impact his assessment of the case, the clerk's involvement could create the appearance of a conflict. As a result, the clerk should immediately raise the issue with the supervising clerk or judge, depending on Chambers protocol, and be walled off from the case as appropriate. The judge determines this on a case-by-case basis.

Many situations can create actual or potential conflicts of interest. For example, a clerk should *immediately* notify his or her supervisor or judge if any of the following is true:[31]

(1)   the law clerk, his or her significant other, or relative[32] has a personal relationship with someone that is a party or is connected to a party in some way[33] (*e.g.*, the law clerk's parent works for the law firm handling the pending case even though the parent is not staffed on the matter);

(2)   the law clerk, his or her significant other, or relative has a financial interest in the case (*e.g.*, the law clerk owns stock in a company that is a party to the litigation);[34]

(3)   the law clerk has a preexisting personal bias concerning a party or an issue in the litigation (*e.g.*, before clerking, the law clerk published a blog post heavily criticizing the business practices of a party to the case);

(4)   the law clerk has personal knowledge of facts at dispute in the litigation (*e.g.*, the clerk witnessed the accident that gave rise to the litigation);

(5)   the law clerk worked on the case prior to the clerkship;

(6)   the law clerk, his or her significant other, or relative has or will serve as a witness in the matter;

(7)   the law clerk, his or her significant other, or relative[35] is related to a party or an "officer, director, or trustee of a party"; and/or

(8)   the law clerk, his or her significant other, or relative has publicly commented on the merits of a case at issue or the legal issue involved therein.

Notably, the list above is non-exhaustive and is at times, more restrictive, than the Code. However, it does paint a clear picture of the kinds of circumstances that could pose a conflict. At the outset of your clerkship, confer with your judge regarding the kinds of circumstances that would warrant your exclusion from a case. Below is another resource adapted from MPT, which provides additional guidance on ethical issues that clerks commonly encounter.

Actual Conflicts

- Prior to your clerkship, you worked on a case now pending before your judge

- A firm at which you worked before your clerkship and to which you plan to return after your clerkship represents the defendant in a matter before your judge

- You served as a material witness in a case now pending before your judge

- You own stock in a company that is a party before your judge

- Your husband or wife represents the plaintiff in a proceeding before your judge

- Your aunt or uncle is a defendant in a wrongful discharge lawsuit pending before your judge

Potential Conflicts

(situations such as these do not necessarily disqualify you from working on a case, but you should always alert your judge to them):

- A close friend or relative may serve as an expert witness in a case pending before your judge

- An attorney you met at speed dating or networking event and with whom you exchanged numbers appears the next day in court before your judge

- An environmental hazard in a case before your judge borders your parents' or grandparents' property

- In your law review note or legal blog, you expressed opinions on the merits of a case now on appeal before your judge

This chart is largely adapted from Maintaining the Public Trust (2011), a publication of the Federal Judicial Center.

What should I do if I suspect a conflict of interest?

Stop. Research. Report. When a conflict arises, stop work and immediately notify your judge or supervising clerk, whichever course that Chambers' protocol dictates.[36] Research the relevant ethics materials to determine if an actual or potential conflict exists. Promptly report the issue and the results of your research to your supervising clerk or judge. Then Chambers "should take appropriate steps to restrict the judicial employee's performance of official duties in such matter so as to avoid a conflict or the appearance of a conflict of interest."[37]

Let's practice.

> 1. Your spouse owns stock in a publicly traded company that is a party to a case pending before your judge. May you work on the case?
>
> 2. What if you worked for a party appearing before your judge prior to law school?
>
> 3. Last summer, you worked at Heath & Wyatt, LLP. You conducted objective research on a patent infringement matter. Now you are clerking for Special Master Asbury, and Heath & Wyatt is appearing before your court handling a vaccine case. May you work on the case?
>
> 4. Your cousin is an immunologist at Cabell Huntington Hospital. You are working on a vaccine case and discover that your cousin is appearing as an expert witness in the case. What do you do?
>
> 5. You attend an ABA networking event, and an attractive attorney asks for your number. You have a few drinks with him after the event. The next day, he appears before your judge. What do you do?

May I engage in outside activities or employment during my clerkship?

It depends. In general, law clerks may engage in outside activities, such as civic, charitable, or recreational activities, or "financial and business dealings" so long as they do not "detract from the dignity of the court, interfere with the performance of official activities, or adversely reflect on the operation and dignity of the court or office the judicial employee serves."[38] Notably, a clerk must obtain his or her judge's permission to engage in law-related outside activity, such as publishing law review articles, contributing to a law-related blog, or teaching at a local law school,[39] as well as "financial and business activities that might reasonably be interpreted as violating the [Code]." Even if the clerk obtains permission, he or she generally cannot accept honoraria—"payments for a single appearance, speech, or article."[40] However, a clerk "may earn compensation from certain outside activities or receive reimbursement for expenses related to those activities . . . [within] limits."[41]

Generally, clerks may not engage in the practice of law, even on a pro bono basis, since doing so might create a conflict or impede the clerk's performance of his or her clerkship duties.[42] Some exceptions may exist, such as providing limited, unpaid legal aid to a family member, but even then, the clerk should confer with the judge *before* offering aid. Nor may clerks accept a paid position with a law firm likely to appear before the court, even if the position does not directly involve the practice of law. Outside political activity raises special concerns that are discussed separately below.

Soliciting funds for outside activities also raises concerns. Canon 4C(1) advises clerks to "avoid activities that exploit their judicial position or associate them in a substantial financial manner with attorneys likely to appear in their court."[43] Nor may a law clerk solicit funds in connection with outside activities; for instance, a clerk may not use the prestige of the clerkship to encourage individuals to donate funds to an activity or organization. A clerk may also not ask other court employees to contribute funds "under circumstances where the staff member's close relationship to the judge could reasonably be construed to give undue weight to the solicitation."[44]

Outside Legal Activities—A Checklist

1. Does the activity interfere with your performance of your official duties? ☐

2. Will the activity exploit your government position? ☐

3. Does the activity present an appearance of impropriety or reflect adversely on the court? ☐

4. Will the activity associate you in a substantial financial manner with attorneys appearing in your court? ☐

5. If the activity involves routine family legal work, does it— involve any appearance in federal court? ☐ [O]ccur while on duty or in the workplace? ☐ [R]esult in compensation (other than in probate proceedings)? ☐

6. If the activity involves the pro bono practice of law, does it—involve any appearance in a federal, state, or local court or administrative agency? ☐ [O]ccur while on duty or in the workplace? ☐ [I]nvolve a matter of public controversy or an issue likely to come before your court? ☐ [R]esult in compensation? ☐

7. Is the activity inconsistent with any additional condition or limitation your judge imposes on law clerks' law-related activities? ☐

If you answer yes to any of these questions, you probably should not engage in the activity absent your judge's express permission.

This checklist is excerpted from Maintaining the Public Trust (2011), a publication of the Federal Judicial Center. It is reprinted herein with the permission of the Federal Judicial Center. It has been altered to include check boxes.

May I engage in political activity during my clerkship?

Generally no. Lawyers play a special role in society and possess a unique skill set. For these reasons, lawyers have often had a pivotal impact on politics at every level. Indeed, as of October 2016, 25 of our 44 presidents have been lawyers, including legendary commanders-in-chief Abraham

Lincoln and Franklin Delano Roosevelt.[45] Many of the Founding Fathers, including Thomas Jefferson and John Adams, were also attorneys.[46] In fact, many of the signers of the Declaration of Independence and framers of the U.S. Constitution were lawyers.[47]

It seems counterintuitive then that Canon 5 of the Code clearly prohibits clerks from actively engaging in partisan[48] or non-partisan[49] political activity, such as publicly endorsing candidates, holding political office, or soliciting funds on a candidate or party's behalf.[50] Indeed, it is oft-quipped that the only political activity in which a clerk can safely engage without running afoul of the Code is simply casting his or her vote! However, these proscriptions are necessary given the clerk's close relationship with his or her judge. Due to this special relationship, a clerk's public opposition or support of a candidate, issue, or organization might be imputed to the clerk's judge, which in turn, could prompt allegations of impartiality in judicial decision-making, however false.

May I interview for jobs during my clerkship?

It depends. Most law clerks are hired for a one or two-year term. Some law clerks have practiced prior to the clerkship and plan to return to their firms when the clerkship concludes. Others plan to pursue a subsequent clerkship or seek post-clerkship employment at a law firm, corporation, non-profit, law school, or government agency. Such clerks should take care to avoid ethical issues that may arise during their job searches, including potential breaches of confidentiality or the prohibited receipt of gifts or compensation. Some exceptions to the general prohibition on accepting gifts do exist, such as ordinary social hospitality, gifts from relatives and friends on special occasions, gifts arising from a spouse's professional connections, invitations to bar-related functions, or some scholarships or fellowships.[51]

Canon 4C(4) permits a clerk to job-seek during a clerkship so long as his or her judge permits it, but not all judges do. Some judges permit clerks to job-seek but not accept any compensation, such as a signing bonus or even travel expenses related to an interview. Others only permit clerks to seek positions with entities that do not do business with or appear before the court. For these reasons, it is important for you to discuss your Chambers' policy regarding job-seeking as soon as you accept the offer to clerk and before you commence your clerkship. If you have a post-clerkship position in place, immediately inform your judge in case your prospective employer presents a conflict of interest.

The application process poses additional ethical concerns. For example, some Chambers may not permit you to list the judge for whom you clerk, only the court, until the clerkship ends. This restriction would not only apply to professional social media sites, but also to paper or electronic resumes and cover letters provided to potential employers during a clerkship. In addition, you may not use any work product produced during your clerkship as a writing sample absent your judge's express permission. According to the Code, clerks may not "solicit or accept a gift from anyone seeking official action from or doing business with the court . . ."[52] Thus, although a prospective employer may offer to purchase you lunch, dinner, coffee, or a drink during an interview, the meal or beverage might constitute a "gift," particularly if the item has more than de minimis value. Furthermore, during interviews with prospective employers, you may not divulge confidential information gleaned as a result of your clerkship duties. For all of these reasons, job-seeking can give rise to a host of serious ethical issues, and you are advised to find employment either before your clerkship commences or after it concludes. If doing so is not possible, then discuss your concerns with your judge and comply with Chambers-specific policies.

Notably, as a clerk, you may not use your connection to your judge to influence prospective employers, such as implying that if the firm offers you employment, you will assess that firm's position more favorably in a pending case. That being said, it is usually permissible to ask your judge to serve as a reference or draft a letter of recommendation. Judges differ in their willingness to serve in these capacities.

B. CHAMBERS CONFIDENTIALITY

Why is Chambers confidentiality important?

A judge must be able to express his or her thoughts freely within Chambers. A judge must also have a safe space to compare competing theories of the case as well as evaluate different types of evidence. Conversations between an attorney and client are confidential so that the client can provide the attorney with all information, whether favorable or adverse, necessary to zealously advocate for the client. Similarly, Chambers confidentiality ensures the free exchange of thoughtful discourse, debate, and even disagreement among a judge and his or her clerks; without the promise of confidentiality, the judge's relationship with his or her law clerks might be compromised as would the judge's ability to impartially and thoughtfully weigh competing arguments in each case. In addition, judges must be free to change their minds without fear of public backlash or a loss of legitimacy in the judiciary. As a result, confidentiality contributes to more informed, thoughtful, and well-reasoned judicial decision-making.

What is the scope of a clerk's duty of confidentiality?

According to Canon 3D, "[a] judicial employee should never disclose any confidential information received in the course of official duties, except as required in the performance of such duties, nor should a judicial employee employ such information for personal gain."[53] Clerks should also not comment on the merits of a pending or impending action. In other words, "what happens in Chambers stays in Chambers."[54] This includes a clerk's friends, family, parents, significant others, spouses, children, etc. It even includes co-workers because Chambers does *not* encompass the entire court; it refers only to members of the Chambers in which you clerk. Thus, you may not discuss confidential information, including pending cases, with clerks or externs from other Chambers within the same court absent your judge's express permission. Nor may you use attorney colleagues, other clerks or judges, or former professors as sounding boards for your recommendations or research for the judge. In fact, some Chambers may implement even more stringent Chambers-specific policies regarding confidentiality.

Although Chambers-specific policies may vary somewhat, a few clear-cut rules delineate what a clerk generally may and may not discuss outside Chambers absent his or her judge's permission. For instance, a clerk generally may not disclose information, orally or in writing, regarding how his or her judge plans to rule or the outcome of a pending case. Nor may a clerk ever discuss or disclose work product relating to a pending case, such as a bench memo, draft opinion, or 11-Day (a memo evaluating another panel's draft opinion before it issues). Any draft work product relating to a case, whether pending or decided, remains confidential for life and cannot be disclosed or discussed. After all, the final issued opinion may differ markedly from clerk work product. Nor may a clerk share the content of his or her discussions with the judge about cases, attorneys, or the judge's observations about a particular case. Indeed, a good rule of thumb is simply to never disclose identifying information obtained during the course of or as a direct result of a clerkship if that information is unavailable to the broader legal community. That being said, a clerk may divulge information to the extent his or her judge expressly permits it so long as doing so does not violate the court's local rules on confidentiality.

This broad proscription also encompasses personal information about your judge. Imagine a scenario in which your old law school friend, David, learns that you are now clerking for Judge Wilkinson. Judge Wilkinson is a prominent judge, and David's law firm often appears before her court. David texts you at home one weekend to ask whether Judge Wilkinson is a member of the gym near the court because he would like to join in hopes of making her acquaintance in an informal setting. David contacted you via your personal telephone number, not office equipment, and the text occurred outside office hours while you were at home. Judge Wilkinson's gym membership is not directly relevant to a pending case. However, you still should not disclose this information because it is personal information that you obtained during your clerkship as a direct result of your special relationship to Judge Wilkinson. It is not widely available to the legal community or public and disclosing it would violate Judge Wilkinson's privacy. It could also be viewed as an abuse of the judge's trust. As a result, you should simply respond to David: "I cannot disclose that kind of private, personal information." Never disclose personal information regarding your judge absent his or her express permission.

On the other hand, some information that you obtain during your clerkship is not necessarily confidential, particularly when you obtained it in the performance of your clerkship duties but not as a direct result of your special relationship to your judge. For example, successful performance of your clerkship will likely require you to acquire mastery of court rules, protocol, and procedures; generally this information is not confidential. You may explain it to friends, family, or discuss it with other attorneys or law clerks. You may also discuss or disclose information that is contained in the public record, such as items listed in a case docket or disclosed in public court proceedings. Of course, this excludes a published decision that is under seal and thus, not publicly available except in a redacted form.[55] For example, after your judge publishes a decision, it is available on Westlaw and other research databases and may be cited in a reporter if it is a reported case. You are permitted to discuss the case so long as your discussion never reveals information regarding the *process* of the judge's decision-making; in other words, you may discuss the issued case, but not any of the discussions, draft, or process that occurred *behind* the scenes unless your judge expressly authorizes you to do so. However, in such instances, it is a best practice simply to refer the individual to the issued opinion, rather than attempting to explain or comment upon it.

Confidential documents include bench memoranda, correspondence with the judge relating to cases, information about the judge's decision-making process, draft judicial opinions, the judge's straw vote on a case, etc. Anything in draft form should be considered confidential. Non-confidential documents typically include court rules, court procedures, information available on the court website, published cases, an oral argument transcript, law review articles, published speeches, and biographical information about your judge that is included in his or her court profile. Notably, however, both of the aforementioned lists are non-exhaustive, and exceptions may apply.

It is important to emphasize that a clerk's obligation to maintain Chambers confidentiality is lifelong.[56] If you are not 100% certain of whether you may disclose information, always ask before you act. Be sure you understand the permissible scope of what you may ask or share. For example, your judge may give you permission to discuss a pending case with a law clerk assisting another judge on the panel deciding the case but may limit the scope of those discussions such that you may not disclose how your judge intends to vote.

Let's practice. Which documents are confidential?

- Appellee's non-confidential brief? ☐
- A published opinion? ☐
- Draft dissent? ☐
- The name of your judge's alma mater? ☐
- Judge's straw vote? ☐
- A bench memo? ☐
- The name of your judge's doctor? ☐
- For whom your judge voted in the last election? ☐
- A copy of an ABA speech that your judge has delivered? ☐
- A draft ABA speech? ☐

May I discuss pending cases with clerks in other Chambers?

It depends. As explained above, what happens in Chambers generally stays in Chambers. Thus, absent your judge's permission, you should not discuss with other clerks how your judge plans to decide a case, his or her decision-making process, or any other personal information you have learned as a result of your relationship with your judge. Typically, you can share this material with your co-clerks within Chambers. Likewise, only with your judge's permission may you share work product, such as bench memoranda or draft opinions, with other clerks at your court. Many appellate judges will permit their law clerks to at least discuss pending cases or information contained within the clerk's bench memo with clerks whose judges are on the same appellate panel. However, always confirm this with your judge prior to disclosing such information or engaging in such discussions.

Let's practice.

You are writing a bench memo in a tax case. You are recommending that the judge reverse. May you discuss the case and your recommendation with:

- Your former tax professor? ☐
- Your former judicial drafting professor? ☐
- Your supervising law clerk? ☐
- A law clerk from another Chambers whose judge is on the panel? ☐
- Another judge who is on the panel? ☐
- Another judge who is not on the panel? ☐
- The court librarian? ☐
- Your former boss who is a tax attorney? ☐
- The court's general counsel? ☐
- The judicial assistant? ☐
- Your spouse? ☐
- Your roommate? ☐
- Your parent? ☐

Why are some briefs marked confidential?

In some instances, a clerk may receive two sets of briefs, one of which is marked confidential.[57] This means that some information pertinent to the judge's decision is highly sensitive. Such information will typically be bracketed and bolded in the text. Only the non-confidential briefs will be made available to the public or posted on the court's intranet. Only the Chambers hearing the case will have access to the confidential briefs. When drafting your bench memo, be sure to note at the outset of the bench memo that it contains confidential information and explain how you will denote such information. It is common to use boldfaced font and double brackets to denote confidential information. It is important to note this information for the judge so that he or she will not mistakenly ask a question at oral argument that divulges confidential information. Moreover, the bench memo is often converted into the final draft opinion, sometimes quite quickly. Clearly demarcating confidential information with boldfaced font and double brackets will better ensure that such information is not accidentally included in the final opinion, particularly if you must transition that assignment to another clerk due to the fact that your clerkship term has come to an end.

What does under seal mean?

Some cases have heightened confidentially protections often due to confidential information they contain, which relates to pricing or national security. For example, as noted above, it is common for cases brought under the National Childhood Injury Vaccine Compensation Act of 1986 ("Vaccine Act") to be litigated under seal when they involve child-petitioners; such cases are often labeled *Doe* and assigned a number that has not been previously assigned to a prior case, such as *Doe 93*.

Cases are filed under seal through special electronic case filing procedures. Even other judges and law clerks within your court will lack access to unredacted case records for cases filed under seal. Only your Chambers will see the unredacted version of the filings, and whenever Chambers issues an order or opinion in the case, it will do so under seal. The parties will be given an opportunity to suggest redactions to the final opinion, and only that redacted version, which omits the sensitive information, will be available to the public. Take special care to maintain confidentiality when handling a case that has been filed under seal.

C. ETHICS AND TECHNOLOGY

In some ways, technology has outpaced available ethical guidelines. Ethics guidance and governing law predate today's technology, which provides everyone with instant access to an international audience via social media sites. The lack of clear-cut guidance regarding social media, email, instant messaging, and blogging in combination with the ease and frequency in which people utilize them raise grave concerns regarding potential ethical violations and breaches of confidentiality. Recent hacks of highly protected email and technological systems only bolster these concerns.

How may I use technology, including social media, during my clerkship without running afoul of ethical guidelines?

Email: In recent years, government agencies and private employers have experienced serious data breaches. In many cases, personal emails have been hacked or stolen. The judiciary is aware of these attacks and has taken special measures to protect against them, utilizing software and other security protocols to better protect the integrity and confidentiality of sensitive court data. However, employees often pose the greatest threat to cybersecurity. No matter how well a security system works, one employee violating protocol can facilitate a massive breach. For this reason, it is critical that you undergo cybersecurity training at the outset of your clerkship. Pay special attention to Chambers-specific and court-wide policies regarding the use of technology and office equipment. Although your Chambers will likely have specific rules, below are some general tips that will better prevent a data breach. To the extent these policies conflict with the guidelines of your court or Chambers, comply with the latter.

Be aware that personal email systems may not have the same security protections in place as the court's system. Therefore, do not email confidential documents to yourself at your personal email address. For the same reason, only email your judge and fellow clerks via the court email, unless your judge instructs otherwise. You may email cases or law review articles that would not divulge the nature of the case pending before your judge. If you must work from home instead of in Chambers, consult your court's technology department to see if there are mechanisms to allow you to connect remotely to the court's email system without imperiling security.

In addition, do not save confidential information on a thumb drive unless you obtain your judge or supervising clerk's express permission to do so. A thumb drive is so small that it could easily be lost, stolen, or switched, making confidential documents available that could then be posted online, sold, shared, etc.

For similar reasons, never take confidential documents outside Chambers, absent your judge or supervising clerk's express permission. This includes taking a *confidential* brief, for example, to read in the courtyard, cafeteria, or library at your court; note that rules might be less restrictive for non-confidential briefs. However, even within your court, you must never take any confidential work product, such as a bench memo or draft opinion outside Chambers absent permission. Even broader restrictions encompass taking confidential documents, whether briefs or work product, outside the court, such as taking a brief home to work on a bench memo over the weekend. If a roommate, friend, or guest were to see the information or if it were to be lost or stolen on the way home, that could potentially constitute a serious confidentiality breach. Notably, however, there may be instances when you receive permission to take such documents outside the court. For example, perhaps your judge is sitting by designation at a court in another state. Your judge may direct you to bring copies of the bench memo in the case he or she will hear. Take special care to keep the document in a carry-on bag, and never take it out in the car, plane, train, elevator, etc., to read or discuss. Someone might easily view and read the document without your knowledge.

Let's practice.

> You want to work on your bench memo from home. What materials, if any, may you take home:
>
> A. Nothing absent the judge's permission
> B. Cases so long as they don't contain case-related notes arising from discussions with the judge
> C. Non-confidential briefs

Instant Messaging, Texting, and Social Media: Courts typically do not permit clerks to use court technology for personal reasons. This rule is easy to follow with regard to the copier, scanner, and office telephone.

The computer that Chambers provides is a different story. New clerks and externs often believe that while they cannot make a long-distance telephone call using their office phone, it is perfectly permissible for them to use their court-provided computer to instant message friends who work outside the court, surf the Internet, or post on social media sites. Nothing could be further from the truth. Restrictions regarding the use of technology and office equipment are not implemented solely for financial reasons; rather, many of the rules aim to preserve confidentiality and maintain cybersecurity. Thus, a good rule of thumb is to avoid using office equipment, including your computer, for personal reasons, such as sending personal emails, instant messaging friends outside Chambers, or posting on or perusing social media.

Enterprising clerks may mistakenly believe that they can comply with this rule simply by logging onto such sites using their personal smartphones or texting friends during the workday rather than instant messaging them. Yet this, too, is ill-advised for several reasons. First, it is a best practice to keep your personal phone turned off while working and to turn it on to check messages, etc., only during breaks. This will improve your productivity by minimizing distractions and will also prevent you from distracting others. For example, a fellow clerk might find it quite distracting to sit near a co-clerk whose phone buzzes and bings repeatedly throughout the day, while a supervisor might infer that the clerk is focusing more on personal matters than on completing his or her work.

Setting aside these important professionalism concerns, using your smartphone only during designated breaks may also make you less likely to quickly respond to a text message or social media post and thereby inadvertently disclose confidential information. Consider this scenario:

> Judge Lycans is sitting on tomorrow's panel in a very important international trade case. The judges on the panel will not be revealed until the morning of the oral argument. You turned in your bench memo to Judge Lycans several days ago, but this morning after you met with the judge, she observed some important gaps in the parties' arguments and asked you to complete some supplemental research. You must get it to her by tomorrow morning before the hearing. While you are experiencing this "fire drill," your phone begins buzzing. You have been included on a group text message inviting you and twenty other friends from law school to an impromptu happy hour that evening. At first, you ignore the messages, but then you quickly respond, "Can't make it. Gonna be researching countervailing duties all night for an early hearing. Have fun!"

While your quick response may at first seem benign since you did not include identifying details about the case, you have indeed disclosed confidential information. You have implicitly shared with over twenty people that Judge Lycans will be hearing an international trade case the next day. Your law school friends may work at firms that appear before your court, and they could easily forward your text to others. They have no reason to know that the information is confidential. There is no way to recall the text once read. Thus, in your haste to answer the text and get back to the business at hand, you have inadvertently breached Chambers confidentiality. Yet this would never have occurred had your phone been turned off and you only had turned to it later during a break when you could have thoughtfully crafted a proper response. This same scenario is equally applicable to posting on social media.

As explained above, according to Canon 3D, a clerk may never discuss cases pending before the court, the judge's decision-making process, the work of the court, the judge's personal life, etc., on social media absent the judge's express permission. Such discussions constitute "public comment[s] on the merits of a pending or impending action," even if the clerk's profile contains strict privacy settings. If information is obtained due to your special relationship with your judge, then it remains confidential even after your clerkship ends. Thus, absent your judge's permission, you may not blog or post about it on any social media site for your lifetime.

Social media sites can also give rise to additional professionalism concerns. In everything, the clerk represents not just his or her judge but the entire judiciary. Thus, a clerk's words and actions can create a positive public perception of the judiciary or in the alternative, tarnish the court's image with the public. Unethical or unprofessional conduct may cause the public to perceive the judiciary as broken, unfair, illegitimate, or inaccessible. Perhaps for this reason, Canon 4A observes that "[a] judicial employee's activities outside of official duties should not detract from the dignity of the court, interfere with the performance of official duties, or adversely reflect on the operation and dignity of the court or office the judicial employee serves." Imagine a scenario in which Heather has added "friends" on her social media site, including attorneys and fellow clerks, who know that Heather clerks for Judge Hancock.[58] Heather posts pictures of herself participating in a wet T-shirt contest during her bachelorette bash in the Bahamas. One could argue that the photographs reflect Heather's participation in an outside activity that "adversely reflect[s] on the operation and dignity of the court or office the judicial employee serves." The same holds true for clerks posting pictures of recreational drug use, whether lawful or not where and when taken, or photographs involving tobacco or alcohol use. Thus, it is critical that any representation a clerk posts reflect the dignity and integrity of the judiciary, particularly if the clerk has granted attorneys and fellow clerks access to the photographs, rather than keeping them private.

In addition, status updates and other social media functions can evince a lack of professionalism or breach confidentiality. For example, if a clerk for the D.C. District Court posts a status update or check-in at 2am at El Centro, a popular Georgetown salsa bar, the night before an 8am hearing, that may reflect poorly on the clerk and relatedly, the court. Even posts that do not breach confidentiality can still reflect adversely on a clerk's professionalism, dedication, and work ethic. For example, posts such as "working all weekend. ☹" or "Since when do externs have to work weekends?" are ill-advised since they denote a poor work ethic and lack of dedication.

Social media sites that require autobiographical information pose additional concerns. Never list that you work for a court or specific judge unless you obtain the judge's express permission. Do not list specific cases you have worked on or documents you have completed absent permission. As explained above, the same holds true for your resume and other application materials. Ask your judge or supervising clerk to review your resume before you exit Chambers to ensure that your resume does not divulge confidential information. Obtain express permission to submit any work product completed during your time in Chambers as a writing sample, and only provide a redacted version that omits identifying details like docket numbers. Never talk to the media, including student publications or your law school's communications director, absent permission.

D. INTERACTING WITH ATTORNEYS AND THE MEDIA

Law clerks, both current and former, may occasionally be asked by attorneys, the media, or prospective employers to share insights from their special relationship with the judge. In such conversations, clerks must be careful not to divulge confidential information. The section that follows provides guidance regarding how to interact with attorneys and the media without running afoul of ethical guidelines.

As a clerk, may I speak to attorneys appearing before the court without committing an ethical violation?

It depends. Such conversations might be permissible so long as you have the judge's permission and the communication is not ex parte, which means that counsel for only one party is privy to the conversation. Most judges will also permit clerks to exchange small talk with attorneys at court proceedings. However, never speak to parties' counsel at a hearing or status conference absent your judge's express permission. At the outset of the clerkship, determine whether speaking frequently to attorneys is within the scope of your clerkship responsibilities. Chambers vary in this regard. For example, as an appellate law clerk, you will rarely if ever directly speak with the attorneys handling a case. More likely than not, attorney inquiries regarding court procedures and protocol will be directed to the Clerk's Office where staff attorneys will explain court procedures and protocol.

The same cannot be said of clerks to trial court judges. As discussed in Chapter 5, the role of a trial court clerk is quite distinct from that of an appellate clerk. A trial court clerk will often speak directly to counsel on a pending matter to schedule hearings and status conferences, answer questions, etc. For this reason, it is critical that trial court clerks understand the scope and contours of their communications with attorneys.

First, clerks may not participate in any ex parte discussions with attorneys on a pending matter. As noted earlier, an ex parte communication occurs when only one attorney on the matter communicates with the court. This could occur if plaintiff's counsel emails the law clerk without copying defense counsel on the email or telephones the clerk without having defense counsel on the line. It could even occur if plaintiff's counsel encounters the clerk at or outside the court and discusses the case with the clerk outside the presence of opposing counsel. Each of these instances constitutes an improper ex parte communication and a potential ethical violation.

Attorneys may attempt to engage in ex parte communications with clerks for various reasons. Inexperienced attorneys or pro se litigants may be unaware that ex parte communications are unethical and inappropriate. Other attorneys may simply hope to gain an inside view regarding the judge's leanings or may try to get an unfair advantage for their clients; this, of course, misunderstands the meaning of zealous advocacy, which must at all times remain ethical. Given the special status of pro se litigants, some judges may permit their clerks to direct pro se litigants to a legal aid agency or volunteer attorney network, but others may not.

At the outset of your clerkship, ask your judge or supervising clerk how to handle an ex parte communication. Each Chambers may handle this situation somewhat differently. In general, the clerk, upon realizing that this is an ex parte communication, must immediately end the communication, even if doing so requires the clerk to interrupt the attorney mid-sentence. If the communication is via telephone, the law clerk should quickly state, "I'm sorry, but this is an impermissible ex parte communication. As such, I must hang up. If you call back, please have opposing counsel present on the line." If the communication occurs via email, the law clerk should stop reading the email and respond, "I am unable to read this email or respond because this is an impermissible ex parte communication. If you wish to contact the court, you must copy opposing counsel on the correspondence. Thank you." Such a no-nonsense response may be difficult, particularly for a young law clerk writing to a prominent attorney. However, the clerk's duty is to protect Chambers confidentiality, uphold the integrity of the court, and preserve the propriety of the proceedings. In some Chambers, the judge or supervising clerk will expect you to alert him or her of the incident; in other Chambers, the judge may simply direct you to draft a dated memo to file documenting the incident and noting how you handled it. Still other judges may require clerks to take both measures out of an abundance of caution.

Even if a communication is not ex parte, a clerk may still be somewhat limited in how he or she may respond. At the outset of the clerkship, confer with your judge or supervising clerk to determine how to respond to soft inquiries from parties, such as when the judge plans to issue a decision, etc. In most Chambers, judges will likely direct clerks to simply respond, "I'm sorry, but I really can't say. You'll just have to wait until the opinion issues."

Let's practice.

> You are handling a case with Judge Violet. The attorneys in the case do not get along well. They have gotten into arguments during conferences, etc. This morning Plaintiff filed an unopposed motion for an extension of time, but within an hour, Defendant opposed the motion. Five minutes later, the irate plaintiff's attorney calls you without having defense counsel on the line and begins accusing defense counsel of going against his promise not to oppose the motion. Plaintiff's counsel claims that defense counsel agreed by phone not to oppose the motion but then filed an opposition to the motion that morning. How do you handle this situation?

May I speak with the media during my clerkship?

Generally no. When you clerk for a prominent jurist or a high-profile case is pending before your judge, the media may contact you. Canon 3D makes clear that you cannot disclose any confidential information or comment publicly on the merits of pending or impending cases.[59] Although ethics resources provide guidance on this issue, it is worth sitting down with your judge when Chambers is first assigned a high-profile matter to quickly review Chambers protocol. For example, some judges might permit their clerks to direct the media to publicly available sources or to provide general comments on court protocol, procedures, or rules that are available to the public. Other judges may simply instruct clerks to respond with "No comment" or to advise members of the media to consult those sources themselves rather than commenting upon or explaining them. However, the vast majority of judges do not permit their law clerks to have *any* contact with the media, either orally or in writing. This is especially true when the court has employees designated to handle media inquiries. Your court or Chambers may also have guidelines for dealing with the press, so be sure to consult them. Even if your judge has no guidelines regarding speaking to the press and no clear prohibition, it is still a best practice to obtain your judge's express permission and to share your planned remarks with the judge for approval. The same rules hold true for student publications and school media directors who may wish to congratulate you on your clerkship. Never act without your judge's permission.

Let's practice.

> You are externing for Judge Brecklin. During your externship, your law school's Director of Communications emails you to seek comment on how Judge Brecklin feels about a recent Supreme Court decision affirming a decision that Judge Brecklin authored. How do you respond?

Must I comply with judicial ethics rules after my clerkship concludes?

It depends. The ethical rules discussed in this chapter primarily apply to *current* judicial employees. These rules are often more restrictive than the general rules that apply to attorneys not currently serving the judiciary, such as former clerks who now work in law firms or as in-house counsel. As a practicing attorney, the Model Rules of Professional Responsibility that your jurisdiction has adopted will govern your conduct and may differ in some extent from the more restrictive rules, which apply to clerks.

That being said, however, the duty to maintain Chambers confidentiality continues even after your clerkship or externship concludes. This duty can often be tested during interviews or in the course of post-clerkship employment. Sometimes interviewers will intentionally ask a former clerk or extern to comment on a pending case or explain his or her judge's decision-making process. The interviewer may aim to discern the information or may simply be testing whether the interviewee understands and will uphold the duty of confidentiality—the same duty to which all attorneys must adhere absent rare and quite limited exceptions. In such instances, a savvy interviewee will simply observe that he or she cannot comment because doing so might divulge confidential information. In other instances, a clerk may join a law firm that appears before the clerk's former judge or court. His or her new supervisors may press the former clerk to illuminate his or her former judge's views on a certain issue, identify which arguments the judge might find most persuasive, or predict how the judge would rule. Rather than divulging confidential information, the former clerk should simply offer to conduct research into the matter or suggest that the attorneys look at the judge's recent cases on the issue to obtain that information. Nor may a former clerk work on a case that was pending before the court during his or her clerkship or of which the clerk has special knowledge as a result of his or her clerkship. In addition, clerks generally may not write scholarly articles or blog posts about cases pending at their courts during their clerkships absent permission.

Ethics Checklist for Law Clerks[60]

The checklist below will help you identify potential conflicts of interest and other possible ethics concerns that may arise during the course of your clerkship. You should review the checklist, note applicable points, and discuss them with your judge. Your judge may have stricter standards than required by the Code or statute. If so, you must follow the policies of your chambers.

Potential conflicts

Do you have any of the following potential conflicts—

- personally own one or more shares of stock or some other financial interest in a company involved in the litigation? ☐
- have an equitable interest (e.g., as a vested beneficiary) in an estate or trust that has a financial interest in the company? ☐
- serve as an officer, director, advisor, trustee, or active participant in the affairs of the company? ☐
- serve as a fiduciary of an estate or trust that has a financial interest in the company? ☐
- have a power of attorney that conveys an ownership interest in stock or other property? ☐
- does your spouse, minor resident child, or other close relative have any of the foregoing potential conflicts? ☐

Actual conflicts

With regard to your potential involvement in a case before your judge—

- do you have personal knowledge of disputed evidentiary facts? ☐
- have you previously served as counsel in the matter? ☐
- has your previous or future law firm served as counsel in the matter? ☐
- are you a party? ☐
- do you have an interest that could be substantially affected by the outcome? ☐
- are you likely to be a material witness? ☐
- have you previously served in government employment as counsel, advisor, or material witness in the matter, or expressed an opinion concerning the merits? ☐

> With regard to the potential involvement in a case before your judge of your spouse or any third degree relative of you or your spouse, to your knowledge—
>
> - is your spouse or relative a party or counsel in the matter? ☐
> - is your spouse's law firm counsel in the matter? ☐
> - does your spouse or relative have an interest that could be substantially affected by the outcome? ☐
> - is your spouse or relative likely to be a material witness? ☐
>
> **Potentially inappropriate outside activities**
>
> Do you engage in any of the following activities—
>
> - serve as a member or on the board of a professional or law-related organization? ☐
> - serve as a member or on the board of a civic, charitable, or social club? ☐
> - belong to an organization that litigates frequently in the court? ☐
> - belong to an organization engaged in lobbying or political activities? ☐
> - raise funds for your outside activities? ☐
> - engage in partisan political activities, either as a candidate or on behalf of others? ☐
> - engage in nonpartisan political activities, either as a candidate or on behalf of others? ☐
>
> With respect to law-related or other professional activities, do you—
>
> - speak, write, or teach on law-related subjects? ☐
> - speak, write, or teach on other subjects? ☐
> - practice law on a pro bono basis or otherwise? ☐
> - engage in any other law-related pursuits? ☐
>
> With respect to outside employment, are you—
>
> - engaging in paid outside employment for attorneys, law firms, or others with an interest in your performance of official duties? ☐
> - engaging in any other outside employment? ☐
> - applying to or interviewing with prospective employers for a legal position? ☐
> - receiving offers of gifts or benefits from attorneys, law firms, or others with an interest in your performance of official duties? ☐

Observing your judge's requirements

Discuss with your judge any specific requirements he or she may have as to the following:

- dealing with the press, including—restrictions on any communications with the press, procedures to follow when contacted by the press, and the availability of written guidelines for press inquiries

- dealing with counsel, including—restrictions on any communications with counsel, procedures to follow when contacted by counsel, and case-related discussions with anyone outside chambers, including other law clerks

When seeking future employment—

- applying to or interviewing with prospective employers before your clerkship ends

- using writing samples from your clerkship

- discussing your contributions to your judge's work

- discussing your judge's office procedures and proclivities

- accepting meals and other benefits given to candidates during the interview process

- formally accepting a job offer before your clerkship ends

- accepting bonuses from a future employer before your clerkship ends

- working on matters handled by law firms with whom you are seeking employment

- engaging in outside employment during your clerkship for attorneys, law firms, or others with an interest in your performance of official duties

- engaging in other forms of outside employment during your clerkship

- practicing law on a pro bono basis or otherwise

- speaking, writing, or teaching on law-related subjects

- engaging in professional, charitable, and other activities during your clerkship, including—
  - using office equipment and services
  - engaging in such activities while on duty or in your workplace

This Ethics Checklist derives from Maintaining the Public Trust (2011), a publication of the Federal Judicial Center. It is used herein with the permission of the Federal Judicial Center.

Although the information contained in this chapter heavily relies upon resources pertaining to federal clerkships, similar ethical rules govern the conduct of law clerks at state and local courts. For more information on clerkship ethics, see Appendix B.

E. SUPPLEMENTAL RESOURCES

1. CODE OF CONDUCT FOR JUDICIAL EMPLOYEES (2013), http://www.uscourts.gov/rules-policies/judiciary-policies/code-conduct/code-conduct-judicial-employees.

2. *Maintaining the Public Trust: Ethics for Federal Judicial Law Clerks*, FEDERAL JUDICIAL CENTER (2013), https://oscar.uscourts.gov/assets/Maintaining_Public_Trust.pdf.

3. *Comment, The Law Clerk's Duty of Confidentiality*, 129 U. PA. L. REV. 1230 (1981).

Notes

---

[1] DENIS STEVEN RUTKUS, CONG. RESEARCH SERV., RL31989, SUPREME COURT APPOINTMENT PROCESS: ROLES OF THE PRESIDENT, JUDICIARY COMMITTEE, AND SENATE 1, 2 (2005).

[2] *How the Federal Courts are Organized*, FEDERAL JUDICIAL CENTER, http://www.fjc.gov/federal/courts.nsf/autoframe?openagent&nav=menu1&page=/federal/courts.nsf/page/183 (last visited June 13, 2016).

[3] Gerhard Peters & John Woolley, *George Bush: Statement on Signing the Ethics Reform Act of 1989*, THE AMERICAN PRESIDENCY PROJECT, http://www.presidency.ucsb.edu/ws/?pid=17885 (last visited June 13, 2016).

[4] Ethics Reform Act, Pub. L. No. 101–194, 103 Stat. 1716 (1989).

[5] 18 U.S.C. § 201.

[6] 18 U.S.C. § 641.

[7] 18 U.S.C. § 287; 31 U.S.C. § 3729.

[8] 18 U.S.C. § 2071.

[9] 31 U.S.C. § 1344.

[10] CODE OF CONDUCT FOR JUDICIAL EMPLOYEES (2013), http://www.uscourts.gov/rules-policies/judiciary-policies/code-conduct/code-conduct-judicial-employees.

[11] *Id.*

[12] *See, e.g.*, CODE OF CONDUCT FOR LAW CLERKS AND STAFF ATTORNEYS OF THE SUPREME COURT OF TEXAS (2002), http://www.txcourts.gov/All_Archived_Documents/SupremeCourt/AdministrativeOrders/miscdocket/02/02904100.pdf.

[13] Notably, Justices of the United States Supreme Court and all Supreme Court employees are exempt from the canons, and judges, as opposed to employees, are subject to a separate code of conduct particular to them. *See* CODE OF CONDUCT FOR UNITED STATES JUDGES (2014), http://www.uscourts.gov/judges-judgeships/code-conduct-united-states-judges. AO and Federal Judicial Center employees are subject to agency codes. *See* CODE OF CONDUCT FOR JUDICIAL EMPLOYEES, *supra* note 10. Nor are contractors covered. *Id.*

[14] *Governance & the Judicial Conference*, UNITED STATES COURTS, http://www.uscourts.gov/about-federal-courts/governance-judicial-conference (last visited June 27, 2016).

[15] *Id.*

[16] *Id.*

---

17   *About the Judicial Conference*, UNITED STATES COURTS, http://www.uscourts.gov/about-federal-courts/governance-judicial-conference/about-judicial-conference (last visited June 27, 2016).

18   *Id.*

19   *Id.*

20   *Id.*

21   FEDERAL JUDICIAL CENTER, http://www.fjc.gov (last visited June 14, 2016).

22   Federal Judicial Center, *Maintaining the Public Trust: Ethics for Federal Judicial Law Clerks*, (2013), https://oscar.uscourts.gov/assets/Maintaining_Public_Trust.pdf.

23   Such research may require you to go beyond this chapter and look closely at the primary sources outlined above.

24   Notably, all inquiries to the Committee on Codes of Conduct remain confidential. *Maintaining the Public Trust*, *supra* note 22, at 4. Advisory opinions can be found at PUBLISHED ADVISORY OPINIONS (2009), http://www.uscourts.gov/rules-policies/judiciary-policies/code-conduct/published-advisory-opinions.

25   PUBLISHED ADVISORY OPINIONS, *supra* note 24.

26   CODE OF CONDUCT FOR JUDICIAL EMPLOYEES, *supra* note 10, at Canon 3C.

27   *Id.* at Canon 3C.

28   *Id.* at Canon 3E.

29   *See, e.g.*, Gerald Lebovits, *Ethical Judicial Writing—Part III*, 79 N.Y. ST. B.J. 64 (Feb. 2007); Gerald Lebovits, *Ethical Judicial Writing—Part II*, 79 N.Y. ST. B.J. 64 (Jan. 2007); Gerald Lebovits, *Ethical Judicial Writing—Part I*, 78 N.Y. ST. B.J. 64 (Nov./Dec. 2006).

30   CODE OF CONDUCT FOR JUDICIAL EMPLOYEES, *supra* note 10, at Canon 3F.

31   According to Canon 3F(5), "[a] member of a judge's personal staff should inform the appointing judge of any circumstances or activity of the staff members that might serve as a basis for disqualification of either the staff member or the judge, in a matter pending before the judge." *Id.*

32   For purposes of this book, the term "relative" encompasses relatives by blood, adoption, and marriage. The Code references "a person related . . . within the third degree of relationship." *Id.* In many Chambers, judges will also wish to be made aware of the involvement of former relatives, such as ex-spouses or former stepparents.

33   The Code defines this "third degree of relationship" as including a "parent, child, grandparent, grandchild, great grandparent, great grandchild, sibling, aunt, uncle, niece, and nephew." *Id.* Although the Code does not explicitly specify, this presumably includes both biological and adopted relatives and step-relatives.

34   "'Financial interests' include stocks and other ownership interests, however small, but generally do not include bonds and mutual funds." *Maintaining the Public Trust*, *supra* note 22, at 11. This is because a law clerk has no control over the performance of mutual funds, bonds, etc. Notably, Canon 3F(4) defines "financial interest" quite broadly to include "ownership of a legal or equitable interest, however small, or a relationship as director, advisor, or other active participant in the affairs of a party, except that: (i) ownership in a mutual or common investment fund that holds securities is not a 'financial interest' in such securities unless the employee participates in the management of the fund; (ii) an office in an educational, religious, charitable, fraternal, or civic organization is not a 'financial interest' in securities held by the organization; (iii) the proprietary interest of a policy holder in a mutual insurance company, or a depositor in a mutual savings association, or a similar property interest, is a 'financial interest' in the organization only if the outcome of the proceeding could substantially affect the value of the interest; and (iv) ownership of government securities is a 'financial interest' in the issuer only if the outcome of the proceedings could substantially affect the value of the securities." CODE OF CONDUCT FOR JUDICIAL EMPLOYEES, *supra* note 10, at Canon 3F(4).

35   Although the Code uses the term "spouse," it is advisable to alert the judge of a conflict if the same holds true for a significant other, even if not a spouse.

36   *Id.* at Canon 3F(3).

37   *Id.*

38   *Id.* at Canon 4A (discussing "civic, charitable, religious, professional, educational, cultural, avocational, social, fraternal, and recreational activities . . . speak[ing], writ[ing], and teach[ing]"); *id.* at Canon 4C(1) ("A judicial employee should refrain from outside financial and business dealings that tend to . . . exploit the position, or associate the judicial employee in a

substantial financial manner with lawyers or other persons likely to come before the judicial employee or the court or office . . .")

[39]   *Id.* at Canon 4A. Canon 4E permits law clerks to receive "compensation and reimbursement of expenses for outside activities" so long as: (1) their judge permits it; (ii) doing so does not run afoul of governing law; and (iii) they report compensation and reimbursement as required by relevant law. "Expense reimbursement should be limited to the actual cost of travel, food, and lodging reasonably incurred by a judicial employee and, where appropriate to the occasion, by the judicial employee's spouse or relative. Any payment in excess of such an amount is compensation." *Id.* at Canon 4E; *see also* 5 U.S.C. App. §§ 101–111; 5 U.S.C. App. §§ 501–505.

[40]   *Maintaining the Public Trust, supra* note 22, at 22.

[41]   *Maintaining the Public Trust: Ethics for Federal Judicial Law Clerks,* http://www.lawschool.cornell.edu/publicservice/upload/Federal-Judicial-Center-Ethics-Brochure.pdf,   20 (2011).

[42]   CODE OF CONDUCT FOR JUDICIAL EMPLOYEES, *supra* note 10, at Canon 4D (defining "judicial employees" broadly and permitting them to engage in the practice of law under limited circumstances; however, such circumstances likely do not apply to judicial clerks given the special nature of their clerkship duties and their close relationship with their respective judges). *But see Maintaining the Public Trust, supra* note 22, at 12–13 (one exception to the general prohibition permits law clerks to provide legal services on a pro bono basis "in certain civil cases" so long as it does not "take place on duty or in the workplace, . . . result in compensation, . . . involve any appearance in a federal, state, or local court or administrative agency, . . . [or] involve a matter of public controversy or an issue likely to come before your court.").

[43]   *Maintaining the Public Trust, supra* note 22, at 12.

[44]   CODE OF CONDUCT FOR JUDICIAL EMPLOYEES, *supra* note 10, at Canon 4B.

[45]   Dan Slater, *Barack Obama: The U.S.'s 44th President (and 25th Lawyer-President!),* WALL STREET J.: L. BLOG (Nov. 5, 2008, 9:16 AM), http://blogs.wsj.com/law/2008/11/05/barack-obama-the-uss-44th-president-and-24th-lawyer-president/.

[46]   *America's Founding Fathers: Delegates to the Constitutional Convention,* NATIONAL ARCHIVES,   http://www.archives.gov/exhibits/charters/constitution_founding_fathers_overview .html (last visited June 15, 2016).

[47]   *Constitution of the United States: Questions & Answers,* NATIONAL ARCHIVES, http://www.archives.gov/exhibits/charters/constitution_q_and_a.html (last visited June 15, 2016).

[48]   "A judicial employee should refrain from partisan political activity; should not act as a leader or hold any office in a partisan political organization; should not make speeches for or publicly endorse or oppose a partisan political organization or candidate; should not solicit funds for or contribute to a partisan political organization, candidate, or event; should not become a candidate for partisan political office; and should not otherwise actively engage in partisan political activities." CODE OF CONDUCT FOR JUDICIAL EMPLOYEES, *supra* note 10, at Canon 5A.

[49]   A judicial clerk "should refrain from nonpartisan political activity such as campaigning for or publicly endorsing or opposing a nonpartisan political candidate; soliciting funds for or contributing to a nonpartisan political candidate or event; and becoming a candidate for nonpartisan political office." *Id.* at Canon 5B.

[50]   Significantly, Canon 5 is more restrictive for judicial clerks than other judicial employees because judicial clerks are "members of a judge's personal staff." *Id.* As such, clerks must even refrain from non-partisan political activity in which other judicial employees may sometimes engage so long as doing so does not reflect adversely on the court's integrity or impede the performance of the employee's duties. *Id.* at Canon 5B.

[51]   *Maintaining the Public Trust,* supra note 22, at 18–19.

[52]   CODE OF CONDUCT FOR JUDICIAL EMPLOYEES, *supra* note 10, at Canon 4C(2).

[53]   *Id.* at Canon 3D.

[54]   MARY L. DUNNEWOLD, BETH A. HONETSCHLAGER, & BRENDA L. TOFTE, JUDICIAL CLERKSHIPS: A PRACTICAL GUIDE, 282 (2010).

[55]   A case that is *under seal* is one in which identifying information is redacted to protect the identities of the parties or other highly sensitive information. Such cases are filed using a special, separate electronic case filing procedure. They are often denoted with case names like *Doe 90*, which make it impossible to connect the decision with the individuals involved. It is critical to preserve confidentiality when handling any pending case, but the duty of confidentiality is heightened in cases that are under seal.

[56]   CODE OF CONDUCT FOR JUDICIAL EMPLOYEES, *supra* note 10, at Canon 3D ("A former judicial employee should observe the same restrictions on disclosure of confidential information that apply to a current judicial employee, excepted as modified by the appointing authority.")

[57]   In addition, not all filings are public, even if they are not marked confidential. For example, a trial court clerk may work on an ex parte motion or a motion filed under seal.

[58]   Perhaps for this reason, some judges require clerks to limit off-duty socializing with attorney friends who appear before the court. DUNNEWOLD, *supra* note 54, at 291.

[59]   CODE OF CONDUCT FOR JUDICIAL EMPLOYEES, *supra* note 10, at Canon 3D.

CHAPTER 7

EFFECTIVE DOCKET AND
TIME MANAGEMENT

■ ■ ■

Effective time management and good organization are both critical to performing well as a law clerk. Your judge is far too busy to remember filing deadlines or hearing dates. It is up to you and the judicial assistant to know exactly what needs to be done and by when. This is particularly true for trial court clerks for whom each day is fast-paced and often unpredictable.

A. TOOLS AND TECHNIQUES FOR EFFECTIVE TIME MANAGEMENT

To determine if you are managing your time wisely, for the first month of your clerkship, consider tracking your hours on a sample hours log akin to the data time entry systems that many law firms use to track attorney's billable hours. This case log will serve dual purposes. First, you can review it on your own or with a clerk who manages his or her time wisely to determine how you can improve your efficiency and time management skills. This is especially pertinent for judicial externs and interns who are still cultivating good time management skills. Second, if you continue to maintain this log, your judge may permit you to later use it as a conflicts list when you obtain subsequent employment. Over the years, you will work on many different matters, and it may become difficult, if not impossible, to remember every single case. Thus, keeping a case log will prevent you from inadvertently violating ethical rules involving conflicts of interest after your clerkship concludes.

Strategic planning is also essential to effective time management. Keep a running action item list of tasks that must be accomplished for each day or each week. Prioritize items that are time-sensitive or of heightened importance. As you complete each item throughout the day, delete the item and add any new items that now must be completed. Revise the list as appropriate based on whether this new item is time-sensitive or especially important. At the end of each day, review the list. Think about the most efficient way to complete the remaining tasks for the next day. Complete whatever preliminary matters must be completed in order for you to hit the ground running on those tasks the next day. When you enter the next day, work through the list for that day strategically. Do not reorder the list since it has already been prioritized but be flexible as required. At the end of each week, set aside at least fifteen to thirty minutes to assess your case log and your action item list to determine which items must be completed for next week and in which order. Create an action plan and hold yourself accountable. Now apply these principles of good time management to work through the hypothetical below.

Let's practice.

> You have the following tasks on your May 22 to-do list: finalizing an 11-day on an opinion that will issue on May 27; cite-checking and editing a co-clerk's opinion that must go to the judge by day's end; research for a bench memo for July's Court Week; buying a birthday card for your co-clerk who turns thirty tomorrow; and meeting with your judge at 3pm about a speech you must help him draft for a judicial conference he is attending next week. How do you prioritize these tasks?

Assume that you commence your day at 9:00 am. With these items on your desk, you might turn first to:

> 9:00–9:15am: Reading and archiving emails
>
> 9:15–11:00am: Cite-checking and editing your co-clerk's opinion since that must go your judge by day's end *(Unless you turn to this early in the day, it will not allow sufficient time for your co-clerk to incorporate your feedback.).*
>
> 11:00–1:15pm: Finalizing 11-Day Memo *(You should provide this to your judge no later than May 25, or earlier if you recommend taking action; thus, this is relatively time sensitive.).*
>
> 1:15–2:00pm: Lunch and picking up a birthday card for co-clerk's birthday tomorrow; reading and archiving emails
>
> 2:00–3:00pm: Preparing to meet with your judge regarding his speech; outlining ideas for the speech
>
> 3:00–3:45pm: Meeting with your judge about his speech; inputting notes from meeting into speech outline
>
> 3:45–5:30pm: Completing research for bench memo for July Court Week *(Since the bench memo is for a July case, the final version will not be due to your judge until late June. Thus, this action item moves to the bottom of the list since it is not as time-sensitive as the other items. This is not to suggest that all research can be completed in such a short time. However, you can devote time to it each day.).*
>
> 5:30–5:45pm: Updating your case/hours log and action item list; revising list for tomorrow so you can hit the ground running; reading and archiving emails

In this way, you have strategically managed your time to maximize your efficiency. You begin the day by assessing your email to ensure that no unexpected tasks have arisen overnight that will require you to revise your action plan. Then, you show care and consideration of your co-clerk's schedule by taking into account your co-clerk's time as well. Instead of making two separate trips out of Chambers, which would waste time, you picked up the card while also picking up your lunch, preferably along the way. Yet you still took time out of your day to show kindness to your co-clerk; this is critical to relationship building. You allowed yourself ample time to prepare for your meeting with your judge so that the meeting was productive; this demonstrates respect for your judge's time. You have set reasonable internal deadlines for the July bench memos as evidenced by the fact that you are already beginning the initial research for those memos. You ended the day by reflecting on what you accomplished and what remains to be done so that the next day is equally efficient. You have listed out your *known* tasks for the next day in the order in which it will be most efficient to complete them. In every respect, you have managed your time well and still managed to leave Chambers at a reasonable hour, ideally with zero unopened emails in your inbox.

As illustrated above, efficiency enables you to maintain a healthier work/life balance without compromising the quality of your work product. Working smarter usually means the opposite of working longer. Maintaining a balance is essential to performing your clerkship duties well. Clerking can be stressful at times. The work you do is incredibly important. The stakes are high, and mistakes may have far-reaching implications. Managing your stress in healthy ways and making time for the people and things you love will only enrich your performance as a law clerk. Failure to do so may result in mental health issues, such as anxiety and depression, or stress-induced personality changes, such as irritability or withdrawal, which could damage your relationship with your judge and fellow clerks and perhaps even harm the quality of your work product.

To avoid these issues, make time for the things you love. Exercise. Many courts have gyms either in the courthouse or nearby. Eat well and pack your lunch if eating out is too much temptation to order unhealthy food. Get at least eight hours of sleep per night. Spend time with your significant other, friends, family, and your pet(s). Get to know your fellow clerks outside the office by inviting them to after-hours happy hours or other events. Read a book for pleasure or binge watch your favorite television show. Take a day trip. Seek spiritual fulfillment or actively practice your faith. If your personal relationships suffer because of your clerkship duties, so will your work product. Make time for fun and relaxation. In other words, carve out meaningful time for yourself.

A healthy balance also requires you to know how to keep your professional life (and its accompanying pressures) distinct from your personal life. As a general rule of thumb, keep personal problems *outside* Chambers to the maximum extent possible. Put differently, leave your problems at the door. Doing otherwise undercuts professionalism and may interfere with your ability to produce good work and maintain positive workplace relationships. Likewise, do not take professional problems home to your loved ones. Doing so may not only violate Chambers confidentiality in some instances but also may harm your personal relationships.

B. TOOLS AND TECHNIQUES FOR EFFECTIVE DOCKET AND CASE MANAGEMENT

If you are a trial court clerk, you will often be involved in scheduling matters. You may conduct conference calls with attorneys to establish a schedule that is mutually acceptable to the parties and the court and then draft a corresponding scheduling order, which establishes filing deadlines and hearing dates in the matter. In so doing, it is very important for you to take into account your judge's professional and personal commitments. For example, do not schedule a hearing on your judge's birthday or on the day that his or her son is returning home from being stationed abroad. In both cases, your judge may prefer to take the day off, work from home, or at least have a light caseload that day. Be thoughtful. Just because a party suggests a date or time frame, that does not mean the court must accept it, although the court should work diligently with the parties to establish a mutually convenient schedule.

In addition, both appellate and trial court clerks must be able to accurately gauge how much time they may need to adequately assist the judge in preparing for hearings, trials, or oral argument. This involves assessing the complexity of the case, the time needed for drafting a bench memo or performing other preparatory measures, evaluating the impact on the schedule of other professional or personal commitments, and predicting how much time the judge will need to review the materials necessary to prepare. As a good rule of thumb, always assume that any task will take longer than you first expect. By setting a deadline that is more generous than you may need, you will likely preempt the problem of having to request an extension; depending on your Chambers culture and on your judge, requesting an extension may be perceived as inconvenient or unprofessional. Sometimes an extension is impractical or impossible to grant given pressing time considerations. Avoid this issue by asking for more time than you believe you will need; in this regard, you are much likelier to either meet the deadline or to exceed expectations by submitting your work product ahead of schedule. This is especially true for new law clerks as well as judicial externs who may lack a strong sense of how long a task will take and do not yet possess well developed time management skills.

Do not procrastinate. Set manageable internal deadlines for each project and hold yourself accountable. In some situations, as with a judicial externship, you may be able to submit portions of a lengthy document on a rolling basis, such as submitting the background section of your bench memo to your supervising clerk for review while you complete the discussion section. Setting and keeping reasonable internal deadlines will preempt an eleventh hour panic that may result in shoddy or incomplete work product or the inability to meet a hard deadline.

Setting internal deadlines is also a good way to prepare for the unexpected. A clerk cannot always know which time-sensitive task may lie ahead. For example, a clerk at the United States Court of Federal Claims who has promised to get a draft opinion to his or her judge by Friday afternoon must maintain internal deadlines throughout the drafting cycle. In this way, even if an emergency bid protest lands on the clerk's desk late Wednesday afternoon, he or she will still have made sufficient progress on the opinion such that turning to the bid protest for the entirety of Wednesday will not substantially impede the clerk's ability to meet the Friday deadline for the opinion. Planning for contingencies may also obviate the need for pulling all-nighters or working weekends when unexpected circumstances arise, which in turn, allows the clerk to maintain a healthier work/life balance.

Although some Chambers hold regular status meetings to discuss the status of all pending matters in Chambers, other judges spontaneously require status updates and conferences. Always be prepared. While you must keep apprised of your judge's personal and professional schedule, that obligation is not a two-way street. Do not expect your judge to know what you are working on, which current deadlines you aim to meet, or anything about your personal commitments outside Chambers unless you have notified Chambers of the obligation and added it to the Chambers calendar. As such, you must be prepared at a moment's notice to apprise your judge of the status of all pending matters at the judge's convenience. After all, you serve at the pleasure of your judge; it is not the other way around. For this reason, it is important to always stay up to date on the status of all pending, open matters.

There are several effective tools for docket and case management, some of which are discussed below. The key to each is organization and consistent updating. Staying well organized is essential to managing your caseload and professional schedule.

Case folders and subfolders: The easiest case management tool is the use of electronic case folders and subfolders. At the trial court, one case may have many pending motions, etc. Thus, create a main folder that is labeled with the case name and docket number. Subsumed within the main folder, create a subfolder for each independent matter, such as "Docket,"

"Materials Relating to the Pending Motion to Dismiss," etc. Within the "Motion to Dismiss" folder, you might include further sub-folders, such as "Opinion Drafts," which could include all versions of each draft of the pending Order and Opinion Granting the Motion. Each version should include a version number and date to better ensure that you are working on the current draft but also so that you can return to older drafts to reinsert previously deleted material. Another folder labeled "Key Cases" might include highlighted versions of the key cases cited in the motions and/or opinion. Create as many folders and subfolders as you need to help you efficiently store and quickly locate materials. Because good organization is critical to successful performance in any type of clerkship, the use of folders and subfolders is equally helpful in appellate and trial court clerkships.

On the other hand, some tools, such as the case status charts and status update memos mentioned below, are much more, if not exclusively, beneficial at the trial court level since only law clerks at those courts play a more active role in managing the docket.

Case Status Chart: As shown below, a *case status chart* indicates the case name, general nature of the case, docket number, an overview of the procedural posture and status of the case, impending deadlines, and whether the case is active/open or inactive/closed. The format and content of a case chart varies. A law clerk may create the chart exclusively for personal use or the law clerk may opt to share it on a regular basis with the judge, judicial assistant, or other law clerks in Chambers. As such, style, format, and content vary by law clerk. Choose the style, format, and content that work best for you.

A case status chart is an excellent organizational tool that you can quickly peruse and print when a spontaneous status update meeting has been called; it is equally useful when a status update meeting is on the calendar. The key, however, is to *consistently* update the case status chart each time a status change occurs in each case. You can allot a certain time each day for case status chart updating or simply input updates as soon as you become aware of them. Choose the method that works best for you but be consistent. While it is easy to update the chart one update or day at a time, it is a gargantuan task to input all updates that have piled up over several weeks. Doing so is impossible when a spontaneous status update meeting has been called, and then the case status chart will prove useless because you failed to consistently populate it.

Here is a sample case status chart.

Case	Docket No.	Status	Deadlines	Open
Smith v. HHS (Vaccine Act, adult, flu vaccine, TM)	16–0911	Mot. SJ filed 3.14.17 Response received 4.1.17 **Reply due 4.8.17 OA 5.8.17**	**Bench memo due 5.1.17**	Y

Here, the case status chart indicates the abbreviated name of the case as well as general facts regarding the nature of the case. The chart shows that this is a case brought under the National Childhood Vaccine Injury Compensation Act of 1986, which is commonly referred to as the Vaccine Act. It further reveals that the alleged victim of the vaccine injury is an adult, not a child as in many cases. The petitioner alleges that he or she suffers from transverse myelitis ("TM") as a result of receiving the flu vaccine. The chart next indicates the docket number and shows the current procedural history of the case. To emphasize upcoming deadlines, use capitalization, highlighted text, or boldfaced type. The sample uses boldfaced type to emphasize that while Chambers has received a motion for summary judgment and response to that motion, Chambers should expect to receive the reply on April 8, 2017. It further notes that oral argument ("OA") will be held on May 8, 2017. Once the law clerk receives the reply brief, he or she would return the reply brief deadline to regular type and change "due" to "received." The law clerk would do the same after the court had held oral argument. Thus, the status column indicates the parties' obligations and deadlines as well as which materials Chambers has already received. The "Deadlines" column reveals the law clerk's internal deadlines. Here, the chart indicates that the law clerk will provide a bench memo to the judge by or before May 1, 2017. That bench memo will discuss the motion for summary judgment that will be argued on May 8, 2017, and recommend whether the court will grant or deny the motion. Finally, the final "Open" column indicates whether the case is open/active or inactive/closed. Here, the law clerk uses a "Y" to state that "Yes, the case is open and active." Other law clerks might use "A" for active, "I" for inactive, "O" for open, or "C" for closed. Choose the terminology that is clearest for you. There is no single right way to create a case status chart. As an additional safeguard, provide a copy of the chart to your judicial assistant and the clerk covering for you if you must be out of the office for a day or more. It will also prove incredibly helpful to your law clerk successor.

Status Update Memo: A *status update memo* is a short memo to your judge that succinctly summarizes the most pressing upcoming deadlines in your open matters. The memo is an effective organizational tool that will not only reassure your judge that you are staying on top of Chambers scheduling but also will allow the judge to plan his or her schedule accordingly. In some instances, submitting a status memo at a regular interval, such as on a weekly or biweekly basis, may altogether alleviate the need for lengthy status update meetings. Utilize your case status chart to draft the status update memo. You may provide it in a regular memo format, a case chart format, or in a bullet-point format. Choose the style and format that work best for you and your judge. Do not include all of the information on your case status chart; to the contrary, select only the most pressing upcoming matters that will occur between now and your next submission of a status update memo. The memo should include only important matters, such as expected filings, any hearings, status conferences, trials or arguments, and any substantive materials, such as a draft opinion, that you plan to provide to the judge. In rare instances, include holidays or other personal information on the memo as well. For example, if you will be out of town with limited or no email access for a long weekend camping trip, politely and gently remind your judge of those dates at the bottom of your status update memo. Such gentle reminders will help the judge plan his or her schedule accordingly, and as such, will enable Chambers to function smoothly.

Calendar Updates: Technology has greatly impacted the daily function of Chambers. However, many Chambers still rely upon an old-fashioned tool to keep things on schedule: the Chambers Master Calendar. This calendar will often either hang in a prominent location in Chambers or will be available on the judicial assistant's desk. Whenever any member of Chambers schedules an event, he or she is obligated to promptly (preferably immediately so that it is not forgotten) input that event on the calendar. Typically, the Master Calendar includes both professional and personal commitments. Thus, it might indicate when the judge will be out of town on vacation, the date and time of the oral argument in *Smith v. HHS*, the date and time of a telephonic status conference in *Ansel v. Davol*, the date and time of an ABA Conference at which the judge will speak, the judicial assistant's birthday, the date and time of a special networking reception that the judge will host for current and former law clerks, a court holiday when Chambers will be closed, and the date and time of the judge's medical appointments so that the law clerks know to avoid scheduling meetings or conferences during those times, etc.

Some Chambers have now moved away from using a paper Master Calendar and instead input all such information into an electronic Master

Calendar to which all members of Chambers have access; in other Chambers, the judge, clerks, and judicial assistant electronically share individual calendars with one another. Still other Chambers do some combination thereof. One huge advantage of electronic calendars is the ease with which you can invite other individuals to an event so that it is added to their calendars. In addition, you can also set an event reminder for yourself and your invitees, hours or even days before the event. It is typically a good rule of thumb to set a reminder reasonably in advance of each event, particularly for something small, such as a meeting with another clerk or a telephonic conference that you might easily forget during a hectic day.

Always consult the Master Calendar, whether paper, electronic, or both, before scheduling any conference, hearing, vacation day, or other matter. Consult it before providing a draft scheduling order to your judge or before requesting a vacation day. Avoid scheduling blunders and conflicts by using the calendar(s)—both your personal calendar and the Master Calendar—diligently. It is usually a best practice to also confirm any dates with the judicial assistant.

However, as with any other docket management tool, the calendar is only useful if everyone consistently, accurately, and promptly updates it as soon as they schedule or cancel an event or appointment. So be thoughtful and professional enough to update the calendar as soon as you schedule an event or receive approval for a vacation day, etc. Do not delay. Promptly revise rescheduled events and remove canceled events. Do this on all calendar formats that your Chamber uses whether paper or electronic. Be equally diligent in updating your personal calendar.

Most judges and law clerks also now carry telephones with calendar and reminder capabilities. However, syncing the calendar on your personal telephone with the Chambers electronic calendar may pose ethical, confidentiality, and security concerns. Thus, do not sync your calendar without your judge's express permission, if such syncing is even possible. Additionally, confer with the Information Technology Specialists at your court to see if syncing may raise security-related or other concerns. Even if you cannot sync the court calendar with the personal calendar on your phone, consult with your judge to determine if you may manually input deadlines and set reminders on your telephone that do not include identifying information. Such an event might say "SM BM due to judge." This somewhat cryptic reminder might intend to remind you that the bench memo in *Smith v. HHS* is due to your judge that day. However, because the use of initials such as "SM" and "BM" could potentially be reverse engineered to determine which item and which case it refers to, some judges may not permit you to enter such information onto your personal calendars. Never act without your judge's permission. It is a best practice to also confer with your Court's Technology Officer or Information Technology specialists.

CM/ECF Alerts: Today, most, if not all, federal courts and many state courts have converted to electronic case management and case filing ("CM/ECF"). While CM/ECF offers many advantages over paper filing, one major advantage is the ability to set up CM/ECF alerts in your pending cases. If you establish an alert and provide your email address to CM/ECF, an email alert will be sent to you each time anything is electronically filed in the case. This will alleviate the need to actively check the regular docket to determine if any motions, especially time-sensitive, unexpected filings, such as a motion for sanctions, have been filed. That being said, CM/ECF does not alleviate the need to regularly check the case docket and to work closely with the Clerk's Office. Never exclusively rely upon CM/ECF alerts as technical and other issues occasionally occur. This is particularly true if the case status chart indicates that a party should have filed a document, but Chambers has not yet received it. As a final note, in some if not all courts, *pro se* litigants do not use CM/ECF.

Judicial Assistant and Clerk's Office: No amount of technology can replace the value of working closely with the judicial assistant and the Clerk's Office. These capable individuals have years of expertise in running a Chambers and a court, respectively. Consult them before scheduling important events and never hesitate to ask them questions about case management. A clerkship is a collaborative endeavor, and your judicial assistant and members of the Clerk's Office are critical members of that team. In particular, your judicial assistant is an incredibly special and important resource given his or her extremely close relationship with and knowledge of the judge.

CHAPTER 8

PROFESSIONALISM AND DECORUM

■ ■ ■

When you become a law clerk, you represent your judge and your court in everything you do, whether inside or outside the courthouse. As such, it is your duty to conduct yourself in a way that exemplifies the dignity and prestige of your court and your judge, not just for the duration of the clerkship but for your lifetime. For this reason, it is essential that you consistently display professionalism and proper decorum during and after your clerkship.

A. PROFESSIONALISM

Professionalism is a term that means different things to different people. As used herein, professionalism refers broadly to the conduct, knowledge, skill, attitude, and discernment necessary to perform commendably as a law clerk and to preserve, if not promote, the judiciary's reputation. Put differently, professionalism encompasses more than simply *what* one knows, but also how one behaves. Among other things, it embraces whether a law clerk maintains Chambers confidentiality, possesses a positive attitude, handles constructive feedback well, interacts with others in a respectful, collegial manner, and produces high-quality, accurate work within reasonable time frames. Furthermore, a professional is always punctual, polite, polished, and prepared. Displaying professionalism is equally, if not more, important to a clerk's success than possessing strong research and writing skills or knowledge of the subject matter within the court's jurisdiction.

Accordingly, the *Code of Conduct for Judicial Employees* ("Code") states that law clerks and other judicial employees should exemplify patience, respect for others, courtesy, and dignity to everyone that they encounter from a prominent attorney at a prestigious law firm to an impoverished prisoner proceeding *pro se*.[1] The Code defines professionalism as setting one's personal views, stereotypes, and biases aside and performing the duties of one's office "in a prompt, efficient, nondiscriminatory, fair, and professional manner."[2]

Professionalism is important because your actions and behavior, whether inside or outside the courthouse, will influence public perception of you, your judge, and your court. Your actions could even impact perception of the court's legitimacy and its ability to maintain impartiality.

Every party that appears before the court should leave feeling as if his or her arguments have been heard and thoughtfully considered. The parties and public should have confidence in your judge's competence and objectivity. To accomplish this, below is a non-exhaustive list highlighting important hallmarks of professionalism in the context of the judiciary.

In your role as a law clerk, professionalism will generally encompass all of the following:

(1)   arriving punctually for work and to meetings both inside and outside Chambers absent an acceptable excuse or extenuating circumstances;

> *Your judge and fellow clerks are exceptionally busy; tardiness wastes their valuable time and as such, is inconsiderate and disrespectful. If you are late for good cause, email, text, or telephone as soon as you know you might be late so that they can plan their schedules accordingly, and when you do arrive, apologize for being tardy. If you know you must be late for work or another obligation, let your judge or co-clerk know reasonably in advance.*

(2)   dressing and grooming appropriately and wearing proper business attire during Court Week, hearings, trials, etc.;

> *Appropriate dress and grooming are important to making a positive impression. You want to be remembered for what you say and do, not the unprofessional way you look. Improper dress and grooming will distract your audience, shifting the focus away from what you say to how you appear. Be sure your appearance never diminishes the reputation of your judge or your court.*
>
> *Attire, jewelry, and makeup should be minimal and conservative. Avoid noisy jewelry as well, such as digital watches that beep loudly. Confer with your judge before your first day of work to determine if you should cover or remove visible tattoos, piercings, or other body art at work.*
>
> *Keep stain remover at your desk in case you accidentally stain your clothes during the workday. It may also be a good idea to keep a suit in your office in case of an unexpected hearing; this is especially true of trial clerks.*
>
> *Do not wear anything that is ill-fitting (e.g., too tight, too low-cut, etc.). Sleeveless blouses and dresses may be permissible in some Chambers, but not in others; at present, most Chambers do not permit strapless or*

spaghetti strap blouses and dresses. Skirts and dresses should be of appropriate length. Use good judgment.

This is a non-exhaustive list of suggested guidelines for appearance and grooming. Your specific court or Chambers may have its own guidelines and preferences, which may be more or less stringent or specific. Confer with your Chambers before commencing your clerkship so that you understand the grooming and dress expected of you. If there are no written guidelines or the guidelines are ambiguous, then err on the conservative side until you get a sense of the Chambers culture from your fellow clerks. Nothing in this list should be construed so as to conflict with appearance and grooming practices that reflect a clerk's bona fide religious beliefs and practices. Promptly confer with your judge if any questions arise regarding proper dress and grooming at work.

(3) drafting professional emails and other communications;

In Chambers, every communication, even an email or instant message to a fellow clerk, should exemplify professionalism and courtesy. Edit every communication carefully. Ensure that each communication is clear, concise, precise, accurate, well organized, and well written. The tone should always be polite, respectful, objective, and sophisticated. Avoid Internet acronyms, slang, profanity, and anything else inappropriate for a professional communication. For more information, please see Chapter 13.

(4) avoiding profanity and other inappropriate language in Chambers;

It takes a long time to build a good reputation and only an instant to destroy it. There is no better way to do that than to use inappropriate language in Chambers, which is offensive to your judge, judicial assistant, fellow clerks, etc. Profanity is never appropriate in Chambers or at any work-related events, such as a Chambers reception or at a Chambers happy hour. In addition, avoid off-color jokes and offensive language. For example, many courts have court softball teams that play against one another. Such language could damage a law clerk's reputation at the court and hurt his relationships with other judges or fellow clerks. Choose your words carefully. If you do accidentally use profanity or inappropriate language, immediately apologize.

(5)   turning off your phone and other electronic devices during work hours;

> *Turning off your devices will not only minimize the distraction they may cause to other clerks who can hear them ringing, beeping, or vibrating, but it also helps you to better focus on your work and be more efficient. In addition, answering a call or text quickly while at work may increase the chance of you writing something that could breach Chambers confidentiality, such as a seemingly innocent text like "Can't make it tonight. Gotta bench memo due Tuesday." While this seems innocent enough, it signals to the recipient that your judge is likely hearing oral argument the following Tuesday. Although federal appellate panels are usually assigned the day of the case argument, you have just inadvertently divulged that your judge is on a Tuesday panel, perhaps the only Tuesday panel. Because you are in a hurry and at work, you may be less likely to stop and think before you send, possibly divulging confidential information. Finally, common sense dictates that you should focus on work while you are at work. If your phone is constantly ringing and buzzing, it signals to everyone around you, including the judge and judicial assistant if they are within hearing distance, that you are not 100% focused on your work but instead are juggling professional and personal obligations all day long. So turn off your phone. Turn it on during breaks or at lunchtime. Check it at points when you have stepped away from your desk and are in "break mode."*

(6)   only using office equipment for official work purposes and not visiting social media or other non-work-related Internet sites during the workday;

> *Using office equipment for non-work purposes that are more than de minimis is unprofessional and in some circumstances, unethical. Office supplies are expensive and publicly funded. It is improper to use taxpayer funded ink, toner, and paper for purely personal reasons, such as printing flyers for an upcoming party. Occasional, minimal use may be permissible so long as you have the permission of Chambers.*

(7)   meeting deadlines or if impossible, requesting an extension for good cause reasonably in advance of the deadline;

   (8) being prepared for all meetings and submitting high quality, polished, and complete drafts with properly formatted and accurate citations;[3]

Preparedness and polish are two hallmarks of a professional. According to Lebovits et al (2008), everything you write in Chambers must comport with "high ethical standards, . . . ensure accuracy and honesty in research, facts, and analysis[,] . . .[and] must exhibit the qualities of good moral character: candor, respect, honesty, and professionalism." The order, opinion, etc., must maintain a tone of objectivity and make clear that all parties' arguments were thoughtfully and equally considered and that the decision was made in the absence of personal feelings, bias, stereotypes, or any other improper considerations. Never take credit for work that is not original; always support your assertions with properly formatted and accurate citations. Attribute quotes to the original author. For more information regarding effecting writing and editing, refer to Chapters 11 and 12.

---

   (9) giving and receiving constructive feedback effectively;

  (10) arriving early, staying late, and working weekends as necessary to ensure a job well done;

  (11) being a team player who proactively offers to chip in to assist other clerks or the judge to finalize work;

  (12) mentoring externs or new clerks in Chambers and treating them as colleagues instead of competition;

  (13) maintaining confidentiality and impartiality;

Immediately alert the judge of any potential conflict of interest, even something minor, such as having gone to law school with one of the attorneys involved in a pending matter. Refer to ethics guidelines and consult with the ethics counsel for the court as necessary. Even if you know an attorney in a case, do not openly interact with the attorney so as to avoid the appearance of impropriety or favoritism. Do not compliment the attorney on his or her performance or comment on the nature of the briefing. Such personal connections cannot influence your recommendation to the judge or handling of the case, and you should avoid any conduct that might give the opposite impression. Indeed, some judges ask law clerks to avoid socializing with any attorneys who have cases pending at the court for the duration of the clerkship. Confer with your judge to determine his or her policy in this regard. By no means may you accept any "gift" from an attorney with a case pending before the court.

(14) otherwise complying with ethical guidelines; and

(15) not doing anything inside or outside Chambers that would reflect negatively on the judge or the court, such as drinking and driving, posting inappropriate pictures on a social media site, committing a crime, or using illegal substances. Note that even in jurisdictions that have legalized the recreational use of marijuana, judges prohibit use of such substances at the courthouse, and many may also prefer that clerks not engage in the practice outside Chambers, at least during the pendency of the clerkship.

You are your court's ambassador inside and outside Chambers. Whether at a hearing or a happy hour, conduct yourself as a professional. Do not use profanity, make off-color jokes, or use any other inappropriate language. Dress appropriately. If you drink at all, do not drink to excess; limit yourself to no more than one drink per hour, and drink a glass of water for every glass of alcohol you consume. Pace yourself and eat a snack as well.

With regard to social media, do not post any pictures, remarks, etc., that will damage the prestige of your court or judge. This includes photographs of you or fellow law clerks using any illegal substances, drinking alcohol, or using tobacco products. Make sure that your social media sites are private and do not become social media friends with your judge or co-workers before or during your clerkship. This will help you better maintain important boundaries between your personal and professional life. For example, there is nothing wrong with you posting a photo of yourself in a swimsuit at the beach, but you may not want other judges or clerks on the court to see such a photograph. You can avoid this simply by keeping your social media site private. If you do wish to "connect" with coworkers during your clerkship, only do so using a professional networking site. Always confer with your Chambers and your court to determine the nature of any social medial policy, concerning what you may or may not post, whether you may list the judge for whom you clerk on your social media profile(s), etc. Such policies vary by judge.

The non-exhaustive list above outlines some of the ways that a law clerk should exemplify professionalism. In addition, a professional also exercises basic etiquette. For example, always refer to judges as "Judge," never "Sir" or "Ma'am." Refer to the Chief Judge as "Chief Judge." Address the judicial assistant as "Mr." or "Ms." unless and until you receive the judicial assistant's permission to refer to him or her by first name. Typically you will address other law clerks on a first name basis. However, formality and culture vary significantly with some Chambers being quite formal and others operating more casually; at the Office of Special Masters, for instance, some special masters permit clerks and externs to address them by their first name. For this reason, it is important to observe Chambers culture before erring on the side of informality.

No matter how informal Chambers culture may be, practice proper etiquette. Always open the door and elevator for your judge, whether male or female, and allow him or her to exit first, unless otherwise instructed. Be polite and respectful to every judicial employee, from the janitor to the judicial assistant, and treat everyone with the same level of respect from the judicial extern to the Chief Judge. Be collegial and considerate. If and when you answer the phone, remember that your treatment of the caller reflects on your judge; it may positively or negatively impact public perception of both your judge and the judiciary as a whole. So be polite and patient. Simply put, exercise the Golden Rule, treating others as you would like to be treated.

B. DECORUM

Another facet of professionalism is maintaining proper courtroom decorum at all times. What constitutes appropriate courtroom decorum may vary by judge and by court. However, the guidelines of the United States Court of Appeals for the Federal Circuit are typical of most courts.[4] These guidelines are excerpted below and available on the court website. Peruse your court's website and confer with your Chambers to determine the scope and guidelines of the proper decorum for your Chambers and your court.

The dignity of the Court is to be respected and maintained at all times.

Attire for counsel and spectators should be restrained and appropriate for the dignity of the Court of Appeals of the United States.

Court security officers and Court staff are authorized to open and inspect any item carried into the courtroom.

Everyone in the courtroom, unless physically challenged, must rise when the judges enter and remain standing until the presiding judge invites everyone to be seated. Similarly, when court adjourns, everyone stands in place until the judges are no longer visible. Standing in the courtroom may be permitted only at the discretion of the Clerk. Areas marked as reserved are for Court staff and Federal Circuit law clerks.

Counsel may address the Court when invited to do so. Only counsel associated with the appeal being argued may address the Court, unless a judge directs otherwise.

Coat racks in the hallways outside the courtrooms are to be utilized.

Only material related to the Court's business can be read in the courtroom while Court is in session.

When Court is in session, no one should be heard except for counsel making argument or a judge.

The following items are prohibited in the courtroom and adjacent lobby area:

- Recording or broadcast devices

- Cameras, including those contained in computers and other electronic devices

- Food and drink except for the water provided at the counsel table

- Computers (except those to be used by counsel in argued cases)

- Phones must be turned off

- Inappropriate facial gestures or exaggerated gesticulating is forbidden

- Repeated entrances and departures are to be avoided

- Doorways and passageways should be kept clear at all times

C. SUPPLEMENTAL RESOURCES

1. CODE OF CONDUCT FOR JUDICIAL EMPLOYEES (2013), http://www.uscourts.gov/rules-policies/judiciary-policies/code-conduct/code-conduct-judicial-employees.

2. CODE OF CONDUCT FOR UNITED STATES JUDGES (2014), http://www.uscourts.gov/judges-judgeships/code-conduct-united-states-judges.

3. CALVERT G. CHIPCHASE, FEDERAL DISTRICT COURT LAW CLERK HANDBOOK (2007).

4. MARY L. DUNNEWOLD, BETH A. HONETSCHLAGER, & BRENDA L. TOFTE, JUDICIAL CLERKSHIPS: A PRACTICAL GUIDE (2010).

5. FEDERAL JUDICIAL CENTER, JUDICIAL WRITING MANUAL (1991).

6. SYLVAN SOBEL, ED., LAW CLERK HANDBOOK: A HANDBOOK FOR LAW CLERKS TO FEDERAL JUDGES (2d ed. 2007).

7. JOSEPH LEMON, FEDERAL APPELLATE COURT LAW CLERK HANDBOOK (2007).

8. JENNIFER L. SHEPPARD, IN CHAMBERS: A GUIDE FOR JUDICIAL CLERKS AND EXTERNS (2012).

Notes

---

[1] CODE OF CONDUCT FOR JUDICIAL EMPLOYEES (2013), http://www.uscourts.gov/rules-policies/judiciary-policies/code-conduct/code-conduct-judicial-employees.

[2] *Id.* at Canon 2.

[3] Gerald Lebovits et al., *Ethical Judicial Opinion Writing*, 21 GEO. J. LEGAL ETHICS 237 (2008).

[4] http://www.cafc.uscourts.gov/argument/court-decorum.

CHAPTER 9

TECHNOLOGY AND THE JUDICIARY

■ ■ ■

In recent years, technology has revolutionized the practice of law and with it, the judiciary. For example, today most federal courts use an automated case management and docketing system known as Case Management/Electronic Case Files ("CM/ECF").[1] Courts increasingly use technology like CM/ECF to enhance the ease, convenience, and efficiency of litigation. Effective use of technology can also result in significant cost savings.

On the other hand, misuse of technology can have dire consequences. It could result in something as serious as the inadvertent disclosure of confidential information to something more minor like accidentally transferring a party to the wrong individual. Yet in both instances, the law clerk's ineptitude and carelessness will reflect poorly on the public perception of the judge and the court. As a result, the party may lose faith in the judge's decision-making and relatedly, the court's legitimacy.

For this reason, it is essential for a law clerk to develop proficiency with frequently used technology early in his or her clerkship. Thus, at the outset of your clerkship, undergo training in how to use CM/ECF, the court's email management system, the telephones, the scanner and copier, and any other commonly used technology. Detailed instructions regarding how to use each type of technology exceed the scope of this chapter in part because each court utilizes distinct technologies each of which work differently. However, the sections below will provide a brief overview of CM/ECF and *Microsoft Outlook 2013*™.

A. ELECTRONIC CASE FILING AND MANAGEMENT

CM/ECF is an automated case management and docketing system that allows parties to electronically file pleadings, motions, and other documents in PDF form with the court twenty-four hours a day. CM/ECF also enables parties to file or access documents remotely from any location, provides secure, long-term document e-storage, and immediately notifies parties of case activity. For example, a law clerk can request an email alert whenever any party files a motion in the matter, which makes it very easy to keep abreast of case activity. However, confirm that your email account will accept emails from CM/ECF rather than automatically sending them to your SPAM folder. Also turn off your pop-up blocker to permit pop-ups from the CM/ECF system.

Electronic filing simultaneously generates an electronic docket available to the public via a system known as Public Access to Court Electronic Records ("PACER").[2] Members of the public must pay for access to PACER, but it is available free to the parties involved in the matter as well as to members of the federal judiciary.[3] Court opinions are also available for free at the Government Printing Office's FDSys website.[4]

With regard to CM/ECF, each electronic docket entry contains a hyperlink to each electronically filed document, which obviates the need for paper filing. Most federal courts began transitioning to CM/ECF within the last decade, if not more recently, so a complex case with a lengthy history will likely only contain such hyperlinks for documents filed after the court transitioned to CM/ECF.[5]

Filing a document in CM/ECF requires a court-issued login and password.[6] Some courts permit others to file electronically. Notably, some courts do not permit pro se litigants to e-file.[7] For example, at the United States Court of Federal Claims, most cases are filed electronically, but pro se litigants must generally file paper pleadings with the Clerk's Office.[8] At the outset of your clerkship, speak with your Clerk's Office to understand your court's specific practice with regard to pro se litigants. For more information on this issue, please review Chapter 18.

Although each court requires training regarding how to use CM/ECF, the section that follows will briefly explain some hallmarks of the system. In addition, PACER training is available on the PACER Service Center website, and it is wise to complete the training prior to commencing your clerkship or at the outset of your clerkship term.[9]

That being said, the judiciary is in the process of transitioning to a new version of CM/ECF.[10] Indeed, this phase has already been implemented for testing in pilot courts like the United States Court of Appeals for the Second Circuit. Thus, be sure to determine which version of CM/ECF your Chambers uses and always have a senior clerk or judicial assistant monitor you the first time you file an order or other document to ensure that you are performing each step correctly.

To file a document on CM/ECF, first confirm that the document is the final version and that it is properly labeled. All documents must be submitted in a searchable PDF format.[11] You can create a searchable PDF by printing a word-processed document to a PDF printer and uploading the searchable PDF version.[12] "However, exhibits submitted as attachments to a document may typically be scanned and attached if you do not possess a word processing file version of the attachment."[13] Always confirm this with your Chambers before filing.

Be especially careful to ensure you are filing in the proper matter. This is especially important when you have the same party at issue in multiple pending litigations. Also be doubly careful that you are filing the proper version of the document and that it contains no typographical errors, visible track changes, version numbers, or any other errors, no matter how small or insignificant. Failure to do so could result in the inadvertent disclosure of confidential information. Also remember that what you are filing may be available for the public to see, and in some cases, will be precedential. Thus, even an error as small as misplacement of a comma may become highly relevant. Moreover, it is crucial that you are careful and thorough in properly filing so that you do not harm the reputation and credibility of your judge or your court.

After you click *Logout*, a pop-up will appear asking you to confirm that you wish to log out of CM/ECF. Click *OK* or *Cancel* depending on which action you wish to take.[14] Once you log out, the parties will receive notice of the filing.[15] It is important to make sure that the notice is timely sent and to confirm that the link will take the parties to the proper document.[16] Check its formatting, etc. If you discover any errors, then follow proper Chambers' protocol. In some Chambers, your judge may permit you to file an amended version of the document correcting the error, if it is minor such as a small typographical error; in other Chambers and for any significant error, your judge will likely want you to notify him or her before taking any action to amend the filing.

Note that documents filed under seal require a special procedure. Before filing a document under seal, confer with a more senior clerk or the judicial assistant. Failure to follow this protocol may result in the confidential filing becoming publicly available. Even when filing a document that is not under seal, it is advisable to request supervision the first time you file.

B. EMAIL MANAGEMENT

In addition to CM/ECF, most federal and many state courts also use *Microsoft Outlook 2013*™ as the Chambers' email management technology. Although an exhaustive discussion of *Microsoft Outlook 2013*™ exceeds the scope of this chapter, the section that follows will highlight some of the most critical features of that system. Each clerk should undergo training on the Chambers' email management system at the outset of the clerkship, either officially as part of clerkship orientation or unofficially by requesting an overview from the judicial assistant. Such training is important because misuse of technology, even inadvertent, can result in a breach of Chambers confidentiality or other serious issues that could not only impede your clerkship but might even result in your termination.

What are commonly used features of Microsoft Outlook 2013™, and how do I use them?

Law clerks commonly use the following features of *Microsoft Outlook 2013™*: (1) marking an email confidential; (2) requesting delivery and read receipts; (3) recalling an email; (4) sharing a calendar; (5) setting up out of office alerts; and (6) creating email folders. Each of these features will be discussed in more detail below.[17]

Marking an Email Confidential: Among other things, *Microsoft Outlook 2013™* permits a sender to mark an email as confidential, important, private, or sensitive.[18] If you mark an email confidential, the recipient will see "Please treat this as Confidential" in the information bar.[19] To change the sensitivity level, click *File*. Under Outlook, choose *Options*. Click *Mail*. Then under *Send Messages*, select *Confidential*. Since most of the messages you send from your work email will be confidential, consider making the confidential setting your default setting so that all outgoing messages are marked this way. Marking an email confidential is important for two reasons. First, if you accidentally send an email to the wrong recipient, the recipient is likelier to stop reading it or never open it at all because it is marked confidential. Second, if the proper recipient does receive it, he or she is less likely to forward it or share it before realizing its sensitive nature.

Requesting a Delivery and/or Read Receipt:[20] In many instances, it is critical to confirm that an email has been delivered and/or read. To request a notification that an email has been delivered and/or read, click *File*. On the left side of the screen, choose *Options*. Click *Mail*. Check the box, which states *Delivery receipt confirming the message was delivered to the recipient*. Now check the box asking for a *Read receipt confirming the recipient viewed the message*. Next, select whether you *always* want a read receipt sent or whether Outlook should ask you each time whether to send one. For ease and convenience, it is best to ask your email system to always send receipts. Notably, you can select one type of receipt or both; for purposes of clerking, however, both are advisable. In this way you will know that the email has actually been delivered and whether the recipient has opened it.

How to Recall an Email:[21] At some point during your clerkship, you may inadvertently send an email to the wrong recipient; doing so may breach Chambers confidentiality. In the alternative, you may email a message that contains a typographical error or forget to attach a document to an email. Although doing so does not endanger confidentiality, it may still reflect poorly on you and perhaps your judge. Fortunately, in such instances, the *Recall* feature is invaluable. It enables you to quickly and discretely correct your error, minimizing any fallout. To recall a message, go to *Mail* and then choose *Sent Items*. Open the sent message you want to recall. Look in the *Message* Tab in the *Move* group. Then choose *Actions* in the drop-down menu and next select, *Recall this Message*. Next, click *Delete Unread Copies of this Message*. Note, however, that this feature only enables you to recall *unread* messages, not an erroneous message that the recipient has already opened.

How to Share a Calendar:[22] In order to schedule hearings or to determine when to provide your judge with a bench memo, etc., you must keep apprised of your judge's personal and professional schedule. In some Chambers, sharing your calendar facilitates this. For instance, if you share your office calendar with the judicial assistant, it makes it much easier for him or her to compile a Master Calendar for Chambers that includes items from each clerk's docket, court events and holidays, and the judge's personal obligations. To share a calendar by email, go to the *Home* tab; in the *Share* group, select *E-mail calendar*. Then in the *Calendar* box, select the calendar you wish to send. Be careful to send the correct one. In the *Date Range* Box, choose the time period that you wish to share. Then click *OK*.

How to Set Up Out of Office Alerts:[23] When you are going to be out of the office for more than a few hours, it is courteous and responsible to set up an out of office alert. The alert will respond to any emails you receive with a message notifying the recipient of your absence and inability to immediately respond to the message. This will ensure that if your judge, counsel for a party, or anyone else has a time-sensitive request, he or she will know why you are not immediately responding and can seek assistance elsewhere as necessary, such as from the judicial assistant or your co-clerk. To set up an out of office message, go to *Tools* and select *Out of Office Assistant*. Choose a start date and time when your email account should begin providing the alert and an end date and time when it should stop. Two message boxes will appear. In the *Inside My Organization* box, type the message that you wish to be sent when someone *within* the court emails you while you are away. A sample message might say: "I am currently out of the office with limited or no email access. If your inquiry is time-sensitive, please contact Ms. Rachel Alaina at alainar@ao.uscourts.gov. Thank you." It is a best practice to include an emergency contact in your out of office message and that contact's office email address or telephone number. In the *Outside My Organization* tab, draft the message you wish to be sent to persons *outside* the court, such as counsel on cases pending before the court, who may email you while you are out of the office. In most instances, it is permissible to use the same message for each type of sender. Finally, click *OK*.

How to Create Email Folders:[24] Creating an email folder for each pending case as well as for other personal emails will help you effectively manage your email and stay organized. As such, it will also better prevent you from accidentally overlooking an important email. To create a new email folder, click on the *Inbox*. Then click *Folder* and *New Folder*. A dialog box will open. Type a descriptive folder title into the box. Finally, click *OK*. The new folder should appear in the list of email folders, and you can begin moving messages into the folders.

Notably, the instructions above pertain only to *Microsoft Outlook 2013*™, so confer with your judicial assistant and Information Technology department to determine which email management system your court uses. Never be afraid to ask for help. It is far better to seek assistance than to commit an error.

C. ANSWERING THE TELEPHONE

In addition to CM/ECF and email management, some clerks, such as those working at trial courts, will often be tasked with answering the phone. It is important to practice proper etiquette in answering these calls because in so doing, you represent your judge. Your conduct must never reflect adversely on your judge's dignity and integrity. In particular, learn how to place a call on hold and to transfer a call as you will frequently be required to do so, particularly as a trial court clerk. Losing a call in the process or transferring a party to the wrong individual may not only reflect poorly on Chambers but also may be off-putting or frustrating to the caller.

In addition, practice proper telephone etiquette. Be polite and courteous when answering the phone. Introduce the Chambers first and then yourself. For instance, you might say, "Good morning. You've reached the Chambers of the Honorable Maxine Wilkinson. This is her law clerk, Christine Hope, speaking. How may I help you?" Speak clearly and slowly. Never eat, drink, chew gum, or type while using the telephone. Not only might the speaker be able to hear you doing so, but also such multitasking may impede your ability to listen carefully to the speaker. One exception is if you are taking notes regarding the call. If you do so, explain that clearly up front and apologize in advance for any typing-related noise. When speaking with the caller, avoid slang or poor grammar. Address the caller properly by title, such as "Mr. Turner" or "Dr. Alexander." Never address a person that you do not know well by his or her first name unless and until he or she requests that you do so. Maintain a proper level of decorum. Be patient and helpful. Even if the caller is hostile or rude, never respond in kind. Diffuse the situation; do not exacerbate it.

Always ask if you may put a caller on hold before doing so and never leave the caller on hold for more than a few minutes. When you return to the call, apologize for the wait. Close your office door before commencing a call. Do not speak to anyone else in Chambers during a call. If someone does stop by while you are on the phone, simply gesture to the phone to let the person know you are unavailable. It is important that the caller feels that he or she enjoys your complete and undivided attention during the call. Before you transfer a call, jot down the caller's phone number so you can telephone him or her back in case the transfer fails. Before concluding the call, thank the caller and wish him or her a good afternoon or evening as appropriate.

Be especially careful not to partake in *ex parte* communications, which occur when one party to a case pending before the court telephones Chambers in the absence of the other party. Such communications are generally prohibited. For more instructions on how to handle an *ex parte* telephone call, see Chapter 6.

Notes

---

　　¹　*Case Management / Electronic Case Files*, PACER, https://www.pacer.gov/cmecf/ (last visited July 31, 2016); *FAQS: Case Management / Electronic Case Files (CM/ECF)* ("FAQS"), US COURTS, http://www.uscourts.gov/courtrecords/electronic-filing-cmecf/faqs-case-management-electronic-case-files-cmecf (last visited July 31, 2016).

　　²　PACER, https://www.pacer.gov/ (last visited July 31, 2009).

　　³　*Registration Wizard*, PACER, https://pacer.psc.uscourts.gov/pscof/regWizard.jsf (last visited July 31, 2016).

　　⁴　*United States Court Opinions*, U.S. GOVERNMENT PUBLISHING OFFICE, https://www.gpo.gov/searchwebapp/browse/collection.action?collectionCode=USCOURTS (last visited July 31, 2016).

　　⁵　R. Lainie Wilson Harris, Esq., *Ready or Not Here We E-Come: Remaining Persuasive Amidst the Shift Towards Electronic Filing*, 12 LEGAL COMM. & RHETORIC: JALWD 83, 87–88 (2015).

　　⁶　FAQS, *supra* note 1.

　　⁷　*Id.*

　　⁸　*Frequently Asked Questions*, U.S. COURT OF FEDERAL CLAIMS, http://www.uscfc.uscourts.gov/faqs (last visited July 31, 2009) ("You must be an attorney who is a member of the U.S. Court of Federal Claims bar to obtain a CM/ECF account. If you are not an attorney, you cannot normally obtain a CM/ECF account or file electronically.").

　　⁹　*CM/ECF Filer or Pacer Login*, U.S. COURTS, https://dcecf.psc.uscourts.gov/cgi-bin/login.pl (last visited July 31, 2009).

　　¹⁰　*Electronic Filing (CM/ECF)*, U.S. COURTS, http://www.uscourts.gov/courtrecords/electronic-filing-cmecf (last visited July 31, 2009).

　　¹¹　*CM/ECF FAQs*, PACER, https://www.pacer.gov/psc/efaq.html (Follow "General" hyperlink; then click on "I tried to file a document, but it says 'format not recognized.' What am I doing wrong?").

　　¹²　*CM/ECF User Guide* 7 (9th Cir. 2016), http://cdn.ca9.uscourts.gov/datastore/uploads/cmecf/ecf-user-guide.pdf.

　　¹³　*Id.* at 8.

　　¹⁴　*Id.* at 14.

　　¹⁵　*Id.* at 167.

　　¹⁶　ALAN WRIGHT ET AL., 16A FED. PRAC. & PROC. JURIS § 3950.6 n. 37 (4th ed. 2016).

　　¹⁷　As noted above, these instructions may not apply to all email management systems. For specific information on your Chambers' email management system, consult your judicial assistant or your court's information technology resources.

　　¹⁸　*Mark an E-mail as Important, Private, or Sensitive*, MICROSOFT, https://support.office.com/en-us/article/Mark-an-email-message-as-important-private-or-sensitive-f480dcea-59a9-48da-b7ed-3b3e0ab27a62#feedbackText (last visited July 31, 2016).

　　¹⁹　*Id.*

[20]   *How to Request a Delivery/Read Receipt in Outlook 2013*, HOW TO GEEK, http://www. howtogeek.com/171023/how-to-request-a-deliveryread-receipt-in-outlook-2013/ (last visited July 31, 2016).

[21]   *Recall or Replace an E-mail Message that you Sent*, MICROSOFT, https://support.office .com/en-us/article/Recall-or-replace-an-email-message-that-you-sent-81c1ae4a-1ea3-4355-b05f-91785773ac15 (last visited July 31, 2016).

[22]   *Share an Outlook Calendar with Other People*, MICROSOFT, https://support.office.com/en-us/article/Share-an-Outlook-calendar-with-other-people-cafb9303-1b1e-40d3-839d-b6abac03a5e8 (last visited July 31, 2016).

[23]   *How to Use the Out of Office Assistant in Outlook*, MICROSOFT, https://support.microsoft .com/en-us/kb/290846 (last visited July 31, 2016).

[24]   Diane Poremsky & Sherry Kinkoph Gunter, *Managing E-mail in Microsoft Outlook 2013™*, QUE PUBILSHING (Oct. 30, 2013), http://www.quepublishing.com/articles/article.aspx?p =2130298.

CHAPTER 10

PRACTICAL TIPS FOR EFFECTIVE
LEGAL RESEARCH

■ ■ ■

As a law clerk, you will often conduct legal research into issues pending before the court. It is critically important that your research is thorough, thoughtful, and accurate. You may be asked to conduct independent research regarding a question from your judge or simply to verify the accuracy of a party's contention in a motion or brief. Whatever the case may be, the judge relies on you, even more so than the attorneys appearing before the court, to confirm that the court has all of the accurate information it needs to render the best decision.

The process of performing legal research as a law clerk differs somewhat from the process you may have used during law school or as a practitioner. Typically, you will not start from scratch. In most instances, unless you are dealing with a question that you or your judge has independently raised, you should use the authorities cited in the briefing as a starting point. Ethical rules of practice require attorneys to apprise the court of any controlling, binding authority, so it is the attorneys' duty to cite to such authority in the brief. That being said, however, some briefing is more well researched than others. So you cannot simply assume that everything an attorney cites is accurate, correct, or exhaustive. You must start with those authorities, verify them, but then go further, conducting your own independent research to ensure that the court has the entire relevant legal landscape necessary to issue the right decision. In addition, attorneys are not necessarily required to apprise the court of non-controlling authority, even if on point. Thus, an attorney may not cite a case from another circuit when arguing an issue of first impression; however, as a law clerk, aim to give your judge everything that might be helpful to him or her, and an on-point case from another circuit might certainly fall into that category. For all of these reasons, it is very important that you assess the accuracy of cases cited and then do your own digging. Although you are generally limited to the factual record that the parties provide to the court, you are permitted to conduct additional *legal* research.

A second key difference is that the parties have usually identified the issues for you in the briefing. Thus, you typically do not need to discern which arguments the parties could make, etc.; it is not the court's job to make arguments for the parties. However, it is sometimes helpful to alert your judge to a lurking, important issue that the parties may have missed, especially if the issue is something that the court could or should raise *sua sponte*, or on its own motion, such as whether the court has jurisdiction to hear the case. In such instances, a judge might request that the parties submit supplemental briefing on the issue or be prepared to address it at oral argument on a motion.

In addition to the research required to draft orders, bench memoranda, opinions, etc., some judges require law clerks to conduct additional research to assist with the judge's scholarly writing, speeches, etc. Other judges require law clerks to stay abreast of developments in certain areas of the law. For example, a judge in the Eastern District of Texas might ask his or her law clerk to track all key patent decisions issued by the United States Court of Appeals for the Federal Circuit or U.S. Supreme Court and to circulate case summaries within Chambers a few weeks after each case issues. The law clerk might track those in a patent law handbook or other Chambers-owned document or even give luncheon capstone talks to Chambers regarding the developments. In this way, both the law clerk and the Chambers stay abreast of legal developments in areas of law that dominate the court's docket.

Your judge may also ask you to track any cases issued from the court and report on subsequent developments, such as how the lower court decided the case on remand or whether the U.S. Supreme Court granted certiorari in the case. The easiest way to do this is to set an electronic alert to apprise you of any activity in the case's docket.

A. CONDUCTING RESEARCH EFFECTIVELY

How do I understand the proper scope of research?

To understand the scope of the assignment, use the assignment memo contained in Chapter 5. In many instances, your judge or supervising law clerk will telephone or email you to request a meeting with you during which he or she intends to give you an assignment. The conversation or email may provide some general information about the assignment. Use that information to complete the questions on the assignment memo and to tweak it as necessary before the meeting. In some instances, you will add or delete questions. Take a copy of the assignment memo with you to the meeting to better ensure that you understand the scope and nature of the research necessary to complete the assignment. In particular, ask your judge or supervising clerk where you should focus your research, whether any existing research on the issue exists, the deadline for the assignment, and in what format you should present your research.

What are the hallmarks of effective research?

Strong writing hinges upon thorough research. How well you say something will not matter if what you say is incorrect or incomplete. As such, effective research must be comprehensive, current, accurate, and well organized. It makes no difference if you find every case, unless you can keep track of where you have searched, what you have found, and what it says. Also check the history of each source of law to make sure that all sources cited remain good law. Keep track of that as well so that no case or other source of law is inadvertently overlooked. In addition, actively read each source of law so that you do not misconstrue its meaning.

What, if any, research assistance may I consult?

Look to the briefing first. Sometimes it will include a secondary source that is useful; alternatively, the briefing will cite a case, which in turn leads you to a wonderful secondary source. If you are still hitting a dead end, do not spend too much time spinning your wheels. Speak with your fellow law clerks to see if they are familiar with the issue or area of law or have suggestions for helpful resources. Ask them if there is anything in particular that you should read to get up to speed on that issue or area of law. Next, ask your law librarian. Law librarians are an incredible wealth of knowledge. They possess immense expertise in legal research and can often pinpoint the best source you need. However, your request should be general enough not to breach Chambers confidentiality and only consult the law librarian after you have obtained your judge's permission.

What are some common research sources?

Below is a non-exhaustive list of commonly used research tools.

Type of Resource	Example(s)	Notes
Search Engines	Google	This is a great free starting place but beware that it will not provide an exhaustive list of sources. So it may be a starting point but **never** an ending point.
Portals	USA.gov	
Metasites	Cornell Law School's Legal Information Institute Findlaw Justia	
Legal Research Databases	Westlaw LexisNexis Bloomberg Casemaker Ravel Law	
Other Databases	Heinonline JSTOR Psycinfo	
Government Sites	Thomas.gov www.uscourts.gov	Thomas is an excellent place to research legislative history and pending legislation.
Law Library Sites	Library of Congress Wake Forest Law Library	
Works-in-Progress	Bepress Legal Repository Social Science Resource Network	
Bar Association Sites	www.abanet.org New York Bar Association	
Other	Federal Judicial Center PACER Reputable Law Blogs	
Print Resources	Reporters Treatises Books Law Reviews	

How do I get started with legal research?

Actively Read the Briefing: Read the parties' submissions. If you are very unfamiliar with the relevant area of law, review a treatise or secondary source to become more comfortable with the relevant area of law. Review the Record, comparing every factual assertion in the briefing against the Record and noting inconsistencies, mischaracterizations, quoting words out of context, etc. Read all of the authorities cited in the briefing, comparing each legal citation in the briefing against the source and noting inconsistencies, mischaracterizations, etc. As you read, jot down potential issues that may require further independent research, such as a case that the party did not cite but which is mentioned as a seminal case in the treatise on the subject. Also write down potential search terms that may be helpful to you as you read.

Devise a Plan: Now devise a research plan. Determine the scope of the search—where you should look, in what time frame, and for what issue. Perform targeted research for each issue or sub-issue instead of a single very broad search, the results of which might be vast and unwieldy. Be flexible and revise the plan as necessary. If you get stuck, speak with a law librarian to get back on course. Also be open to alternative search locations, such as reputable blogs such as Patently-O, which may discuss policy implications of potential decisions or provide insight into the thoughts of the relevant bar.

Choose Effective Search Terms and Sources: Finalize your search terms and verify the spelling of each. Create a quick checklist of which sources you may use and compare it to the authorities cited in the briefing. Are you using all of the databases the attorneys use? As necessary, consult with a librarian to see if there are any other places you should look.

Perform Targeted Searches: One advantage of being a law clerk is that you can perform unlimited searches in electronic databases, so you need not perform a very broad search and then narrow it. Instead, you can do a series of targeted searches. Keep track of where you have looked and what search terms you have used so that you do not waste time performing duplicative searches. In the alternative, you can also perform a single broad search and then run targeted, advanced searches to locate specific cases within your broad results.

Be Selective: After you have used a secondary source to familiarize yourself with the subject matter as applicable, prioritize controlling authority. Then move to persuasive authority, such as an on-point precedential case from another circuit. Then move to an on-point case from within the circuit, albeit not controlling, and cases in other circuits. Next, move to cases to which an analogy may be drawn, such as a Supreme Court opinion on a different statute but with a similar remedial purpose or analogous facts.

Organize your Research: Create folders and subfolders on your computer where you can store the research. For example, one folder might be titled *Thompson v. Foster* and a subfolder inside might be labeled "Motion to Dismiss." Within that folder, you might create multiple folders—one for draft opinions, one for highlighted versions of the cases, and another for your accompanying case chart.

To further assist you in organizing the case law you plan to use in the opinion, a case chart may be useful. To create your case chart, populate each column with the appropriate information. Customize it for your personal use. For each element or factor, you must synthesize various authorities to explain the law. Typically, one case or statutory cite cannot adequately explain the contours of the law. Indeed, one case may outline the factors, while other subsequent cases expand or explain the contours of each factor. As you read each case, ask yourself: (1) What is the governing law? Where does it come from? (2) How are the cases that address this alike factually? Different? Are certain facts more relevant than others? Weighed more heavily? (3) How is the legal reasoning in the case similar? Different? Are the courts establishing a trend or prevailing view? and (4) How does this case compare to our case legally? Factually?

Then organize your paragraphs by column. To make the drafting process easier, include the citation information after each fact or statement. Bold, highlight, or asterisk facts that appeared especially important to the court or that were weighed more heavily. Summarize each column with the rule of law or key takeaway point you can extrapolate. In another variation, create a separate column for the key rule(s) of law. Find the charting system that works best for you. Below is an example of a possible case chart in a case regarding whether a wage discussion ban might violate the National Labor Relations Act ("NLRA").

Case (*Include the proper citation*)	Key facts	Adversely impact Section 7 rights	Substantial, legitimate business justification	Balancing test	Holding	Comparison to our case (*How are the cases alike? How are they different?*)

Actively Read Each Case: When you find a good case or other source of law, actively and carefully read it. Save it as a Word document and highlight its relevant parts. Use Track Changes to make electronic notes to yourself. Develop a personal rating system for each case. For example, you might use "VH" for "very helpful" cases that may warrant a case illustration and "SH" for "somewhat helpful" cases that merely warrant a single cite or explanatory parenthetical.

> **Case Rating Scale**
> - **VH** = a very important and helpful case that you will likely use multiple times as a case illustration and/or in parentheticals
> - **SH** = a somewhat helpful case that you will use primarily as an explanatory parenthetical or to provide additional support in a string cite; you may use it several times or just once
> - **NH** = a case that although it turned up in your research, proved not to be helpful upon reading it. A case may not be helpful for various reasons. Perhaps the facts are too distinguishable, the outcome undermines your position, the procedural posture is too distinct, etc.

A critical reader thinks and analyzes while reading.[1] First, get context. To get context, review the caption and factual background closely. Is it a published case or unpublished? Is it a decision from a single judge, a panel, or an en banc panel? Is it a split or unanimous decision? Ask yourself who the key parties are, what court decided the case, when was it decided, what was the case generally about, etc. In other words, ask the who, what, when, why, and where of the case. Make notes in your case chart or on the case itself as you read.

Now skim the opinion. The first time you read the case, read to gain the big picture; do not simply read for a specific purpose since that may cause you to overlook material information. The second time you read, read critically, actively, and with your purpose in mind. Have your pen, highlighter, or flags in hand to highlight important points or make notes in the case margins. Have your case chart open and populate it as you slowly read. Dissect the case. Pay special attention to key words, such as "and," "or," "either," "unless," "except," "if . . . then," "shall," "must," "shall not," "may not," "must not," or "provided that" as these words can fundamentally alter the meaning of a statute, case, or other legal document.[2] Be sure to distinguish dicta or statements in the Background from the actual holding of the case. Also be sure to distinguish statements in the concurrence or dissent from the holding. Focus on punctuation; the simple placement of a comma sometimes alters the meaning of a holding or a statutory requirement. At this point, you will know the legal issue you are handling, and you will read the case to determine how this case relates to your issue, if at all.

Include a quick summary at the top of the case indicating which legal issue the case addresses and whether it supports or undercuts your recommendation. Feel free to write this on the top of the first page of the case. Never simply rely upon an argument synopsis or headnotes when conducting legal research; these are not part of the opinion and should not be cited or quoted.

As you read, ask yourself:
(1) What issues did the opinion address? Which issues did the parties raise but the court opted not to resolve? Why?
(2) Is the opinion precedential?
(3) What did the court decide?
(4) Why did the court make that decision?
(5) Did the court reject or adopt a party's argument or develop an argument of its own?
(6) Is the opinion correct?
(7) How do the facts and law compare to your case or issue?
(8) How does the case fit into the existing body of law?
(9) What are the implications of this decision?

How do I actively read a statute or regulation?

The same process above works equally well when actively reading a statute or regulation. However, be sure to go to the print version because statutory and regulatory provisions must be read in context. Always read the title, the definitions, and the surrounding sections. Do not simply pull the provision at issue and read it in isolation. To understand the provision, you must understand where it fits in the statute as a whole. Each statutory section speaks to the other sections. Never interpret one provision such that it contradicts another within the same statute or regulation.

How do I actively read a judicial opinion?

With regard to reading judicial opinions, remember that an opinion is a court's written decision. It typically has several components. The caption indicates the parties involved in the dispute. Under the caption is the legal citation that tells you the name of the court that decided the case, where the case can be found, and the year the court issued the opinion. The opinion's author is typically denoted with the author's initials.

The body of the opinion usually begins with a brief statement of the issue(s), general factual background, and then a succinct overview of the procedural posture. Note whether this information is a factual finding of a trial court or merely a recitation of the factual background. Next, the opinion will discuss the court's reasoning. As you read the case, be careful to distinguish a party's argument with the court's reasoning. Also note when a statement is a holding essential to the case or mere dicta that is not legally binding. Finally, also always note whether the statement is contained within the majority opinion, a dissent, or concurrence; dissents and concurrences lack the force of law and must be denoted as such if cited. The disposition tells you how the court disposed of the case.

According to Professor Orin Kerr, when you actively read a case, always aim to acquire: (1) a thorough understanding of the facts and disposition of the case; (2) an understanding of the arguments that each party argued to the court and the relevant source(s) of law; (3) a strong grasp of the legal reasoning in the majority opinion, as well as the reasoning of any concurring and/or dissenting opinions. (*e.g.*, Why did the court reach this decision? How did the court frame the issue and attempt to resolve it? On what sources of law did the court rely to reach its decision?); and (4) the holding as well as its scope and significance. Furthermore, as Professor Kerr observes:

> [Y]ou should accept that some opinions are vague. Sometimes a court won't explain its reasoning very well, and that forces us to try to figure out what the opinion means. You'll look for the "holding" of the case, but you'll get frustrated because you can't find one. It's not your fault; some opinions are written in a narrow way so that there is no clear holding, and others are just poorly reasoned or written. Rather than trying to fill in the ambiguity with false certainty, try embracing the ambiguity instead. One of the skills of top-flight lawyers is that they know what they don't know: they know when the law is unclear.[3]

A Checklist on How to Actively Read a Case

1. Note whether the case is controlling or persuasive and whether it was in effect at the time of the events giving rise to the litigation. Check its subsequent history. Is it still good law?

2. Always note the precise issue that the court is considering. Is it the same or different from the issue in your case?

3. What is the holding relevant to your issue?

4. Consider the procedural posture of the case. A case at the same procedural posture as your case is likely more compelling since standards of review differ at each stage of litigation.

5. It is very important that you thoroughly and carefully read the facts of the case. As you read, note any relevant facts. Do not read the case with tunnel vision, looking only for the facts that support your position. At this point, you need to know all the facts. Note whether each fact is similar to a fact in your case or distinguishable. Use your judgment to determine what is relevant and what is not.

6. It is very important that you understand how and why the court reached its decision. Once you understand that reasoning, you can apply the rules of law to the facts of your case. You can also use the reasoning to assess each party's legal arguments. Note how and where you can use the case.

7. What is the holding? The disposition? A case is often more persuasive when the court disposes of the case in the same way that you want it to dispose of your case.

8. Always review any dissenting opinions and concurring opinions. A dissenting opinion is not controlling, and you must specially designate it as a dissenting opinion. The same is true of concurring opinions, which agree with the outcome of the case but not the reasoning.

9. After you finish actively reading the case, think about the big picture. Does the case support or undermine a party's argument? If yes, how?

Know When to Quit: When you start pulling the same cases over and over again (typically the ones that the parties have also cited), then it is probably safe to stop your search. Remember that not every question has a clear answer. Perhaps you have not found the perfect, on point case because such a case does not yet exist.

Outline: Before you draft, create an outline. The outline should be organized around points of law, such as legal issues that you need to address, elements, or factors. Do not just have one case summary after another. Find an outline format that works for you. Feel free to include visual representations, too, such as timelines or flow charts. Timelines are especially useful where timeliness is an issue. If you decide not to outline but later encounter difficulty when organizing your authority, stop and outline; it is never too late. Nor does your outline bind you. You do not necessarily have to organize your analysis section in the way you outlined it if you later realize that another organizational structure is clearer. At the same time, do not use the outline to procrastinate and avoid actually putting pen to paper.

Here is a sample outline of an opinion discussing whether an employer may ban employees from discussing their wages in the workplace without violating Sections 7 and 8 of the NLRA:

I.   Proposed policy likely infringes upon EEs' Section 7 rights and thus, is presumptively invalid.

    a.   Sections 7 and 8 prohibit unfair labor practices that interfere with EE's Section 7 rights—Cite statute.

    b.   Wage prohibition policies infringe upon Section 7 rights and thus, are presumed invalid *See Jeannette* at 435; *Wilson Trophy* at 345.

    c.   Key facts: Proposed policy is unqualified rule that bans wage discussions all over workplace; unclear whether written or not.

    d.   Conclusion: Policy will likely be found to violate Section 8.

II. Proffered justifications for proposed policy—preserving morale and preventing dissent—are likely insufficient to rebut policy's presumed invalidity.

    a.   Avoiding dissent and EE jealousy are insufficient. *See Jeannette* at 436.

    b.   Key facts: Proposed justifications are preserving morale and preventing dissent.

    c.   Conclusion: Proposed justifications will be insufficient.

III. No need to reach balancing test because ER's justifications are insufficient.

    a.   *See Jeannette* at 456; *IBM* at 345.

For additional tips regarding how to effectively conduct, organize, and incorporate legal research, please see the chart below.

Tips for Effective Legal Research

Develop a Research Strategy and Plan

- Don't start from scratch. Use the briefing as a starting point but do independent research as needed.
- Ask the questions on your assignment memo regarding where to look, etc., so that you know the expected scope and time frame of the research.
- Determine if anyone has worked on this issue. Do not reinvent the wheel.
- Read the briefing available, etc., to help you formulate effective search terms.

Choose the Best Source

- Use books for statutory research so you can more easily see how all of the pieces of the statute fit together from the section title to the definitions.
- Use *Get a Document* to pull up a specific case or article if you already know its name.
- If you are starting from scratch, search in federal and state cases and law review articles *combined*.
    - *TIP: Don't forget to check out the treatises that sometimes appear.*
- If you are very unfamiliar with an area of law, read law review articles from credible authors *first* as they often provide succinct case summaries and may lead you to cases that your search might have missed.

Miscellaneous

- Shoot for more recent cases (2000 to present) to determine the current state of the law, unless there is a seminal case upon which all recent cases rely.
- Shoot for cases from higher courts with more authority where possible (*e.g.*, U.S. Supreme Court).
- Shoot for *controlling* authority (*e.g.*, cases within your jurisdiction)—where possible and where a jurisdiction is provided.

Developing Search Terms

- Begin with a broad search unless you know exactly what you want. (Then just use *Get a Document*.)
- The "Advanced Search" option will likely pull back more precise results.

- "And" pulls up documents with both of your search terms anywhere in the document.
- "Or" pulls up documents with one OR the other of your search terms anywhere in the document.
- "w/s" will pull up documents with your two search terms in the same sentence.
- "w/p" will pull up documents with your two search terms in the same paragraph.
- "!" is an extender that you can place at the end of a word. For example, Gene! will pull up documents containing words like gene, genes, genetic, genetics, etc.
- "w/25" will pull up documents with your two search terms located 25 words apart.
- If your search turns up an excessive number of results, then narrow the search. For example, employ "w/5" instead of "w/s" or "w/s" instead of "w/p."
- If your search turns up "No documents found," then broaden the search. For example, use "and" instead of "w/p."

FOCUS

- Once you pull up your results, it is often impossible to read every case or article. Type a narrower search string into the Focus or Locate box, which allows you to search *within your results*.
  - *TIP: You can always click the back arrow to return to your original broad search.*

Headnotes

- Sometimes a heading summarizes the legal principle for which you search. Click "More like this headnote" to find other cases discussing the same principle. This is another effective research tool.

Check History

- Before you cite a case or other source of law, *always* check its subsequent history to make sure it has positive treatment.
- If a case has been overturned *or* superseded, it is "bad law," meaning that it stands for a precedent that can no longer be supported. One exception is if the case was overturned on other grounds than the point for which you wish to cite it.
- If a case has been questioned within its jurisdiction, avoid citing it to support your position.

- Shoot for a case with a + sign, meaning that it has been followed, or case with a yellow triangle that says "No negative subsequent appellate history."

- Sometimes you can research other cases that have cited to your original case in order to find a case that more closely fits with the facts of your specific case. This is another effective research tool.

B. SUPPLEMENTAL RESOURCES

1. JDS ARMSTRONG & CHRISTOPHER A. KNOTT, WHERE THE LAW IS: AN INTRODUCTION TO ADVANCED LEGAL RESEARCH (3d ed. 2008).

2. Timothy L. Coggins, *Legal, Factual, and Other Internet Sites for Attorneys and Legal Professionals*, 15 RICH. J.L. & TECH. 13 (2009).

3. CHRISTINE COUGHLIN, JOAN MALMUD ROCKLIN, & SANDY PATRICK, A LAWYER WRITES: A PRACTICAL GUIDE TO LEGAL ANALYSIS (2d ed. 2013).

4. DIANA R. DONAHOE, TEACHING LAW, https://www.teaching law.com/.

5. MARY DUNNEWOLD, BETH A. HONETSCHLAGER, & BRENDA L. TOFTE, JUDICIAL CLERKSHIPS: A PRACTICAL GUIDE (2010).

6. LAURA GRAHAM & MIRIAM E. FELSENBURG, THE PRE-WRITING HANDBOOK FOR LAW STUDENTS: A STEP-BY-STEP GUIDE (2013).

7. LAUREL CURRIE OATES & ANNE ENQUIST, JUST RESEARCH (2d ed. 2009).

8. Jackie Woodside, *Introducing Students to Online Research Guides*, 17 PERSPECTIVES 171 (2009).

Notes

---

[1] CHRISTINE COUGHLIN, JOAN MALMUD, & SANDY PATRICK, A LAWYER WRITES: A PRACTICAL GUIDE TO LEGAL ANALYSIS 33–34 (2008) (advising readers to read critically by "getting context", "skimming the text", "read[ing] the text closely", and questioning it).

[2] *Id.* at 41.

[3] Orin S. Kerr, *How to Read a Legal Opinion: A Guide for New Law Students*, THE GREEN BAG: AN ENTERTAINING JOURNAL OF LAW (2007), http://www.volokh.com/files/howtoreadv2.pdf (last visited July 23, 2016).

CHAPTER 11

PRACTICAL TIPS FOR EFFECTIVE JUDICIAL DRAFTING

■ ■ ■

Effective judicial drafting is critical to performing well as a law clerk. It is exceptionally important because the words that you draft may ultimately become part of an order or opinion that has a legally binding effect not just on the parties but sometimes upon the public as a whole. Furthermore, improper grammar diminishes your credibility with the reader. For this reason, it is essential that whatever you draft is accurate, clear, thorough, thoughtful, concise, and precise. Notably, *what* you say is no more important than *how* you say it. Every word counts, so choose your words wisely. Years later, practitioners and other jurists may quibble over the mere placement of a comma in their earnest attempt to discern what a court intended. As a law clerk, you must be able to clearly convey complex ideas. Drafting and editing will likely consume the bulk of your time and are arguably the most important functions of a law clerk. Accordingly, strong writing skills are often the number one thing that judges seek when hiring a law clerk.

A. HALLMARKS OF EFFECTIVE JUDICIAL DRAFTING

Effective judicial writing is clear, accurate, concise, and precise. It is tailored to its audience, maintains a proper tone and level of sophistication, and effectuates the document's spirit and purpose. It is well researched, well reasoned, well organized, and well supported. It is properly formatted and visually pleasing on the page. It avoids grammatical, spelling, typographical, stylistic, and citation errors.

How is judicial drafting distinct from objective and persuasive writing?

Judicial drafting is similar to and distinguishable from the objective and persuasive writing that you studied during law school. In a purely objective memorandum or client letter, your goal is to educate and inform. By comparison, in persuasive writing, you aim to zealously advocate for your client—to persuade the reader that your position is correct. In many ways, judicial drafting must do both. It must maintain a neutral tone so that parties feel that their arguments have been fairly considered. Like a memo, one goal of an opinion is to inform the parties of the court's decision and reasoning. On the other hand, the tools of persuasive advocacy also play a limited role in helping the court to more effectively explain why it found one position more compelling. Yet the use of persuasive tools must never undermine the perception of the court's impartiality. For this reason, judicial drafting is, in some ways, a hybrid that incorporates elements of both objective writing and persuasive advocacy.

Another notable distinction is that, unlike memo writing, judicial orders and opinions, once issued, are not confidential.[1] To the contrary, they enjoy a wide audience comprised of individuals with varying degrees of familiarity with the issue. Thus, choose your words wisely because in a precedential opinion involving an issue of first impression,[2] those words may not only become the law of the case but also the definitive law on the issue, unless and until the case is overturned or superseded. Despite the unique nature of judicial drafting, many, if not most, of the hallmarks of effective writing are equally applicable in any context, whether objective, persuasive, or something in between. Some of these hallmarks are explained in more detail below.

How do I tailor my drafting to the document's audience and purpose?

Before you commence drafting, consider the audience and purpose of the document. Audience, tone, and purpose vary significantly depending on the document, and they often shape how you draft, whether the document is confidential, and what the document includes. Tailor your tone to your audience. Customize the content so that the document best effectuates its intended purpose. Documents not for consumption outside Chambers are highly confidential and should be designated as such with a confidential header. For example, the audience for a bench memo is usually just your judge; thus, your tone is deferential while recognizing your judge's legal expertise. By contrast, a letter to a pro se litigant who is not an attorney would be quite different. The purpose of the letter is to explain what the court wants the litigant to do and why the court requires this action. This explanation must be customized to the litigant's experience. Presumably, he or she is unfamiliar with legal doctrines, so the letter should include more explanation, even of basic legal terminology and procedure.

What, if any, steps should I take before I begin drafting to ensure an effective final product?

Before you begin drafting, discern your audience, purpose, format, and time constraints. Meet with your judge or the clerk who assigned the work to be sure you understand his or her expectations regarding the format, time constraints, scope, etc., of the assignment. Then plan your schedule accordingly, establishing reasonable internal deadlines to keep you accountable. Actively and critically review the briefing, record, and sources of law. Check their subsequent history. Note outstanding questions that these documents raise. Conduct thorough and thoughtful factual and legal research as appropriate. Create a case chart that outlines the relevant portions of each case you plan to discuss. Use your case chart and factual research to craft a detailed outline with headings and sub-headings.[3] For more information on effectively conducting, organizing, and incorporating research, read Chapter 10.

How do I draft an effective paragraph?

To draft an effective paragraph, follow the *ILEAC Approach*: Issue or Idea, Law, Explanation of the Law, Application of the Law to Fact, and Conclusion. Begin each paragraph with a clear topic sentence that either states the issue or idea the paragraph will address. When writing a judicial opinion, the topic sentence should state the conclusion you want the reader to reach after reading the entire paragraph or section (*e.g.*, an iteration of *ILEAC* known as *CLEAC*).

Micro-Organization: Internal Organization of Each Paragraph

I	State the **issue** or **idea** in an effective topic sentence (*Organize each paragraph around a single main idea*)
L	State the relevant **law** (*e.g., the relevant statute, regulation, or rule of law synthesized from cases*)
E	**Explain** and/or **expound** upon the rule of law using case illustrations, citation sentences, and/or explanatory parentheticals
A	**Apply** the law to the relevant facts (*Introduce the application with a transition word like "here" or a phrase like "in this case." To avoid an overly long paragraph, place the application and conclusion in a separate paragraph.*)
C	Clearly state the **conclusion** you wish the reader to reach

Use transitional phrases, such as "next," "furthermore," "likewise," "similarly," etc., to link paragraphs and sentences as appropriate and to ensure that the paragraphs and sentences flow logically and cohesively. Use "here" or "in this case" to signal to the reader that the paragraph is transitioning from a discussion of the relevant law to the application of law to the facts of the case. Make one key point per paragraph and fully develop that point. Put differently, organize each paragraph around one main idea or issue. Do not include too many distinct ideas in a single paragraph because this prevents the drafter from fully developing each individual point or idea. Avoid overly short or overly long paragraphs. For instance, a paragraph should not be a single sentence; nor should it consume an entire page. Once you have drafted all the paragraphs in a section, also make sure that those various paragraphs are in a logical order and flow well together.

How do I draft an effective sentence?

To draft an effective sentence, vary your sentence length, structure, and word choice. Shorter sentences tend to be clearer and more effective. A good rule of thumb is that your sentence should be 25 words or less although exceptions exist. The best way to determine if a sentence is too long is to read it aloud. Include only one main thought or idea per sentence; including too many distinct thoughts may make the sentence unwieldy or confusing. Use active voice unless passive voice is necessary to achieve greater clarity or add persuasive value.

B. TECHNIQUES TO IMPROVE JUDICIAL DRAFTING[4]

Use gender-neutral language: In the past, grammar rules dictated that the masculine forms of language, such as "he," always be used as the default when the sex of the subject was unknown. As attitudes toward equal rights for both sexes dramatically changed, so did our language. The use of "he" as the default arguably manifested the androcentrism of American society, which means that the male or masculine experience is viewed as the "norm" or "default" while the female or feminine experience is treated as "other."[5] In some instances, such as when certain nouns, such as "judge," "doctor," "lawyer," "police officer," "soldier," etc., were automatically paired with a masculine pronoun, doing so perpetuated gender stereotypes rooted in gender polarization.[6] Today, it is a best practice to use gender-neutral language, such as "person," "individual," "employee," "plaintiff," "he or she," "his or her," etc. Failure to do so may be perceived as gender stereotyping, especially by female readers, such as female attorneys, judges, or law clerks.

Be positive: Speak in the affirmative. Avoid double negatives. Showcase the reasons why your position is correct, rather than writing in a defensive posture that elucidates why your argument is not incorrect. The intentional use of that double negative illustrates just how confusing double negatives can be.

Use proper agreement: Always ensure that your subject and verb agree and keep them close together in the sentence if possible. Such sentences are often clearer and easier to read. Also be sure that your subject and pronoun agree. Improper agreement is one of the most common errors in legal drafting. For example, "court" is a collective noun, so typically the corresponding pronoun is "it," not "they." A correct sentence might say, "**The court** [subject] sitting en banc reversed the panel decision. **It** [pronoun] concluded that the Vaccine Act is subject to equitable tolling."

Be concise: Remove wordy constructions and long-winded preambles. Microedit the sentence to remove any words that add no value or are imprecise. Make every word count. However, do not remove words where doing so fundamentally alters the meaning of the sentence or introduces confusion and inaccuracy.

One easy way to do this is to avoid unnecessary use of passive voice and to utilize powerful, active verbs rather than nominalizations. A nominalization typically converts a base verb into a multi-syllabic noun ending in -ion that must be paired with a supporting verb, article, and preposition. For example, use "examine," which is an active verb, instead of a phrase involving a nominalization—"conduct an examination of." Other common endings, which are red flags for nominalizations, include but are not limited to: -al, -ence, -ancy, -ity, -me, -ant, -ent, and -ance. Nominalizations are nearly always less clear and succinct than simply using the active verb from which the nominalization derives.

Use plain language: Avoid unnecessary legalese. Speaking in plain English nearly always leads to clearer, more succinct writing. Thus, as a general rule, avoid words like "aforesaid," "forthwith," "arguendo," "heretofore," "inasmuch as," "hereinabove," "in order to," etc. Except in rare circumstances, such legalese impedes clarity and conciseness without adding value.

Use elegant variation: With the exception of party designations,[7] avoid redundancy in word choice, sentence length and structure, and key phrases. For example, instead of starting each sentence with "Furthermore," employ various transitional words, including "next," "moreover," "likewise," "similarly," "additionally," etc. Rather than beginning each explanatory parenthetical with the same -ing verb, utilize a vast array of base verbs, such as "determining," "concluding," "stating," "reasoning," "explaining," "elucidating," "opining," "expressing," "remarking," "observing," etc. Use a thesaurus to maintain refreshing elegant variation and avoid pure repetition. One notable exception to elegant variation is a designation. For example, once you have designated a party as "Plaintiff," use that designation consistently for the remainder of the document; any variance will likely confuse the reader.

Avoid spelling errors: Do not rely on spellchecking software exclusively as it may miss common spelling errors, such as statute/statue, its/it's, there/their, to/too, and facie/face. Nor does it generally capture usage issues, such as "The dear crossed the road."

Use "that" and "which" correctly: A comma precedes "which." No comma precedes "that." Please see an example below:

Phrase One: The furniture that Plaintiff purchased
Notice that there is no comma preceding Plaintiff.
Phrase Two: The furniture, which Plaintiff purchased,
Notice the proper use of commas with which.

Use words of authority with care: Be cautious when using words of authority since improper word choice may cause you to misstate the law or confuse the reader.

Must: Use "must" when an action is required. "Will" and "shall" also typically denote a requirement.

Must not: Use "must not" when an action is prohibited.

May: Use "may" or "could" when an action is permissible, and the actor has discretion in performing the action.

May not: Use "may not," "shall not," or "will not" when the action is impermissible.

Is entitled to: Use "is entitled to" when an action is permissible, not required, but the actor has a right to the action or thing at his or her option.

Should: Use "should" when the actor ought to perform the action but is not required to do so.

Use active voice: Use active voice unless passive voice adds clarity, precision, or offers some other strategic advantage. For example, in brief writing, defense counsel may not want to emphasize the fact that his or her client hit the plaintiff. Thus, defense counsel might write, "Because Plaintiff was jaywalking, she was struck accidentally by a vehicle" rather than "Plaintiff jaywalked, and as a result, Ms. Smith's car accidentally struck Plaintiff." This is a purely stylistic choice, but some writers might opt to use passive voice to deemphasize Ms. Smith's role and avoid mentioning her in the sentence.

Typically, however, drafters use active voice in part because it encourages them to speak in the affirmative and be more concise. Consider the following two sentences:

Sentence One: The case was decided by the judge.

This sentence uses passive voice. The judge is the actor. The case is the thing upon which the judge acts. However, passive voice alters the order, giving emphasis to the thing acted upon rather than the actor. In this way, it effectively takes the action out of the sentence. To do so, it must also add additional words "by the," which are a red flag of passive voice.

Sentence Two: The judge decided the case.

Use of active voice reorders the parts of the sentence to clearly emphasize the actor first and then the subject of the action. It is clearer and shorter since three words—"was," "by," and "the"—are no longer necessary.

How do I use authority effectively?

To use authority effectively, be judicious in which sources you rely upon in your analysis. Use recent cases unless an older case is seminal, remains good law, and has been cited in all or most subsequent cases. For example, the Supreme Court decided *Brown v. Board of Education* in 1954,[8] but it is the seminal case on racial integration of public schools. Thus, if your draft pertains to that issue, you would cite *Brown* as well as its progeny to explore how the law on school integration has evolved. Failure to cite a seminal case would diminish your draft's credibility because it would not appear sufficiently thorough.

On the other hand, solely relying on older cases can be dangerous since they may not adequately reflect changes or recent trends in the law. For example, if your draft pertains to disability discrimination, citing to cases decided under the Americans with Disabilities Act of 1990 ("ADA") prior to January 1, 2009, would not reflect the impact of the ADA Amendments Act of 2008, which took effect on that date. As such, the analysis might well be outdated and inaccurate in part because the ADA Amendments Act superseded key Supreme Court cases interpreting the ADA. For this reason, it is critical to check the subsequent history of every source of law—whether a statute, case, regulation, etc.—to guarantee it remains good law.

For similar reasons, rely upon precedential cases rather than non-precedential cases if possible. Choose cases in the relevant jurisdiction that are the most factually and legally on point where such cases exist. Select cases with positive treatment; generally avoid cases with negative treatment, especially if distinguished, criticized, or questioned by other courts within the same jurisdiction. One exception occurs when the case has been overturned on grounds unrelated to the legal point relevant to your case. If no controlling law on point exists, as with an issue of first impression, then use persuasive authority from the relevant court of last resort, then the appellate courts, and finally other trial courts in that order.

Quote key excerpts from the law as explained below. Paraphrase accurately; when you put information into your own words, it should still convey the text accurately. Paraphrasing should not alter the meaning of the words.

Eliminate unnecessary string citations.[9] However, exceptions to this rule do exist. For example, string cites are generally permissible to: (1) establish that a point of law is well settled or longstanding; (2) explain a legal trend or majority/minority approach; (3) indicate which courts or circuits have agreed or disagreed on a point of law; or (4) elucidate the historical basis for a proposition. For example, to show that many states agree that animal cruelty should be prohibited, you may follow that assertion with a string cite referencing each state's animal anti-cruelty statute(s). Typically begin such string cites with "*See, e.g.,*". Use them sparingly and only as appropriate. After explaining the legal point you wish to make in the first parenthetical, simply include "same" in subsequent parentheticals to avoid redundancy. If a single case states that, for instance, three jurisdictions have adopted a limited duty rule applicable to the owners of hockey arenas, include that in the parenthetical to make your string cite even more authoritative. For example, such a cite might read: *Barker v. Maxim*, 123 F.3d 456, 459 (S.D.N.Y. 2016) (explaining that the Second, Fourth, and Sixth Circuits have applied a limited duty rule to assess negligence claims brought against owners of hockey arenas). The informative parenthetical eliminates the need to cite a separate case from each of those circuits.

Do not allow your discussion to lapse into a series of case illustrations. To the contrary, use a case illustration only where the case is legally and factually on point and where a more in-depth explanation of the case is necessary to best elucidate how it supports your assertion. In such cases, still only include the relevant aspects of the case. Use case illustrations sparingly, if at all.

In all other situations, use explanatory parentheticals, citation sentences, or quotes to support a rule of law and explain how it supports your position. Begin each parenthetical with an active -ing verb, such as those listed earlier in this chapter. Use elegant variation in selecting these introductory verbs. Use "holding" only if describing the court's holding in the case, and use "finding" only when discussing a factual finding. If a parenthetical only contains a direct quote, then there is no need to use an -ing verb to introduce the quote. Do not embed an important rule of law in a parenthetical the first time used. State the rule of law in the text and use the parenthetical to expound upon or illustrate it. Tailor the information in the parenthetical to explain only the specific assertion or proposition in the sentence it supports. Omit unnecessary information, and keep your explanations precise and concise. As a good rule of a thumb, a parenthetical should be no longer than two lines.

If a parenthetical will exceed two lines but does not warrant a full-scale case illustration, then use a citation sentence. Here is an example:

> In *Oncale*, the U.S. Supreme Court concluded that same-sex sexual harassment is actionable under Title VII in part because nothing in Title VII's legislative history or in precedent interpreting Title VII indicates that conduct must be motivated by sexual desire to constitute sexual harassment. 523 U.S. at 79–81.

Deploying various methods to explain authority, such as case illustrations, explanatory parentheticals, direct quotes, and citation sentences will also improve the diversity and elegant variation of your writing, making it more interesting and refreshing to read.

Finally, support each legal assertion with an accurate and properly formatted citation.[10] Never misstate or mischaracterize a holding. Do not use a quote from dicta,[11] a dissenting opinion, or a concurrence without stating that clearly to the reader; otherwise, the reader may mistakenly assume that the dicta, dissent, etc., constitutes controlling authority. Use accurate pinpoint citations. Use footnotes sparingly, if at all, and resist footnoting substantive case discussions.[12] If such a discussion is important enough to include, then it should likely be placed in the main body of the document.

How do I draft more succinctly?

To be more concise, microedit carefully. Microediting involves going through each paragraph line by line and each sentence word by word to ensure that each is necessary and/or adds value. Put differently, make every word count. If you can convey the same meaning in fewer words without losing clarity and precision, do so. Trim the foliage. To do this, minimize "glue words." Avoid compound constructions, such as "at that point in time," "inasmuch as," "in order to," etc. Replace compound constructions with single words that convey the same meaning. For example, replace "inasmuch as" with "since" and "by means of" with "via" or "by." Use active voice. Avoid nominalizations and legalese. Convert phrases, such as "the case filed by John" to "John's case," which conveys the exact same meaning in fewer words. Also avoid word-wasting idioms, such as "despite the fact that"; use "although" instead. However, do not remove or rephrase words or sentences where doing so alters the meaning, power, or message of the sentence, introduces ambiguity, imprecision, or inaccuracy, or otherwise weakens the drafting.

How do I improve clarity and organization?

Outline before you draft. Repeat the same organizational approach throughout the document. For instance, if you discuss Issue X and then Issue Y in the Introduction of your opinion, you should address them in the exact same order in the Discussion section. If you outline Element A, Element B, Element C, and Element D in the legal landscape for Issue X, then you should also analyze the elements in that same order later in the opinion. The ideas in your explanation of the law and again in the application section should follow that same order as well.

Use headings and subheadings as appropriate. With regard to paragraphs outside the overarching legal landscape of your opinion and not contained in the Statement of Facts, use the ILEAC or CLEAC Approach explained earlier as a guideline for internal paragraph organization. Include only one main idea per paragraph. Fully develop it. To ensure that your paragraph does not contain too many distinct concepts, designate a color for each idea. Then use various colored highlighters to highlight your paragraph. Ideally, each paragraph will be a single color revolving around a single idea. If instead your single paragraph looks more like a rainbow than a solid color, then you have included too many disparate ideas.[13] Notably, sometimes even a single sentence will contain multiple, distinct ideas. This visualization allows drafters to more easily sort the content and input it into the section where it best fits.

Another technique that I often use to explain organization to my students is to compare content organization to the shape-sorting toys that toddlers commonly use to learn their shapes. The toys typically involve a box with a wooden lid. The lid has holes in the form of various shapes from circles to triangles cut into it. Inside the box are wooden blocks also in various colors, shapes, and sizes, including rectangles, circles, squares, triangles, etc. Once someone pours all of the blocks out of the box and places the lid back onto the box, the blocks are jumbled and mixed much like the ideas in a disorganized piece of work product. To place them back into the box, the child must sort the various shapes and make decisions regarding where they fit. Drafters perform this same thought exercise when they decide where content fits best. Drawing from the shape sorting exercise that nearly all drafters played as children, I recommend that students assign each distinct idea a shape, such as a triangle, circle, or square. Read each section, placing the appropriate shape over the appropriate section; a well-organized paragraph will be entirely composed of "circles."

Use a strong roadmap sentence or paragraph at the beginning of each section, which explains what you will discuss in that section. Similarly, begin each paragraph with a strong topic sentence that explains what that paragraph will discuss. Include transitional phrases throughout the paragraph to improve flow. Good examples include "furthermore," "first," "here," "for example," or "additionally."[14]

Avoid making logical, inferential leaps; explain things in a step-by-step manner. With regard to word arrangement, place conditions and exceptions where they are clearest and easiest to read. Use bullet points and lists as necessary. Avoid wide gaps between a subject, verb, and object. Similarly, place modifiers close to the words modified and avoid nested modifiers where possible. Be careful to clarify the scope of modifiers. For instance, "Women and men over 40" is ambiguous as to whether the modifier—"over 40" applies to only men or to women as well. If the sentence aims to include *all* women, revise the sentence to read "Men over 40 and women . . ."

Here is an example of a poorly constructed sentence:

> A petition, which in the case of the Vaccine Act must allege that an injury on the Vaccine Table caused an alleged injury within the proper time frame, must be filed by the petitioner with the Office of Special Masters within three years.

Now let's revise it.

> A petitioner alleging a vaccine-related injury must file a Vaccine Act petition with the Office of Special Masters within the three-year statute of limitations.

How and when should I use quotations?

Use quotations sparingly and judiciously. Excessive quoting, particularly block quoting, reflects the inability to synthesize ideas into your own words and detracts from clarity. However, in some instances, quoting is appropriate. For example, if a statute, constitutional provision, regulation, contract provision, etc., is at issue, quote the relevant language. In a case involving allegations of a hostile work environment, you may wish to quote the harassing remarks that the victim endured to underscore the magnitude and severity of the harassment. Use good judgment.

Be especially careful when selecting block quotes of 50 words or more.[15] Consult the *Bluebook* to format them correctly. Indent the block quote on both sides, use full justification, and do not surround the quoted text with quotation marks. Include the citation on the far left of the next line.

Whenever you quote, indicate any deletions, alterations, omissions, or additions, including emphasis added, in the supporting citation as noted in the latest addition of the *Bluebook*.[16] For example, one might write, "[Plaintiff] failed to arrive on time to work *three* times this week . . . [and]

missed two days of work last week without advance notice." J.A. 15 (emphasis added). Brackets indicate an insertion, while ellipses indicate an omission. Including "emphasis added" in a parenthetical following the citation makes clear that the drafter has italicized "three" to emphasize the number of times Plaintiff has been tardy to work.

How and when should I use footnotes?

Confer with your judge or fellow clerks to determine whether your judge permits the use of footnotes. As explained earlier, even when footnotes are permitted, use them sparingly, if at all. Do not relegate key, substantive information to a footnote. Keep them precise and concise. Although not in the main text, footnotes should be just as sophisticated and well written as text in the main body of the document. Unless otherwise instructed, justify footnotes and use one size smaller font (*e.g.*, use 10-point font for footnotes if 12-point font is used in the body). Use the same font in the footnote as in the body of the main text. Footnotes should be complete sentences, but a footnote typically should not exceed more than three to four lines. Support the assertions in a footnote with properly formatted and accurate factual and/or legal citations as necessary.

There are certain circumstances in which footnotes are recommended. For example, one might include a footnote in a draft opinion if the court will only address a single, dispositive issue even though the parties raised multiple issues. This clarifies to the parties that the court did not overlook the other issues raised and that their omission is intentional. Likewise, include an explanatory footnote if one party raised an issue in its brief that was not raised below since parties typically are not permitted to raise an issue for the first time on appeal. In addition, if the opinion raises an issue *sua sponte*, such as lack of jurisdiction, include a footnote explaining why. Similarly, if a bench memo, opinion, etc., discusses scientific or other terminology with which the reader is likely unfamiliar, the drafter may include a footnote that explains that concept in more detail or defines the term using a credible source, such as *Dorland's Medical Dictionary*.

C. THINGS TO AVOID

Avoid improper capitalization:[17] Always capitalize the deciding court in your case (*e.g.*, "Court") as well as designations (*e.g.*, "Plaintiff," "District Court," etc.). Do not capitalize common nouns from other cases, such as a court that made a holding in a different case. For example, you might write, "There, the court held that the plaintiff had failed to exhaust his administrative remedies." Proper capitalization signals to the reader that you are discussing a *different* case, not the instant one.

Avoid double negatives: As noted above, double negatives are grammatically incorrect and quite confusing to the reader.

Avoid using "to be" verbs: Standing alone, to be verbs lack power and often signal use of passive voice. By way of illustration, compare "The court's decision is incorrect because" with "The court erred because . . ." Using the action verb "erred" is stronger, more powerful, and also allows the sentence to be more precise and concise.

Beware absolutes: In most areas of the law, exceptions exist to nearly every rule. Thus, be very careful in using absolutes, such as "never," "always," etc. Doing so can misstate the law and mislead the reader.

Avoid inflammatory language: For the most part, judicial drafting should maintain a neutral tone. Use of inflammatory language, such as "shocking," "vexatious," or "fatally defective" undermines an objective tone and may diminish the drafter's credibility with the reader. Moreover, inflammatory phrases usually cross the line, even in persuasive writing, and may be off-putting to the reader.

Avoid parenthetical numerals:[18] To avoid redundancy and promote conciseness, do not use parenthetical numerals after you write out a numeral (*e.g.*, one (1) dog, two (2) kittens, etc.). Including the parenthetical numeral is purely repetitive, consuming space without improving clarity or adding value.

Avoid contractions: Contractions, such as "don't," etc., have no place in formal writing. Write out each word in full.

Avoid sexist language: As explained above, use gender-neutral language. For example, use a universal default statement, such as "any person who" or "one who" instead of "any man who." Instead of using "he," "his," and "him" as the default when a person's sex is unknown, use "he or she," "his or her," or "him or her." Avoid using s/he or He/She. Do not alternate the order of "he or she" throughout the document. Avoid expressions that imply a value judgment based on sex or gender and that may perpetuate sex and gender stereotypes (*e.g.*, "gentler sex," "woman's work," "manly effort," etc.). Use gender-neutral language, such as "reasonable person," "plaintiff," "employee," "perpetrator," etc., where possible.

Below are some additional tips for effective judicial drafting.

<u>Organization</u>
- Think before you draft. Outline your content *before* you begin drafting.
- Use a logical structure that includes headings.
- List each question or issue separately.
- Use bullets or numbering for lists.
- Insert page numbers, except on the first page. Page number font should match text font.

- Break long sentences into shorter sentences.
- Use smooth transitions.
- Avoid overuse of words like "However," "Moreover," and "Accordingly." Do not break up a sentence with such a word.
- Use the structure of a sentence to clarify its content (*e.g.*, "To constitute the tort of intentional infliction of emotional distress ("IIED"), Plaintiff must prove the following four legal elements: (1) intent; (2) extreme or outrageous conduct; (3) causation; and (4) emotional distress.").

Tone

- Determine the purpose of the piece (*e.g.*, persuasive v. objective, etc.).
- Remember your audience (*e.g.*, needs, understanding of the law, level of education, time constraints, etc.).
- Watch your tone.
- Show respect/deference as appropriate.

Substance

- Choose your words carefully. Consider connotation.
- Distinguish assumptions from facts.
- Always write out the full name of a party or entity the first time you use the name. Identify abbreviations or designations in parentheses with quotation marks (*e.g.*, Federal Bureau of Investigation ("FBI")).
- State only the relevant facts but err on the side of over-inclusion.
- Avoid using unsupported legal conclusions (*e.g.*, "Ryan's conduct clearly constitutes unlawful sexual harassment.")
- Do not incorporate facts merely by referring to exhibits. Use proper citation to the record or joint appendix.
- In intra-office communications, note missing facts, perhaps by using boldface font or bracketing.
- Note to the judge in brackets and bold font any facts that a party has designated as confidential or under seal.
- State the applicable standard of review, if necessary. Verify it.
- At the beginning of the argument or discussion section, provide any necessary background on the area of law, but do not go overboard.
- Discuss *controlling authority* (*i.e.*, cases decided by a court with higher authority, such as the United States Supreme

Court, and/or in the same jurisdiction (*e.g.*, same state, circuit, or locality)).

- Generally avoid citing to persuasive and/or secondary authority (*e.g.*, cases from another country, circuit, or state; treatises; law review articles; periodicals, etc.) unless necessary.

- Use quotes, especially block quotes, sparingly and use proper formatting.

Grammar & Style

- Generally avoid using passive voice.
- Use powerful verbs.
- Speak in the affirmative.
- Avoid pure repetition.
- Be precise and concise.
- Write out numerals one through ten. Use numerals for 11, etc.
- Never start a sentence with "whether" or "but."
- Avoid run-on sentences.
- Do not break up a sentence with a phrase, such as "however." Place such phrases at the beginning of the sentence.
- Generally avoid the use of legal jargon, such as "arguendo."
- Use gender-neutral language.
- Use designations consistently.
- Use proper agreement.
- Avoid grammatical, spelling, and typographical errors.
- Use a comma before "which" but not "that."

Citation

- Use string cites sparingly. Here is an example: *See, e.g., Buckner v. Bell*, 208 F.2d 132 (2d Cir. 2008); *Bell v. Mobley*, 218 F.2d 145 (2d Cir. 2007); *Tucker v. Drobe*, 215 F.2d 199 (2d Cir. 2003).[1]
- Use proper signals.
- Order authorities correctly.
- Include subsequent history.
- Use proper italicization.
- Include an accurate pincite.
- Distinguish between a finding, a holding (*i.e.*, the Court's decision), and dicta (*e.g.*, extraneous language in the decision that is not essential to the holding).

- Avoid citing dicta where possible. Here is an example of dicta: In writing for the Court, Justice Moss states, "This case involves a male supervisor allegedly harassing his male subordinate. *Were the case to have involved two non-employees, surely the outcome would be different.*" The italicized statement constitutes dicta. It is not controlling law.

- Cite and discuss the "best" cases first (*i.e.*, cases decided by the same judge in the same jurisdiction at the same stage of litigation under the same law and with similar facts).

- Provide concise explanations of why you are citing a case or other authority after the citation. Here is an example: *Buckner v. Bell*, 208 F.2d 132, 136 (2d Cir. 2008) (holding that same-sex harassment is actionable under Title VII).

- Avoid lengthy footnotes that contain critical substantive information; include such substance in the main body of the document. Use footnotes sparingly, if at all.

- Check the subsequent history early and often to make sure that the law remains good law.

- Comply carefully with the latest edition of *The Bluebook*.

Editing

- Edit, edit, edit! After you finish writing a document, edit it immediately for typos, grammatical errors, etc. Then put it away for a few hours before editing it again.

- Edit with purpose, reading once solely for substance, once exclusively for citation, etc.

- Print out a hard copy to edit.

- As permitted and proper, ask a peer to review your work.

- Eliminate unnecessary words.

- Do not use unusual fonts.

- Use spellcheck.

- Read the document aloud. If a sentence is hard to read or say aloud, then it is probably poorly constructed or too long.

- For more information on editing, please read Chapter 12.

D. SUPPLEMENTAL RESOURCES

A full discussion of the hallmarks of effective drafting, grammar, and citation exceeds the scope and purpose of this book. For additional information or practice, please consult the excellent supplemental resources below.

1. LINDA J. BARRIS, UNDERSTANDING AND MASTERING THE BLUEBOOK: A GUIDE FOR STUDENTS AND PRACTITIONERS (3d ed. 2015).

2. CHRISTINE COUGHLIN, JOAN MALMUD ROCKLIN, & SANDY PATRICK, A LAWYER WRITES: A PRACTICAL GUIDE TO LEGAL ANALYSIS (2d ed. 2013).

3. CHRISTY DESANCTIS & MICHAEL MURRAY, LEGAL WRITING AND ANALYSIS (2015).

4. MARY L. DUNNEWOLD, BETH A. HONETSCHLAGER, & BRENDA L. TOFTE, JUDICIAL CLERKSHIPS: A PRACTICAL GUIDE (2010).

5. ANNE ENQUIST & LAUREL CURRIE OATES, JUST WRITING: GRAMMAR, PUNCTUATION, AND STYLE FOR THE LEGAL WRITER (2d ed. 2005).

6. BRYAN GARNER, THE REDBOOK: A MANUAL ON LEGAL STYLE (2d ed. 2006).

7. LAURA P. GRAHAM & MIRIAM E. FELSENBURG, THE PRE-WRITING HANDBOOK FOR LAW STUDENTS: A STEP-BY-STEP GUIDE (2013).

8. AUSTEN PARRISH & DENNIS YOKOYAMA, EFFECTIVE LAWYERING: A CHECKLIST APPROACH TO LEGAL WRITING & ORAL ARGUMENT (2007).

9. RICHARD WYDICK, PLAIN ENGLISH FOR LAWYERS (5th ed. 2005).

10. THE BLUEBOOK: A UNIFORM SYSTEM OF CITATION (20th ed. 2015).

Notes

---

[1]   As noted elsewhere in the book, bench memoranda are confidential as are drafts of any Chambers work product, such as draft opinions, Chambers correspondence, etc.

[2]   An *issue of first impression* is a novel issue that the jurisdiction has not squarely addressed.

[3]   For more information on pre-writing, see Chapter 10 as well as *The Pre-Writing Handbook for Law Students: A Step-by-Step Guide* by Laura P. Graham and Miriam E. Felsenburg.

---

[4]   The information contained herein draws heavily upon Richard Wydick, PLAIN ENGLISH FOR LAWYERS (5th ed. 2005).

[5]   Sandra Lipsitz Bem, *Dismantling Gender Polarization and Compulsory Heterosexuality: Should We Turn the Volume Down or Up?*, 32 J. SEX RES. 329, 329–34 (1995).

[6]   *Id.* (defining *gender polarization* as the separation of sex and gender into opposite ends of a spectrum derived from socially constructed notions of masculinity and femininity, maleness and femaleness).

[7]   As used herein, *designation* refers to how the drafter has decided to refer to a party or entity. For example, a drafter might designate Plaintiff Rachel Alaina as "Plaintiff" and for the sake of clarity and efficiency, should then refer to Ms. Alaina as "Plaintiff" consistently throughout the document.

[8]   Brown v. Bd. of Educ. of Topeka, 347 U.S. 483 (1954).

[9]   *See generally* LINDA J. BARRIS, UNDERSTANDING AND MASTERING THE BLUEBOOK: A GUIDE FOR STUDENTS AND PRACTITIONERS (3d ed. 2015).

[10]   *Id.*

[11]   *Dicta* is language in a judicial opinion that is not essential to the holding. "Use dictum sparingly and only if it serves or promotes the public interest or judicial administration." ABA, JUDICIAL OPINION WRITING MANUAL, 34 (1991). A *dissent* is an opinion that disagrees with the majority's reasoning and disposition. A dissent is not controlling. A *concurrence* is an opinion that agrees with the court's disposition but would have reached the conclusion on different grounds. Reasoning in a concurrence does not constitute controlling authority. Follow special rules contained in the latest edition of *The Bluebook* regarding how to cite dissenting and concurring opinions.

[12]   When a drafter uses footnotes excessively, a "reader's eyes must constantly move from text to footnotes and back again . . . This is distracting and wastes time. For this reason, some judges object to any footnotes . . . Most judges use them to expand on the text . . . Follow your judge's practice." SYLVAN A. SOBEL, ED., LAW CLERK HANDBOOK: A HANDBOOK FOR LAW CLERKS TO FEDERAL JUDGES, 98 (2007); *see also* ABA, *supra* note 11, at 34 (advising drafters to never "place in a footnote any material necessary to an understanding of the opinion").

[13]   The use of colored highlighters to edit content and organization first appeared in MARY BETH BEAZLEY, A PRACTICAL GUIDE TO APPELLATE ADVOCACY 92–96 (2002). Later texts expand upon this idea, which I have used often in teaching. *See* CHRISTINE COUGHLIN ET AL., A LAWYER WRITES: A PRACTICAL GUIDE TO LEGAL ANALYSIS 245 (2008).

[14]   For an excellent table of transitional phrases, see page 255 of *A Lawyer Writes*, *supra* note 13, which in turn attributes L. Oates, A. Enquist, and K. Junsch, *The Legal Writing Handbook: Analysis, Research and Writing*, 613–22 (3d ed. 2002), and Bryan A. Garner, *Legal Writing in Plain English: A Text with Exercises* 68 (2001).

[15]   *See generally* BARRIS, *supra* note 9.

[16]   *Id.*

[17]   *Id.* at 139–43.

[18]   *Id.* at 145–48.

CHAPTER 12

PRACTICAL TIPS FOR EFFECTIVE EDITING

■ ■ ■

A good law clerk must be a strong, detail-oriented editor who knows how to give and receive constructive feedback and who exercises wise judgment in determining which suggested edits to incorporate. Editing is one of the most important functions a law clerk performs.[1] Good editing leads to clarity, precision, enhanced credibility, and also exhibits care and respect for the reader. Whether it is an order or opinion, editing is critical to prevent substantive errors, imprecise language, confusion of the body of law, and embarrassment for your judge. Editing can preempt the kinds of mistakes that could injure the professional reputation of you and your judge and even harm the prestige and legitimacy of your court. Thus, failure to edit carefully and thoroughly, both for substantive and non-substantive errors, constitutes a failure to fulfill your duties to your judge, fellow clerks, the court, the parties, and perhaps even to the public.

Stringent, careful editing is not just necessary for documents that will be issued to the public; to the contrary, edit your bench memoranda and other work product just as carefully for the very same reasons. To do otherwise signals carelessness, a lack of respect, and as such, destroys the credibility of your work product. For example, if you have typographical errors and misspelled a party's name within your bench memo, that could indicate that you do not take pride in your work, respect the reader, or thoroughly review your written work product. As such, the reader is less likely to trust the credibility and accuracy of your legal research and in turn, is less likely to follow your recommendation. In such instances, your judge may either return the work product to you to revise or reassign the task to a different law clerk. To avoid this, afford editing the ample time, care, and thoughtfulness it requires.

A. TIPS FOR EFFECTIVE EDITING

The following is a non-exhaustive list of suggestions for effective editing.

Allow yourself ample time: Oftentimes, new law clerks do not allow themselves sufficient time for editing. Perhaps they erroneously believe that they will be able to observe and correct all errors with only one to two rounds of editing. Nothing could be further from the truth. Thus, establish a drafting timeline that builds in ample time for editing, beginning at least one full week before the final deadline. Note that the time allotted for editing varies depending on the subject. Allow more time for a lengthy opinion that will have precedential authority and a public audience than to a one-page 11-Day Memo that will only go to the judge. Although the time allotted varies, a strong law clerk will edit every document extensively no matter the audience or impact.

Edit in Stages: Do not reserve all editing for the end of the drafting process. To the contrary, edit in stages. For example, edit each paragraph or section immediately after you draft it. Then, edit it again after you complete the entire section. After you complete your Discussion section, return to the Background to delete extraneous facts that you did not use in the Discussion. Finally, perform the targeted editing of the entire draft described below.

Perform Targeted Review: Edit with purpose. Read the document once through just to review big picture issues, such as whether the document handles all issues and contains all relevant substance. Next, macroedit, determining if the document has all major components in the right order and that the large subsections are also in the proper order. Then edit the paragraphs, ensuring that they are also in the right order. Next, edit within each paragraph, making sure each paragraph possesses a strong topic sentence, states the law, explains the law, applies the law to the facts, and ends with a clear conclusion. Next, edit exclusively for proper citation. Then, edit only for grammatical and spelling errors. This list could go on, but targeted editing like this will better enable you to catch errors. However, it is a time-intensive endeavor, so allow yourself ample time to complete it.

Read the Document Multiple Times in Multiple Ways: Read the document several times in different mediums to catch formatting and other errors. Print a hard copy to view the margins on the page, whether headings are orphaned, etc. Read it aloud to hear whether sentences are too long or awkwardly structured. Read it from the end to the beginning since readers tend to string the key words in a sentence together to gain meaning from the sentence; this is less common when you read the document out of order, such as reading the last paragraph first.

Use Computer Resources: Use spellchecking software and other computer tools to catch spelling and grammatical errors. However, do not rely on these features exclusively. As some say, spellchecking flails! This example illustrates that spellchecking software is unable to capture whether a word is used out of context. Nor does a computer know if you intend to write "their" or "there," "its" or "it's," "complement" or "compliment," "statute" or "statue", etc. As such, use these tools to *supplement*, not replace, your own editing, which should catch such mistakes.

Put It Away: After awhile, a drafter can become so immersed in his or her work product that he or she is likelier to overlook errors, especially minor ones. To avoid this, allow yourself sufficient time to step away from the work product for a few hours, or even an entire day, and return to it with rested eyes and a fresh perspective. When you are tired or have reviewed the draft three to four times in a row, each subsequent review is likely to have diminishing returns. It is better to put the draft away and return to it later.

Seek Peer Review: Your fellow clerks are some of the most talented attorneys with whom you will ever have the privilege to work, and they are likely all very strong editors. Given that they lack your familiarity with the document's subject matter, however, they will not only notice grammatical and other errors you may have missed, but also they may observe points at which you have erroneously assumed audience knowledge, made logical leaps, or explained something in a confusing manner. They may also have insightful suggestions regarding other possible solutions, policy implications, or legal or factual analogies you may draw. As such, seeking peer review from a strong editor whom you trust and respect will almost always strengthen your work product. In turn, graciously accept their feedback and only incorporate suggestions that will enhance the draft. You need not automatically make every revision. Be judicious. Never take suggested edits personally, and always be gracious and appreciative. After all, editing someone's work takes significant time, diplomacy, and care. Be sure to thank your editor(s) in person and also by sending a follow-up thank you email or note, depending on the significance of the review.

How do I know which edits to incorporate and which to reject? Do I automatically make any edit that my judge or another judge suggests?

You need not automatically input any suggested revision, not even one suggested by your judge. If your judge or another judge suggests a revision that you believe will make the draft imprecise, misleading, inaccurate, or erroneous, you should gently, respectfully, and promptly explain that to the judge. Elucidate your concern, and if your judge disagrees, then input the revision, since the judge, not you, is the author. However, be certain that the judge makes a well informed decision. Memorialize your objection in a memo to file that you email to yourself, simply to protect yourself in the event that the case is later reversed or otherwise challenged because of the revision. Never take your judge's suggested revisions personally, but instead, welcome them as it is the judge's opinion or correspondence, not yours, and his or her suggestions will likely strengthen the final work product. Your judge writes the final opinion; you merely provide a draft. Thus, understand and honor the scope of your supporting role in Chambers.

The same general principles apply with regard to suggested revisions from co-clerks. In some Chambers, your judge will ask you to share your near-to-final draft with one or all of your co-clerks for source-checking, cite-checking, and other review. This is especially common in trial courts. Allow ample time for this, and be mindful of your co-clerks' busy schedules. As with your judge, do not take a co-clerk's comments personally. Your co-clerks are incredibly bright, so be open to their suggested revisions; the incorporated edits will likely strengthen the opinion. Again, exercise good judgment in accepting and rejecting edits, only incorporating suggested revisions that will strengthen the opinion.

Be aware that the editing process of appellate opinions requires additional collaboration between Chambers because three-judge or en banc panels decide appellate cases. Thus, once an appellate opinion has been finalized in all respects, you will submit it to the other judges on the panel for review. Those Chambers may provide substantive edits or purely stylistic ones, suggested edits or mandatory ones. If a judge disagrees with the wording of a majority opinion, he or she may indicate that either a substantive change be made, such as an insertion drafted by the judge, or he or she will dissent or draft a separate *dubitante* opinion. In other cases, a judge may indicate that he or she will not require the changes so long as the other panelists agree to make the decision non-precedential. In other instances, a judge may implore the other panelists to simply use a non-precedential per curiam affirmance without an opinion to dispose of the case or risk issuing a fractured opinion with a lengthy dissent or concurrence. You may have to serve as your judge's diplomat during such discussions between Chambers, unless and until they are escalated from the law clerks to the judges.

B. EDITING OTHERS' WORK

When editing someone else's work, determine at the outset the intended purpose, nature, and scope of the review, desired format for comments (*e.g.*, track changes, handwritten remarks, comments by email or via an in-person discussion, etc.), and hard deadline by which the edits must be received. Do not assume that "editing" simply means reviewing citation format or mere proofreading for typographical errors. In Chambers, "editing" usually includes a much more intensive, comprehensive review.

If you do make edits via track changes, always be 100% certain that you have saved the original document under a new, appropriately titled name before you commence your review. Do not risk altering the original.

When editing the work of others, it is often helpful to utilize the same editing tips above that you would utilize when reviewing your own work. The main difference, however, is in how you convey such changes. When reviewing another person's work, it is incredibly important that you are diplomatic, deferential, and clear. Do not make the change; suggest the change and explain the reason for suggesting it. In this regard, the "comments" feature in many word processing programs is especially useful.

As noted above, do not be a "yes person." You are not meaningful as an editor if you are afraid to notify the drafter that language is unclear, that a holding has been misstated, etc. The drafter sought your assistance as an editor because he or she trusts that you will catch mistakes that the drafter missed; deliberately overlooking such errors because you do not want to upset or insult the drafter constitutes a failure to fulfill your duty as a law clerk and to satisfactorily do what the drafter asked of you. Do not be afraid to point out issues. That being said, be judicious and tactful in your comments. For example, do not make purely stylistic changes, such as changing "observed" to "noted" simply because you prefer the latter. Purely stylistic revisions typically exceed the scope of editorial duties.

What duties are typically within the scope of peer review?

Generally an editor will check the document just as thoroughly as he or she would edit his or her own work. This means that the editor will review the briefing to verify that the draft accurately discusses all relevant substance. The editor will also read each case cited, confirming the pincite, ensuring that the holding is properly stated, etc. The editor will also confirm that every case, statute, regulation, etc., cited remains good law and has not been repealed, reversed, criticized, etc. Editing may also mean reviewing the Record, when it is available, to ensure that all relevant facts are included, properly cited, and accurately explained. The editor will also consult the latest edition of *The Bluebook* to determine that citations are properly formatted. Finally, the editor will proofread for typographical, grammatical, and spelling errors. Be thorough and thoughtful.

As noted earlier, good editing is not just about *what* errors you find but also about *how* you suggest revisions to the drafter. Gently and diplomatically convey your suggested comments. A strong editor provides constructive, not destructive, criticism. Any suggestions provided should be clear and well supported. Limit your suggested edits to meaningful edits that will enhance the opinion. For instance, rather than stating, "The case doesn't say this. It says X," you might suggest, "Perhaps review the opinion at page 23. I read this a bit differently to indicate X. I'm happy to discuss this with you if you'd like." Finally, when you submit your edits to the drafter, include a kind message, such as this:

Dear Violet,

I really enjoyed reading your draft opinion. Great job! Per your request, I have attached my edits in the form of track changes below. Please let me know if you have any questions about my suggestions. I'm happy to discuss them with you, and I hope they are helpful. Good luck!

Kind regards,

Lambie

Effective Editing Checklist

1. Macroedit first.
   a. Is it well researched and well supported? ☐
   b. Is it effective? ☐
   c. Is it clear, easy to understand, and well written? ☐
   d. Do I have all major components in the proper order? ☐
   e. Is all of the relevant factual and legal substance covered? ☐
      i. Fully developed? ☐
      ii. Accurate? ☐
      iii. Supported by proper citations? ☐
      iv. Remains good law/has positive treatment? ☐
   f. Is it clear and well organized? Are sections and paragraphs clearly organized? ☐
      i. Have I properly used headings and subheadings? ☐
      ii. Have I avoided making logical leaps or skipping steps? ☐
   g. Do I have the proper tone? ☐
   h. Have I taken into account the knowledge base of my audience? ☐
   i. Is it confidential? If yes, do I have an appropriate header and clearly denote any confidential information with boldfaced font and double brackets? ☐
   j. Am I accomplishing the document's purpose? ☐
   k. Is my formatting correct? ☐
      i. Page numbers? ☐
      ii. Margins? ☐
      iii. Font? ☐
      iv. Footnotes? ☐
      v. Quotations? ☐
      vi. No orphaned headings? ☐

vii. Proper page breaks? ☐

viii. Justification? ☐

2. Microedit paragraphs.

    a. Are my paragraphs in a logical order? ☐

    b. Does each paragraph have a clear opening sentence that states what I will address in that paragraph? ☐

    c. Does the paragraph have clear internal organization? ☐ Do I avoid making logical leaps? ☐

    d. Does the paragraph have a clear conclusion? ☐

    e. Does the paragraph use transition phrases? ☐

    f. Is it not overly long? ☐

    g. Does this paragraph fit well here within the body of the document? ☐

    h. Is it under the proper subheading? ☐

    i. Am I explaining too many distinct concepts in a single paragraph rather than just addressing and fully developing a single point or idea? ☐

3. Then microedit sentences, going word by word.

    a. Is the language precise? ☐ Did I use the proper word here? Is the word's connotation appropriate? ☐

    b. Is the sentence structure clear and not awkward? *(Read it aloud.)* ☐

    c. Does the sentence fit well here in the body of the paragraph? ☐

    d. Do I use the proper party designation? ☐

    e. It is clear and easy to understand? ☐

    f. Is the tone correct? ☐

    g. Does it use elegant variation? ☐

    h. Is this sentence necessary? ☐ Could it be more concise? ☐ Does every word have value? ☐

    i. Have I avoided use of passive voice unless necessary? ☐

    j. Is this a run-on? ☐ Do I need a semi-colon or to break this into separate sentences? ☐

    k. Have I avoided any issues with grammar, spelling, or typographical errors? ☐

    l. Are all citations accurate and properly formatted? ☐ Am I missing any citations? ☐

4. Have I run any spellchecking and grammar checking software and corrected any errors that those programs uncovered? ☐

5. Have I read it aloud? ☐

6.   Have I reviewed a hard copy? ☐

7.   Have I performed targeted review? ☐

8.   Have I put it away and returned to it? ☐

9.   Have I edited it out of order, one section at a time, or from back to front? ☐

10. Have I obtained peer review from a strong editor and incorporated the edits from that review that will strengthen the opinion? ☐

11. Have I reviewed it at least five times? ☐ Have I reviewed it over a period of at least three to four days? ☐ (*This varies depending on the size of the document as a shorter document may require much less intense review than a longer document that will have precedential effect and a public audience such as an opinion.*)

For a more targeted editing checklist tailored to a specific document, please review the checklist for drafting a bench memo in Chapter 16 and the checklist for drafting an opinion in Chapter 17.

C. SUPPLEMENTAL RESOURCES

1.   CHRISTINE COUGHLIN, JOAN MALMUD ROCKLIN, & SANDY PATRICK, A LAWYER WRITES: A PRACTICAL GUIDE TO LEGAL ANALYSIS (2d ed. 2013).

2.   AUSTEN L. PARRISH & DENNIS T. YOKOYAMA, EFFECTIVE LAWYERING: A CHECKLIST APPROACH TO LEGAL WRITING & ORAL ARGUMENT (2d ed. 2014).

3.   MICHAEL D. MURRAY & CHRISTY H. DESANCTIS, LEGAL WRITING AND ANALYSIS (2d ed. 2015)

4.   BRYAN GARNER, REDBOOK: A MANUAL ON LEGAL STYLE (3d ed. 2013).

5.   MARY L. DUNNEWOLD, BETH A. HONETSCHLAGER, & BRENDA L. TOFTE, JUDICIAL CLERKSHIPS: A PRACTICAL GUIDE (2010).

6.   RICHARD C. WYDICK, PLAIN ENGLISH FOR LAWYERS (5th ed. 2005).

7.   THE BLUEBOOK: A UNIFORM SYSTEM OF CITATION (20th ed. 2015).

Note

---

[1]   In *A Lawyer Writes*, the authors distinguish editing from polishing, but herein the term "editing" should be read broadly to encompass all aspects of the editing process, including content editing, polishing, and proofreading. *See* CHRISTINE COUGHLIN, JOAN MALMUD ROCKLIN, & SANDY PATRICK, A LAWYER WRITES: A PRACTICAL GUIDE TO LEGAL ANALYSIS (2d ed. 2013).

CHAPTER 13

DRAFTING AND MANAGING CHAMBERS CORRESPONDENCE

■ ■ ■

One of the most critical responsibilities of a law clerk is to draft and manage Chambers correspondence. You represent Chambers in *what* you say and *how* you say it. Thus, take every email and every letter seriously. Edit them for substance, tone, and typographical errors just as carefully as you would edit an order or opinion.

A. EFFECTIVE EMAIL MANAGEMENT

During your clerkship, you will likely draft, send, and receive countless emails each day. Thus, dutiful email management and organization are critical to ensure a timely response to each email received and to better guarantee that an important, time-sensitive email is not overlooked.

Inbox Zero: *Inbox Zero* is an email management strategy that encourages each clerk to have zero emails in his or her Inbox at the end of each workday.[1] According to productivity expert, Merlin Mann, there are five actions one should take with each email: "delete, delegate, respond, defer, and do."[2] Specifically, he encourages email recipients to: (1) process email intermittently during the day; (2) "delete or archive as many new messages as possible"; (3) immediately forward any email that is best dealt with by someone else to the proper recipient; (4) respond immediately to inquiries that can be answered in just a few minutes; (5) "move new messages that require more than two minutes to answer . . . to a separate 'requires response' folder"; and (6) allocate ample time each day to respond to those messages rather than allowing them to clog your Inbox.[3]

Email Folders: In addition, create folders within your email system that are appropriately labeled with each case name. Create additional folders for non-case related correspondence, such as emails from your judge relating to an ABA speech he or she will give next month. As noted above, each time you receive an email, respond to it or delete it as necessary. If you do not delete it, then immediately move it into the appropriate folder. At the end of each day, be sure that your Inbox contains zero emails. Also check your spam folder once daily in case it accidentally captured relevant emails. If you are dutiful in your email management and organization, then it will be quite easy for you to locate important emails, and there is far less chance that important emails will be accidentally deleted or overlooked.

To create a new email folder, click on the *Inbox*. Then click *Folder* and *New Folder*. This will open a dialog box and allow you to type a name into the box. Finally, click *OK*. The new folder should appear in the list of email folders, and you can begin moving messages into the folders.[4] For more information on how to create an email folder, see Chapter 9.

B. DRAFTING AN EFFECTIVE EMAIL

Technology has revolutionized the judiciary in countless ways only one of which is the way that attorneys communicate with Chambers and the way that Chambers communicate with each other. Today, the bulk of that communication occurs via email. We email daily from our laptops and smartphones. Email allows users to bridge time zones and geographical divides. In part because email brings people together quickly, efficiently, and inexpensively, it has become the preferred mode of communication in many Chambers. Sometimes, it is even used for communication between a clerk and his or her judge or between co-clerks.

The ease and speed with which one can send an email, however, has a downside. That downside is that oftentimes, new law clerks mistakenly believe that because an email is easy and quick to send, it should be easy and quick to draft. Perhaps for this reason, too many law clerks send emails without affording them the care, time, and editing they deserve. Law clerks forget that an email is a professional communication and that as such, it must be appropriately formal, well written, and well edited.

In general, the content of an email should be concise, precise, easy to read, and easy to absorb. It should also be accurate, well organized, and written in plain language. Brevity is even more important in an email than in other forms of communication. Ideally, an email will be no more than one screen long.[5] A professional email should maintain the same formal tone that you would use in any other professional communication to your judge, a fellow clerk, or an attorney, such as a letter. Below are some more specific guidelines for drafting professional emails.

Recipient(s): Be especially careful that you are sending the email to the correct recipient and are using his or her most current email address. Be diligent in avoiding spelling and typographical errors. Be especially careful when your email system automatically populates a name; this is especially likely to generate errors when recipients have a common name such as "Smith" or "Jones." Also be careful to only use the person's office email address instead of a personal email address that might also be in your email contacts.

List the recipients in the order of the professional hierarchy. In Chambers, this would include the judge first, then the clerk who has been working in Chambers the longest, the other clerks from oldest to newest, the judicial assistant, and then any externs or interns from the one who has been externing the longest to the newest extern to join Chambers.

Do not overuse the general Chambers email; tailor your recipients to the intended audience. Be especially wary of "Reply All." Otherwise, you are unnecessarily clogging others' emails, which is inconsiderate. Be especially careful not to inadvertently send an email to the entire court, to another court, or to the wrong person as this could result in a serious breach of Chambers confidentiality. Be very careful to include the attorneys for all parties, as accidentally omitting a party could constitute an improper *ex parte* communication.

In the event this happens, alert the judge and the individual immediately, by telephone if possible. Ask the person to delete the email without reading it. Likewise, if you inadvertently receive a confidential correspondence, simply alert the sender that you received the message in error and are going to delete it without reading it.

As explained above, most email systems permit you to require read receipts to achieve confirmation that an email has been sent, delivered, and read. Always confirm that your email has reached its intended destination, and if you have not received a response in the expected time frame, confirm with the recipient that the email has been opened and read.

From: Never send an email from any address other than your secure work email address. This is critical to maintaining Chambers confidentiality. As such, many courts employ special highly secure email networks. If you email your judge or a co-clerk from your personal email account, you may risk the integrity of Chambers security, possibly leading to infection by a virus or even facilitating a security or confidentiality breach.

Use "reply" and "reply all" with extreme care. Email strings can become unwieldy, and a reply all may go to unintended recipients. This is especially true if you are replying to a single person in an email thread; if that person responds to your individual email by replying to all, then all readers of the thread will see the email that you intended to be between you and one other person. In such cases, it is safer to begin a new, independent email thread with a new subject line to the sole, intended recipient.

CC: Only copy an individual if the person should be aware of the email but is not the direct recipient. For example, it is typically a good idea to CC the judicial assistant on any emails with the judge or parties in which you are attempting to schedule an event as the judicial assistant is most well versed in the judge's personal and professional schedule and is often in charge of managing the calendar. Use the CC feature sparingly, carefully, and deliberately.

BCC: Beware the BCC feature. There are few instances in which blind copying is appropriate. Typically a reader wants to know if anyone else is privy to the email conversation. In addition, if the individual replies to you or replies all, it will not necessarily go to all of the individuals who have been blind copied, which can lead to communication mishaps. One exception when BCC may be useful is when you wish to keep a copy of the correspondence, so you BCC yourself. However, this is somewhat redundant since you can always retrieve sent messages from the "Sent" folder.

Subject Line: Include a proper subject line that adequately reflects the subject and purpose of the email. Oftentimes, it is helpful if the subject includes the case name and number. If an email is time-sensitive, include something such as "IMPORTANT," "ACTION REQUIRED," or "TIME-SENSITIVE" in the subject line to alert the reader that this message is a priority. Some email systems also permit you to flag such emails for the reader.

Salutation and Header: Include a proper salutation and confidential header, if the communication is confidential. A salutation may be unnecessary once you have exchanged emails on the same topic.[6] Communications within Chambers and between Chambers are confidential; communication with attorneys representing the parties is confidential with respect to non-parties. However, avoid any *ex parte* communications as mentioned above.

Formatting and Organization: Do not capitalize all of the words in the email since readers may perceive that as hostile or angry. If you or your reader may have difficulty reading small font, use a larger font. Use regular size font in a normal typeface and font color; do not switch to unusual fonts or atypical font colors, such as blue or purple; those may be hard to see and appear unprofessional. Use the same spacing and organization that you might you use in a letter. Do not clump every paragraph together; create separate paragraphs. Some emails may warrant other organizational tools, too, such as numbering, bullet points, boldfaced or underlined headings or subheadings, etc. If an email will discuss several issues, it may be helpful to list them in order of most to least important in a single overview topic sentence and then discuss each one in turn.[7]

Body: Follow the same general principles of formatting and organization mentioned above. With regard to tone, be appropriately formal and respectful. Use sophisticated language. Avoid slang and emoticons. One rule of thumb is never to write anything in email that you would not be willing to post on a billboard in Times Square. Follow the same rules of effective legal drafting explained in Chapter 11. Being concise and precise is even more important in an email. Do not draft overly long emails. If an email will take more than three full paragraphs, consider including a short message in the actual email and attaching a longer analysis. Typically close each email with a sentence such as, "Please let me know if you have any questions or concerns" in case anything in your email is unclear.

Closing: Use an appropriately formal closing, such as "Regards," "Kind regards," or "Best." Avoid overly intimate closings, such as "Affectionately yours" or "Sincerely."

Attachments: Include a sentence briefly describing any attachments. List them in order of most to least important. Attach pertinent materials in the same order as listed in the email. Check to make sure that the attachments are the correct version without track changes showing, are not too large to send, and do open. Only attach pertinent materials, such as highlighted versions of key cases. Always confirm that any attached items have actually been attached before sending as this is a common error. Some email programs will alert you if your email contains the word "attached" but does not contain an attachment. Clearly name the attachments. For example, if you attach cases, rename them "*Smith v. Jones,*" etc., rather than simply using the less helpful reporter cite.

Proofreading: Be careful and take your time. Allow yourself ample time to edit. Read the email aloud. Have a peer or co-clerk review it or print out a hard copy. Edit the email several times just as carefully as you would edit a letter or order. Recall that a single typographical error, such as inadvertently omitting the word "not," could fundamentally alter the meaning of the email. Such carelessness could result in confusion or other serious implications. Use spellchecking software but do not rely upon it exclusively; for example, it cannot distinguish between "there" and "their," "its" and "it's," etc. Follow the same rules of effective editing discussed in Chapter 12.

Other Tips: Always stop and think before you send. Never send an email when you are emotional, angry, or do not have time to fully consider what you are writing. Do not write an email when you are on the go or distracted. Be especially careful when you send an email from your phone. Avoid Internet acronyms like LOL and BTW. Use proper capitalization, grammar, and spelling.

Checklist for Drafting an Effective Email

1. Would this message best be conveyed by email or in some other form, such as in person or over the phone? ☐

2. Do I have the time to write this email thoughtfully? ☐ Am I in a hurry, on my phone, or on the go? ☐

3. Is the main point stated in the first one to two sentences? ☐

4. Am I too emotional, upset, tired, or distracted to send this? ☐ Do I need time to step away and think before I respond? ☐

5. Am I sending this from my secure work email? ☐

6. Have I noted whether the email is confidential or time-sensitive? ☐

7. Do I have the proper recipient? ☐ Am I sending this to a secure work email address, not a personal email? ☐ *Triple-check this.*

8. Do I have a proper CC if one is necessary? ☐

9. I have not listed anyone as BCC, right? ☐

10. Do I have a proper subject line with no errors? ☐ Does it include the case name and docket number? ☐ A brief description of the substance? ☐ A notation of "time-sensitive," etc., if it is time-sensitive? ☐

11. Do I have a proper salutation? ☐

12. Does the body cover the main substance? ☐ Is it accurate, clear, concise, precise, easy to read, and well organized with headings or bullet-points as appropriate? ☐ Does it avoid typographical, spelling, and grammatical errors? ☐ Does it take less than one screen to read? ☐

13. Does the email have the proper tone? ☐ Is it professional? ☐

14. How will the reader perceive the email? ☐

15. Did I include a proper closing? ☐

16. Have you signed the email? ☐

17. Does the email include proper attachments in the proper order? ☐ Are they appropriately named? ☐

18. Does the email avoid typos? ☐ Emoticons? ☐ Spelling errors? ☐ Formatting errors? ☐ Grammatical errors? ☐ Internet acronyms? ☐ Words written in all caps? ☐

19. Does the email have the proper format? ☐ Font? ☐ Font color? ☐ Font size? ☐ Indentation? ☐

20. Have I edited this carefully? ☐ Have I read it aloud? ☐ Printed it? ☐ Reviewed it at least three times? ☐

21. Have I ensured the recipient(s) are correct and listed in the proper order? ☐

Here is an annotated sample email.

To: marylycans@ao.uscourts.gov
From: rachelalaina@ao.uscourts.gov
Date: April 12, 2017
Re: Draft Opinion in *Gray v. Montgomery*, 09–HA–2016
Dear Judge,

 I hope you are doing well. Attached herein for your review is my draft opinion granting summary judgment in *Gray v. Montgomery*, 09–HA–2016, the parties' submissions, and highlighted versions of the key cases cited therein. Please let me know if you have any questions or suggested revisions. I look forward to hearing from you.

  Best,

  Rachel

C. DRAFTING AN EFFECTIVE LETTER

 On occasion, judges send letters for a vast array of reasons, such as to communicate with the parties regarding scheduling and other matters. Although a letter is not an opinion or order, it is still a communication from the court. As such, each letter should be well written, well researched, and well organized. Your judge may ask you to take a first cut at the letter. Below are some guidelines that will assist you in drafting an effective letter.

 Components: Typically, a letter will contain the following components: (1) date sent; (2) judge's title, name, and Chambers' address; (3) a "regarding line" (Re:) that states the case name and docket number, as applicable, and summarizes the letter's basic subject or purpose; (4) an appropriate salutation; (5) a sentence that provides a basic overview of the purpose of the letter; (6) the remaining body of the letter; (7) an appropriate closing; (8) a signature; and (9) enclosure(s), if applicable.

 Formatting: Before drafting the letter, ask the judicial assistant or supervising clerk for a sample letter of this type or review the case file to see if other letters have already been sent in the matter to which you can refer for form. Include the official court header as applicable. Insert page numbers on the bottom center of the page if the letter has multiple pages. Unless otherwise instructed, use full justification, Times New Roman black 12-point font, and one-inch margins. Generally avoid footnotes. Feel free to use boldfaced type, headings, subheadings, etc., to enhance organization. Include any header as appropriate.

Address: Include the official court address. Include the judge's name as "The Honorable . . ." and then include the full official name of the court. Confirm that there are no spelling or grammatical errors. Double-check that the date is correct and update the date before you issue the final letter since days may have elapsed between submitting the draft for review and issuing the final letter. Typically, the letter will also identify the method of transmittal, such as facsimile or express mail.

Salutation: Use an appropriately formal salutation such as "Dear" or "To Whom It May Concern." Follow the salutation with a colon. Always triple-check to ensure that you have addressed the letter to the proper recipient and spelled his or her name correctly. Err on the side of formality, referring to the recipient as "Mr." or "Ms.," rather than using the more intimate first name only.

Body: The first one to two sentences of the letter should clearly state the purpose of the letter and provide an overview of its contents. As with all legal writing, the body should be accurate, clear, well organized, and easy to read. Maintain a neutral and professional tone. Know your audience and tailor your explanation and depth to the audience; for example, you may go into more explanation of legal terms when writing to a non-lawyer than an attorney. Explain things in sufficient detail that the reader need not refer back to other materials to understand the letter's meaning. "[L]etters should be complete, self-contained, and independently understandable without having to refer to other documents."[8] Use plain, sophisticated language and support assertions with accurate, properly formatted citations as necessary. Use the same principles of organization that you might use in other settings, such as boldfaced headings or bullet point format. Be appropriately formal and respectful. Follow the same rules of effective legal drafting explained in Chapter 11. Brevity and precision are even more important in a short letter than in a long opinion or bench memo, so make every word count. Do not draft an overly long letter. Generally, you will close each letter with a sentence such as, "Please contact Chambers at the email address below if you have any questions or concerns." Bear in mind that if the case goes up on appeal, this letter may end up in the Record on appeal for perusal by other judges and law clerks.

Closing: Use an appropriately formal closing, such as "Regards," "Kind regards," or "Best." Avoid overly intimate closings, such as "Affectionately yours," or "Sincerely." Confer with your judge as he or she may have a preferred closing.

Signature: Do not forget to obtain the judge's signature. Confer with your judge, judicial assistant, or another clerk to determine whether your judge prefers to sign each letter or permits insertion of an electronic signature on file with the judicial assistant. If the latter, be sure to confirm whether that is permissible for only some letters or all letters and which types of letters fall into which categories. If you must obtain your judge's signature, do not wait until the eleventh hour to do so. Work with the judicial assistant to understand your judge's personal and professional schedule so that you can schedule a convenient time for the judge's review of and signing of the letter. You may even want to schedule a short five-minute meeting with the judge just for the purpose of signing. Your Chambers may have helpful, yellow "Sign Here" flags that will signal to your judge where to sign the document. Do not ask your judge to sign a final letter until it is an absolute final form. This means that you have inputted your judge's revisions, reviewed it for formatting, typographical errors, etc., and it is perfect.

Enclosures: If your letter also contains enclosures, indicate them. List them in order from most to least important. Attach pertinent materials in the same order. Check to make sure that the attachments are the correct version without track changes showing. Only attach pertinent materials. Always confirm that any attached items have actually been enclosed in the proper order before sending as this is a common error.

Editing and Proofreading: Be careful and take your time. Allow yourself ample time to edit. Read the letter aloud. Have a peer or co-clerk review it or print out a hard copy. Edit the letter several times just as carefully as you would edit an order. Recall that a single typographical error, such as inadvertently omitting the word "not" could fundamentally alter the meaning of the letter. Such carelessness could result in confusion or other serious implications. Use your computer program's spellchecking feature but do not rely upon it exclusively; it cannot distinguish between "there" and "their," "its" and "it's," etc. Follow the same rules of effective editing discussed in Chapter 12.

After you have conducted your own edits, submit the letter to the judge for review. Discuss any suggested edits with your judge and do not automatically input an edit that you believe will weaken the letter, make it inaccurate or imprecise, etc. In such cases, discuss your concerns with the judge respectfully and diplomatically, but if the judge disagrees, input the edit. After all, the judge is the author, sender, and signer of the letter; you play merely a supporting role enabling the judge to write a strong letter. If you are especially concerned, memorialize your objections in a memo to yourself that you keep on file.

Once you have inputted your judge's edits, complete the editing and proofreading process all over again. When the letter is in final form, place it on the official court header and print it on special letter paper. Provide it to your judge for signing pursuant to the considerations above.

Addressing the Letter: Always confirm the accuracy of the recipient's address. Check the spelling and confirm that it is the most current address on file. Even if your judicial assistant mails the letter, you should still confirm the recipient's information as two eyes are always better than one. Include the court address on the envelope in case the letter is returned.

As with everything else, the drafting process of a letter is confidential for your lifetime. You may never share the content of draft letters or any discussions relating to that content. Furthermore, the court may not send a letter to one party to a litigation without providing the letter to the other party; doing so would constitute an unethical *ex parte* communication. Thus, be very careful to stay within ethical rules when drafting and sending letters and emails.

Below is a sample clerkship rejection letter.

The Honorable Violet S. Sofia
Address

Recipient's Name
Address
Subject: Clerkship Application
Letter Date

Dear John,

Thank you for you applying to clerk in our Chambers for the 2018–2019 term. Unfortunately, we are unable to offer you a clerkship at this time. Although we are unable to hire you, we were impressed with your credentials and wish you all the best in your future endeavors.

Regards,

Judge Violet S. Sofia

The Honorable Violet S. Sofia

Below is a sample scheduling letter. (*Many Chambers invite applicants to interview by telephone, but this scheduling letter can serve as a guide for scheduling other appointments as well.*)

The Honorable Judge Violet S. Sofia

Address

Recipient's Name

Address

Subject: Clerkship Application

Letter Date

Dear Janet,

Thank you for your interest in serving as my law clerk during the 2018–2019 term. I was very impressed with your credentials and would like to interview you as soon as possible. To schedule an interview, please contact my Chambers at (304) 212-4567. I look forward to meeting you.

Regards,

Judge Violet S. Sofia

The Honorable Judge Violet S. Sofia

Checklist for Drafting an Effective Letter

1. Have I included an accurate, well-edited return address? ☐
2. Is the date current? ☐
3. Does my regarding line include a succinct, accurate overview of the letter's subject? ☐
4. Does the letter have a proper header if confidential? ☐
5. Does the letter have a proper CC if one is necessary so as to avoid being an ex parte communication? ☐
6. Is the letter properly formatted? ☐
7. Does the letter include properly formatted page numbers if it has multiple pages? ☐
8. Does it include an appropriate salutation to the correct recipient? ☐ Is the recipient's name spelled correctly? ☐
9. Does the letter maintain a formal, professional, neutral tone? ☐
10. Is the main point stated in the first one to two sentences? ☐
11. Does the remainder of the body cover the main substance? ☐ Is it accurate, clear, concise, precise, easy to read, and well organized? ☐ Does it avoid typographical, spelling, and grammatical errors? ☐
12. Does the letter include a proper closing? ☐

13. Does the letter include the proper title for the sender? ☐

14. If applicable, does the letter include "Enclosures" in the proper version and order? ☐

15. Does the letter avoid typographical errors? ☐ Contractions? ☐ Spelling errors? ☐ Formatting errors? ☐ Grammatical errors? ☐

16. Print out a hard copy of the letter to review the format. Does the letter have the proper format? ☐ Font? ☐ Font color? ☐ Font size? ☐ Indentation? ☐ No widowed headings? ☐

17. Have I edited this letter very carefully? ☐ Have I read it aloud? ☐ Printed it? ☐ Reviewed it at least three times? ☐ Sought peer or judge review as applicable? ☐

18. Has the letter been signed? ☐

19. Does the envelope have an accurate, current mailing address for the recipient? ☐ Does the envelope content avoid any errors, typographical or otherwise? ☐

D. SUPPLEMENTAL RESOURCES

1. CHRISTINE COUGHLIN, JOAN MALMUD ROCKLIN, & SANDY PATRICK, A LAWYER WRITES: A PRACTICAL GUIDE TO LEGAL ANALYSIS (2d ed. 2013).

2. MARY DUNNEWOLD, BETH A. HONETSCHLAGER, & BRENDA L. TOFTE, JUDICIAL CLERKSHIPS: A PRACTICAL GUIDE (2010).

3. SYLVAN A. SOBEL, Ed., LAW CLERK HANDBOOK: A HANDBOOK FOR LAW CLERKS TO FEDERAL JUDGES (2007).

4. Gerald Lebovits, *E-mail Netiquette for Lawyers*, 81 N.Y. ST. B.J. 64 (2009).

Notes

---

[1] Productivity expert Merlin Mann is credited with coining the term "Inbox Zero" and advocating the approach to email management that it describes. *See* http://whatis.techtarget.com/definition/inbox-zero (last visited July 22, 2016).

[2] *Id.*

[3] *Id.*

[4] *See* http://www.quepublishing.com/articles/article.aspx?p=2130298 (last visited June 22, 2016).

[5] CHRISTINE COUGHLIN, ET AL, A LAWYER WRITES: A PRACTICAL GUIDE TO LEGAL ANALYSIS 271 (2008) ("The optimal length for an email is one screen.").

[6] *Id.* at 275.

[7] *See generally* MATTHEW BUTTERICK, TYPOGRAPHY FOR LAWYERS: ESSENTIAL TOOLS FOR POLISHED AND PERSUASIVE DOCUMENTS (2d. ed. 2015).

[8] AUSTEN L. PARRISH & DENNIS T. YOKOYAMA, EFFECTIVE LAWYERING: A CHECKLIST APPROACH TO LEGAL WRITING & ORAL ARGUMENT 87 (2007).

CHAPTER 14

DRAFTING ORDERS

■ ■ ■

An *order* announces a court's ruling.[1] Orders often direct parties to do (or not do) something. Orders may be oral or written; the latter are more common. Notably, oral rulings have the same force and effect as written orders.

If the court issues an oral ruling during a telephonic conference, the law clerk will typically draft and file a short *minute entry* afterwards to memorialize the ruling. However, this practice differs by court. For example, in some courts, this responsibility falls to the judicial assistant. The minute entry will appear in the case docket to apprise all parties of the oral ruling. Because the docket provides the court, case number, presiding judge, and names of the parties, the minute entry that the law clerk drafts and files generally need only explain the date, nature of the proceedings, and the court's ruling. Before drafting a minute entry, examine samples in the case docket or the docket of another case. At least at the outset of your clerkship, write out the minute entry on paper for your judge's review unless instructed otherwise. Edit carefully. The minute entry will become public record. A sample minute entry might read:

> 8/31/2017: **DENYING** the parties' oral joint motion to stay the proceedings because the parties failed to establish good cause to do so.

A court may also issue an order in response to a party's motion or on the court's own motion. A *motion* is an application or request for the court to issue a decision or take an action. In trial courts, an attorney making the motion may be required or expected to attach a sample order to his or her motion. However, the court is not required to adopt the sample order. Instead, the court can modify the submitted order or draft an entirely new one. Likewise, local rules may require the inclusion of other additional documents as well. For example, they might require a party to append a copy of the proposed amended complaint to its accompanying motion to amend the complaint.

Courts issue orders for various reasons from scheduling oral argument to denying a motion to stay. In response to more complex motions, such as a motion to dismiss or a motion for summary judgment, an order is usually accompanied by a judicial opinion explaining the basis for the order. This document is called an *Order and Opinion*. Opinion drafting is discussed in Chapter 17.

A. TYPES OF ORDERS

As a law clerk, you will be responsible for effectively drafting, filing, and managing orders for your judge. Although an exhaustive list of the various types of orders exceeds the scope of this chapter, common orders include the following:

Interlocutory Order: An *interlocutory order* decides an intervening matter and as appropriate, will sometimes afford temporary relief. For instance, an interlocutory order might establish the child support and custody arrangements that will prevail while a custody case is pending.

Restraining Order: A *restraining order* or *temporary restraining order* ("TRO") may be issued if a party seeks to enjoin a party from certain conduct. These orders are most common where the action subject to the injunction would moot its need. For example, when a party files a bid protest to challenge a government's contract solicitation process, the aggrieved party will likely request a TRO to stop performance on the contract where failure to do so might moot the case or greatly amplify the injury.

Scheduling Order: A *scheduling order* establishes a litigation schedule that the parties must follow. In drafting a scheduling order, it is important to first consult the parties. It is common for parties to file a joint motion suggesting a discovery schedule, and some judges may require this. In the absence of a joint motion, the court can convene a status conference to ascertain mutually convenient dates for discovery and the filing of motions. As a law clerk, it is critical that you do not simply accept the dates that the parties suggest. Instead, carefully consult your judge's personal and professional schedule as well as your own to ensure that the scheduling order establishes reasonable deadlines that will not conflict with the judge's existing personal and professional obligations. These include speaking events, trials, oral arguments, and other pending matters as well as personal commitments, such as vacations, family visits, or medical procedures.

Sometimes an unavoidable conflict emerges after issuance of a scheduling order. In such a case, issue an amended scheduling order. The parties can also request an amendment for good cause shown, or the court may amend the order on its own motion for any reason.

Once a schedule is established, it is critically important to immediately enter the dates into your personal and professional calendars and to share them with the judicial assistant for inclusion in the judge's personal calendar and the Chambers Master Calendar. To avoid breaching confidentiality, do not use identifying information when entering dates into your personal calendar or syncing a calendar on a smartphone or other device with your work calendar absent your judge's express written permission to do so as this could potentially give rise to confidentiality issues. Set email and reminder alerts that will give you ample time to prepare for each filing and scheduled event. This will enable you to alert the judge and parties if a filing deadline is missed and to adequately prepare both yourself and your judge for scheduled events, such as status conferences or oral arguments.

Although scheduling orders are among the easiest to draft, establishing a mutually convenient schedule may be quite difficult. This is particularly true if Chambers has a busy docket or the parties are quite contentious. In ascertaining mutually convenient dates, a party may reach out to you via telephone or email. Never communicate with a party outside the presence of the other. Doing so constitutes an impermissible *ex parte* communication. This is true even if the subject matter of the communication is as mundane as scheduling and the other party is immediately notified. For this reason, it is important to remind the parties to never call or email Chambers, unless both parties are on the line or included in the email. Further encourage them, in lieu of a phone call, to file a joint scheduling order.

Final Order: A *final order* is one that announces a final decision about an issue pending before a court. Such orders often terminate the case entirely and are generally accompanied with an opinion explaining the basis for the order. For example, in a civil action, if one party moves to dismiss for failure to state a claim, the court might issue a final order granting that motion. This order would end the case and result in a final judgment that would permit the losing party to file an appeal.

B. DRAFTING AN EFFECTIVE ORDER

To draft an order, first do a search of the docket to determine if a similar order has already been issued in the case. If you have been asked to draft something other than a final order, then an existing order likely exists. Use that order as a template only. Be careful to ensure that it does not contain any typographical or substantive errors. Be especially mindful of the caption as a party may have been dismissed from the action since issuance of that order; this will require you to modify the caption to reflect that change.

If no similar order has been issued in your case, then consult with a more senior law clerk or the judicial assistant to locate a sample order in another case to use as a template. Try to find a case that is as similar as possible to your case but also do independent research to ensure that your order uses the proper statute and contains the proper form. Some

Chambers maintain a folder with sample orders to which new law clerks can refer. This chapter also includes a sample order that may serve as a guide. Below is a brief explanation of the typical components of an order.

Caption and Title: An order begins with a case caption. This caption lists the parties and their designations (*e.g.*, Plaintiff, etc.), states the court hearing the case, notes the date of issuance, lists the docket number, and sometimes states the general nature of the motions at issue. Below the caption, most orders will include a brief title explaining the nature of the order. This title is often in all caps, boldfaced, underlined, and centered. The nature of the order will explain the motion the court has considered or the order's purpose. For example, the title might say **SCHEDULING ORDER** or **ORDER DENYING DEFENDANT'S MOTION TO DISMISS**. This title should also reflect whether an order is amended or is responding to an amended motion or pleading. For example, a title might say **AMENDED SCHEDULING ORDER** or **ORDER DISMISSING AMENDED COMPLAINT**.

Nature of the Matter and Disposition: Next an order will generally state the pending matter, which the order will address. Rather than explaining the reasons in a full opinion, a short, stand-alone order may then use a catchall phrase such as "for the reasons discussed below," "for the reasons stated on the record," or "for the reasons stated in the accompanying opinion." It will then state the disposition, often in all caps and boldfaced type (*e.g.*, **DENIED, GRANTED**, etc.).

Body: The content and length of the main body of the order varies depending upon the nature of the matter being decided.

Closing and Signature: Each order concludes with the phrase **IT IS SO ORDERED**. The order usually restates the date of issuance and includes the judge's standard signature block. Depending on court rules and practices, an order may require the judge's actual signature, rather than an electronic version. Be sure you know what type of signature is required well in advance. Because orders must often be issued in a time-sensitive manner, it is important for you to be able to provide a finalized version of the order to the judge for signing when the judge is available. For example, if your judge is leaving on Friday to go out of town for a week, be sure to get the final order to your judge no later than Thursday for his or her signature, even if the order is not due until the following week while the judge is away. As a law clerk, it is your duty to stay apprised of dates and deadlines and be familiar with your judge's schedule so that you can properly anticipate and preempt such issues. When you do provide the judge a final order to sign, it is helpful to use "sign here" flags on each page that requires a signature. This is especially helpful if the judge must sign multiple documents in one sitting. Edit carefully and be certain that the version your judge signs is the final version. It is inefficient to ask the judge to sign an order only to discover after the fact that it contains a typographical error. If you do discover an order, correct it and ask your judge to sign the new version.

C. FILING AN ORDER

An order does not take effect until issued. Upon issuance, the order will be reflected on the docket and becomes part of the procedural history of the case. If the case was filed using the CM/ECF system, the electronic docket will link the docket entry to the order so it is easily accessible to the parties and other law clerks in the future.

Edit each order very carefully before issuance, devoting special attention to dates and party names. However, if you do notice an error after issuing an order, the court may file an amended order in response to a motion or on the court's own motion.

When issuing an order, be mindful of the nature of the matter. If a case involves sensitive material, such as a vaccine case involving a child or a government contracts case involving confidential business information, be sure to determine in advance of issuance whether the order must be filed under seal. An order filed under seal will be unavailable to the public except in a redacted form that removes confidential information. For example, a redacted order might replace a party's name with a generic designation such as John Doe. A distinct mechanism is used to file an order under seal. Upon determining that an order must be filed under seal, confer with your Clerk of the Court, fellow co-clerk, or judicial assistant to understand the proper court protocol for filing under seal and out of an abundance of caution, file the order with their supervision if it is your first time filing under seal.

Below is a sample scheduling order.

IN THE UNITED STATES DISTRICT COURT FOR THE
SOUTHERN DISTRICT OF WEST VIRGINIA

No. 16–1951

RACHEL ALEXANDER,	)	
	)	
Plaintiff,	)	
	)	
v.	)	**SCHEDULING ORDER**
	)	
HOPE WILKINSON,	)	
	)	
Defendant.	)	
	)	

THIS MATTER having come before the Court for a scheduling conference pursuant to Rule 16 of the Federal Rules of Civil Procedure on March 17, 2017, and the parties having reviewed the Court's Civil Case Management Order as well as the Local Civil Rules, and for good cause shown,

IT IS on this day of March 31, 2017,

ORDERED that this matter will proceed as follows:

1. **Fact Discovery Deadline**: Fact discovery is to remain open through August 31, 2017. All fact witness depositions must be completed by the close of fact discovery. No discovery is to be issued or engaged in beyond that date, except upon application and for good cause shown.

2. **Motion for Summary Judgment:** Any motion for summary judgment must be electronically filed no later than September 30, 2017.

3. **Local Rules**. The parties are directed to the Local Civil Rules for any other matter not addressed by this Order.

/s/ **VIOLET SOFIA**
THE HONORABLE VIOLET SOFIA
UNITED STATES MAGISTRATE
JUDGE FOR THE SOUTHERN
DISTRICT OF WEST VIRGINIA

Let's practice.

You have just concluded a telephonic status conference with your judge and the attorneys on the matter. Your judge asks you to draft a minute entry and scheduling order based on the call.

Here is a transcript of the call:

Judge: Good morning. We are on the record. This is a telephonic status conference in the matter of *Smith v. ABC Electronics, Incorporated*, docket number 07–CIV–2017. The parties requested the call to establish a mutually convenient schedule both for discovery and the filing of the motions. Counselor for Plaintiff, you may proceed.

Plaintiff's Counsel (Ms. Thompson): Thank you, Your Honor. We requested a status conference because we have been unable to work out a mutually convenient schedule in the case that would enable us to file a joint scheduling motion. Ms. Reyes insists upon a discovery schedule that is unreasonable for my client.

Judge: Why is it unreasonable counselor? What's the issue?

Plaintiff's Counsel: Well, Your Honor, Ms. Reyes wants us to complete discovery in just three months and be prepared to file a motion for summary judgment just four weeks after that. It's unreasonable . . .

Judge: Ms. Reyes, are there any circumstances in this case that warrant limiting discovery to just three months?

Defense Counsel (Ms. Reyes): Respectfully, Your Honor, this is a small, single-plaintiff employment discrimination case involving an employee who worked for our client only six weeks. Thus, we feel that it is reasonable to complete discovery within three months, and my client would like to expedite the process so it can move forward and hire someone new to take the position. Plaintiff has requested reinstatement, so it's impossible for the client to move forward until this issue is resolved.

Judge: Ms. Thompson, on what basis do you believe your client will be unable to complete discovery in three months?

Plaintiff's Counsel: Respectfully, Your Honor, even though this is a single-plaintiff case, it involves allegations of race, sex, and religious discrimination as well as retaliation. And although my client only worked at the Defendant's place of business for six weeks, during that time, she estimates that she sent and received over 20,000 emails and hundreds of instant messages and other correspondence that we must pore over carefully. She also worked with 36 other employees we may want to depose and worked with over 30 clients. In addition to the scope of discovery, I would also like to note that I am a solo practitioner with only one paralegal and a busy caseload, including three trials set for this summer. Ms. Reyes is one member of an eight-person team exclusively devoted to this case and backed by the resources of a large law firm. I have far more limited resources and may need more time to serve my client in the way that she deserves. As for the reinstatement issue, it is my understanding that Defendant has already hired a temp to replace my client and that three other employees handled the same job duties as my client. I see no reason why her workload could not be allocated among them or completed by the temp during the pendency of the litigation. Although that may not be ideal for Defendant, it certainly does not warrant expedited discovery.

Judge: Is this true Ms. Reyes? Is a temp currently handling Plaintiff's former job duties?

Defense Counsel: Yes, Your Honor, but a temp lacks the expertise that a full-time hire would bring.

Judge: In any event, Ms. Reyes, I agree with Ms. Thompson that these circumstances don't warrant such an expedited schedule. So let's meet in the middle. Ms. Thompson, will four months be sufficient?

Plaintiff's Counsel: Yes, Your Honor. Thank you.

Judge: Ms. Reyes?

Defense Counsel: Yes, Your Honor.

Judge: So discovery will close on July 30. And motions for summary judgment will be due on September 15. Does that work for everyone?

Plaintiff's Counsel: Yes, Your Honor. Thank you.

Defense Counsel: Yes, Your Honor. That works for Defendant.

Judge: Is there any other business to attend to during this conference?

Plaintiff's Counsel: None from us, Your Honor.

Defense Counsel: No, Your Honor.

Judge: Ok, well thanks to both of you. Have a good afternoon. This concludes our conference.

Plaintiff's Counsel: Thank you, Your Honor. Goodbye.

Defense Counsel: Thank you, Your Honor. Goodbye.

D. SUPPLEMENTAL RESOURCE

1. MARY L. DUNNEWOLD, BETH A. HONETSCHLAGER, & BRENDA L. TOFTE, JUDICIAL CLERKSHIPS: A PRACTICAL GUIDE (2010).

Note

----

[1]   The author wishes to thank Karon Fowler for her contributions to this chapter.

CHAPTER 15

DRAFTING 11-DAYS AND PFRS

■ ■ ■

In some appellate courts, when an appellate panel is ready to issue a precedential opinion, the panel circulates the finalized opinion as well as any corresponding dissent and/or concurrence to the entire court for review. The other judges on the court will have a set number of days to review the opinion before it issues; the issuance date is known as the "drop date." The name of the document—*11-day*—derives from the number of days typically allotted for such review, but the name and number of days may vary from one court to another.

A. DRAFTING AN 11-DAY

An *11-Day* is a short one to two page single-spaced memo, which assesses an unissued opinion. The purpose of an 11-Day is to alert the author(s) if the opinion is inconsistent with controlling precedent, could have serious adverse implications on the body of law, or is otherwise erroneous or ill-advised in whole or in part. For instance, an 11-Day would notify the author(s) if the opinion overlooks a key fact of law or misunderstands controlling precedent. The 11-Day review process aims to prevent error, reversal, and embarrassment not only for the panel but for the entire court. It also provides each judge and reviewing law clerk with an opportunity to provide meaningful feedback to the drafters, which may strengthen the opinion.

What are the audience and tone of the 11-Day?

Your judge is typically the exclusive audience for the 11-Day. Use a deferential and respectful tone because you are evaluating another judge's opinion.

Is an 11-Day confidential?

Yes. An 11-Day is highly confidential because it pertains to an *unissued* opinion; in some instances, the panel will hold the opinion, rescind it, or heavily revise it. Without the cloak of confidentiality, the panel would likely be less inclined to circulate a draft for feedback from the other judges on the court. Yet this review process only refines and enriches judicial opinions.

Significantly, the confidentiality surrounding 11-Day review is a lifetime obligation. As such, include a boldfaced, capitalized "Confidential" header on each page of the 11-Day. Even after your clerkship concludes, you may not discuss the content of 11-Days that you prepared during your clerkship, such as divulging that an issued opinion had been revised as a result of an 11-Day review.

What are the components of an 11-Day?

The format and content of an 11-Day vary by Chambers, so confer with your supervising clerk before you begin drafting and ask to see a representative sample 11-Day prepared in Chambers. Typically, however, an 11-Day will include the following: (1) a salutation; (2) opinion with case name and docket number; (3) nature of the case; (4) panel members (often designed with initials only); (5) relevant procedural posture and holding; (6) recommendation; (7) drop date; (8) background; (9) issue(s); (10) applicable standard of review; (11) summary of the reasoning in the majority decision; (12) summary of the reasoning in the dissent and/or concurrence, as applicable; and (13) an explanation for the recommendation if the 11-Day advises the judge to take action.

How do I draft an 11-Day?

To draft an 11-Day, first review the draft opinion. Read it once through to understand the context and then slowly, actively read it a second time. As you do so, review each cited case and confirm that it has positive treatment. Typically, you will not have the briefing or Record available during the 11-Day review so you need not verify Record citations. However, you can and should pull cited cases to confirm that they have been cited, quoted, and used correctly. You should also note factual inconsistencies within the opinion. Source check and cite check. This means that you must ensure that each sentence is well supported by the legal cite *and* that the cite is properly formatted. Be certain that the language is lifted from the majority opinion; it should not be taken from a dissent, concurrence, or dicta unless noted.

You are not just checking for typographical or grammatical errors; the scope of your review is much broader and more significant. It encompasses substance and accuracy as well. Take this task seriously and afford it the time, care, and thoughtfulness it deserves. Nor are you simply briefing the case. Rather, you must determine whether the opinion is well-reasoned and consistent with precedent.

The 11-Day is typically written in the format of a short letter to your judge, not the drafter. In the first paragraph, identify the case and docket number, the general nature of the case, and the members of the panel, sometimes simply with their initials. It is common practice to bold the name or initials of the opinion author and to designate who authored a dissent and/or concurrence as applicable. In the same or subsequent sentence, briefly explain the relevant procedural posture, holding, and disposition. Finally, include your recommendation, usually in boldfaced type, and briefly explain the reasoning underlying it. If you opt not to include the specific reasoning, include a clause such as, "For the reasons below" before stating your recommendation.

Next, include the drop date of the opinion in boldfaced font. Then include the issue(s) discussed in the opinion. You need not frame them in the same way that the opinion does. State them as succinctly, clearly, accurately, and precisely as possible. Place them in numbered or bullet-pointed format. List them in the order in which you will discuss them in the summary or reasoning section.

Then include any relevant background information. Do not include citations to the Record or Appendix since those materials are typically not available to you or your judge during the review process. If necessary, you may be able to request them from the drafter. Generally, however, the background section will be extremely succinct and limited to no more than one to two paragraphs although rare exceptions may exist.[1]

Next, include the applicable standard(s) of review. Review the case law cited carefully to verify that the standard applied is proper. Summarize the key reasoning in the opinion. Avoid legal cites unless necessary. For example, if the opinion involves statutory interpretation, then the 11-Day will likely quote the relevant statutory language and corresponding cite. However, limit the number of other cases cited. Be extremely concise and precise. Indeed, your reasoning section should usually be no longer than three to five paragraphs absent exceptional circumstances, such as a very complex case with many issues on appeal. Include a separate summary of the reasoning section for a dissent or concurrence as applicable. Indicate authorship of each. Follow the same general drafting guidelines explained above for dissents and concurrences.

Do not use the 11-Day to alert your judge to typographical, grammatical, spelling, citation, formatting, or stylistic errors in the draft opinion unless they create substantive errors that could warrant reversal or create confusion. Also note that the content and format of 11-Day Memos vary by judge so review an exemplary 11-Day from your Chambers before you draft.

What recommendations may an 11-Day suggest?

Among other things, an 11-Day may recommend that your judge do one of the following: (1) take no action; (2) place a hold on the opinion such that it cannot issue at this time; (3) call for an en banc poll so that the entire court can hear and resolve the case; or (4) email substantive suggestions or concerns to the panel perhaps suggesting revisions to the language. Because judges and their law clerks take such tremendous care in producing well-written and well-researched opinions, the most common recommendation is that the judge take no action. For this reason, no lengthy explanation is necessary if you simply recommend that the judge do nothing. However, if you do not, then do include a separate section explaining the basis for your recommendation. Do not recommend that the judge take action simply because you disagree with the holding; to the contrary, only suggest that your judge take action if the opinion contravenes clear precedent, would have serious, adverse ramifications, or is otherwise erroneous.

How do I alert the opinion's author of typographical, grammatical, spelling, citation, or stylistic errors?

As noted above, do not alert your judge of purely typographical, grammatical, spelling, citation, or stylistic errors. Instead, send those directly to the clerk who circulated the 11-Day for review. The initials of the law clerk who assisted in drafting the opinion will typically be included on the first page of the opinion so that you know to whom to direct your suggested revisions. Save the electronic version of the unissued opinion as a new document. Title it with the case name and your initials. Use track changes to make comments and correct typographical, spelling, grammatical, and citation errors. Except in rare circumstances, do not suggest purely stylistic changes unless doing so will clarify or enhance the opinion. In some Chambers, the judge will not require you to provide such suggested edits for his or her review prior to submitting them to the law clerk serving the opinion's author. However, confirm this with your judge or fellow clerks at the outset of your clerkship. Provide your comments in the most constructive and polite way possible. Remember the scope of your review and do not be excessive. Your job is not to rewrite the opinion, only to point out blatant errors. In your email to the clerk, always make clear that such revisions are merely suggestive, not required, and that you hope they are helpful.

What are the hallmarks of an effective 11-Day?

Accuracy, brevity, and precision are essential to drafting an effective 11-Day. The 11-Day must also be thoughtful and thorough, considering how the holding fits within the existing body of law and its potential ramifications for the future.

When do I submit my 11-Day to my judge?

Ideally you will submit the 11-Day to your judge *at least* two to three days before the drop date, depending on the complexity of the case and your recommendation. Submit the 11-Day earlier if you recommend that your judge take action to provide him or her with sufficient time to do so. Take into account your judge's personal and professional commitments, so that your judge has ample time for review and sufficient time to take appropriate measures before the drop date. On or after the drop date, your judge will likely be unable to place a hold on the opinion or take any other action; thus, an untimely recommendation is effectively meaningless.

How do I submit an 11-Day to my judge?

Because preferences vary by Chambers, confer with your judge to determine whether he or she prefers to receive the 11-Day via hard copy, email, or both. If you submit your 11-Day via email, include a subject line in your email indicating that it is the 11-Day for the particular case; include the case name, docket number, and drop date in the subject line. In the body of the email, include the case name and docket number as well as a list of the attached documents in the order in which they are attached. Attach the unissued opinion, the 11-Day, and any electronically highlighted version of the key cases or documents that the judge should review along with the draft opinion. Make sure that those attachments are electronically highlighted and have clear names that always include a description of the document or the case name, not just a meaningless reporter cite.

Here is a sample submission email.

Subject Line: 11-Day for *Lycans v. Asbury*, 04–JR–2016; **DD:** 12.10.17

Judge,

I hope you are doing well. Attached herein for your review is my 11-Day Memo for the unissued opinion in *Lycans v. Asbury*, 04–JR–2016, and a copy of the opinion. The drop date of the opinion is **December 7, 2017**. I recommend that you **take no action**. Please let me know if you have any questions or concerns.

Best,

Violet

Here is a sample 11-day based on a fictional case.

CONFIDENTIAL

Judge Hoover,

The opinion attached herein for 11-Day Review (*ABC v. 123*, No. 2017–1234) involves whether the CFC properly allowed ABC to amend its complaint and transfer its infringement claim against 123 to the U.S. District Court for the Eastern District of Virginia. The panel (DJ, MR, and **RC**) reversed the trial court's decision to amend ABC's complaint and transfer the amended complaint to the district court. The panel remanded the case for further proceedings consistent with this opinion. For the reasons explained below, I recommend that you **take no action**.

DD: July 20, 2017

Background: This case has a long and complicated procedural history, but only the most relevant events are recited herein. In *ABC II*, the panel majority in a *per curiam* opinion reversed the trial court's

---

ruling that ABC could allege patent infringement as a Fifth Amendment Taking. On remand, the trial court permitted ABC to amend its complaint to add a claim against 123 for infringement under 35 U.S.C. § 271(g) and to transfer that claim to the Eastern District of Virginia pursuant to 28 U.S.C. § 1631. *ABC III*, 85 Fed. Cl. 323, 328 (2015). This interlocutory appeal followed.

Issues: Whether the trial court should have transferred the case and whether the court should have allowed the complaint to be amended to add 123 as a defendant?

Standard of Review: Under 28 U.S.C. § 1631, transfer is appropriate if (1) the transferor court lacks jurisdiction; (2) the action could have been brought in the transferee court at the time it was filed; and (3) the transfer is in the interest of justice. The court reviews the trial court's grant of a motion to transfer a claim for an abuse of discretion, but issues of law are reviewed *de novo*.

Panel Decision: The panel concluded that the change in law effected by *ABC II*, which limited the scope of § 1498(a) to direct infringement under § 271(a), is in error, and must be corrected to avoid a manifest injustice. The panel was permitted to overturn precedent because the second panel is reviewing the same case as the earlier panel; thus, law of the case doctrine governs. A court has the power to revisit prior decisions of its own. The *ABC II* panel's limitation of § 1498(a) to infringement under § 271(a) is inconsistent with the statute's plain language. The panel found that its decision erroneously relied on dicta and caused 19 U.S.C. § 1337(I) to become ineffective. The panel also found that *ABC II* negated Congress's clear intent to protect products resulting from a patented process, wherever practiced, when it rendered § 1337(I) ineffective, thereby limiting the remedies available in situations similar to ABC's. Because the decision is well reasoned and consistent with controlling precedent, I recommend that you **take no action.**

Best,

Janet

B. DRAFTING A PFR

After a federal appellate court issues an opinion, the parties typically have "14 days after entry of judgment" to petition the court for review by filing a "petition for review" ("PFR"); exceptions exist such as when the United States is a party to a civil action.[2] Parties may request panel review and/or en banc review; a party may not exclusively request en banc review.[3] An en banc decision can overturn an appellate panel decision. For an interesting example of an en banc decision, see *Cloer v. Secretary of Health and Human Services*, 675 F.3d 1358 (Fed. Cir. 2012).

A petition for review by the panel is granted only when the panel overlooked or erred regarding an important fact or misapprehended the law.[4] A petition for en banc review is only granted when the holding is inconsistent with precedent or poses a very important question to which all members of the court should have the opportunity to contribute.[5] As such, PFRs are rarely granted.

Parties seeking redress need not file a petition for review. Instead, they may directly file a petition for certiorari with the Supreme Court of the United States, but such petitions are also rarely granted.

What are the audience and tone of a PFR?

Your judge is typically the exclusive audience for the PFR, and its tone should be respectful and deferential.

Is a PFR confidential?

Yes. A PFR is highly confidential, and its contents must remain so for your lifetime. As such, include a boldfaced, capitalized "Confidential" header on each page of a PFR.

What are the components of a PFR?

The format and content of a PFR may vary by Chambers. Thus, at the outset of your clerkship, confer with your supervising clerk before you begin drafting and ask to see a representative sample PFR. Like the 11-Day, a PFR typically contains the following: (1) a salutation; (2) case name and docket number; (3) the nature of the case; (4) the panel members; (5) the procedural posture and holding; (6) your recommendation; (7) drop date; (8) background; (9) issue(s); (10) the applicable standard of review; (11) summary of the reasoning in the majority decision; (12) summary of the reasoning in the dissent and/or concurrence, as applicable; and (13) an explanation for the recommendation.

How do I draft a PFR?

The process of drafting a PFR is quite similar to that of drafting an 11-Day. To draft a PFR, review the opinion and the special briefing that parties file when seeking review. Read everything once through for context and then slowly, actively read the materials a second time. Verify the facts against any Appendix or Record provided. Review each case and confirm that it has positive treatment, is correctly quoted and cited, and is accurately characterized. Source check and cite check. This means that you must ensure that each sentence is well supported by the legal cite and that the cite is properly formatted. As with the 11-Day, you are not just checking for typographical or citation errors; the scope of your review encompasses substance and accuracy as well. Take this task seriously and afford it the significant time, care, and thoughtfulness it warrants.

Like an 11-Day, a PFR is typically written in the format of a short letter to your judge. Follow the same general method as with an 11-Day. In the first paragraph, identify the case and docket number, the general nature of the case, and the members of the panel, sometimes simply with their initials. It is common practice to bold the name or initials of the opinion author and to designate who authored a dissent and/or concurrence as applicable. In the same or subsequent sentence, briefly explain the relevant procedural posture, holding, and disposition. Finally, include your recommendation, usually in boldfaced type, and briefly explain its reasoning. If you opt not to include the specific reasoning, include a clause such as, "For the reasons below" in the clause preceding your recommendation.

Next, include the deadline for the PFR in boldfaced font. Then include the issue(s) discussed in the opinion. You need not frame them in the same manner that the opinion does. State them as succinctly, clearly, accurately, and precisely as possible. Place them in numbered or bullet-pointed format. List them in the order you will discuss them in the reasoning section.

Then include any relevant background information. Typically, you need not include citations to the Record or Appendix if provided. This Background should be extremely succinct and limited to no more than one to two paragraphs although rare exceptions may exist.

Next, include the standard(s) of review. Review the case law cited carefully to verify that this standard is proper. Summarize the parties' arguments. Provide clear reasons in support of your recommendation. Include legal cites as necessary. Be concise and precise. Typically, a PFR is lengthier and more thorough than an 11-Day. Clearly explain in detail the basis for your recommendation.

What may a PFR recommend?

If your judge was *not* a member of the original panel, the PFR will only recommend that the judge vote to grant or to deny *en banc* review. Only the panel members determine whether to grant or deny *panel* review, and it is rarely granted. Do not recommend that the judge vote to grant review simply because you disagree with the holding; to the contrary, only suggest that review be granted if the opinion contravenes precedent or poses an exceptionally important question of law that the court should address en banc, or as an entire court.

What are the hallmarks of an effective PFR?

Like the 11-Day, accuracy, brevity, clarity, and precision are essential to drafting an effective PFR. It must be thoughtful and thorough, considering whether the decision is inconsistent with the existing body of law or is best addressed en banc.

When do I submit a PFR to my judge?

Ideally you will submit the PFR to your judge at least four days before the deadline, depending on the complexity of the case. Also take into account your judge's existing personal and professional commitments, so that he or she has sufficient time to review your PFR and to take any other appropriate measures.

How do I submit a PFR to my judge?

Confer with your judge at the outset of your clerkship to determine the manner in which he or she prefers to receive a PFR. If you submit a PFR via email, include a subject line in your email indicating that it is the PFR for the particular case. The subject line should note the case name, docket number, and the deadline. In the body of the email, include the case name and docket number as well as a list of the attached documents in the order in which they are attached. Attach the PFR and any electronically highlighted version of the key cases or documents that the judge should review along with it. Make sure that those attachments are electronically highlighted and have clear names that always include a description of the document or the case name, not just a reporter cite. Provide your judge with the hard copy of the PFR briefing as soon as you submit the PFR.

Here is a sample submission email for a PFR.

Subject Line: PFR for *Heath v. Wyatt*, 06–DP–2016; **Vote Due:** 4.12.17

Judge,

    I hope you are doing well. Attached herein for your review is my PFR for *Heath v. Wyatt*, 06–DP–2016. The deadline for the vote is **April 12, 2017**. Because the holding does not contravene precedent or pose an exceptionally important question of law, I recommend that you vote to **deny en banc review**. Please let me know if you have any questions or concerns.

Best,

Violet

Below is a non-exhaustive checklist that will assist you in drafting thoughtful and thorough 11-Days and PFRs.

11-Day or PFR Checklist

*The purpose of this checklist is to generally evaluate the effectiveness of your 11-Day or PFR. There is no single right way to draft an effective 11-Day or PFR. There are many different formats and organizations that are effective. This checklist provides a **non-exhaustive** list of considerations that promote effective drafting. More important factors are identified earlier in each subsection of the list. Edit with purpose, first for formatting, then for citation, etc. Furthermore, this checklist may not be identical to the considerations that your judge deems most important. Thus confer with your judge to determine which factors matter most to him or her.*

Formatting

1. Does the 11-Day (or PFR) have all required sections in the correct order? ☐

2. Does the 11-Day (or PFR) use the specified format, including font size and type? ☐

3. Does the 11-Day (or PFR) only use ONE space after each period? ☐

4. Are the pages numbered appropriately, in the bottom center margin, and in the proper font? ☐

5. Does the 11-Day (or PFR) use proper margins on all sides? ☐

6. Has the drafter eliminated unnecessary "white space" between sections of the brief and between paragraphs? ☐

7. Does the 11-Day (or PFR) avoid orphaned headings? ☐

Citation

1. Does the 11-Day (or PFR) use proper citation format? ☐

2. Does the 11-Day (or PFR) use *Id.* as appropriate, including italicizing the period? ☐

3. Does the 11-Day (or PFR) use proper introductory signals? ☐

4. Does the 11-Day (or PFR) include pincites as required? ☐

5. Does the 11-Day (or PFR) use the proper citation format for short cites? ☐

6. Does the 11-Day (or PFR) use proper italicization? ☐

7. Does the 11-Day (or PFR) use proper abbreviation(s) in case names? ☐

8. Does the 11-Day (or PFR) place the cases in the proper order? ☐

9. Has the 11-Day (or PFR) included the subsequent history of cases in the first full cite when required to do so? ☐

Caption

1. Is the Caption properly formatted? ☐

2. Does the Caption include all components? ☐

3. Does the Caption avoid problems with grammar, punctuation, spelling, and capitalization? ☐

Introduction

1. Does the Introduction include an effective roadmap sentence, which states the case at issue? ☐

2. Are the parties properly designated? ☐ Is the designation used consistently? ☐

3. Is the Introduction well organized? Does it flow well? ☐

4. Is the Introduction clear and well written? ☐

5. Is the Introduction objective and succinct? ☐

6. Is the Introduction easy to read and understand? ☐

7. Is the language precise and concise? ☐

8. Does it succinctly and objectively explain the hub issue(s) organized in the way the 11-Day (or PFR) will discuss them? ☐

9. Are key facts and procedural history included as necessary to briefly describe the basic nature of the case? ☐

10. Does the Introduction briefly summarize the core reason(s) for the recommendation or state "For the reasons explained herein?" ☐

11. Does the Introduction clearly state the disposition? ☐

12. Does the Introduction clearly state the recommendation in boldfaced font? ☐

13. Is the recommendation well supported? ☐

14. Does the Introduction include proper word choice and sophisticated language? ☐

15. Does the Introduction use active and passive voice appropriately? *(Avoid passive voice unless necessary.)* ☐

16. Does the Introduction avoid problems with grammar, punctuation, spelling, and capitalization? ☐

17. Does the Introduction omit quotations and footnotes? ☐

Background (Facts and Procedural History)

1. Are all relevant facts and procedural history included? Has irrelevant information been removed? ☐

2. Are party designations used consistently? ☐

3. Is the Background well organized? ☐ Does it flow well? ☐

4. Is the Background clear and well written? ☐

5. Is the Background objective and thorough? ☐

6. Is the Background easy to read and understand? ☐ Does it avoid overly long paragraphs? ☐

7. Is the language precise and concise? ☐

8. Does the Background omit Argument and legal conclusions? ☐

9. Does the Background use effective topic sentences? ☐

10. Does the Background include proper word choice and use language well? ☐ Does the Background use plain language? ☐

11. Does the Background use active and passive voice appropriately? *(Avoid passive voice unless necessary.)* ☐

12. Does the Background avoid problems with grammar, punctuation, spelling, and capitalization? ☐

13. Are quotations used sparingly but effectively, if at all? ☐ Are they necessary? ☐ Are they formatted correctly? ☐

Issue(s) (if included)

1. Does the 11-Day or PFR accurately explain the issue(s)? ☐

2. Is each issue concise, clear, readable, and objective? ☐

3. Does each issue include proper and precise word choice? ☐

4. Does each issue avoid any spelling, grammar, punctuation, or typographical errors? ☐

5.   Are the issues organized in the same order that the 11-Day (or PFR) will discuss them? ☐

Standard of Review

1.   Does the 11-Day (or PFR) elucidate the proper standard of review? ☐

Discussion/Reasoning/Summary of Reasoning

1.   *Overall effectiveness:* Is the Discussion easy to understand and objective? ☐

2.   *Legal Landscape:* Does the Discussion begin with an overview of the legal landscape, such as the relevant constitutional or statutory provision or seminal case? ☐ Does it clearly, precisely, objectively, and accurately state and explain the relevant overarching law? ☐

3.   *Organization:* Is the Discussion clearly and logically organized? ☐ Does it discuss the issues in the same order that they appeared in the statement of issues? ☐

4.   *Analysis:* Does the Discussion present a sound, proper, and well-developed analysis of each issue and sub-issue that does not make logical leaps? ☐ Are any key legal or factual issues missing? ☐

5.   *Tone:* Is the Discussion objective and appropriately sophisticated? ☐

6.   *Effective application of law to facts:* Does the Discussion effectively apply the law to the facts, adequately developing each point? ☐

7.   *Transitions:* Does the 11-Day (or PFR) use effective transitions between the various points of the Discussion? ☐

8.   *Paragraphs:* Does the 11-Day (or PFR) use strong topic sentences and are paragraphs organized logically? ☐

9.   *Grammar & style:* Does the Discussion avoid problems with grammar, punctuation, spelling, pronouns, and capitalization? ☐ Does the Discussion use active and passive voice appropriately? (*Active voice should be used unless passive voice is necessary or effective.*) ☐

10.   *Quotations:* Are quotations used effectively, if at all? ☐ Are they properly formatted? ☐

11.   *Footnotes:* Are footnotes used sparingly, if at all? ☐ Are they necessary? Are they properly formatted? ☐

12. ***Word Choice:*** Does the Discussion include proper word choice, including precise language? ☐ Does the Discussion use plain language? ☐

13. ***Brevity:*** Is the Discussion concise? ☐

Recommendation

1. Is the Recommendation clear, accurate, and well supported? ☐

2. Is it properly formatted? ☐

3. Does it avoid problems with grammar, punctuation, spelling, and capitalization? ☐

Overall Effectiveness

1. Taken as a whole, is the 11-Day (or PFR) well researched? ☐

2. Taken as a whole, is the 11-Day (or PFR) well written? ☐

3. Taken as a whole, is the 11-Day (or PFR) thoughtful? ☐

4. Taken as a whole, is the 11-Day (or PFR) clear, coherent, and easy to understand? ☐

5. Taken as a whole, is the 11-Day (or PFR) objective? ☐

6. Taken as a whole, is the 11-Day (or PFR) accurate and thorough? ☐

7. Taken as a whole, is the 11-Day (or PFR) well organized? ☐

8. Taken as a whole, is the 11-Day (or PFR) effective? ☐

9. Taken as a whole, is the 11-Day (or PFR) precise and concise? ☐

10. Taken as a whole, is the 11-Day (or PFR) well edited, properly formatted, professional, and polished? ☐

C. SUPPLEMENTAL RESOURCES

1. JOSEPH LEMON, FEDERAL APPELLATE COURT LAW CLERK HANDBOOK (2007).

2. JENNIFER L. SHEPPARD, IN CHAMBERS: A GUIDE FOR JUDICIAL CLERKS AND EXTERNS (2012).

Notes

---

[1]   The term *background* is generally used because appellate courts do not make findings of fact.

[2]   FED. R. APP. P. 40(a)(1). However, in a civil case "the petition may be filed by any party within 45 days after entry of judgment if one of the parties is: the United States; a United States agency; a United States officer or employee sued in an official capacity; or a current or former United States officer or employee sued in an individual capacity for an act or omission occurring in connection with duties performed on the United States' behalf—including all instances in which the United States represents that person when the court of appeals' judgment is entered or files that petition for that person." *Id.* For information on this process at state courts, consult the relevant state rules of appellate practice and procedure.

[3]   FED. R. APP. P. 35(a).

[4]   FED. R. APP. P. 40(a)(2).

[5]   FED. R. APP. P. 35(a).

CHAPTER 16

DRAFTING BENCH MEMORANDA

■ ■ ■

As a law clerk, it is your responsibility to assist your judge in thoroughly preparing for hearings and oral argument. An effective bench memorandum is usually the primary way to accomplish this. A *bench memorandum* is a written analysis that synthesizes all of the briefing, facts, and relevant case law, which relate to the issue(s) that will be discussed at the oral argument or hearing, into one comprehensive, concise document.

Being concise and comprehensive in your bench memo is incredibly important because your judge has a busy docket of *all* the cases assigned to Chambers. The size and complexity of those cases will vary. By contrast, you must become a subject matter expert in only a subset of those cases, which is far more manageable. Remember this when drafting your bench memo and ensure that it only includes relevant information. As Professor Amanda B. Hurst, a former law clerk at the United States Court of Appeals for the Eighth Circuit, recounts:

> Somehow ... I got the idea that the more I could write—the better. The more cases I could cite, the more pages I could fill, the bigger words I could use—all meant that I was a good legal researcher and writer. This came to a crashing halt when [my judge] called me in one day to tell me that ... he couldn't read another of my long bench memos. It was like a light bulb went off. ... I was an expert on a few cases per Court Week,[1] but the judge needed to be an expert on all of the cases for Court Week. So the best thing I could do for him was to answer all the hard questions ... [in] as readable and brief a document as I could. ... In other words, I need to ... rid my legal writing of everything but the necessary.

Because a law clerk focuses on a smaller number of cases, he or she should know each case inside and out. Carefully read all of the briefing, including any amicus briefs. Thoroughly peruse the Record and conduct independent research as necessary and permissible. Pinpoint any issues that the parties may have missed that should be raised *sua sponte*. Then synthesize all of this important information into your bench memo. Put differently, an effective bench memo should be a "one-stop shop" for everything your judge needs or wants to know about the case for the upcoming oral argument or hearing.

Before discussing the general format and content of bench memoranda, it is important to note that not all judges require them. Nor do all cases warrant one. Moreover, the format and content of a bench memo may vary significantly by Chambers, court, and the nature of the matter. Thus, it is important to speak with your judge and/or his or her existing clerks at the outset of your clerkship to determine whether and when your judge prefers a bench memo, what it should include, etc. As a general matter, the use of bench memoranda appears to be more prevalent in appellate courts than in trial courts, but many trial judges may still require some sort of written synthesis akin to a bench memo before hearings and oral argument. In appellate courts, law clerks typically draft a bench memo for nearly every argued case.

While non-exhaustive, the advice contained in this chapter generally applies with equal force to bench memoranda drafted for any judge whether state or federal, trial or appellate. However, as noted above, your judge may require additional information or a unique format not discussed herein. Therefore, it is important that you consult your judge or supervising clerk *before* drafting your first bench memo and examine a representative sample of an effective bench memo.

A. PRE-DRAFTING AND OTHER PRELIMINARY MATTERS

What is a bench memo?

As noted above, a bench memo is a comprehensive document that, at a minimum, synthesizes the following: (1) all briefing relevant to the oral argument or hearing, including amicus briefs; (2) determinative facts derived from the Record, Appendix, and/or Joint Appendix (hereinafter collectively referred to as the "Appendix"); and (3) the relevant law, including cases, statutes, and regulations.

In many ways, a bench memo is a hybrid of the purely objective memoranda and purely persuasive briefs that you drafted in law school. Like an objective memo, a bench memo aims to inform your judge about a factual or legal issue that may be relatively unfamiliar, such as a complex issue of first impression or a new technology in a patent case. In this regard, follow the guidelines on objective writing that you likely learned in your first semester of law school. Provide the judge with the legal landscape and all of the facts, without spinning them in one party's favor even if you agree with that party. You must convey both sides of the story objectively, alerting the judge to discrepancies involving material facts. After all, as a representative of the judiciary, you are not a party advocate. Maintain impartiality. On the other hand, a bench memo does require you to assess both parties' arguments, facts, and supporting law and explain which argument(s) should prevail. In this regard, some of the principles that you learned in persuasive advocacy may come into play as you determine which argument(s) are more persuasive and why.[2]

Who is the audience of a bench memo?

A bench memo is typically written for your judge's eyes only, but in some Chambers, your judge may permit (or even require) you to share your memo with a co-clerk for collaborative peer review or discussion. At some circuit courts, your judge may even permit you to discuss the contents of your bench memo with law clerks serving the other judges on the panel. However, be sure to confer with your judge at the outset of your clerkship to clarify with whom you may share your bench memo, if anyone.

Tailor your bench memo to its audience. Given that your audience is usually only your judge, write your bench memo with him or her specifically in mind. For example, if you know that your judge is an expert on sexual harassment law, there is likely no need to provide information in your analysis regarding fundamental sexual harassment law principles of which the judge is already aware. Nor will you need to define basic terminology, such as "adverse employment action." Including such information wastes the reader's time as well as your time in the drafting process. Likewise, you will not need to explain in great detail why *de novo* review is proper when examining the grant of a motion for summary judgment or what *de novo* means as you might when writing a memo to a non-lawyer client or drafting a decision for a *pro se* litigant. On the other hand, if you know that your judge is unfamiliar with the law or technology at issue in the case, take that into account. Provide clear explanations and perhaps even diagrams elucidating how the technology works and include explanatory footnotes defining key technical terms with which your judge may be unfamiliar. Take special care in discussing the legal landscape when drafting a bench memo that pertains to an issue of first impression since no controlling, on-point authority exists. In conclusion, know your audience and match the sophistication and depth of your language to the sophistication and knowledge level of your reader. Put differently, an effective bench memo is a custom fit.

What is the tone of a bench memo?

Given the audience and purpose of your bench memo, its tone should be sophisticated, formal, deferential, and respectful. Your judge decides the case, not you. You play an important supporting role, but you are by no means the ultimate decision-maker. Your judge will decide which questions to ask. Your judge will cast the straw vote. He or she is not bound to follow your recommendation(s). And your judge, not you, authors the opinion. He or she may disagree with your reasoning and reject your conclusion(s). As a law clerk, you merely play a temporary, supporting role, and while that role is critical, you never decide cases or write opinions. Understanding your role is essential to performing well in your clerkship and maintaining a proper tone in your bench memoranda.

Are bench memos confidential?

Typically, yes. A bench memo is highly confidential and as a general rule, cannot be shared outside Chambers absent your judge's express permission. A bench memo is confidential because it contains your legal analysis and suggestions regarding how to resolve each issue. Your judge is obviously not bound to follow your reasoning, so your bench memo could differ markedly from the final issued opinion in the case. For this reason, you must confer with your judge at the outset of your clerkship or drafting process to determine with whom you may share your bench memo. Until then, assume the bench memo and its content are exclusively for your judge.

In appellate courts, a bench memo is also highly confidential because the judges assigned to hear each argued case may not be posted until the day of oral argument; thus, loss of a bench memo (or email or thumb drive containing it) would indicate that your judge is assigned to the case, provide insight into the judge's decision-making process, and perhaps foreshadow how he or she might rule. Such a breach of confidentiality could have devastating implications. Thus, take special care to preserve the confidentiality of a bench memo. For related reasons, you likely will be unable to use a bench memo as a writing sample for future employment unless it is heavily redacted, and you obtain our judge's express permission.

Because a bench memo is confidential, include a boldfaced, capitalized "Confidential" header on each page of the bench memo and be careful never to take it outside Chambers to work on at home or even in other parts of the courthouse. Absent your judge's permission, do not email copies of the bench memo to yourself, especially to your personal email, or save a copy onto a thumb drive for removal from Chambers.

Why do some cases have two sets of briefs? Which set do I use when drafting my bench memo?

In some cases, parties will file two sets of briefs—one that is marked confidential and one that is marked non-confidential. Confidential briefs require special consideration because they contain highly confidential information and/or have been filed under seal. Such briefs are not posted on the court's website where non-confidential briefs might be downloaded. Both sets of confidential and non-confidential briefing submitted are identical in substance except that the confidential information is specially highlighted or designated in the confidential version, and that same information is redacted in the non-confidential (*i.e.*, public) version. Therefore, you must work with the confidential set of briefs delivered to your Chambers when drafting your bench memo since the confidential information found exclusively in the confidential set of briefs may ultimately prove critical to the decision.

Parties typically denote confidential information with boldfaced type and/or brackets. When drafting your bench memo, be sure to also clearly denote any confidential information you have included in bold-faced type and surround it with double brackets. Double brackets are particularly useful because they are more easily distinguishable from single brackets, which reflect alteration of a quote, and make confidential material easier to find electronically.[3] Include a footnote at the outset of the bench memo explaining that it contains confidential information and how you have denoted that information. Emphasize this to your judge so that he or she does not inadvertently breach confidentiality by asking a question at oral argument or a hearing that divulges confidential information or by including such information in the judicial opinion resolving the case. The latter error is especially likely to happen absent the precautions mentioned above since bench memoranda are often converted into judicial opinions.

When is it necessary to draft a bench memo?

As mentioned above, not every case requires a bench memo. Although a bench memo is typically necessary when a relatively complicated case will be argued, bench memoranda are generally not required for submitted cases that will be decided without oral argument. For those cases, you will likely synthesize the briefing, law, and facts directly into a short, unpublished, draft opinion that will be issued *per curiam* on the same day that the case would have been argued.

Nor do most judges require a bench memo for argued cases that are ultimately resolved by a per curiam affirmance without an opinion ("PCA"). For example, at the United States Court of Appeals for the Federal Circuit, Rule 36 enables a panel to affirm a lower court without issuing a full opinion, which explains the court's reasoning. As such, a Rule 36 affirmance lacks precedential authority. Rule 36 is only appropriate where: (1) "the judgment, decision, or order of the trial court appealed from is based on findings that are not clearly erroneous"; (2) "the evidence supporting the jury's verdict is sufficient"; (3) "the record supports summary judgment, directed verdict, or judgment on the pleadings"; (4) "the decision of an administrative agency warrants affirmance under the standard of review in the statute authorizing the petition for review"; or (5) "a judgment or decision has been entered without an error of law."[4] Yet opinions, precedential or not, are often issued in matters that technically satisfy these requirements. Thus, it seems clear that PCAs are most often used when there is a very straightforward case that clearly warrants affirmance and does not justify the investment of judicial resources necessary to author an opinion. Cases ripe for PCA resolution sometimes arise because litigants may appeal as of right to the circuit court, which means that they can appeal whenever they disagree with the outcome of the lower court even if there are not strong *legal* grounds for an appeal. Thus, PCAs are often deployed to quickly dispense of such cases so that the judiciary can invest its time in resolving more complex cases or issues of first impression. Unsurprisingly, PCAs are difficult to reverse because a court is highly unlikely to grant rehearing en banc. Nor is the U.S. Supreme Court likely to grant a petition for certiorari.

Ironically, PCAs are also occasionally used in very complex appellate cases for which the members of the panel simply cannot agree. For example, if each of the judges on a three-judge appellate panel would affirm but all for very different reasons, the panel may opt to simply issue a PCA rather than issue a fractured opinion that could be highly confusing yet still lack precedential power. In conclusion, PCAs are occasionally used in very simple and very difficult cases but are generally inappropriate for cases in between. Perhaps because they promote judicial efficiency, analogous rules permitting PCAs exist at many other federal and state courts as well.[5]

A bench memo may also be unnecessary if a case can be dispensed of due to a dispositive, threshold question. For example, a court must *sua sponte* dismiss a case for lack of jurisdiction even if the parties did not raise the issue below. If you receive a case over which the court no longer has jurisdiction, alert your judge immediately and determine whether a bench memo is no longer necessary since the case will be dismissed on purely jurisdictional grounds. In such cases, some judges prefer that your bench memo only address the dispositive threshold issue, while others expect you to address every issue in case fellow panelists disagree that the issue is dispositive.

Because some cases do not warrant a bench memo, it is critical as a preliminary matter that you review all of the briefing early to assess whether your case is appropriate for a PCA or if there is a single, threshold issue, such as jurisdiction, that is dispositive. Conduct this assessment as soon as possible after you are assigned the case. Do not waste time and judicial resources drafting a bench memo only to determine later that doing so was unnecessary. If you believe your case does not require a bench memo, immediately schedule a meeting with your judge to explain your reasoning. Be prepared to support your case with the briefing, key facts from the Appendix, and any relevant case law. Depending on your judge, this meeting may stand in place of a bench memo.

On the other hand, do not operate under a perhaps false assumption that no bench memo is necessary only to learn in the eleventh hour that your judge disagrees with your assessment and requires a full bench memo. The latter situation would place both you and your judge in a difficult, high-pressure situation, which you should avoid by taking the preemptive measures mentioned above.

How do I determine which style and format my judge prefers?

Individual preferences regarding the style and format of bench memoranda may vary. Some judges impose strict page limits, while others give law clerks more discretion. Before you draft your first bench memo, speak with your judge and co-clerks to get a sense of what your judge prefers. Ask your judge for an example of a strong bench memo. Discuss with your judge or co-clerks why that memo was strong and how it could be improved. With your first bench memo (or perhaps even your first few), find a mentor in Chambers who is a strong writer, analyst, and researcher. If permissible, ask that person to review your bench memo before you present it to the judge. As you become more experienced, this peer review may become unnecessary, but peer review is critically important, especially at the outset of your clerkship.

How should I manage my time when drafting a bench memo?

Time management is critical for effective bench memo drafting. When cases are assigned, promptly conduct a general assessment of each case by reviewing the briefing. Do "clerkship triage," ranking which cases will require the most time due to their size and level of complexity, which cases will require the least time, which cases have one threshold dispositive issue, which cases may be appropriate for a PCA, etc. Then plan your schedule accordingly, turning to the PCA or threshold dispositive issue cases first and preparing to meet with your judge regarding whether to draft bench memoranda for those cases.

Next turn to the most difficult cases. Typically each task takes longer than one assumes, so allow yourself ample time to digest the arguments and become familiar with the issues or technology. Set manageable internal deadlines but also work with your judicial assistant early in the drafting cycle to accommodate your judge's personal and professional schedule. For example, imagine that typically a law clerk would provide her judge a bench memo in a moderately complex takings case on February 25 for an upcoming March 2 oral argument. However, her judge will be vacationing February 25 through February 28. A considerate law clerk will get the bench memo to the judge by or before February 22, so that the judge has ample time to read it and request supplemental research before leaving town. While the judge is away, the law clerk can conduct any supplemental research. Put differently, a law clerk should have the foresight and thoughtfulness to plan ahead.

Unless your judge prefers otherwise, aim to provide your judge with a final bench memo at least one week before the oral argument or hearing. Allow extra time that week to conduct any supplemental research that your judge may require upon reading your bench memo. However, you can often avoid such research by simply anticipating your judge's follow-up questions and making your bench memo as clear and comprehensive as possible. Allow even more time for a particularly complex case, providing it to the judge eight to ten days before argument instead of just a week.

Do not make the mistake of assuming that your judge will only require as much time to review the bench memo as *you* would expect. Every reader is different, and some may require more or less time than you. You serve at the pleasure of your judge. In your supporting role, you should accommodate your judge's schedule, preferences, and needs, not your own.

After you draft a bench memo in an appellate matter, you may want to schedule a meeting to discuss the case with the law clerks serving the other judges on the panel. It is important to build in time for these clerk meetings as they could change the course or direction of your bench memo or prompt you to conduct additional research. Moreover, some judges require law clerks to include information from clerk meetings in the bench memo. Thus, be sure to work with your fellow law clerks early in the argument cycle to schedule such meetings. Allow yourself sufficient time to adequately prepare for those meetings and to incorporate information gained from them into your final bench memo before submitting it to your judge.

B. THE DRAFTING PROCESS

What are the components of a bench memo?

Although the components of a bench memo vary by court and by Chambers, a bench memo typically includes the following: (1) a caption; (2) an introduction; (3) a statement of the issue(s); (4) a list of key documents; (5) the relevant factual and procedural background; (6) an analysis with recommendations; (7) a concise summary of the issues and recommendations; and (8) a list of potential questions to ask at the oral argument or hearing. As will be discussed later, some judges also require additional information either on all cases or particular cases, such as the status of pending related matters, summaries of meetings with other law clerks about the matter, etc.

How do I start drafting a bench memo?

The first step in drafting a bench memo is simply to read all of the briefing to familiarize yourself with the issue(s). Use your judgment to discern whether there are any lurking issues that must be raised *sua sponte* or whether the case might be proper for a PCA.

Now go back and slowly, carefully read each section of each brief. Actively read, perhaps highlighting important points and taking notes. Perhaps create a skeleton bench memo with just headings and use your notes to fill in each component as you actively read. It may be especially helpful to read corresponding sections of each brief together. For example, you might read the issue statement in the appellant's brief and compare it to the issue statement in the appellee's brief to discern the real hub issue(s) in the case. Doing so is not always easy, as both parties may try to frame the issues in the most persuasive way possible, sometimes using smoke and mirrors to distract the court from the real hub issue.

Draft the bench memo one section at a time, continuously editing each section as you read the next. For example, you may take a first cut at drafting your issue section after reading the issue statements in the briefing, but then edit your issue section after reading the other sections in the briefing if doing so uncovers a hidden jurisdictional issue that neither party had raised. Editing is a continual process and eventually each section in your memo should speak to and coalesce with the other sections.

How do I format a bench memo?

Refer to a sample bench memo from your Chambers to determine which format your judge prefers.[6] Bench memoranda are typically single-spaced and often left or fully justified; turn on the hyphenation feature if you use full justification.[7] Unless otherwise instructed, use a proportional font, such as Times New Roman or Century Schoolbook, in 12-point and include page numbers on the bottom center of the page in the same font and size.[8] Use footnotes sparingly, if at all. Reserve them for brief explanatory comments or to define non-legal terms of art as explained in more detail below. Avoid endnotes. Footnotes should be 10-point and in the same font used in the main body unless otherwise instructed. Use only one space between sentences.[9] Italicize; avoid underlining.[10] Activate *kerning* to improve the spacing of letters on the page.[11] To do this, open your word processing software program. Then go to *Format, Font, Advanced,* and click *Kerning for Fonts*.[12] Select point size 8.[13] Include a bold-faced, capitalized "Confidential" header on each page. Bold and double bracket any confidential information. Include capitalized, boldfaced, and/or underlined headings for the Introduction, Issues, List of Key Documents, Background, Analysis, Summary of Issues and Recommendations, and List of Possible Questions. You may bullet point or number each issue or list. You may include sub-headings as appropriate in your Analysis section. Denote headings with Roman numerals and subheadings with capital letters. Avoid orphaned or widowed headings. Italicize case names and use in-text citation. Format all citations according to the latest edition of the Bluebook, using the rules applicable to legal documents rather than law review articles.

For ease and clarity, let's break down the drafting process section by section.

Caption

Start with the caption. Include the full case name as it will be announced at the oral argument or hearing. List the docket number, the attorneys, their law firms, and their professional contact information. In appellate courts, list the judges on the panel or whether the case will be heard *en banc*, which means that the court, as a whole, will render a decision rather than just a three-judge panel. Some judges prefer that you list the panelists' names in order of seniority, designating the senior or presiding judge first. The most senior judge will sit in the middle of the panel and preside over the oral argument unless the chief judge is a panelist in which case he or she will handle those duties. The most senior judge (or chief judge if he or she is a panelist) will also lead the straw vote on the case and will typically assign authorship of opinions, unless he or she is dissenting or concurring in the judgment. Also include the date, time, and courtroom location. As with most captions, use bold-faced type for the generic information like "Date" but do not bold the specific information.

Introduction

Some judges prefer inclusion of a brief Introduction, while others may not. If your judge expects you to include an Introduction, it will likely include the following components: (1) the nature of the matter; (2) a brief introduction of the parties; (3) a succinct overview of the key facts, procedural posture, and hub issue(s); (4) a concise summary of your core reasoning; and (5) your recommendation(s) regarding how to resolve the matter. Some judges will also ask you to flag a close case (*e.g.*, a difficult one that could go either way) in the Introduction so they can plan their preparation time accordingly.

The Introduction typically begins with "This is an appeal of" or "This case involves" so that you can explain the nature of the action before the court. Next, introduce the parties, providing any necessary factual context and using explanatory parentheticals to explain to the judge how you will refer to each party for the duration of the memo. Choose a designation that is clear and succinct and consistently use that designation to refer to the party for the remainder of the bench memo. Use of party names as designations is typically clearer and more helpful to the judge than using generic designations like "Appellant." For instance, if your litigant is ABC Corporation, you might designate the party as "ABC," which is clear, unique, probative, and succinct. Going forward, you will always refer to ABC Corporation as ABC, which will save space and add clarity (*e.g.*, ABC argues, ABC counters, etc.). As noted earlier, it is often helpful to provide at least some factual context when you introduce the parties. For example, if ABC Corporation is the employer at issue in the appeal, you might say something like: "Defendant-Appellant ABC Corporation ("ABC") is a large, Seattle-based telecommunications company, which terminated the employment of Plaintiff-Appellee Jane Doe ("Ms. Doe") in November 2013, due to her habitual tardiness."

After you introduce the parties (or sometimes in conjunction with that introduction as appropriate), you will provide a succinct overview of any key facts and procedural history. For a pure question of law or procedural issue, a recitation of key facts may be largely unnecessary. Likewise, for a fact-intensive inquiry, only very brief coverage of the most relevant procedural posture may be required. Use good judgment. For example, you might write:

> Ms. Doe now alleges that her termination violates the Americans with Disabilities Act of 1990 ("ADA") as amended because her tardiness was due to sleep apnea. It is undisputed that she failed to report that connection to ABC until after she had incurred three tardiness citations and received a notice of termination. The United States District Court for the District of Columbia ("District Court") granted Ms. Doe summary judgment, and ABC appealed.

When drafting the Introduction, the most helpful part of the briefing is usually the Summary of the Argument since the Introduction aims to summarize in very basic terms what the case involves.

Next, briefly pinpoint the hub issue(s) in the case. For example, you might state, "Thus, the issue on appeal is whether an employer may lawfully terminate an employee for tardiness that is an indirect result of a disability where the employer was not made aware of the link until after sanctioning the employee for tardiness and giving her notice of termination." Notice how the issue statement is concise yet still draws from the key facts, the statute at issue, and the procedural history.

Finally, include your recommendation and concisely summarize the key reasons underlying it. For example, you might explain, "Because ABC was unaware of Ms. Doe's disability until *after* issuing her a notice of termination, I recommend that you **REVERSE**." For visual ease and convenience, some judges prefer that you capitalize and/or use bold-faced type for your recommendation.

As mentioned above, your judge may want you to include a final sentence flagging the case as a close case if indeed it is. This will enable the judge to do his or her own "triage" when organizing which cases to review first, when to schedule meetings with you to discuss the issue, etc. For example, if a case is flagged as "close," the judge might look at that bench memo first and schedule a meeting with you earlier since a difficult case may be more likely to require subsequent discussions with you or other judges on the panel as well as supplemental research. The designation as a close case will also signal to your judge that while you ultimately settled on a recommendation, there are strong arguments for both sides. It may further indicate that the straw vote could go either way, and the case could easily give rise to a dissent or concurrence.

Your Introduction section will also include a brief summary of the reasons for your recommendation. Even though the Introduction comes at the beginning of the bench memo, draft the Introduction's summary of reasons *after* the other sections of the bench memo are finalized, particularly the Analysis. Then look at each of the recommendations made in the Analysis as well as the reasons underlying them and include them in the Introduction. The recommendations will likely appear in the topic or conclusion sentences of each of the main paragraphs of the Analysis, so that is a good starting point. For this reason, it is best to begin drafting the first part of your Introduction and then just include a placeholder for your reasoning, recommendation(s), and close case flag. Then once you have finalized your analysis, revisit the Introduction and input these sections as necessary.

Issue Statement

The Issue Statement articulates the key issue(s) that will be discussed at the oral argument or hearing. Typically, you will bullet point all key issues in the case in the order that you plan to discuss them in your Analysis. To draft your Issue Statement, read the issue statement in the appellant's brief and then read the issue statement in the appellee's brief. Compare and contrast them. Do not simply copy them verbatim into your bench memo. It is important for you to process them and determine whether the parties have put up smoke and mirrors in an attempt to craft their issue statements persuasively. You are not required to state the issues as the parties do; to the contrary, you should frame the issues in the clearest, most accurate, and most objective way possible.

Organization is key. Include threshold issues first even if the parties did not; oftentimes the dispositive, threshold issue is the only one the court will decide. Include an explanatory footnote if an issue has been raised on appeal, but you do not believe deciding it is dispositive if the panel agrees on a different issue. Likewise, include a footnote if one party raised an issue in its brief that was not raised below since parties typically are not permitted to raise an issue for the first time on appeal. In addition, if you raise an issue *sua sponte*, such as lack of jurisdiction, add a footnote letting your judge know that the parties did not address it. As a general rule of thumb, use footnotes sparingly, if at all, but these three exceptions are good examples of when a footnote is appropriate. Organize your bench memo so that it tracks your organization of the issues. For example, discuss Issue One first, then Issue Two, and so forth.

Key Documents List

A list of key documents is helpful because, in many cases, the parties fail to effectively remove parts of the Appendix that are irrelevant to the issue(s). In other cases, the parties are unable to work together to compile a single Joint Appendix or believe that material factual discrepancies exist. In such cases, one or both of the parties may file a Supplemental Appendix containing documents that the parties could not agree to include or exclude. For example, imagine a situation where only a few pages of a court transcript are relevant, but the parties provide the entire three hundred page transcript instead of proffering only the twenty relevant pages. In every case, but especially in a case such as this with a voluminous, unwieldy Appendix, it is especially important to assist your judge by listing the most important portions of the Appendix. Simply list the name or general nature of the document and the page range where it can be found in the Appendix. Use good judgment. Only select documents that the judge should be sure to review because they are most relevant to the case and may likely be referenced or quoted at the oral argument or hearing.

Especially where the Appendix is so voluminous that it has multiple volumes, provide highlighted versions of only the key documents when you submit your bench memo. Scan or photocopy the key documents so that they are readily available to your judge. This will save your judge the time and trouble of digging to find the key pages or searching on a page to find a single relevant word or quote. Remember in your supporting role, your job is to make the judge's preparation as easy and efficient as possible. Always keep that in mind.

To be clear, listing the key documents in the Appendix in the Key Documents List does not alleviate your need to fully summarize the relevant facts and procedural history later in the bench memo. Furthermore, while your bench memo will likely rely heavily upon the key documents, you must review the entire Appendix, and your bench memo must draw from *all* of the relevant information it contains. While the Key Documents List will usually precede the Background, you will only be able to draft the list *after* you have completed a thorough review of the Appendix and finalized your Background section. After all, you cannot discern which documents are key documents until you have thoughtfully reviewed the entire Appendix.

Background

Facts: The Background explains the facts and procedural posture relevant to resolving each issue. To draft the factual background, carefully review the Appendix, which is the compilation of factual information pertaining to the oral argument or hearing. In an appellate court, the Appendix is typically not the entire Record of the case but instead has been honed down to only include factual documents material to resolving the issue(s) on appeal. In a trial court, only a portion of the Record will likely be relevant to the issue(s) subject to the upcoming oral argument or hearing. As mentioned earlier, sometimes the parties will work together to create a Joint Appendix, which means that the parties agree that these portions of the Record from the proceedings below are all that the appellate court will require to render a just decision. A Joint Appendix is especially helpful to law clerks and judges as it saves time and expense. To assist the court, attorneys at the trial court may append the relevant portions of the Record to their motions, either separately or jointly.

As you read the Statement of the Facts and/or Statement of the Case in a brief, look up each Appendix cite. Compare and contrast the statement in the brief to the document cited to make sure that the assertion in the brief is accurately stated and supported. Note any mischaracterizations, material omissions, or inaccuracies. Do not simply rely on one party's version of the "story"; in an attempt to be persuasive, the party may have minimized, omitted, or mischaracterized a fact or even taken it out of context. Thus, it is important for you to do your own thorough factual investigation and know the facts of each case cold.

Use the information from the briefs and your own investigation of the Appendix to draft an objective statement of the facts and procedural history for the bench memo. Omit unnecessary facts and procedural posture. In some cases, an illustration or timeline of events can be helpful to visualize that the events happened outside the statute of limitations, etc. Use such demonstrative tools as appropriate.

In addition, know your audience. Include an explanatory footnote defining terminology with which the judge may be unfamiliar. Always include properly formatted and accurate Appendix cites and quotations, if appropriate, for every factual assertion in your bench memo. While some judges do not require factual cites in the Analysis portion of the bench memo, unless directly quoting, others prefer cites throughout all portions of the bench memo.

As with everything else, use the parties' Statement of Facts, Findings of Fact, or Background as a starting point, but you are not bound to tell the story in the exact same way. Choose your own organizational method, whether chronological, topical, perceptual, or some combination thereof. Include clear topic sentences, headings, and transitions. If you do not include all facts, open with: "Only the key facts are recited herein." This signals to the reader that you have omitted some information that you deemed unnecessary to resolve the issue(s). Never copy and paste a party's Statement of the Facts from the briefing into your bench memo. Do not rely exclusively on one party's recitation of the facts. Read both. Compare their assertions to the Appendix itself and note discrepancies, omissions, etc., as mentioned above. Material factual discrepancies could have serious implications, such as rendering the issue improper for summary judgment.

If your case involves confidential briefs, be sure to include a footnote at the outset of the memo explaining this and noting how you will designate confidential information. Be sure to bold and/or double bracket it. This will prevent your judge from accidentally disclosing it at oral argument and will prevent that information from finding its way into the opinion.

Avoid doing factual research outside the Record, but one exception may be if the drafter of the brief uses industrial or medical terminology but fails to define it. In such cases, ask your judge if you may use an outside source, such as a reputable dictionary or encyclopedia, to define the term. For instance, imagine a vaccine case in which the party uses medical and scientific terms such as SIDS, telomere, idiopathic, and etiology but fails to define them. In such a case, ask your judge whether you may have permission to look up those terms in a credible source such as *Dorland's Medical Dictionary*, and include an explanatory footnote defining those terms in the factual background of your memo. However, a strong brief will have done that work for you, so cases that require such additional factual research are the exception, not the rule. Also include accurate Appendix cites or other appropriate attribution for information contained in footnotes.

Procedural Posture: The procedural history is the biography of the litigation. It explains all of the relevant procedural events that have occurred to date. Especially when a case has a lengthy or complicated procedural history, only include the procedural history relevant to resolve the issue(s) on appeal. In such a case, commence the procedural posture section with a sentence such as "Only the relevant procedural history is recited herein." Always include properly formatted and accurate Appendix cites to make your memo more accessible.

The same general drafting rules apply to the procedural history as to the factual background. In drafting this section, rely upon the Statement of the Case and the Appendix. Review the clearest Statement of the Case, comparing it to the other party's Statement of the Case. Look up each Appendix cite to ensure that nothing has been misstated, mischaracterized, etc., and that no material information has been omitted or taken out of context. Never copy and paste a Statement of the Case from one of the briefs, but you may use it as a starting point.

With regard to formatting, sometimes a bullet point or timeline format is more helpful to your judge than simply describing the procedural history in paragraph form. In a case involving a pure legal question, such as statutory interpretation, procedural posture may be less important and consume less space in your memo. By contrast, when a procedural issue is on appeal, the procedural posture may take center stage, consuming even more space than the factual background section.

In appellate courts, the procedural posture is also important because it can indicate what the proper standard of review is on appeal, which in turn, strongly influences the appeal's outcome. For example, if a motion for summary judgment was granted and is on review, the appellate court applies *de novo* review, which means that the appellate court can review the issue from scratch and substitute its judgment for that of the lower court.

Analysis or Discussion

The Analysis is arguably the most important part of a bench memo. It synthesizes the parties' arguments and the relevant law. It then applies the law to the facts to determine which argument(s) should prevail. Include a clear, well-supported recommendation regarding how to resolve each issue.

Because of your judge's heavy caseload, he or she may not have time to read every potentially relevant case and every page of the voluminous Appendix with the same degree of careful attention that you can. Nor does the judge have time to check the history of every case to ensure that it remains good law or do independent legal research to guarantee that the parties presented all controlling authority to the court. Instead, your judge depends on you to become the subject matter expert in your subset of cases. Therefore, it is critical that you know the case, the facts, and the law inside out. It is up to you to spot all the issues or potential flaws in the parties' arguments and bring them to the judge's attention.

In your Analysis, you must also decide which argument(s) should prevail and make an appropriate recommendation. In so doing, you must consider the law, the facts, how the law applies to the facts, and the immediate and long-term implications of the decision. What kind of precedent will this decision create, and what ripple effects might it have in other areas? Consider how narrow or broad the decision should be and whether it should be precedential or non-precedential. Contemplate the real-world outcome on the parties, whether the issue should be reviewed *en banc*, etc. In conclusion, think about the forest, the trees, and the weeds. Be thoughtful and thorough. Think in the short-term and in the long-term, both legally and pragmatically.

With regard to organization, use clear, descriptive subheadings to address each issue in the same order that they appear in your Issue Statement. Begin each section with a brief restatement of the issue, such as "The first issue is whether the District Court should have granted Ms. Doe summary judgment." Typically start with threshold issues like jurisdiction and then move to the most important hub issue, second most important issue, etc., in that order.

Note but do not analyze, non-dispositive or frivolous issues unless your judge instructs otherwise. At this point, you will likely have already had a conversation with your judge about whether you must address such an issue in your brief. Even if you do not address it, still remind the judge of its existence by dropping an explanatory footnote and perhaps including a disclaimer sentence in the body of the analysis, such as "Only dispositive issues are discussed herein."

Explain the parties' positions. For example, you might state, "ABC argues that granting Ms. Doe summary judgment was improper because there is a genuine dispute over the date that Ms. Doe informed ABC that her tardiness was due to her medically diagnosed sleep apnea, but Ms. Doe counters that the date is immaterial to whether ABC had to grant her an accommodation."

State the standard of review that the court must apply in resolving the issue. For instance, you might explain, "Courts apply *de novo* review when determining whether a motion for summary judgment was properly granted." Include a legal cite, preferably to a precedential U.S. Supreme Court case, to support your assertion regarding the proper standard of review. This may require independent legal research; do not simply accept the standard of review that the parties proffer as appropriate. Confirm it because the standard of review is critically important to the outcome. After all, judgments likelier to be affirmed under an abuse of discretion standard than when a court applies *de novo* review because, as mentioned above, the latter permits the reviewing court to substitute its judgment for the lower court, reviewing the case from scratch.

Next provide the relevant law necessary to analyze the issue presented. Explain the entire legal landscape underlying the legal issue whether it includes statutes, regulations, case law, or a combination thereof. In some cases, you will begin with a statutory provision but then explain what the statute means via regulations and/or case law interpreting it. In other cases, only common law is available.

Use explanatory parentheticals, citation sentences, and case illustrations as necessary to fully explain the law, taking into account the sophistication and familiarity of your judge. For example, your bench memo may require less explanation if your judge is very familiar with the law in this area and more explanation if he or she is not. Use the latest edition of the Bluebook to ensure that all citations are properly formatted.

Finally, apply the law to the relevant facts. Bold and/or double bracket any confidential information or information that is under seal. Explain which argument(s) should prevail and why. You may want to conclude with "For the foregoing reasons, I recommend that you **AFFIRM**." Many judges prefer that you capitalize and/or use bold-faced type for your recommendation as shown below.

Recommendation: AFFIRM

Include a recommendation for each issue. Then start the whole process again with a new heading for the next issue.

Your analysis will only be strong if it is well researched, well written, and well edited. Thus, when drafting it, draw upon all of the effective writing tools and techniques discussed in Chapters 10, 11, and 12.

Summary of Issues and Recommendations

At the conclusion of an appellate oral argument, the panel will retire to a private conference room and discuss each case. For ease and convenience, many appellate judges prefer that your bench memo include a succinct summary of the issues, recommendations, and key reasoning for each recommendation on a separate sheet of paper or on the last page of the bench memo for use at this meeting. Such a summary is especially helpful in complex cases with several distinct issues and recommendations that might be scattered on various pages throughout the memo. This separate sheet of paper is typically drafted in bullet point or numbered format. Number the issues. Bold and capitalize each recommendation. Summarize the key reasons for each recommendation as succinctly as possible, perhaps include page numbers referencing the location of the full discussion of that point in the bench memo. The judge can use this summary during the straw vote when discussing the merits of the case with other members of the panel. The summary should also remind your judge whether the case is a close case.

Possible Questions

Many judges also ask their law clerks to assemble a list of possible questions for the oral argument or hearing and to append it to the end of the bench memo. However, your judge may ask all, some, or none of them. As you draft your bench memo, create a separate, running list of probative questions that arise out of your review of the briefing, Appendix, and case law. Answer the ones you can; never keep a question on the list that you can answer from your own research. Use the outstanding questions as a starting point for your draft list of potential questions for oral argument. Each question should be probative, precise, succinct, and relevant to the outcome. Make your questions as specific as possible and draft them so clearly that the judge could ask them without changing a single word. Include Appendix or legal cites as necessary. Organize the list by the party to whom the question should be addressed with appropriate bold-faced headings denoting each party. Use good judgment in deciding which party is best suited to address the question.

Questions can relate to, *inter alia*, how cases work together, future implications of a decision, how narrow or broad a holding should be, how a case is distinguishable, how the relief a party requests comports with existing precedent, etc. Sometimes questions can be particularly useful to get parties to concede points that appear disputed but should not be. Only list poignant questions that will fill an important gap in the briefing, the facts, or the body of law. Never ask a question solely for the sake of asking it.

In addition to the core components addressed above, which you will find in nearly every bench memo, some judges have additional requirements, such as asking law clerks to summarize information about related cases. Even if your judge does not typically require this, you will want to include it if either party believes a case should be stayed due to related litigation or if an outcome in another case might be critical to the pending appeal. Use good judgment. In all other cases, only include such information if that is your judge's preference. In addition, some judges may ask you to summarize the insight you gained from meeting with the law clerks working for the other judges on the panel.

C. FINALIZING AND SUBMITTING A BENCH MEMO

How do I edit a bench memo?

Once you are done drafting, spend significant time editing your bench memo to make sure that it is cohesive, clear, and consistent. After you finalize your Analysis, return to the Background, deleting any extraneous information. If your Chambers permits it and time allows, seek peer review from a co-clerk. Discuss any gaps or issues with your peer editor and input his or her edits before submitting the bench memo to your judge. Also apply the editing tips outlined in Chapter 12.

How and when do I submit a bench memo?

As explained above, always submit a bench memo to your judge *at least* one week before the oral argument or hearing, unless instructed otherwise. If you submit it via email, include a subject line in your email indicating that it is the bench memo for the particular case. In the body of the email, include the case name and docket number as well as a list of the attached documents in the order in which they are attached. Append the bench memo and any electronically highlighted version of the key cases or documents that the judge should review along with the memo. Make sure that those attachments are electronically highlighted and have clear names that always include a description of the document or the case name in addition to its reporter cite.

A sample submission email might say something like:

> Judge,
>
>   I hope you are doing well. Attached herein for your review are my bench memo in *Barker v. Bennett*, 09–CV–2017, the parties' submissions, highlighted key portions of the Joint Appendix, and highlighted key cases. The case will be argued on Monday, Nov. 2, at 10am in Courtroom 402. We are scheduled to meet to discuss the case this Thursday at 2:30pm. Please let me know if you have any questions or suggested revisions.
>
>   Best,
>   Nicole

Other judges may prefer a hard copy submission of the bench memo and its accompanying materials. Although preferences may vary, it is usually a best practice to submit the hard copy materials in a small binder with an index or table of contents noting the enclosed materials in the order in which they appear in the binder. At a minimum, include the bench memo first, then the briefing, the documents from the Key Documents List, and finally, any key cases. To make the binder more easily accessible to your judge, label each document with a distinct colored tab that includes its name or designation (*e.g.*, "Bench Memo", "P's Brief," etc.). Print a cover page for the binder that includes the same information that the bench memo's caption provides: the (1) case name; (2) panel members; (3) courtroom; and (4) date and time of the oral argument or hearing.

Below is a sample annotated bench memo based on a fictional case.[14]

BENCH MEMORANDUM

PANEL: **J.A.**, D.K., R.A.

FROM: Christine Hope

DATE: July 23, 2017

CASE #: 17–1982

ORAL ARGUMENT DATE: Aug. 6, 2017

LOCATION: Courtroom 201

NAME OF CASE: TRIAL JUDGE: Wyatt Easton

Violet Sofia,

     Appellant,

v.

Sloan D. Gibson,

     Respondent.

ATTORNEYS:

For Appellant:	For Appellee:
Heath Brecklin	Sandy Alexander
Brecklin & Kilpatrick, Ltd.	Department of Justice
One Brighton Place, Suite 1102	P.O. Box 400
Arlington, VA 22203	Washington, D.C. 20044

NATURE OF THE ACTION

This is an appeal of a decision of the U.S. Court of Appeals for Veterans Claims ("Veterans Court") in *Sofia v. Gibson*, No. 16–8171, 2016 WL 123456, *1 (Vet. App. Aug. 17, 2015). The Veterans Court affirmed the decision of the Board of Veterans' Appeals ("Board"), denying dependency and indemnity compensation ("DIC") benefits to Ms. Sofia.[15] Congress created a limited exception allowing surviving spouses who remarried before enactment of the Veterans Benefits Act of 2003 ("VBA") an opportunity to apply for DIC benefits, the Board followed the plain meaning of the VBA, and the Board's decision is supported by this Court's holding in *Frederick v. Shinseki*, 684 F.3d 1263 (Fed. Cir. 2012). For these reasons, I recommend that the panel **AFFIRM**.

ISSUE: Was it proper to conclude that Ms. Sofia was ineligible to receive DIC benefits under the VBA where she applied for them outside the one-year filing period and had remarried before 2003 at the age of 64?

KEY DOCUMENTS

- *Sofia v. Gibson*, No. 16–8171, 2016 WL 123456 (Vet. App. Aug. 17, 2015)
- Veterans Benefits Act of 2003, Public Law No. 108–183
- Dependency and Indemnity Compensation, 38 U.S.C. §§ 1310–18
- *Frederick v. Shinseki*, 684 F.3d 1263 (Fed. Cir. 2012)

BACKGROUND

Only relevant facts and procedural posture are recited herein. Ms. Sofia is the surviving spouse of Mr. Hank Lambert, a U.S. Army veteran. A13. On February 14, 1992, Mr. Lambert passed away due to complications related to amyotrophic lateral sclerosis ("ALS"), which is a progressive neurodegenerative disease that affects nerve cells in the brain and spinal cord. A15. Two years later, Ms. Sofia remarried at the age of 64. A17.

In December 2003, Congress enacted the VBA, which authorized the award of DIC benefits to surviving spouses who remarry after age 57. *See* 38 U.S.C. § 103(d)(2)(B). The VBA included a retrospective provision, providing for surviving spouses who had remarried before 2003. *See* Pub. L. No. 108–183, § 101(e), 117 Stat. 2651; *see also* 38 C.F.R. § 3.55(a)(10)(ii) (2013). This Court has clarified that § 101(e) applies to *any* surviving spouse who remarried *after* age 57, prior to the VBA's enactment, so long as the spouse applied for benefits by December 14, 2004. *Frederick v. Shinseki*, 684 F.3d 1263, 1273 (Fed. Cir. 2012).

In 2008, the U.S. Department of Veterans Affairs ("VA") promulgated a regulation granting presumptive entitlement to service connection if the veteran had ALS. 38 C.F.R. § 3.318 (2008).

In December 2009, Ms. Sofia filed her first application for DIC benefits, which the Regional Office ("RO") denied. Specifically, the RO determined that Ms. Sofia could not be recognized as a surviving spouse for purposes of DIC eligibility because she had remarried in 1994 when she was 64, her remarriage took place prior to the enactment of the VBA in 2003, and she did not file a DIC benefits application by December 14, 2004—within the applicable one-year filing deadline. Ms. Sofia appealed, and the Board denied her claim for the same reasons. On appeal, the Veterans Court affirmed and entered judgment. This appeal followed.

---

[15] Section 1310 of Title 38 of the United States Code authorizes the award of DIC benefits to a veteran's surviving spouse when the veteran's death is due to a service-connected or compensable disability. 38 U.S.C. § 1310 (2013). To gain eligibility for benefits, the surviving spouse must demonstrate that the disability incurred in or aggravated by active service was the principal or contributory case of death. 38 C.F.R. § 3.312 (2013).

ANALYSIS

Standard of Review

Under 38 U.S.C. § 7292, this Court has jurisdiction to review a Veterans Court decision "with respect to the validity of the decision . . . on a rule of law or of any statute or regulation . . . or any interpretation thereof (other than a determination as to a factual matter) that was relied on by the [Veterans Court] in making the decision." 38 U.S.C. § 7292(a). This Court should set aside any decision of the Veterans Court that it finds to be "(A) arbitrary, capricious, an abuse of discretion, or otherwise not in accordance with law; (B) contrary to constitutional right, power, privilege, or immunity; (C) in excess of statutory jurisdiction, authority, or limitations, or in violation of a statutory right; or (D) without observance of procedure required by law." 38 U.S.C. § 7292(d)(1) (2010). This Court reviews statutory interpretations of the Veterans Court without deference. *See Chandler v. Shinseki*, 676 F.3d 1045, 1047 (Fed. Cir. 2012). However, absent a constitutional issue, this Court may not review a factual determination or an application of law to the facts. 38 U.S.C. § 7292(d)(2) (2010).

Analysis

As a threshold matter, the Court must decide whether Ms. Sofia satisfies the requirements of § 101(e) of the VBA. The Board concluded that because Ms. Sofia met the requirements of this provision, she had to apply for DIC benefits by December 14, 2004. However, Ms. Sofia contends that she does not meet the definition of a surviving spouse under § 101(e) and, as a result, was ineligible to receive DIC benefits until 2008, when the VA relaxed its evidentiary requirements relating to ALS. Appellant's Br. at 7–9. She argues that the Veterans Court's interpretation of § 101(e) "writes the 'but for having remarried' phrase out of the law." Appellant's Br. at 5. The Government counters that the plain language of § 101(e) supports the Veterans Court's decision. Appellee's Br. at 9.

Specifically, § 101(e) of the VBA states:

> In the case of an individual who but for having remarried would be eligible for benefits under title 38, United States Code, by reason of the amendment made by [section 101(a)] and whose remarriage was before the date of enactment of this Act and after the individual had attained age 57, the individual shall be eligible for such benefits by reason of such amendment only if the individual submits an application for such benefits to the Secretary of Veteran Affairs not later than the end of the one-year period beginning on the date of the enactment of this Act.

Veterans Benefits Act, Pub. L. No. 108–183 § 101(e), 117 Stat 2651 (2003). The one-year deadline referenced above is December 14, 2004.

The Veterans Court did not err in its interpretation and subsequent application of § 101(e) because the plain language of the provision applies to surviving spouses who remarried *before* the VBA's enactment of the Act *and after* attaining age 57. Rather than eliminating the "but for having remarriage" aspect of the statute, the Veterans Court applied the plain meaning of the phrase "eligible for." Ms. Sofia correctly indicates that her evidentiary burden during the one-year period between the VBA's enactment and December 14, 2004, was higher than it would have been had the VA earlier passed the presumptive service connection for ALS. However, Ms. Sofia does not provide any basis to support her claim that she was not eligible to apply for benefits. She only asserts that she did not have a lower evidentiary burden during that time and might have been less likely to receive them. Thus, the Veterans Court's interpretation was in accordance with the law.

Further, Ms. Sofia asserts that the Veterans Court incorrectly interpreted *Frederick* and that it should only apply to those surviving spouses who lost DIC eligibility after remarriage. Appellant's Reply Br. at 8. *Frederick* states in pertinent part:

The reference to the amendment made by subsection (a) thus defines a class of surviving spouses who remarry after the age of 57 and who thus become eligible for DIC benefits as a result of the Act.

This class necessarily includes two groups of surviving spouses who remarried after the age of 57: (a) those who previously applied for and received DIC benefits, and whose remarriage before the effective date of the Act destroyed their eligibility for DIC benefits . . . and (b) *those who for whatever reason never applied for DIC benefits upon the death of their veteran spouse, but who remarried before the effective date of the Act, and thereby lost eligibility for DIC benefits.*

684 F.3d at 1266 (citations omitted) (emphasis added).

Based on the above, Ms. Sofia alleges that she was ineligible for benefits regardless of her marital status and did not gain eligibility for DIC benefits until 2008. Appellant's Br. at 10. The Government counters that Ms. Sofia falls into group (b) above, and thus regained status and eligibility for DIC benefits when Congress amended the VBA in 2003. Respondent's Br. at 14. Notably, the Board and Veterans Court agree with the Government. Therefore, the Government contends that the only remaining question for this Court to decide is whether Ms. Sofia filed her application for DIC benefits by December 14, 2004. *Id.* It is undisputed that she did not.

The Veterans Court correctly interpreted *Frederick*. Section 101(e) provides that if a surviving spouse of a veteran meets two conditions: (1) that the person remarried after age 57 and (2) that he or she would otherwise be eligible for benefits, then that surviving spouse must apply for DIC benefits within one year of the VBA's enactment—December 14, 2004. Here, Ms. Sofia lost her DIC eligibility when she remarried because she was over 57 at the time. However, in 2003, she regained her eligibility and had one year to apply for DIC benefits. It is undisputed that her deceased husband, Mr. Lambert, was a military veteran, who died from ALS-related complications. Although Ms. Sofia would likely have needed more substantial proof of her entitlement to DIC benefits before 2008 when the VA promulgated a regulation granting presumptive entitlement to service connection if the veteran had ALS, Ms. Sofia was still eligible *to apply* for those benefits even if she did not ultimately receive them. However, because she did not apply, the Veterans Court correctly affirmed the Board's decision, denying Ms. Sofia's claim.

RECOMMENDATION: AFFIRM

POTENTIAL QUESTIONS FOR MS. SOFIA:

1. Ms. Sofia alleges that she only became eligible for DIC benefits when the VA created a presumptive service connection between service and ALS in 2008. However, DIC benefits may be awarded if surviving spouses meet their evidentiary burden even if there is no presumptive service connection, right?

2. Ms. Sofia never filed or attempted to file for DIC benefits prior to December 14, 2004, right?

3. Should we take into account the purpose underlying the VBA in reaching our decision?

POTENTIAL QUESTIONS FOR THE GOVERNMENT:

1. Shouldn't we resolve any ambiguity in the statute against the drafter, which in this case, is the government?

2. Was Ms. Sofia's only chance to receive benefits to apply for them by 12/04?

3. Just because Ms. Sofia had a lower chance of receiving benefits due to a higher burden of proof does not mean she was barred from applying for them, right?

4. If Ms. Sofia had applied for DIC benefits before remarrying and before the VA promulgated the regulation in 2008 granting entitlement to presumptive service connection for veterans who died of ALS, would she have received DIC benefits?

Bench Memo Drafting Checklist

*The purpose of this checklist is to generally evaluate the effectiveness of your bench memo. There is no single right way to draft an effective bench memo. There are many different formats and organizations that are correct. This checklist provides a **non-exhaustive** list of considerations that promote effective bench memo drafting. More important factors are identified earlier in each subsection of the list. Edit with purpose, first for formatting, then for citation, etc. Please note that this checklist may not be identical to the considerations that your judge considers most important. Thus confer with your Chambers to determine which factors matter most to your judge and revise the list as necessary so that it captures your judge's preferences.*

Formatting

1. Does the bench memorandum have all required sections in the correct order? ☐

2. Does the bench memorandum use the specified format, including font size and type? ☐

3. Does the bench memorandum only use one space after each period? ☐

4. Are the pages numbered appropriately, in the bottom center margin, and in the proper font? ☐

5. Does the bench memorandum use proper margins on all sides? ☐

6. Has the drafter eliminated unnecessary "white space" between sections of the brief and between paragraphs? ☐

7. Does the bench memorandum avoid orphaned headings? ☐

Citation

1. Does the bench memorandum use proper citation format? ☐

2. Does the bench memorandum use *Id.* as appropriate? ☐

3. Does the bench memorandum use proper introductory signals? ☐

4. Does the bench memorandum include pincites as required? ☐

5. Does the bench memorandum use the proper citation format for short cites? ☐

6. Does the bench memorandum use proper italicization? ☐

7. Does the bench memorandum use proper abbreviation(s) in case names? ☐

8. Does the bench memorandum place cases in the proper order? ☐

9. Does the bench memorandum include the subsequent history of each case in the first full cite? ☐

Caption

1. Is the Caption properly formatted? ☐

2. Does the Caption include all components? ☐

3. Does the Caption avoid problems with grammar, punctuation, spelling, and capitalization? ☐

Introduction

1. Does the Introduction include an effective roadmap sentence? ☐

2. Are the parties properly designated? ☐ Are the designations used consistently? ☐

3. Is the Introduction well organized? ☐ Does it flow well? ☐

4. Is the Introduction clear and well written? ☐

5. Is the Introduction objective and succinct? ☐

6. Is the Introduction easy to read and understand? ☐

7. Is the language precise and concise? ☐

8. Does the Introduction succinctly and objectively explain the hub issue(s) organized in the way the bench memorandum will discuss them? ☐

9. Are key facts and procedural history included as necessary to briefly describe the basic nature of the case? ☐

10. Does the Introduction briefly summarize the core reason(s) for the recommended disposition (*e.g.,* affirm, reverse, etc.)? ☐

11. Does the Introduction clearly state the disposition (*e.g.,* affirm, reverse, etc.)? ☐

12. Does the Introduction include proper word choice and sophisticated language? ☐

13. Does the Introduction use active and passive voice appropriately? (*Avoid passive voice unless necessary*) ☐

14. Does the Introduction avoid problems with grammar, punctuation, spelling, and capitalization? ☐

15. Does the Introduction omit quotations? ☐

16. Are footnotes used sparingly, if at all? ☐ Are they necessary? Are they properly formatted? ☐

Background (Facts and Procedural History)

1. Does the Background include an effective impact statement or roadmap sentence? ☐

2. Are all relevant facts and procedural history included? ☐ Has irrelevant information been removed? ☐

3. Are party designations clear and used consistently? ☐

4. Is the Background well organized? ☐ Does it flow well? ☐

5. Is the Background clear and well written? ☐

6. Does the Background tell both sides of the story objectively and thoroughly? ☐

7. Is the Background easy to read and understand? ☐ Does it avoid overly long paragraphs? ☐

8. Are the facts and procedural history properly supported with accurate citations to the Record or Appendix? ☐

9. Is the language precise and concise? ☐

10. Does the Background omit Argument and legal conclusions? ☐

11. Are factual citations properly formatted? ☐

12. Does the Background use effective topic sentences? ☐

13. Does the Background include proper word choice and use language well? ☐ Does the Background use plain language? ☐

14. Does the Background use active and passive voice appropriately? *(Avoid using passive voice unless necessary)* ☐

15. Does the Background avoid problems with grammar, punctuation, spelling, and capitalization? ☐

16. Are quotations used effectively, if at all? ☐ Are they necessary? Are they formatted correctly? ☐

17. Are footnotes used sparingly, if at all? ☐ Are they necessary? ☐ Are they properly formatted? ☐

Issue(s)

1. Does the bench memorandum accurately explain each issue, with references to the governing law, legal question, and key facts or circumstances? ☐

2. Is each Issue Statement concise, clear, and readable? ☐

3. Is each Issue Statement objective? ☐

4. Does each Issue Statement include proper and precise word choice? ☐

5. Does each Issue Statement avoid any spelling, grammar, punctuation, or typographical errors? ☐

6. Is there a separate Issue Statement for each hub issue? ☐

7. Are the issues organized with the threshold or dispositive issue first and then the less important issues in order of importance and in the same order that the bench memorandum will discuss them? ☐

Analysis

1. *Overall effectiveness:* Is the Analysis easy to understand and persuasive? ☐

2. *Legal Landscape:* Does the Analysis begin with an overview of the legal landscape, such as the relevant constitutional or statutory provision(s) or seminal case? ☐ Does it clearly, precisely, objectively, and accurately state and explain the relevant overarching law? ☐

3. *Standard of Review:* Does the Analysis elucidate the proper standard of review and support that assertion with accurate, properly formatted citations to controlling authority? ☐

4. *Organization:* Is the Analysis clearly and logically organized? ☐ Does it discuss the issues in the same order that they appeared in the Introduction or Issue Statement? ☐

5. *Reasoning:* Does the bench memorandum present a sound, proper, and well-developed analysis of each issue and sub-issue without making logical leaps? ☐ Are any key legal or factual issues missing? ☐

6. *Tone:* Is the Analysis objective and appropriately sophisticated? ☐

7. *Effective use of authority:* Does the Analysis use authority effectively, including effective case illustrations and parentheticals? ☐ Is the content of case illustrations and parentheticals properly tailored? ☐

8. *Effective application of law to facts:* Does the Analysis effectively apply the law to the facts, adequately developing each point? ☐

9. *Effective handling of adverse authority and "bad" facts:* Does the Analysis effectively handle opposing arguments or facts that undercut the disposition? ☐ Does

it effectively counter critiques from the concurrence and/or dissent to the extent they exist? □

10. **Headings:** Are headings and subheadings clear, effective, and well placed? □

11. **Transitions:** Does the bench memorandum use effective transitions? □

12. **Paragraphs:** Does the bench memorandum use persuasive and strong topic sentences, and are paragraphs organized logically? □

13. **Grammar & style:** Does the Analysis avoid problems with grammar, punctuation, spelling, pronouns, and capitalization? □ Does it use active and passive voice appropriately? (*Avoid passive voice unless necessary or effective*) □

14. **Quotations:** Are quotations used effectively, if at all? □ Are they properly formatted? □

15. **Footnotes:** Are footnotes used sparingly, if at all? □ Are they necessary? Are they properly formatted? □

16. **Word Choice:** Does the Analysis include proper word choice, including precise language? □ Does the Analysis use plain language? □

17. **Brevity:** Is the Analysis concise? □

Recommendation(s)

1. Is each Recommendation clear, accurate, and easy to understand? □

Overall Effectiveness

1. Taken as a whole, is the bench memorandum well researched? □

2. Taken as a whole, is the bench memorandum well written? □

3. Taken as a whole, is the bench memorandum thoughtful? □

4. Taken as a whole, does the bench memorandum address all issues raised or clearly explain why an issue is not explicitly addressed? □

5. Taken as a whole, is the bench memorandum clear, coherent, and easy to understand? □

6. Taken as a whole, is the bench memorandum objective? □

7. Taken as a whole, is the bench memorandum accurate and thorough? □

8. Taken as a whole, is the bench memorandum well organized? □

9. Taken as a whole, is the bench memorandum effective? ☐

10. Taken as a whole, is the bench memorandum precise and concise? ☐

Bench Memo Tips Sheet

Caption
- ✓ Case Name
- ✓ Docket Number
- ✓ Panel (order of seniority)
- ✓ Date, Time, and Courtroom
- ✓ Attorneys and Contact Info

Introduction
- ✓ Introduce parties and choose designations
- ✓ Hub Issue(s)
- ✓ Overview of Key Facts and Procedural Posture
- ✓ Summarize Key Reasons for Recommendation(s)
- ✓ Recommended Disposition(s)
- ✓ Close Case?

Issue(s)
- ✓ Threshold or dispositive first

List of Key Documents
- ✓ Select from Appendix
- ✓ Include description and page numbers
- ✓ Some also include key cases in the same list or separately

Background
a. Facts
- ✓ Only key facts
- ✓ Define terms or use diagrams as helpful

b. Procedural Posture
- ✓ Summarize key reasoning for decision on appeal

Standard of Review
- ✓ Cite SCOTUS or Published In-Circuit Case with positive treatment
- ✓ Can be a separate section or woven into Analysis; the latter works best when there are multiple issues that each have a different SoR
- ✓ Accuracy is critical since outcome often hinges on SoR. Do independent research to verify this even if parties agree

Analysis
- ✓ Include headings and sub-headings as appropriate

- • They do not have to be persuasive since this is not a brief. However, persuasive or more detailed headings are also permissible. Choose your own style.
- ✓ Overarching legal landscape (main statute or constitutional provision(s), seminal cases to explain the test at issue, etc.)
- ✓ Use cases to explain how those provisions have been construed and apply to our facts
- ✓ Conclusion and Recommendation for each issue

Summary of Issues, Key Reasons, and Recommendations

- ✓ Bulleted or numbered on a separate page
- ✓ Include references to where the issue is discussed in the bench memorandum

List of Possible Oral Argument Questions

- ✓ Number or bullet point
- ✓ Organize by party to whom the question should be addressed

D. SUPPLEMENTAL RESOURCES

1. MARY L. DUNNEWOLD, BETH A. HONETSCHLAGER, & BRENDA L. TOFTE, JUDICIAL CLERKSHIPS: A PRACTICAL GUIDE (2010).

3. JOSEPH L. LEMON, FEDERAL APPELLATE COURT LAW CLERK HANDBOOK (2007).

4. JENNIFER L. SHEPPARD, IN CHAMBERS: A GUIDE FOR JUDICIAL CLERKS AND EXTERNS (2012).

Notes

----

[1]   *Court Week* refers to the first week of each month when a federal circuit court hears oral argument on all of the cases to be argued that month. Some circuits, including the Fourth, First, and Federal, hear oral arguments during a monthly Court Week, which is usually held at the beginning of each month with some exceptions. Other circuits hear arguments throughout the month. To determine when your court hears oral argument, consult the court calendar on the court's official website. By comparison, trial courts schedule oral arguments throughout the month and do not hold an official Court Week. To determine when your court will hear oral argument in a matter, consult the master calendar for Chambers or the docket in the case of interest. The date should be listed on a scheduling order.

[2]   Once you submit your bench memo to your judge, he or she may wish to meet with you so that you can defend your analysis. Principles of persuasive oral advocacy may prove valuable at this meeting as well.

[3]   The author attributes this helpful suggestion to Professor Dan Brean of the University of Akron School of Law.

[4]   Federal Rules of Appellate Procedure and Federal Circuit Rules of Practice (Mar. 2016), http://www.cafc.uscourts.gov/sites/default/files/rules-of-practice/MASTERFederalCircuitRulesOf Practice-9.21.16.pdf/.

[5]   *See generally* Philip Marcus, *Affirmance Without Opinion,* 6 FORDHAM L. REV. 212 (1937); Amy D. Ronner and Bruce J. Winick, *Silencing the Appellant's Voice: The Antitherapeutic Per Curiam Affirmance,* 24 SEATTLE UNIV. L. REV. 499 (2000).

[6]   *See generally* MATTHEW BUTTERICK, TYPOGRAPHY FOR LAWYERS: ESSENTIAL TOOLS FOR POLISHED & PERSUASIVE DOCUMENTS (2d ed. 2015).

[7]   Matthew Salzwedel, *10 Takeaways from Typography for Lawyers,* LAWYERIST.COM (Oct. 26, 2015), https://lawyerist.com/91911/10-takeaways-typography-lawyers/.

[8]   *But see* Butterick, *supra* note 6 at 110 (criticizing Times New Roman as "the font of least resistance").

[9]   *Id.*

[10]   *Id.*

[11]   *Id.*

[12]   Salzwedel, *supra* note 7.

[13]   *Id.*

[14]   The sample is derived from student work product and has been reprinted herein with the authors' permission.

CHAPTER 17

DRAFTING JUDICIAL OPINIONS

■ ■ ■

A strong judicial opinion will articulate the court's reasoning and disposition clearly, concisely, and precisely to the parties and the public.[1] Although some judges write all of their own judicial opinions, in most Chambers, law clerks play a critical role in opinion drafting.[2] Indeed, it is the task for which law clerks are perhaps most needed and best known.

Drafting a judicial opinion is a tremendous responsibility that should not be taken lightly. This is because the holding contained in the opinion, unless vacated or reversed, will become the *law of the case*.[3] As such, it has an incredibly significant impact upon the parties to the litigation. Some opinions are also precedential, which means that they will not only affect the parties to the litigation but also will have far-reaching implications for subsequent, similar cases and the public at large. Indeed, *common law* consists of the body of law developed from custom and judicial precedent; in America, common law fills the innumerable gaps and questions left unanswered by statutes and regulations.[4] For this reason, a well written judicial opinion may shape the body of law, clarifying, expanding, and enriching it. On the other hand, a poorly written or poorly supported opinion may confuse the law. As a law clerk, you play a pivotal role in ensuring that the court makes the right decision and conveys that decision in the clearest possible way.

Your judge authors many opinions in many cases; yet opinion-writing is only *one* of his or her numerous responsibilities. As a law clerk, you are your judge's first line of defense against drafting an erroneous or ineffective opinion. It is your duty to ensure that each opinion is factually and legally sound and clearly supported by controlling precedent. Sometimes you must conduct independent research to uncover controlling law or key issues that the parties may have missed. It is also your duty to discern the key facts and apply the law correctly to those facts. It is your duty to select the most precise wording and to draft a holding that is appropriately tailored to the issue(s) and the case; an overly broad holding could have serious, unintended consequences for the parties and/or the public. As such, the stakes in opinion drafting are incredibly high, and one error, however slight, could have disastrous implications. Worse still, any mistakes will have a wide audience in part because courts are required by law to post their judicial opinions on their court websites.[5]

In conclusion, given their audience and import, draft opinions are likely the most important and most difficult documents you will craft during your clerkship. Afford every draft opinion the significant time, effort, and care that it deserves.

A. PRE-DRAFTING AND OTHER PRELIMINARY MATTERS

What is the purpose of a judicial opinion?

The purpose of a judicial opinion is to educate the audience about the issue(s) and to explain why the court made its decision. For this reason, an opinion should be precise, clear, and thoughtful.

Although a judicial opinion aims to educate, it should usually avoid pure dicta. *Dictum* is a statement in a judicial opinion that is not binding because it is not essential to the holding or resolution of the case. Dicta can be problematic because readers can misconstrue it as legally binding or as an essential part of the holding. As such, dicta may confuse readers or the body of law as a whole and even give rise to an appeal. For example, in *DiMare Fresh v. United States*,[6] the Tomato Producers appealed in part because the lower court judge allotted significant space in her decision to opining that the claim should have been brought as a tort rather than as a regulatory taking.

However, in exceptional instances the use of dicta may be important and appropriate, such as when the court wishes to send a clear signal to the legislature regarding how to correct a statute that has been overturned on appeal. For example, in *U.S. v. Stevens*, Chief Justice John Roberts, writing on behalf of the majority, overturned Section 48, a law banning, *inter alia*, the creation or sale of depictions of unlawful animal cruelty, as unconstitutionally overbroad. However, in dicta, Chief Justice Roberts advised that the majority nowhere concluded whether a statute prohibiting depictions of "extreme animal cruelty" would pass constitutional muster.[7] Congress took the hint,[8] and parroting the majority opinion's language, enacted a revised law, which prohibits depictions of "extreme animal cruelty" that, among other things, are obscene and lack socially redeeming value.[9] Dicta may also be useful to state the narrow scope of the holding and preempt its extension beyond what the court intends.

As a general rule, however, it is a best practice to resist the temptation to draft opinions that include dicta and are broader than necessary to support the judgment. If you believe that some dicta may be necessary, helpful, or appropriate, be sure to discuss it specifically with your judge to ensure that he or she can fully consider the implications of the dicta.

Who is the audience for a judicial opinion?

A draft trial court opinion is typically reserved for your judge and/or co-clerk(s). In some Chambers, clerks exchange and spade drafts before issuance. At the appellate level, your judge is the primary audience for your draft opinion, but it will also be circulated to the other panel members and in some instances, to the entire court for review before issuance.

By comparison, the audience of an *issued* judicial opinion can be incredibly broad. It will include the parties and their attorneys, other judges on the court, other courts, even outside the United States, other attorneys, law professors, law students, and all other members of the public since opinions are posted on the court's website.

What is the tone of a judicial opinion?

The tone of a judicial opinion may vary somewhat depending on the judge and nature of the case. Some scholars argue for the utility of therapeutic jurisprudence, meaning that even if a party loses the case, the party may still benefit somewhat from simply enjoying an opportunity to be heard.

Tone is especially critical for certain types of cases, such as those involving veterans, children, and medical injuries. In these human-oriented cases, it may be especially important for the opinion to set an empathetic, therapeutic tone. For example, in a veteran's case, the factual background might begin with a sentence, such as "Mr. Herbert served his country honorably in the United States Army from 1943 to 1945." Even if the court ultimately rejects Mr. Herbert's claim, the court has still signaled an appreciation of Mr. Herbert's service and let him know that his claims were heard and seriously considered. By contrast, the tone might be quite different in a case in which the court is awarding sanctions against an attorney who has engaged in misconduct. In sum, tailor the tone of the opinion to your judge's voice and to the nature of the case.

How is drafting an opinion different from drafting a bench memorandum?

There are several key ways that opinion drafting is distinct from bench memo drafting. First, a law clerk is typically only required to draft a judicial opinion on a case that he or she has "prepped" for oral argument or otherwise been handling. Of course, exceptions do exist as when a new law clerk inherits a case that has already been argued from an outgoing clerk or when a law clerk drafts an opinion regarding an issue for which no oral argument has been held. Typically though, the law clerk has conducted independent research, drafted a bench memo, developed a list of potential oral argument questions, discussed the case with fellow clerks and the judge, and attended oral argument or the relevant hearing in the case. Thus, by the time the law clerk must draft the opinion, the clerk is a true subject matter expert on the case; the "heavy lifting" in understanding the case and synthesizing the relevant facts and law should be complete, and there is no reason to reinvent the wheel. For this reason, most law clerks, particularly at the appellate level, will simply convert the bench memo into the draft opinion. In this regard, bench memo drafting is often far more difficult because it requires a synthesis of all of the briefing, the record on appeal, and all of the relevant case law, while opinion drafting merely requires the law clerk to repackage a well-researched and well-written bench memo into a slightly different format. As a result, seasoned law clerks will always draft the bench memo with an eye toward flipping it into an opinion, taking extreme time and effort to choose precise wording, edit carefully, etc., to minimize the work required during the subsequent opinion drafting process. In fact, some judges prefer their law clerks to prepare a draft opinion for each case prior to oral argument, rather than a bench memo, although this is rare.

Second, a judicial opinion has a very different audience and impact than a bench memo. The bench memo is confidential and typically shared only with the judge. It has no precedential power. In stark contrast, the audience of the opinion is the court, the parties, and the public as a whole. Given the shift in audience, the tone of a judicial opinion is far more authoritative and less deferential than the tone of a bench memo. The opinion will be posted on the court's website, added to electronic databases, such as Westlaw, and if published, it will also be included in a reporter. Unless overturned, it will become the law of the case, directly impacting the parties. If it is precedential, it may control subsequent on-point cases in the relevant jurisdiction. For these reasons, the stakes are much higher with opinion drafting than with bench memo drafting. As such, word choice must be even more precise. Editing must be even more rigorous. A typographical error in a bench memo should be avoided, but a typographical error in a judicial opinion could have devastating consequences, depending on the nature of the error.

Third, the scope and coverage of the bench memo may be broader and more in-depth than in the opinion. For this reason, the bench memo is often longer and more comprehensive than the opinion in the same case. This is because the bench memo may address *all* issues that concern the court, while the opinion may only address the single dispositive or threshold issue. For example, perhaps your appellate case involves a threshold jurisdictional issue that is a close call as well as two additional issues relating to the merits. Since it was unclear whether all panelists would agree to dismiss the case on jurisdictional grounds, you briefed all three issues in your bench memo. However, if after oral argument, all three panelists agree to dismiss the case on jurisdictional grounds, the opinion need not address issues two and three. Since only the single jurisdictional issue is discussed, the issue section, factual background, and analysis must all be appropriately trimmed to focus exclusively on the law and facts relevant to jurisdiction. The opinion will no longer address all of the parties' arguments on the other issues or include facts or law irrelevant to jurisdiction. For this reason, the fifteen-page bench memo on three issues could easily result in a six-page opinion exclusively addressing jurisdiction. However, in such a case, the opinion would likely include a sentence or footnote explaining that the court did not reach the remaining issues because the threshold jurisdictional issue was dispositive. This signals to the parties that the court is aware of their additional arguments but deems it unnecessary to reach them.

How is drafting a trial court opinion distinct from drafting an appellate opinion?

For the most part, the general principles of opinion drafting discussed in this chapter apply with equal force to trial and appellate opinions at both the state and federal levels. However, some distinctions do exist when drafting a trial court opinion or an appellate opinion. For example, trial courts typically include similar information in the caption, but only one judge—the author—is listed since trial court cases are not resolved by panels. As such, there is never a dissent, concurrence, or dubitante opinion. Nor do trial courts hear cases en banc.

Pre-drafting may also differ significantly where no oral argument or hearing required a law clerk to prepare a bench memo. If no bench memo exists, then simply follow the pre-drafting steps explained in Chapter 16 regarding how to synthesize the briefing, Appendix, and law. Then follow the instructions herein to directly incorporate that information into a judicial opinion.

Both trial court and appellate opinions usually include an Introduction that contains similar information, but when trial court opinions involve fact-findings, the factual background is usually referred to as "Findings of Fact." The factual background will still be called "Background" when a court resolves motions to dismiss or other issues where factual findings have not yet been made.

Trial court opinions typically use headings, such as "Opinion and Order," whereas most appellate opinions do not. Like appellate opinions, they may also include subheadings as appropriate. Trial court opinions typically refer to the analytical portion of the opinion as the "Discussion" and again use subheadings to denote why the court has jurisdiction in the first instance. In other instances, however, the trial court may refer to its legal conclusions as "Conclusions of Law." Furthermore, in trial court opinions, the standard of review is not typically included in a separate section as in some appellate opinions. However, the same general principles of drafting, organization, and citation still apply in the

Discussion. Finally, trial court opinions usually conclude with an Order, as shown below:

Order

1. Defendant's Motion for Judgment on the Administrative Record is **GRANTED.**

2. Intervenor's Motion for Judgment on the Administrative Record is **GRANTED.**

3. Plaintiff's Motion for a Permanent Injunction and request for declaratory relief are **DENIED.**

4. Prior to the release of this opinion to the public, the parties shall review the opinion for competition-sensitive, proprietary, confidential or other protected information. The parties shall file proposed redacted versions of this decision or, in the alternative, file a notice indicating the party's intent not to file proposed redactions, on or before **January 14, 2017.**

5. The Clerk is directed to enter judgment on the Administrative Record in favor of Defendant and Intervenor consistent with this opinion.

The purpose of a trial court opinion also differs from the purpose of an appellate opinion. As the court of first instance, the trial court will typically explain all reasons for its disposition so that if the case is appealed, the appellate court can hopefully find at least one reason to affirm. In addition, the trial court will typically go into much greater detail in discussing the facts and law. As such, trial court opinions are often much longer and more detailed than appellate court opinions. They often resolve a whole host of complex issues, whereas parties generally raise a smaller subset of issues on appeal. Indeed, *Stobie Creek* is a trial court tax opinion that exceeds seventy pages![10] The trial court will likely issue many opinions and orders in the litigation, some on simple issues such as a discovery motion or motion *in limine* and some on more complex motions, such as a Motion for Judgment on the Administrative Record or a Motion for Summary Judgment. Trial courts also handle the day-to-day management of a litigation, such as issuing scheduling orders and holding status conferences. They resolve discovery disputes, and district courts even see a small number of cases through to a jury trial. By comparison, only bench trials are held at some specialty courts, such as the United States Court of Federal Claims.

Finally, a trial court opinion is usually not prepared in consultation with others. Only the judge and perhaps a co-clerk provide input into the draft opinion. While drafting, they do not confer with other judges or those judges' law clerks.

Does opinion drafting differ in federal courts versus state courts?

For the most part, no. The same *general* principles of effective opinion drafting apply equally to state court and federal court opinions. For this reason, most existing resources that discuss opinion drafting, such as the *Judicial Opinion Writing Manual*[11] and *Judicial Clerkships: A Practical Guide*[12]—draw no major distinction between the essentials of drafting a state court versus federal court opinion. Nor is such a distinction drawn herein. That being said, confer with your judge or supervising clerk at the outset of your clerkship to determine your judge's preference and approach to opinion drafting and review exemplary opinions that your judge has authored to better understand his or her expectations for your draft opinion. Also familiarize yourself with your court's local rules.

Why are a law clerk's duties limited to opinion "drafting" rather than opinion "writing"?

In your supporting role as a law clerk, you never author an opinion. Nor do you ever issue a ruling or decide a case. In fact, your name is never listed anywhere in an opinion, not even in a footnote acknowledging your contribution no matter how significant.[13] Your judge is the author of the opinion. Thus, your judge "writes" it, and you merely provide a "draft." This is a particularly important distinction when preparing your resume, designing your social media profiles, or interviewing for subsequent positions. Any claims of "writing," authorship, or decision-making will seriously mischaracterize your role and the scope of your duties. After all, no decision issues absent the judge's review and approval. To imply otherwise is misleading. Doing so could impede your ability to obtain future employment and damage your relationship with your former judge and fellow clerks. So choose your words carefully and always accurately convey the limited scope of your role and duties.

What happens if my judge disagreed with my recommendation in the bench memo or changed his or her mind after oral argument?

A strong bench memo is written objectively and comprehensively; it goes narrow and deep, thoughtfully exploring each party's arguments, supporting facts, and all relevant law. For this reason, your bench memo will still serve as a good starting point for drafting the opinion, even if your judge has changed his or her mind or disagreed with the recommendation(s) made in the bench memo, so long as it was well written, well researched, and well supported. Do not reinvent the wheel.

How is an opinion concerning an issue of first impression distinct from an opinion regarding a well settled question of law?

An *issue of first impression* is a novel issue that a jurisdiction has not squarely addressed. Issues of first impression are often more complex and difficult to decide because there is no controlling law directly on point to guide the court. Thus, the court may go to greater lengths to explain its reasoning, draw analogies to persuasive authority, and perhaps even rely on relevant law review articles or secondary sources to support its conclusions. Such opinions may also be likelier to discuss policy implications, which often play a more influential role when resolving novel issues.

Is a draft judicial opinion confidential?

Yes. Like a bench memo, a draft judicial opinion is highly confidential because it contains the judge's reasoning and disposition. Both may change or evolve dramatically during the drafting process. For this reason, it is incredibly important that *all* versions of a draft opinion as well as discussions or correspondence about the drafting process remain confidential. This obligation persists even after your clerkship concludes; it is a lifetime obligation. You may never discuss the iterations of the opinion without your judge's permission. Nor may you ever divulge discussions regarding the drafting process, the oral argument, the straw vote conference, etc. You may not provide identifying information on your resume, on social media sites, in interviews, to future employers, or anyone else, including spouses, family, and friends. Never disclose that you drafted a decision in a particular case or worked on a particular matter absent your judge's express permission. In short, what happens in Chambers stays in Chambers forever.

Is an issued judicial opinion confidential?

No. Once an opinion has been issued, it is public record. It will be provided to the parties, posted on the court's website, and included in electronic research databases like Westlaw. However, *your role* in drafting the opinion must remain confidential along with your insight into the decision-making process. The opinion will not attribute or acknowledge your contribution in any way; nor should you.

How do I successfully speak in my judge's voice?

Every judge speaks in a unique voice and employs a different style. Adopting that voice and style is essential to strong opinion-drafting. Before you draft your first opinion, speak with your judge and co-clerks to get a sense of what your judge prefers. Inquire about your judge's decision-making process and ask him or her for the names of his or her five most well written opinions. Read these opinions to discern your judge's voice, tone, and style and to determine key phrases that your judge often uses. If possible, discuss with your judge or co-clerks why these opinions were strong and how they could be improved. With your first opinion (or perhaps even your first few), find a mentor in Chambers who is a strong writer, thinker, and researcher. If your judge permits it, ask that person to review your draft opinion before you present it to the judge. In some Chambers, especially at the trial court, judges may require each law clerk to review the other law clerk's draft opinion before the judge reviews it. This appears less common in appellate courts. As you become more experienced, peer review may become less necessary, but it is essential at the outset of your clerkship. During the editing process, your judge will also likely suggest stylistic and word choice changes that better effectuate the judge's voice. Over time, it will be easier and easier to write and speak in your judge's voice, diminishing the need for such edits.

Who decides whether to make an opinion precedential?

The judge or panel makes that decision, but judges commonly confer with their law clerks when doing so. Each court's internal operating procedures may provide guidance regarding which cases are more suitable for publication and which are not. Argued cases often result in precedential opinions, and submitted cases usually result in unpublished opinions. Yet this is not always the case. Where a case involves a very important question or an issue of first impression, it is usually precedential whether argued or not. This is particularly true in appellate courts if the panel is unanimous or believes there is value in explaining its reasoning to the public as well as the parties. On the other hand, if an opinion may draw a dissent or concurrence, sometimes the panel will reach a compromise, withdrawing a dissent or concurrence on the condition that the opinion not be precedential. This avoids the problems inherent in issuing a fractured opinion that could confuse the body of law. There are many other considerations as well, such as whether the disposition is just based on the unique facts of the case, but the judge does not want the reasoning extended to other situations.

How do you decide whether to write an opinion or issue a per curiam affirmance without an opinion?

As noted earlier, local rules often exist that enable courts to issue a non-precedential PCA that resolves a case without issuing a full opinion, which explains the court's reasoning. PCAs are appropriate whenever there is a very straightforward case that clearly warrants affirmance and does not justify the investment of judicial resources to author a lengthy, precedential opinion. PCAs are an important tool of judicial efficiency often used to quickly dispose of such cases so that the judiciary can invest its time in resolving more complex cases, such as issues of first impression. Interestingly, PCAs are also occasionally used in very complex cases in which panel members simply cannot agree, such as a controversial issue of first impression. For example, if each of the judges on a three-judge appellate panel would affirm but all for very different reasons, the panel may opt to simply issue a PCA rather than issue a confusing, fractured opinion.

How is authorship of an appellate opinion assigned?

Although court procedures may vary, the presiding judge on the panel usually assigns authorship of each opinion. The presiding judge is either the chief judge or, if the chief judge is not on the panel, then the most senior judge on the panel. That judge will assign authorship of the submitted cases shortly after they are assigned to various Chambers. The judge will assign authorship of the argued cases during the straw vote conference. An exception sometimes exists when the presiding judge has resolved to author a dissenting, concurring, or dubitante opinion. Then the presiding judge may permit the next most senior judge joining the majority to determine who will draft the majority opinion.

What is the time frame for drafting an opinion?

The time frame for drafting varies. According to the Federal Judicial Center:

> Although there is no statutory requirement that opinions be issued within a fixed time or in any particular order, judges generally determine priority based on three criteria: the importance and urgency of the decision; the nature of the appeal, giving direct criminal appeals priority over civil cases; and the order in which appeals were argued to the court (or in which briefing was completed).[14]

At the outset of your clerkship or the case, speak with your judge about reasonable expectations regarding the drafting timeline for each opinion. Complex issues will likely take longer than less difficult ones. Also allow more time when the opinion requires substantial revision. Likewise, turnaround may be slower if the judge has an especially busy docket. A good best practice is to anticipate this by getting the first draft of an opinion to your judge within 45 days of the last filing in the matter, such as the reply brief, or the date of oral argument if one was held.

Timing is especially critical in an appellate court. For an appellate opinion, the author of the opinion often strives to timely circulate a draft to all panel members within 60 days of argument. In turn, that will generally allow for at least one month to receive comments and incorporate changes from other members of the panel, absent unusual circumstances such as a panelist deciding to dissent. As discussed in Chapter 15, in some circuit courts, an appellate opinion will be placed into the 11-Day process.[15] In addition, some courts circulate a list of outstanding opinions at regular intervals to encourage judicial efficiency.

As when drafting a bench memo, know your judge's personal and professional schedule and accommodate it. For a trial court opinion where you need not circulate an opinion to an entire panel, confer with your judge to establish appropriate drafting deadlines. Also be mindful that some opinions, such as in bid protests, must be expedited.

B. OPINION-DRAFTING TERMINOLOGY AND TYPES OF OPINIONS

As a threshold matter, it is important to note that not all cases require an opinion. Trial judges resolve some motions, such as motions *in limine*, exclusively with short, written orders or sometimes even with oral rulings. Likewise, some appeals may be resolved via a per curiam affirmance without an opinion.

Furthermore, the content and style of a judicial opinion varies by judge, court, and nature of the matter. Thus, it is important to speak with your judge and/or his or her existing clerks at the outset of the opinion-drafting process to determine which format to follow, how to best speak in your judge's voice, etc. Always review sample opinions from Chambers before you begin to draft.

What are the hallmarks of an effective opinion?

The hallmarks of an effective opinion are similar to those of an effective bench memo. Thus, draw on *all* of the effective writing tools and techniques that you learned in your legal writing courses and that are reiterated in this book. Your opinion will only be strong if it is well researched, well written, *and* well edited.

Among other things, an effective opinion is clear, cohesive, thoughtful, and comprehensive. It is well organized and easy to follow. It is precise and concise. It is also well edited. Specifically, it deploys elegant variation and avoids grammatical, spelling, typographical, and other errors. It includes all necessary substance and uses authority effectively. It is well researched, and its conclusions are well supported. It contemplates its audience and maintains the proper tone. It is always respectful to other jurists and to the parties. It avoids dicta and other extraneous language or facts. It fully develops each point made, and the internal organization of each paragraph is also clear and logical. It does not make logical leaps or skip important inferential steps. It utilizes appropriately formal and sophisticated word choice and effectively rebuts potential criticisms of its conclusions. It relies upon footnotes sparingly, if at all, and also avoids excessive quoting. All assertions are accurate, precise, and properly supported with legal or factual citations, which are also accurate and properly formatted.

What are the various types of opinions?

There are various types of opinions, although some are far more common than others. Below is a non-exhaustive list of Chambers terminology often used in relation to opinion-drafting.

Argued: An oral argument was held in an opinion resulting from an *argued case.*

En Banc: In an appellate court, an *en banc* decision is one issued by the court as a whole rather than a three-judge panel. However, because the Ninth Circuit is so large, an en banc opinion by the Ninth Circuit will only include a representative number of judges on the court rather than the full court.[16]

Published or Unpublished: Opinions may be *published* (*i.e.,* reported) or *unpublished* (*i.e.,* unreported). A published opinion is precedential, while an unpublished opinion is not. Published cases typically involve issues of legal significance, such as issues of first impression.[17] They aim to expand and meaningfully contribute to the existing body of law. Unpublished cases are not published in a reporter. Although unpublished cases lack precedential value, Federal Rule of Appellate Procedure 32.1(a)(i) requires federal appellate courts to permit citation to unpublished cases issued on or after January 1, 2007.[18] Other federal and state courts have followed suit, but citation to precedential cases is still preferred where possible.

Note that the term "published" does not refer to whether the case is posted on court websites or appears in an electronic database like Westlaw. This is because Section 205 of the E-Government Act of 2002 requires covered courts to provide access to their written opinions, whether published or unpublished, on the court's website.[19] Legal research databases like Westlaw also include both published and unpublished decisions in their databases, although unpublished cases are always clearly designated as such and only have an electronic database cite rather than a cite to a print reporter.

Panel: In an appellate court, a three-judge *panel* renders a decision. It may be precedential or non-precedential, unanimous or fractured (*i.e.,* including a concurrence and/or dissent, etc.).

Per Curiam: *Per curiam* means "by the court" and refers to an appellate opinion for which no single judge takes credit for authorship. Rather, the whole panel assumes responsibility for authoring the opinion, even if one judge does take the lead in writing it.

The manner in which authorship of a per curiam opinion is assigned may vary by court. However, in some appellate courts, the senior judge on the panel or chief judge will assign authorship shortly after the cases are assigned. The presiding judge may assign one case to each of the other judges on the panel or assume authorship of one of the cases.

According to the Federal Judicial Center, "[m]ost appellate courts issue signed opinions in only a minority of cases."[20] Per curiam opinions most typically occur in straightforward cases the resolution of which will not meaningfully contribute to the existing body of law. This often includes cases that have been decided without oral argument or that involve pro se litigants.[21] Such cases often occur because parties may appeal as of right to the appropriate circuit court, which means that the circuit court must allow the appeal to go forward so long has it has jurisdiction, even if the appeal lacks merit. Such cases are easily disposed of and are often decided without oral argument. A court may also issue a precedential opinion per curiam because it wishes to speak in a single, unified voice on an issue of singular importance to the public. In rare instances, a judge may attach a concurring or dissenting opinion to a per curiam opinion. For example, in *CSX Transportation, Inc. v. Hensley*, 556 U.S. 838 (2009), the U.S. Supreme Court issued a per curiam opinion, but Justice Stevens and Justice Ginsburg dissented. Per curiam opinions are typically shorter than other opinions unless they discuss a complex, important issue.

To promote judicial efficiency, some per curiam affirmances do not include an opinion that explains the court's reasoning. For example, Federal Circuit Rule 36 permits the Federal Circuit to affirm without an opinion, and analogous rules exist at other state and federal courts. Such per curiam affirmances simply state the disposition. For this reason, they are difficult to overturn since a higher court is unlikely to review a decision when it is unable to discern whether the lower court's reasoning was improper.

Pro Se: A *pro se* opinion is one drafted in a case in which a party self-represents. *Pro se* opinions are typically shorter and often tailored to a non-lawyer audience. *Pro se* cases give rise to many special issues, which are addressed in Chapter 18.

Submitted: A *submitted case* is decided "on the briefs," meaning without oral argument. Opinions in submitted cases are often unreported. Usually law clerks do not draft bench memoranda in submitted cases.

At the trial court . . .

Order and Opinion: A trial court may wish to issue an Order, such as an order granting a motion to dismiss, with an accompanying opinion explaining the reason underlying the Order. As will be discussed below, a trial court *Order and Opinion* follows much the same format as an appellate majority opinion with a few exceptions noted below. Such opinions are also known as an Order and Memorandum of Law where the court is exclusively deciding a legal issue rather than sharing factual findings. They will include a background section where the court has not yet made factual findings, as in an Order and Opinion resolving a Motion to Dismiss in lieu of an Answer. An Order and Opinion is most typically used for important cases that involve issues of precedential or social significance.

Findings of Fact and Conclusions of Law (also known as "Findings of Fact, Conclusions of Law, and Order" or "Findings of Fact, Conclusions of Law, and Order for Judgment"): In a bench trial in which the judge, not a jury, acts as the fact-finder, the court may be called upon to issue *Findings of Fact* as well as *Conclusions of Law*. This document explains which version of the facts the judge accepts as true and which legal conclusions the judge reaches when applying the law to those facts. The structure is quite similar to the Order and Opinion, although a factual background section is likely redundant. Since the factual findings may overlap with the legal conclusions, some judges include a disclaimer at the outset of the document, which states, "To the extent the findings of fact may be considered conclusions of law, they will be deemed conclusions of law. Similarly, to the extent that the matters expressed herein as conclusions of law may be considered findings of fact, they will be deemed findings of fact."[22] Always cite to the Record and to the law as appropriate. Where a fact is undisputed, the court should state that clearly; where facts are in dispute, the court should explain why it accepted one factual assertion over another or why one factual assertion is more credible. While some judges explain this decision in more detail, others simply observe that the fact has been proven by preponderant evidence, which is the applicable legal standard in civil litigation. As noted above, some also include an accompanying Order.

At the appellate court:

Summary Order or Per Curiam Affirmance: Opinions are usually reserved for important cases that involve complex, important questions and will contribute to the development of the body of law. In other cases, a *summary order* or *per curiam affirmance without an opinion* ("PCA") promotes judicial efficiency. A summary order or PCA states the court's disposition without explaining the basis for its decision. Such orders typically do not include a statement of findings or conclusions, although they may do so. Summary orders and PCAs are not precedential. Because summary orders are quite formulaic and straightforward, if you are asked to draft one, ask your co-clerk for a form or example to follow before proceeding. In other Chambers, the judicial assistant or Clerk's Office drafts them.

Majority Opinion: A *majority opinion* explains the majority's reasoning and states the controlling disposition on the issue(s). It may be published or unpublished.

Dissenting Opinion: A *dissenting opinion* is one in which a judge (or several judges) disagree(s) with the majority opinion. Only single-judge dissents occur in appellate panel decisions, but multi-judge dissents may occur in *en banc* or Supreme Court decisions. Dissenting opinions are typically shorter than the majority opinion. A judge may dissent in full or in part.

The late Justice Antonin Scalia's memorable prose earned him the fitting title—"The Great Dissenter." For example, in *PGA Tour, Inc. v. Martin*, Justice Scalia observed, "We Justices must confront what is indeed an awesome responsibility. It has been rendered the solemn duty of the Supreme Court of the United States, laid upon it by Congress in pursuance of the Federal Government's power '[t]o regulate Commerce with foreign Nations, and among the several States . . . to decide What Is Golf."[23] Likewise, in *Lee v. Weisman*, Justice Scalia quipped, "I find it a sufficient embarrassment that our Establishment Clause jurisprudence regarding holiday displays has come to require scrutiny more commonly associated with interior decorators than with the judiciary."[24] For other examples of provocative dissents, review the dissenting opinions of the Federal Circuit's very own "Great Dissenter," Judge Pauline Newman, whose insightful dissents "demonstrate the coherence of her specialized judicial philosophy."[25]

Concurring Opinion: A *concurring opinion* is an opinion by one or more judges on the court who agree(s) with the disposition of the majority but disagree with all or some of the majority's reasoning in support of the disposition. Concurring opinions are typically shorter than dissenting opinions. A judge may concur in full, in part, or concur dubitante, which means with doubt. For an example of an impactful concurrence, review Justice Robert H. Jackson's concurring opinion in *Youngstown Sheet & Tube Co. v. Sawyer*.[26]

Dubitante Opinion: A *dubitante* (d[y]oo-bi-tan-tee) *opinion* is one in which a judge has grave doubts regarding the soundness of the majority opinion but not to the extent that he or she feels compelled to dissent.[27] Dubitante opinions are so rare that many lawyers are unaware of their existence.[28] Indeed, since 1950, only Justice Douglas and Justice Frankfurter have issued a separate dubitante opinion instead of merely joining dubitante, which means signing "dubitante" after one's name.[29]

One of the most memorable examples of a dubitante opinion comes from Judge Jimmie V. Reyna of the Federal Circuit. In *Wi-Lan v. LG Electronics*, Judge Reyna, an avid fisherman, issued a separate, one-page dubitante opinion utilizing vivid nautical imagery to explain his skepticism of the majority's reasoning. His opinion states in pertinent part:

> The majority embarks on a winding course as it explores Ninth and other regional circuit case law. . . . the majority discerns a trend in the law . . . I examine the trend and find in it no gates that lead to secure blue water. Indeed, I find that even a route that lies opposite the route charted by the majority is as good a route as any. . . . Thus, while instinct tells me the majority could

be correct, I am concerned that our heading is not based on an accurate bearing. As I cannot prove or disprove our result, I go along with the majority-but with doubt.[30]

Given that a judge may join the majority opinion dubitante without writing separately, why would any judge choose to issue a dubitante opinion? First, a dubitante opinion signals to readers that perhaps a better, but not yet conceived, legal argument may exist. Drafting a dubitante opinion may also better preserve judicial collegiality, promote efficiency, and conserve judicial resources. It may also avoid the confusion caused by a fractured, plurality opinion. On the other hand, some argue that dubitante opinions can result in confusion since they technically constitute a vote with the majority for the purposes of whether the opinion has precedential power. Yet if a dubitante opinion is necessary for a majority, the opinion may be ripe for reversal.

C. THE DRAFTING PROCESS

How do you begin drafting a judicial opinion? What are the steps in the drafting process?

When drafting an opinion in which no oral argument will be held, speak with your judge after reviewing the last filing to determine his or her initial thoughts on the matter. Because you had no reason to prepare a bench memo, follow the pre-drafting process outlined in Chapter 16 but compile the information directly into an opinion rather than a bench memo.

Alternatively, if oral argument or another proceeding has been held, then speak with your judge shortly after the proceeding to determine if there were any issues raised or concerns quashed that will impact the opinion. For example, your judge might advise you to limit the decision to just the jurisdictional issue because all judges agree that it is dispositive. By comparison, in a complex patent case, the judge might observe that you cannot limit the opinion to the patent eligibility issue, without inviting a concurrence, dubitante, or dissent, since one of the judges on the panel remains unconvinced that the eligibility issue is dispositive. Each judge usually takes notes during the straw vote conference, and as your judge permits, it may be useful for you to review those notes and/or the straw vote conference sheet to see how the panelists voted and what issues, facts, or law were most important to them. Save your bench memo as a new document and then incorporate your notes, perhaps in the form of track changes, to reflect this discussion of post-argument considerations.

Next, review your own notes from the proceeding and if a recording of the argument is available, listen to the recording. At some circuit courts, a recording is posted to the court website shortly after oral argument so that it is available to the public. Once again, save your bench memo as a new document if one exists and then incorporate your notes from the recording, perhaps in the form of track changes.

Now ask yourself whether anything from the proceeding warrants additional independent research, either legal or factual, assuming such research is permissible. For instance, did a party rely upon a new case that had been issued after the party had filed its appellate brief? If yes, confer with your judge and with his or her approval, pull and read the case. Include it in your synthesis as necessary. Flag for the judge that the case was not included in the original brief and was first mentioned at the proceeding.

Next consider what you should remove from your bench memo before converting it to an opinion. For instance, will your opinion only address patent eligibility, allowing you to remove analysis relating to the obviousness issue that the court need not reach to resolve the case? Likewise, which portions of your background pertain only to obviousness? All such sections can likely be removed unless they are necessary for context or clarity. Now delete the following portions of the bench memo, as applicable: (1) the list of key documents and/or key cases: (2) the summary of recommendations; (3) the list of possible oral argument questions; (4) information pertaining to the statement of related cases; and (5) notes from meetings with other law clerks. The remaining portions of the bench memo will serve as a helpful starting point for the corresponding sections in the judicial opinion. Remove any irrelevant information from the remaining sections.

Now you are ready to begin converting the bench memo into the opinion. First, save your bench memo as a descriptively titled new document, such as "Connor v. Bracis Draft Opinion Version One 6.25.17". Use of version numbers and dates will ensure that you are always working in the most current version of the document. Add a "CONFIDENTIAL DRAFT OPINION: NOT FOR CIRCULATION" header to each page of the document. Insert page numbers. Each time you begin working on the opinion, save the document with a new version number and/or date so that you may always return to a prior version to retrieve deleted information that you have subsequently decided to include.

What information must you incorporate into the opinion that is not in the bench memo you drafted for the case?

You will incorporate any information that arose between your submission of the bench memo and the onset of the opinion drafting process. This includes relevant information that arose at oral argument, such as an oral concession or a new case, or during your post-argument debriefing with your judge. It also includes any relevant intervening authority issued after oral argument as appropriate.

What information must you remove from your bench memo?

You must remove confidential information that was essential to prepare the judge for oral argument but that cannot be included in a publicly issued opinion. You should also delete information that is no longer necessary to support your legal conclusions or disposition, such as when several issues were raised on appeal, but the opinion will only discuss a single, dispositive issue. Finally, remove all portions of the bench memo improper for inclusion in the opinion, such as the list of key documents and potential questions.

What are the parts of a typical opinion?

Content varies by court and opinion type. However, every opinion typically contains a caption, an Introduction, Background (or Findings of Fact as applicable), Discussion or Analysis (or Conclusions of Law as appropriate), and Disposition (or Order at a trial court). Each of these components will be discussed in more detail below.

How do I format a judicial opinion?

For specific information on formatting, refer to a sample opinion from your Chambers to determine which formatting style your judge and/or court prefer(s).[31] Typically, draft opinions are single-spaced and fully justified. Turn on the hyphenation feature. Unless otherwise instructed, use a proportional font like Times New Roman or Century Schoolbook in 12-point. To ensure proper spacing, go to "Format," "Font," "Advanced," and select "Kerning" and "8 point." Include page numbers on the bottom center of the page. Use in-text citation, not endnotes. Be sure that the font of the page number matches the font of the main text. Footnotes should be used sparingly, if at all. They should appear in 10-point and in the same font as used in the main body. Include a boldfaced, capitalized "Confidential" header on each page of the draft opinion but be careful to remove it before you provide the final opinion to the Clerk's Office for issuance to the public. Include properly formatted headings for each section of the opinion. You may include headings and sub-headings as appropriate in your Discussion section. Denote headings and sub-headings according to your judge's preference. Avoid orphaned or widowed headings that have insufficient space to include two lines of text beneath them. Absent instructions to the contrary, italicize case names and use in-text citation, not footnotes or endnotes. Format all citations according to the latest citation rules regarding legal documents, not law review articles. Include one space after a period.

For ease and clarity, let's break down the drafting process step by step.

The section that follows is quite comprehensive. Rather than reading the entire section in one sitting, read each section before you draft that corresponding section in your opinion. Read slowly and critically, so that you can more easily absorb all of the information provided.

Caption

Unless drafting a dissent, concurrence, or dubitante opinion, start your opinion with a Caption. The content of the caption varies by court, so view a sample before you begin the opinion to determine which information your caption should include. Typically, however, a caption will identify each of the following: (1) the case name, parties, and their designations; (2) the deciding court; (3) the case identification number or docket number; (4) the attorneys' names, affiliations, and addresses; (5) the date of the argument, if applicable, and decision; and (6) the judges' names and authorship (or en banc or per curiam as appropriate) in order of the chief judge or most senior judge to the least senior judge.

The caption lists the full names of each party (or parties) and their party designations. At the Supreme Court, the party that files the petition for certiorari is the *Petitioner*, and the party who responds is the *Respondent*. At the circuit court, the party that files the appeal is the *Appellant*, and the party that responds is the *Appellee*. If a party files a cross-appeal, the party can be both an Appellee and Cross-Appellant and vice-versa. At the trial court level, the party that filed the Complaint is the *Plaintiff*, and the party that defends against the Complaint is the *Defendant*. Party labels differ in specialty courts. For example, at the Office of Special Masters, the party that files a petition is the *Petitioner*, and the Government, specifically the Secretary of Health and Human Services, is always the *Respondent*.

The caption also includes the docket number, the day, month, and year of the oral argument, if applicable, and the day, month, and year the case was decided (*i.e.*, the date the opinion was issued). It also includes the deciding court. The caption of your opinion will not have a reporter or database cite because it will not yet be available. The opinion will also typically list the attorneys, their contact information, and which party each attorney represents. Every opinion will list the author of the opinion. Appellate opinions will also list the other members of the panel joining in the opinion and note any dissent(s), concurrence(s) or dubitante opinion(s).

After the caption but before the Introduction, some opinions, typically trial court opinions, will list the nature of the opinion, such as "Opinion and Order Granting Summary Judgment" in boldfaced, capitalized, and centered letters. Such titles are typically not required in appellate court opinions since they are always a review of an appeal. Some opinions may succinctly state the procedural posture of the appeal as well as the disposition of the appeal.

Here is an example of a case caption.

■ APPEAL from a Judgment of the District Court of the Eastern District of Texas, JUDGE JOHN D. LOVE. *Affirmed.*

Representing Appellant: Heath Brecklin of Brecklin & Asbury, LLP, Austin, Texas.

Representing Appellee: Wyatt Easton of Easton & Turner, LLP, Tyler, Texas.

■ Before PROST, CHIEF JUDGE, and REYNA and HUGHES, JUDGES.

■ HUGHES, JUDGE, filed a dissenting opinion.

■ PROST, CHIEF JUDGE.

Rather than reinvent the wheel, you may be tempted to recycle a caption used from a prior opinion in the same case. However, before doing so, verify that the case caption has not changed. After all, parties may be added to or removed from a case, and party names may change over time. Always confirm that the case caption remains accurate before using it. Failure to do so is a common error.

Now let's turn to the Introduction.

Introduction

Most opinions include a brief Introduction. It aims to apprise the reader generally of what the case involves. At the outset of your clerkship, peruse samples of strong introductions before you begin to draft to get a sense of which style of Introduction your judge prefers.

The Introduction generally includes each of the following: (1) the nature of the case or appeal and/or issue presented; (2) a brief introduction of the parties; (3) a succinct overview of the key facts, procedural posture, and hub issue(s) in the order that they will be discussed; (4) a concise summary of the core reasoning; and (5) the disposition(s). For these reasons, the Introduction drafted for your bench memo is typically a good starting point, but you cannot merely copy and paste it. You must revise it accordingly to make it suitable for the opinion.

The Introduction will usually begin with a sentence such as "This is a case about," "This case involves," "This case presents the question of," "This appeal presents the question of," or "This is an appeal from." Such a sentence will succinctly and precisely explain the basic nature of the action before the court. This sentence will often pinpoint the hub issue(s) in the case usually in a generic or abstract fashion. For example, the opinion might state, "This appeal presents the question of whether an employee claiming a violation of Title VII of the Civil Rights Act of 1964 ("Title VII") must expressly state that he or she has filed a Charge of Discrimination ("Charge") with the Equal Employment Opportunity Commission

("EEOC") in his or her Complaint in order to withstand a Motion to Dismiss for Failure to Exhaust Administrative Remedies."

Notice how the sentence is concise yet still draws from the key facts, the statute at issue, and the procedural history. The opinion need not state the issues as the parties do; to the contrary, it should frame the issues in the clearest, most accurate, and most objective way possible. State the issues in the same order in which they will be discussed in the opinion, drawing from the Issue Statement in your bench memo to the extent one exists. With regard to organization, include threshold issues first, even if the parties did not, and include a footnote if the court will only address a single, dispositive issue even though the parties raised multiple issues. Likewise, include an explanatory footnote if one party raised an issue in its brief that was not raised below since parties typically are not permitted to raise an issue for the first time on appeal. In addition, if the opinion raises an issue *sua sponte*, such as lack of jurisdiction, include an explanatory footnote. Although footnotes should be used sparingly, in such circumstances a footnote is warranted.

Next, introduce the parties, providing any necessary factual context and using explanatory parentheticals to explain to the judge how you will refer to each party for the duration of the opinion. For example, the opinion might state, "Plaintiff-Appellant ABC Corporation ("ABC")." Going forward, the opinion will always refer to ABC Corporation as ABC, which will save space and add clarity (*e.g.,* ABC argues, ABC counters, etc.). Choose a designation that is clear and succinct and consistently use that designation to refer to the party for the remainder of the opinion. In opinions, the use of party names as designations may be clearer and more helpful to the reader than using generic designations like "Appellant." Choose precise labels that connote impartiality and promote clarity.

It is often helpful to provide at least some factual context when introducing the parties. For example, if ABC is the employer at issue in the appeal, you might state: "Defendant-Appellant ABC Corporation ("ABC") is a pet food manufacturer, which terminated Plaintiff-Appellee John Smith's employment in July 2017, allegedly due to his recurring failure to perform his duties satisfactorily."

After you introduce the parties (or sometimes in conjunction with that introduction as appropriate), provide a succinct overview of any key facts and the key procedural history that is specific to the case. For a pure question of law or a procedural issue, a lengthy recitation of the facts may be unnecessary. Likewise, for a fact-intensive inquiry, only very brief coverage of the most relevant procedural posture may be required. Use good judgment. For example, you might write, "Mr. Smith alleges that he was terminated due to his race in violation of Title VII of the Civil Rights Act of 1964 ("Title VII"). The United States District Court for the Eastern

District of Virginia ("District Court") granted ABC's Motion to Dismiss for Failure to Exhaust Administrative Remedies, and Mr. Smith timely appealed."

The next section is perhaps the most important part of the Introduction. Here, the opinion will explain the disposition(s) and concisely summarize the core underlying reasons supporting each one. The reasoning section should be a succinct analysis of the primary reasons for the disposition. For example, the opinion might explain, "Because it is undisputed that Mr. Smith did not timely file a Charge with the Equal Employment Opportunity Commission ("EEOC") or receive a right-to-sue letter before bringing suit as required by law, we **AFFIRM**." For visual ease and convenience, some judges prefer that you capitalize and/or use boldfaced type for the disposition. Ironically, although the Introduction comes at the beginning of the opinion, you can only finalize it *after* the other sections of the opinion are entirely complete. Thus, after the rest of the opinion is complete, return to finalize and edit the Introduction.

Here is an excellent sample Introduction excerpted from *Association for Molecular Pathology et al v. Myriad Genetics, Inc.*, 133 S.Ct. 2107 (2013).

Respondent Myriad Genetics, Inc. (Myriad), discovered the precise location and sequence of two human genes, mutations of which can substantially increase the risks of breast and ovarian cancer. Myriad obtained a number of patents based upon its discovery. This case involves claims from three of them and requires us to resolve whether a naturally occurring segment of deoxyribonucleic acid (DNA) is patent eligible under 35 U.S.C. § 101 by virtue of its isolation from the rest of the human genome. We also address the patent eligibility of synthetically created DNA known as complementary DNA (cDNA), which contains the same protein-coding information found in a segment of natural DNA but omits portions within the DNA segment that do not code for proteins. For the reasons that follow, we hold that a naturally occurring DNA segment is a product of nature and not patent eligible merely because it has been isolated, but that cDNA is patent eligible because it is not naturally occurring. We, therefore, affirm in part and reverse in part the decision of the United States Court of Appeals for the Federal Circuit.

Explain the key issues in the order that the opinion will discuss them, placing threshold or dispositive issues first. Do not simply copy the Issue Statement from a party's brief or your bench memo verbatim into your opinion. It is important for you to process them and craft an objective, clear, and accurate statement of each issue. You are not required to state the issues as the parties do or as you did in your bench memo. To the contrary, you should frame the issues in the clearest, most accurate, and most objective way possible. In addition, statements made at oral argument or concerns raised during the straw vote conference may warrant revision of the issue statement(s).

Organization is key. Include threshold issues first even if the parties did not; often the dispositive, threshold issue is the only one the court will decide. Include an explanatory footnote if an issue has been raised on appeal but you do not believe deciding it is necessary because the panel agrees on a different issue. Likewise, include a footnote if one party raised an issue in its brief that was not raised below since parties typically are not permitted to raise an issue for the first time on appeal. As a general rule of thumb, use footnotes sparingly, if at all, but as mentioned earlier, these three exceptions are good examples of when a footnote is appropriate. Organize your opinion so that it tracks your organization of the issues. For example, discuss Issue One first, then Issue Two, and so forth.

Now let's turn to the Background section.

Subheadings

Use subheadings where doing so will make the opinion clearer, better organized, and easier to read. Subheadings are especially useful in complex cases involving multiple issues, particularly if each issue is subject to a distinct standard of review or relates to different portions of the factual background. Always avoid an orphaned or widowed heading and subheading; only include a heading or subheading if there is sufficient space to include at least two lines of text below it.

The nature and format of headings and subheadings varies by judge and by court. Before you begin drafting, confer with your judge or co-clerks and view sample opinions to determine which style and format your judge prefers. Some judges will include a longer, descriptive heading; others will include succinct subheadings that are mere sentence fragments. Still others simply denote headings and subheadings with letters, numbers, or Roman numerals. For example, in *Myriad*, Justice Clarence Thomas used boldfaced, capitalized Roman numerals (*i.e.,* **I**, **II**, etc.) instead of main section headings, such as Background, and boldfaced, capitalized letters (*i.e.,* **A**, **B**, **C**, etc.) to denote subsections of the opinion.

Background

The Background explains the facts and often the procedural posture relevant to resolving each issue. In a trial court opinion where a fact-finder has made factual findings, this section is appropriately titled "Findings of Fact."

Draft the Background objectively and comprehensively, maintaining a neutral tone. Be judicious in your selection of which facts to include. Only include: (1) legally relevant facts; (2) contextual facts essential to understanding the background of the case; and (3) facts essential to establishing a proper tone for the opinion (*e.g.*, in a veteran's case, the dates and nature of a veteran's service, receipt of medals, and the date of his or her honorable discharge). Omit facts that are clearly irrelevant. Draft broadly, including all potentially relevant facts. After you have completed your Analysis, remove all facts from the Background that you did not use in your Analysis or that are unnecessary for context or tone.

As a general rule, avoid lengthy quotations of trial testimony, the Record, etc., Support each assertion with proper cites to the Record or oral argument transcript as appropriate. Use footnotes sparingly, if at all. Define terminology with which the average person would be unfamiliar, such as technological lingo or medical terms in a footnote or in the text. For instance, imagine a medical malpractice case in which the party uses medical terms such as "idiopathic" but fails to define them. Confer with your judge regarding whether you should include an explanatory footnote defining those terms via a credible source, such as *Dorland's Medical Dictionary*.

Choose your words carefully. Be precise and succinct. Avoid legal conclusions or legally loaded terminology, such as "Mr. Doe repeatedly harassed Ms. Smith at the office." After all, harassment is a legally loaded term that must be established by applying law to fact. Be especially mindful that courts of last resort and appellate courts do not "find" facts; the opinion recites facts from the Record, rather than finding them, and views them according to the applicable standard of review.

Acknowledge factual discrepancies. Material factual discrepancies could have serious implications, such as rendering the issue improper for summary judgment. Always include properly formatted and accurate Record cites.

Include headings, subheadings, roadmaps, and transition words as appropriate. Sometimes inserting a roadmap paragraph at the outset of the Background provides an additional organizational tool. Strong topic sentences will serve as additional mini-roadmaps to lead readers as they journey through the background of the case. The reader's journey should always be a clear and direct path, not a winding road.

As noted earlier, a comprehensive recitation of the facts is not always necessary. For example, perhaps the appeal will be resolved solely on the basis of a procedural question, so the opinion might include an extremely succinct version of the facts and begin with "Only the relevant facts are recited herein." This signals to the reader that you omitted some information that you deemed unnecessary to resolve the issue on appeal. In an unpublished decision, your judge may permit you to heavily condense the facts since the parties are familiar with them.

Organization of the Background varies by case. The most common organizational methods are chronological, topical, perceptual, or some combination thereof. The chronological approach tells the "story" of the case in the order in which it occurred. Chronological organization is typically the clearest manner in which to explain the factual background, and perhaps for this reason, is most common. Topical organization recounts the factual background by topic. Some cases specifically lend themselves to this organizational approach. For example, in the factual background of a vaccine case, the opinion might first address the topic of the vaccine, including how it is produced, etc. Next, the opinion might discuss the background of the medical injury at issue. Finally, the opinion might explore the chronology of the specific case, such as the age of the individual who received the vaccine, why, when, where, and how he or she received it, etc. Similarly, in *Myriad*, Justice Thomas utilizes a topical approach, first discussing general principles of genetics before turning to the specific facts relating to the patents at issue in the case. Finally, perceptual organization explains the factual background from the various perspectives of the parties involved. It is the least commonly used approach.

In some cases, a diagram or other graphical illustration can be helpful to visualize or illustrate key facts. However, use such demonstrative tools sparingly and only as appropriate.

If your case involves confidential briefs, be sure to remove all confidential information from the opinion. Confidentiality is typically limited to the Chambers reviewing the case. Thus, an opinion cannot even be circulated on the 11-Day process if it contains confidential information. And it certainly cannot be issued to the public, posted on the court's website, or added to an electronic database like Westlaw if it contains confidential information. Thoroughly review the draft opinion to ensure that all such information has been removed from the draft opinion. One exception is for opinions filed under seal. Those opinions will be submitted to the parties for suggested redactions before being issued to the public, so it is their duty, not the court's, to decide which information to remove before issuance.

Use the factual background from your bench memo, if one exists, as a starting point, but do not simply copy it verbatim. Review it, incorporating relevant information gained at the oral argument, subsequent discussions, or supplemental research. Avoid any mischaracterizations, material omissions, or inaccuracies.

Procedural Posture

The procedural history is the biography of the litigation. It encompasses the procedural events that have occurred to date. Especially when a case has a lengthy or complicated procedural history, only include relevant procedural history relevant to resolve the issue(s) on appeal. In such a case, commence the procedural posture section with a sentence, such as "Only the relevant procedural history is recited herein." Always include properly formatted and accurate Record cites.

The same general drafting rules apply to the procedural history as to the factual background section. If you employed a timeline or bullet point format to explain the procedural history in the bench memo, convert your notes into full sentence, paragraph form. In a case involving a pure legal question, the procedural posture may be less important, so afford it less space. By contrast, when a procedural issue is on appeal, the procedural posture may take center stage. For example, in *Myriad*, the procedural posture is so relevant that Justice Thomas devotes several paragraphs to it in a separate section.

The procedural posture is also important because it can indicate what the proper standard of review is on appeal, which in turn, strongly influences the appeal's outcome. For example, if a motion to dismiss was granted and is on review, the appellate court knows to apply *de novo* review, which means that the appellate court can review the issue from scratch and substitute its judgment for that of the lower court.

Now let's turn to the Standard of Review.

Standard of Review

The Standard of Review states the applicable legal standard that the court must apply to resolve the issue(s). In appellate courts, the standard of review illuminates the level of deference that the reviewing court must afford the lower court. In some opinions, the standard of review appears in a separate section preceding the Discussion or Analysis. This is especially true for opinions in which there is a single issue or where the same standard of review applies to all issues. In cases involving multiple issues, each with its own distinct standard of review, the opinion will likely explain the applicable standard of review at the outset of the discussion of each issue within the larger Analysis section. In support of the standard of review, always cite to a Supreme Court opinion or to a controlling, precedential opinion within the circuit. Conduct independent research to confirm that the parties applied the proper standard of review in their briefing.

The Standard of Reviews differs by issue. Typically, greater deference is given to decisions regarding facts, which means a reviewing court is less likely to reverse them. This is because the trial judge or jury likely had the opportunity to hear witness testimony, observe witness demeanor, etc. Thus, trial courts are better suited to making factual findings and in turn, fact-based decisions. Less deference is given to decisions of law, which means that they are more vulnerable to reversal. This is because either court is equally well suited to reach a sound legal conclusion. Choosing the proper standard of review and applying it properly are critical since the disposition often hinges on the standard of review.

While an exhaustive discussion of all standards of review exceeds the scope and purpose of the chapter, common standards of review include the following:

Abuse of Discretion: The abuse of discretion standard of review applies to discretionary decisions, such as those involving the admissibility of evidence or imposition of sanctions. This highly deferential standard presumes that the trial judge is better suited to render on-the-spot judgments. Thus, it is difficult to prevail on an issue to which this extremely deferential standard applies unless exceptional circumstances exist.[32]

Clearly Erroneous: A clearly erroneous standard applies to factual findings. Rule 52(a) of the Federal Rules of Civil Procedure states: "Findings of fact, whether based on oral or documentary evidence, must not be set aside unless clearly erroneous, and the reviewing court must give due regard to the trial court's opportunity to judge the witness' credibility." As the Supreme Court emphasized in *United States v. Gypsum Co.*, 333 U.S. 364, 395 (1948), clear error exists only when there is "a definite and firm conviction" that the court erred.

De Novo: *De novo*, or plenary review, means that the reviewing court may review the issue(s) from scratch without affording any deference to the lower court. Thus, the reviewing court may substitute its judgment for that of the lower court. This standard applies to pure questions of law as well as to mixed questions of law and fact, such as the question of whether the facts are sufficient to satisfy a legal standard.

Analysis

The Analysis or Discussion (collectively referred to hereinafter as "Analysis") is arguably the most important part of the opinion. It synthesizes the parties' arguments, the relevant law, and the key facts. It then applies the law to the facts to explain which argument(s) prevail and why. It also includes a clear, well-supported disposition for each issue. As you draft the Analysis, consider how narrow or broad the decision should be and whether it should be precedential or non-precedential. Be thoughtful and thorough. Consider both short-term and long-term implications.

With regard to organization, use subheadings, as appropriate, to organize the analysis of each issue in the way that it appeared in your Introduction, addressing threshold issues and dispositive issues first. Some opinions merely designate each section with a Roman numeral; others use a descriptive heading. Use whatever style or format your judge prefers.

If the opinion does not resolve every issue raised, include a sentence or explanatory footnote signaling to the reader that this omission is intentional, not an oversight. Such a sentence might say, "Only dispositive issues are discussed herein" or "Because this issue is dispositive, the Court need not reach the remaining issues raised on appeal." Likewise, some opinions observe: "The Court has considered the other issues on appeal and concluded that they do not warrant relief" or "The Court has considered all other issues raised and concluded that they are without merit."

Begin the Analysis with an effective overview roadmap paragraph. With regard to the internal organization of each subsection or perhaps even each paragraph, consider following my *ILEAC Approach*. The ILEAC Approach encourages the drafter to: (1) state the issue or idea that will be discussed in the paragraph or section **(I)**; (2) provide the relevant law for the issue **(L)**; (3) explain and expound upon the relevant law as necessary, using citation sentences, case illustrations, and/or explanatory parentheticals **(E)**; (4) apply the law to the facts **(A)**; and (5) state the well-reasoned conclusion that you want the reader to draw after reading the paragraph or section **(C)**. To avoid lengthy paragraphs, drafters may address the ILE in one paragraph and the AC in another, as appropriate. Drafters may also use the related *CLEAC Approach*, in which the topic sentence states a compelling conclusion instead of objectively stating the issue or idea that the paragraph will discuss.

Within each subsection, state the issue clearly, perhaps by saying "The first issue is whether." Then, as applicable, state the proper standard of review that the court must employ when reviewing this issue, unless you have included that information in a separate standard of review section.

Next provide the relevant legal landscape for the issue. For example, if the first issue involves an Equal Protection violation, the discussion will likely begin by quoting the Equal Protection Clause of the Fourteenth Amendment and briefly explaining the spirit, history, and purpose of the clause. Next, the opinion may include seminal case law, defining the contours of equal protection law.

After you have stated the relevant law, use regulations, case law, and perhaps other sources of law to explain how the law has been interpreted or applied in similar factual situations. Put differently, explain what the law means in a practical sense and what it requires. Doing so is necessary whenever the text of the law, standing alone, does not squarely resolve the issue presented. Use properly formatted citations to the statutes, cases, etc.

Do not rely upon non-controlling secondary sources, such as law review articles. Use controlling, precedential law with positive treatment. To determine this, review the litigation history of each case upon which you rely to ensure that it has not been criticized, questioned, overturned, or superseded. Confirm that regulations and statutes have not been amended or repealed and that they were in effect during the time period relevant to the litigation. Choose cases that are current and on point, both legally and factually. Do not cite to unpublished cases or cases outside the circuit if possible.

Furthermore, it is incredibly important to explain the relevant rules of law accurately and precisely. Not only must the sources of law upon which you rely remain good law that is controlling and on-point, but also your statement of the rules of law gleaned from those sources should not misconstrue precedent. Use positive, affirmative statements from case law rather than inferring a rule of law from context or dicta.

Next, explain each party's arguments but employ the skills learned in your persuasive advocacy course to quickly and effectively dispel arguments that the court considers unconvincing. However, as you do so, remember that the primary tone of the opinion must be impartial. Parties should feel that the court has thoughtfully considered all of the issues, the law, and the facts. Briefly explain the parties' arguments, stating "ABC contends" or "ABC counters." For purposes of elegant variation in word choice, use various verbs, including but not limited to "argues," "contends," "counters," "states," "observes," "reasons," "maintains," and "disputes." In other words, utilize your thesaurus. Be aware of the connotation of words, such as "claims" or "alleges," which may be construed as calling one party's contentions, factual or otherwise, into doubt. Be especially careful to avoid such word choice where the standard of review dictates that you view all of the facts in a specific way, such as in the light most favorable to the non-movant, etc. Be precise.

Afford less space and discussion to the losing party's arguments and reasoning. Embed them in dependent clauses in the middle of the paragraph or page. Do not place them in positions of emphasis such as the very beginning or very end of a paragraph or section. Surround them with facts, law, and reasoning that strongly support the prevailing party's position. Anticipate and rebut counterarguments to the prevailing party's position. Again, however, temper your persuasive techniques so that they do not undermine a strong, pervasive tone of impartiality.

Next, apply the law to the facts of your specific case. You may indicate a transition from a general discussion of the law to a specific discussion of the case with transition signals, such as "here," "in this case," or "in the instant case." For the reader's convenience, cite to the Record and law as appropriate. All cites should be accurate and properly formatted. See the example below:

> Here, it is undisputed that Mr. Smith's Complaint nowhere alleges that he timely filed a Charge of Discrimination with the EEOC before filing his Complaint in federal court. JA 8. Nor did he append a copy of the Charge to his Complaint or in any other

way notify ABC of such filing. JA 15. Not surprisingly, ABC contends that to date it has never received any Notice of a Charge of Discrimination filed by Mr. Smith. Appellant's Br. at 6.

Conclude with a takeaway summation that indicates the court's final disposition on that specific issue. For example, the opinion might conclude, "For these reasons, the District Court properly granted ABC's Motion to Dismiss for Failure to Exhaust Administrative Remedies, and we AFFIRM."

In sum, do not reinvent the wheel. Borrow from your bench memo as much as possible, revising and rewriting as necessary. Provide all of the reasons for the decision to guard against a successful appeal. Be clear, thoughtful, and thorough. Use proper, precise word choice, such as "The Court holds" to describe a legal holding and "The Court finds" to discuss factual findings. Be concise. Edit carefully.

Now let's turn to the Conclusion.

Disposition and Conclusion

The disposition and conclusion explain how the court will dispose of the case. For instance, if the appellate court holds that the district court properly dismissed Ms. Smith's complaint, then the disposition states how the appellate court will dispose of the case—by affirming. Common dispositions include but are not limited to dismissing, affirming, reversing, vacating, and remanding. A court may dispose of a case in full or in part. This occurs when a court either dismisses one claim but allows the remaining claims to proceed or affirms one aspect of a decision (perhaps the grant of a motion for sanctions) but reverses another (perhaps the grant of a motion for summary judgment). The conclusion typically begins with a sentence, such as "For the foregoing reasons, we [INSERT DISPOSITION]." Then a trial court opinion will note, "IT IS HEREBY ORDERED" explaining the judicial order that will effectuate the court's conclusion. This portion of the opinion involves special formatting as shown below.

Signature Block

A signature is not required for federal appellate opinions. When a signature block is required, it usually contains the judge's title, signature, court, the court address, and the date of issuance. At some trial courts, the final decision will require the judge's signature before being sent to the Clerk's Office. In such cases, be sure that the opinion is 100% final and perfect before presenting it to the judge for a signature. Also carefully consider your timing well in advance of the signing. For example, if a decision must be sent to the Clerk's Office on Monday, do not wait until Monday to provide your judge with a final draft to sign if she is not going to be in the office that day. Instead, plan ahead and know your judge's schedule. Determine well in advance when the decision must issue and when the judge will be available for signing; then plan your schedule accordingly. If possible, set up a short meeting on the Chambers calendar for the signing. In an emergency when you are unable to obtain your judge's signature, contact your judge and/or the Clerk's Office immediately to determine how to proceed or whether an electronic or authorized surrogate signature will suffice.

How do I draft a dissenting opinion?

In appellate courts, a dissenting opinion is one authored by a judge (or group of judges in an en banc matter) who disagrees with the disposition and rationale of the majority opinion. Dissents have no precedential power. According to some scholars, Supreme Court dissents typically occur due to "the ideological distance between the justice and the majority opinion writer."[33] It is unclear whether this holds true in other courts.

To draft a dissent, follow the same steps mentioned above. However, unless you disagree with the majority's background or statement of the issues, those sections may be heavily condensed or even omitted. Review the majority opinion and directly address the parts of the opinion with which your judge disagrees. However, always do so with proper respect or deference for the author of the majority opinion and those joining it. Once finalized, your Chambers will circulate the dissent to the other judges on the panel so that the majority and/or concurring opinions may be revised to address it. This back-and-forth revision process may last for weeks or even months. In some instances, revisions ultimately make the dissent unnecessary, such as when the majority eventually adopts some of the reasoning of the dissent, makes the case non-precedential, issues a per curiam affirmance without an opinion, or significantly narrows the holding. In an en banc or Supreme Court case, a dissenting opinion may be so persuasive and powerful that more judges or justices opt to join it, converting it to the majority opinion; however, such instances are incredibly rare.

How do I draft a concurrence?

A concurring opinion is one written by a judge or justice (or a group of judges in an en banc opinion or justices in a Supreme Court opinion) that agrees with the disposition of the majority opinion but for different reasons. Put differently, the judge would reach the same conclusion but on different grounds.

There are different kinds of concurring opinions. Some authors distinguish a regular concurrence from a special concurrence. In a regular concurrence, the judge agrees with the disposition as well as the content of the opinion. In a special concurrence, the judge agrees with the disposition but not the rationale. More specifically, an expansive concurrence aims to expand or supplement the reasoning, while a doctrinal concurrence offers an entirely different theory or rationale for the disposition. A limiting concurrence limits the holding, while a reluctant concurrence or concurrence dubitante indicates that a judge does not want to join the majority opinion but feels compelled to do so, perhaps because of stare decisis. Such opinions often ask the Court to reexamine the doctrine at issue. An emphatic concurrence aims to emphasize and clarify one or more specific aspects of the opinion. Finally, an unnecessary concurrence is one that does not elucidate the underlying reasoning, but which does serve to fracture the opinion. Witkin (1977) cautions against the use of such concurrences as they "produce all the evils of a concurring opinion with none of its values."[34]

Concurrences respond directly to the content of the majority opinion but usually also articulate independent, distinct reasons in support of the disposition. According to Maveety, "concurring voices produce the legal debate that furthers the intellectual development of the law on the Supreme Court."[35] In some instances, a law clerk will begin drafting a concurrence shortly after the oral argument and straw vote in reliance upon the judge's impressions of the reasoning on which the majority opinion will rely. In other instances, a judge will ask the law clerk to wait until both have reviewed the full majority opinion before drafting the concurrence since the majority opinion may reflect the concurring judge's concerns so as to make a concurrence unnecessary. In either case, a concurring opinion cannot be completed until the Chambers has reviewed the full majority opinion and discussed with the author whether he or she will modify it so as to obviate the need for a concurrence.

A concurrence is not controlling precedent but may still have a significant influence on the body of law. Indeed, Corley (2010) argues that "concurrences are a form of judicial signaling, where [lower court] judges use the signals contained in concurring opinions to interpret the majority opinion and apply it to the case before them."[36]

A concurring opinion is an important tool for compromise because unless the author of the majority opinion agrees to modify the opinion to quash the need for a concurrence, then the concurring opinion can convert the majority opinion into a fractured plurality opinion. A plurality opinion is one in which the disposition stands but no majority agrees with the underlying rationale for the disposition. Such a fractured opinion confuses the body of law, making it unclear whether the majority's rationale is binding. Perhaps not surprisingly, according to Corley (2009), lower courts are less likely to follow Supreme Court plurality opinions.[37] Spriggs and Hartford (2001) also found that a Supreme Court opinion with many concurrences is likelier to be subsequently overruled.[38] Likewise, plurality opinions lack the clarity, weight, and force of a single, unanimous opinion. That being said, concurrences like Justice Jackson's opinion in *Youngstown* sometimes do meaningfully contribute to the evolution of the law.

Finally, responding to the critiques and nuances of a sophisticated and well supported concurrence may enrich the majority opinion. According to the late Justice Antonin Scalia, "[t]he dissent or concurrence puts my opinion to the test, providing a direct confrontation of the best arguments on both sides of the disputed points. It is a sure cure for laziness, compelling me to make the most of my case."[39] His friend and colleague, Justice Ruth Bader Ginsburg similarly observed, "it heightens the opinion writer's incentive to 'get it right.' "[40]

To draft a concurrence, follow the same general steps for majority opinion drafting that are outlined above. However, unless you disagree with the majority's background or statement of the issues, those sections may be heavily condensed or even omitted. For this reason, a concurrence is often shorter than the corresponding majority opinion although exceptions exist. Review the majority opinion and any dissent(s) and directly address the parts of the opinion(s) with which your judge disagrees. However, always do so with proper respect or deference for the opinion's author as well as those joining the majority. Once finalized, your Chambers will circulate the concurrence to the other judges on the panel so that the majority and/or dissenting opinions may be tweaked to address it. As with a dissent, this collaborative peer review process may last for weeks or even months.

As with a dissenting opinion, revisions to the majority opinion sometimes make the concurrence unnecessary. For example, the majority may adopt at least some of the reasoning of the concurrence or make the case non-precedential. Likewise, in exceptional instances, an especially cogent and persuasive concurring opinion in an en banc or Supreme Court case can become the majority opinion.

Interestingly, in the beginning when the U.S. Supreme Court heard a case, each justice separately delivered a seriatim opinion. Chief Justice John Marshall ended that tradition because he felt that speaking in a single, unanimous voice would increase the Supreme Court's legitimacy and prestige. However, in the last fifty years, the number of concurring and dissenting opinions appears to be on the rise. Still, concurring opinions appear to be somewhat less common than dissenting opinions.[41] According to Chief Justice John G. Roberts, Jr., "nowadays, you take a look at some of our opinions and you wonder if we're reverting back to the English model where everybody has to have their say. It's more being concerned with the jurisprudence of the individual rather than working toward a jurisprudence of the Court."[42]

D. FINALIZING, EDITING, AND SUBMITTING A DRAFT OPINION

How and when do I submit my opinion to my judge?

Ideally you will submit your draft opinion to your judge no more than 30 to 45 days after the last filing, proceeding, or oral argument in the matter, depending on the complexity of the case and the other circumstances explained above. If you submit the draft opinion via email, include a subject line in your email indicating that it is the draft opinion for the particular case. In the body of the email, include the case name and docket number as well as a list of the attached documents in the order in which they are attached. Attach the draft opinion and any electronically highlighted versions of the key cases or documents that the judge should review along with the draft opinion unless instructed otherwise. Make sure that those attachments have clear names that always include a description of the document or the case name, not just a reporter cite.

A sample submission email might say something like:

> Judge Asbury,
>
> I hope you are doing well. Attached herein for your review are my draft opinion in *Thompson v. Foster*, 09–CV–2017, the parties' submissions, highlighted key portions of the Joint Appendix, and highlighted key cases. Please let me know if you have any questions or suggested revisions.
>
>   Best,
>
>   Janet

Some judges may prefer a hard copy submission, and if that is the case, then follow the instructions for hard copy submission outlined in Chapter 16.

What is the typical editing process for an opinion?

Once you are done drafting, spend significant time editing each section of the draft opinion to make sure that it is cohesive, clear, and consistent. After you finalize the Analysis, return to the Background, deleting any extraneous information. Print out the draft and review a hard copy. Read it aloud. Put it away and return to it. Edit each time with a distinct purpose, once for organization, once for typographical errors, etc. Use spellchecking software but do not rely on it exclusively. Apply all of the tips contained in Chapter 12. If your Chambers permits it and time allows, seek peer review from a strong writer in your Chambers. Discuss any gaps or issues with your peer and input edits *before* submitting the opinion to your judge.

The back-and-forth editing process with your judge is extremely collaborative and can go on for weeks or even months depending on your judge, the quality of the draft(s), the judge's style, and the complexity, size, and import of the case. Indeed, many opinions will go through five to ten drafts. Save each draft under a new name, such as Version Three, and include a date so that you always input your edits into the most current draft. Promptly input edits and provide the judge with a revised draft within a few days after the judge has provided suggested edits, depending on the breadth and difficulty of the suggested revisions.

Do not take the judge's constructive feedback personally. Welcome the feedback since it will only strengthen the opinion. If you disagree with a suggested revision for substantive reasons, respectfully and politely explain why you believe it will make the opinion inaccurate, misleading, imprecise, or otherwise subject to reversal. Use good judgment in accepting or rejecting edits. If the judge does not share your concerns, then make the change. After all, the judge authors the opinion and decides the case, not you. However, you may also memorialize your objection in a memo to file to protect yourself in the event that the case is later reversed or otherwise challenged because of the revision.

In some Chambers, the judge will ask you to share the near-to-final draft with one or all of your co-clerks for source-checking, cite-checking, and other review. This is especially common in trial courts. Allow ample time for this and be mindful of your co-clerks' busy schedules. As with your judge, do not take their comments personally. Your co-clerks are incredibly bright, so be open to their suggested revisions; incorporating them will likely strengthen the opinion. Again, exercise good judgment in accepting and rejecting edits, only incorporating suggested revisions that will strengthen the opinion.

The editing process of appellate opinions requires additional collaboration between Chambers. Thus, once an appellate opinion has been finalized in all respects, submit it to the other judges on the panel for review. Those Chambers may provide substantive edits or purely stylistic ones, suggested edits or mandatory ones. If a judge is particularly displeased with the majority opinion, he or she may indicate that either a substantive change is made, such as an insertion drafted by the displeased judge, or that judge will dissent or draft a separate dubitante opinion. In other cases, the judge may indicate that he or she will not require the changes so long as the other panelists agree to make the decision non-precedential. In still other instances, a judge may implore the other panelists to simply use a per curiam affirmance to dispose of the case or risk issuing a fractured opinion with a lengthy dissent or concurrence. You will often serve as your judge's diplomat during such discussions between Chambers unless and until they are escalated from the law clerks to the judges on the panel. Sometimes you will be able to revise the decision in such a way that another panelist will withdraw his or her concurrence, dissent, or dubitante opinion.

If another judge drafts a concurrence or dissent, the judge will provide it to you after reviewing the majority opinion, so the majority opinion can be revised to address the concurrence and/or dissent. Then the revised majority opinion will undergo additional rounds of editing and review.

As discussed in Chapter 15, in some appellate courts, a panel will circulate a final opinion (including any concurrence or dissent) to all Chambers for additional review before issuance. Chambers can respond in several ways: (1) taking no action; (2) noting purely proofreading or cite-checking edits; (3) offering suggested or required substantive or stylistic edits; (4) calling for an en banc poll to determine whether the case should be heard en banc even before the parties have requested it; or (5) placing a hold on the opinion. A hold will prevent the opinion from being issued. To have effect, these actions must take place *before* the date that the opinion will be sent to the Clerk's Office for processing, which is known as the "drop date" of the opinion. For more information on this process, see Chapter 15.

How do I decide which edits to incorporate from other Chambers?

Only incorporate edits that strengthen the opinion and are acceptable to your judge. As a general rule, you may incorporate any typographical, grammatical, or other proofreading or citation edits without first conferring with your judge. However, for stylistic edits, such as suggested changes to word choice, consult your judge if you believe those changes will significantly alter the meaning of the opinion or result in imprecision. For any other substantive changes, confer with your judge before incorporating them. Do not meet with your judge until you have received and reviewed *all* of the feedback from other Chambers and have determined which edits are questionable. For the sake of efficiency, discuss the suggested revisions with your judge in a single sitting rather than in a piecemeal fashion. Always note if changes are suggested versus required. Only the judge may decide whether to modify the opinion to preempt a concurrence or dissent or to simply keep the opinion as is.

What, if any, post-drafting issues must I consider?

After an opinion is drafted, there may still be post-drafting decisions to consider. You and your judge may want to revisit whether the opinion should be precedential or unpublished. For certain cases, such as those brought under the National Childhood Vaccine Injury Compensation Act of 1986, you will likely need to issue the opinion under seal to preserve the confidentiality of the parties and then provide the opinion to the parties for suggested redactions before it is made available to the public.[43]

In addition, once the opinion has been issued, you or the judicial assistant will typically track the opinion to determine whether it has prompted parties to file a petition for review, an appeal, or a petition for certiorari at the U.S. Supreme Court. You can usually do this by setting an alert with CM/ECF or with an electronic database, such as Westlaw, which will notify you if the parties seek further review.

In some appellate courts, a losing party may file a petition for review ("PFR"), asking the panel or entire court to reconsider the decision. As noted in Chapter 15, a PFR can request panel and en banc review; interestingly, a party may request only panel review but cannot exclusively request en banc review. A PFR should only be granted in exceptional circumstances where the panel overlooked a material fact or misapprehended the law. En banc review may be granted even if panel review is denied. En banc review is proper when the case presents a very important question of law or the case outcome appears to be inconsistent with the law of the circuit or with other controlling precedent. PFRs are rarely granted. Similarly, the U.S. Supreme Court typically grants certiorari in fewer than 10% of all petitions.[44]

What happens after the opinion is in its final form?

At the trial court, you may need to obtain your judge's signature as discussed above. This is not required at the appellate level. When the opinion is in final form and ready to issue, work with your judicial assistant to provide it to the Clerk's Office. Be sure that any metadata has been removed before sending files to the Clerk's Office.[45] *Metadata* refers to information regarding the document revisions, versions, etc.[46] After an opinion is issued, the original is filed with the Clerk of Court who, as necessary, prepares a judgment in accordance with the opinion.[47] Usually, the Clerk of Court also arranges for posting the opinion on the court's website and distributing it in accordance with court procedure.[48]

What, if any, post-drafting confidentiality and ethical obligations persist?

Drafting an opinion is a much more collaborative endeavor than drafting a bench memo. This is fitting since the opinion also has a much wider audience and may establish precedent that will impact the body of law. All of the discussions and written work product generated during this process must remain confidential for your lifetime. You may not share them with anyone at any time, absent your judge's express permission.

Opinion Drafting Checklist

The purpose of this checklist is to generally evaluate the effectiveness of your draft opinion. There is no single right way to draft an effective opinion. There are many different formats and organizations that are correct. This checklist provides a **non-exhaustive** *list of considerations that promote effective opinion drafting. More important factors are identified earlier in each subsection of the list. Edit with purpose, first for formatting, then for citation, etc. Please note that this checklist may not be identical to the considerations that your judge considers most important. Thus, confer with your judge to determine which factors matter most to him or her. Also consult local court rules and review representative opinions that your judge has recently authored.*

Formatting

1. Does the opinion have all required sections in the correct order? ☐
2. Does the opinion use the specified format, including font size and type? ☐
3. Does the opinion only use one space after each period? ☐
4. Are the pages numbered appropriately, in the bottom center margin, and in the proper font? ☐
5. Does the opinion use proper margins on all sides? ☐
6. Has the drafter eliminated unnecessary "white space" between sections of the brief and between paragraphs? ☐
7. Does the opinion avoid orphaned headings? ☐

Citation

1. Does the opinion use proper citation format? ☐
2. Does the opinion use *Id.* as appropriate, including italicizing the period? ☐
3. Does the opinion use proper introductory signals? ☐
4. Does the opinion include pincites as required? ☐
5. Does the opinion use the proper citation format for short cites? ☐
6. Does the opinion use proper italicization? ☐
7. Does the opinion use proper abbreviation(s) in case names? ☐
8. Does the opinion place the cases in the proper order? ☐
9. Do cites include subsequent case history as required? ☐

Caption

1. Is the Caption properly formatted? ☐
2. Does the Caption include all components? ☐
3. Is the Caption accurate? ☐

　　4.　Does the Caption avoid problems with grammar, punctuation, spelling, and capitalization? ☐

Introduction

　　1.　Does the Introduction include an effective roadmap sentence? ☐

　　2.　Are the parties properly designated? Is the designation used consistently? ☐

　　3.　Is the Introduction well organized? Does it flow well? ☐

　　4.　Is the Introduction clear and well written? ☐

　　5.　Is the Introduction objective and succinct? ☐

　　6.　Is the Introduction easy to read and understand? ☐

　　7.　Is the language precise and concise? ☐

　　8.　Does it succinctly and objectively explain the hub issue(s) in the order in which the opinion will discuss them? ☐

　　9.　Are key facts and procedural history included as necessary to briefly describe the basic nature of the case? ☐

　　10.　Does the Introduction briefly summarize the core reason(s) for the disposition or state "For the reasons explained herein"? ☐

　　11.　Does the Introduction clearly state the disposition (*e.g.,* denied, granted, affirm, reverse, etc.)? ☐

　　12.　Does the Introduction include proper word choice and sophisticated language? ☐

　　13.　Does the Introduction use active and passive voice appropriately? *(Do not use passive voice unless necessary.)* ☐

　　14.　Does the Introduction avoid problems with grammar, punctuation, spelling, and capitalization? ☐

　　15.　Does the Introduction omit quotations? ☐

　　16.　Are footnotes used sparingly, if at all? ☐
Are they necessary? ☐ Are they properly formatted? ☐

Background (Facts and Procedural History)

　　1.　Does the Background include an effective impact statement or roadmap sentence? ☐

　　2.　Are all relevant facts and procedural history included? Has irrelevant information been removed? ☐

　　3.　Are the parties properly designated? Is the designation used consistently? ☐

　　4.　Is the Background well organized? ☐ Does it flow well? ☐

　　5.　Is the Background clear and well written? ☐

6. Does the Background tell both sides of the story objectively and thoroughly? ☐

7. Is the Background easy to read and understand? ☐
Does it avoid overly long paragraphs? ☐

8. Are the facts and procedural history properly supported with accurate citations to the Record or Appendix? ☐

9. Is the language precise and concise? ☐

10. Does the Background omit Argument and legal conclusions? ☐

11. Are the citations to the Record or Appendix properly formatted? ☐

12. Does the Background use effective topic sentences? ☐

13. Does the Background include proper word choice and use language well? ☐ Does the Background use plain language? ☐

14. Does the Background use active and passive voice appropriately? *(Avoid passive voice unless necessary.)* ☐

15. Does the Background avoid problems with grammar, punctuation, spelling, and capitalization? ☐

16. Are quotations used effectively, if at all? ☐ Are they necessary? ☐ Are they formatted correctly? ☐

17. Are footnotes used sparingly, if at all? ☐ Are they necessary? ☐ Are they properly formatted? ☐

Discussion

1. ***Overall effectiveness:*** Is the Discussion easy to understand? ☐

2. ***Legal Landscape:*** Does the Discussion begin with an overview of the legal landscape, such as the relevant constitutional or statutory provision or seminal case? ☐
Does it clearly, precisely, objectively, and accurately state and explain the relevant overarching law? ☐

3. ***Standard of Review:*** Does the Discussion articulate the proper standard of review and support that assertion with accurate, properly formatted citations to controlling authority? ☐

4. ***Organization:*** Is the Discussion clearly and logically organized? ☐ Does it discuss the issues in the same order that they appeared in the Introduction? ☐

5. ***Analysis:*** Does the Discussion present a sound, proper, and well-developed analysis of each issue and sub-issue that does not make logical leaps? Are any key legal or factual issues missing? ☐

6. ***Tone:*** Is the Discussion objective and appropriately sophisticated? ☐

7. ***Effective use of authority:*** Does the Discussion use authority effectively, including effective case illustrations and parentheticals? ☐ Is the content of case illustrations and parentheticals properly tailored? ☐

8. ***Effective application of law to facts:*** Does the Discussion effectively apply the law to the facts, adequately developing each point? ☐

9. ***Effective handling of adverse authority and "bad" facts:*** Does the Discussion effectively handle opposing arguments or facts that undercut the disposition? ☐ Does the Discussion effectively counter critiques from the concurrence and/or dissent to the extent they exist? ☐

10. ***Headings:*** Are headings and subheadings clear, effective, and well placed? ☐

11. ***Transitions:*** Does the opinion use effective transitions between the various points of the Discussion? ☐

12. ***Paragraphs:*** Does the opinion use persuasive and strong topic sentences, and are paragraphs organized logically? ☐

13. ***Grammar & style:*** Does the Discussion avoid problems with grammar, punctuation, spelling, pronouns, and capitalization? ☐ Does the Discussion use active and passive voice appropriately? (*Active voice should be used unless passive voice is necessary or effective.*) ☐

14. ***Quotations:*** Are quotations used effectively, if at all? ☐ Are they properly formatted? ☐

15. ***Footnotes:*** Are footnotes used sparingly, if at all? ☐ Are they necessary? Are they properly formatted? ☐

16. ***Word Choice:*** Does the Discussion include proper word choice, including precise language? ☐ Does the Discussion use plain language? ☐

17. ***Brevity:*** Is the Discussion concise? ☐

Conclusion and Disposition

1. Is the Conclusion clear, accurate, and easy to understand? ☐

2. Does the Conclusion accurately and precisely state the appropriate disposition and impact of the decision? ☐

3. Is the Conclusion properly formatted? ☐

4. Does the Conclusion avoid problems with grammar, punctuation, spelling, pronouns, and capitalization? ☐

5. Does it include a properly formatted signature block? ☐

Overall Effectiveness

1. Taken as a whole, is the opinion well researched? ☐
2. Taken as a whole, is the opinion well written? ☐
3. Taken as a whole, is the opinion thoughtful? ☐
4. Taken as a whole, does the opinion address all issues raised or clearly explain why an issue is not explicitly addressed? ☐
5. Taken as a whole, is the opinion clear, coherent, and easy to understand? ☐
6. Taken as a whole, is the opinion objective? ☐
7. Taken as a whole, is the opinion accurate and thorough? ☐
8. Taken as a whole, is the opinion well organized? ☐
9. Taken as a whole, is the opinion effective? ☐
10. Taken as a whole, is the opinion precise and concise? ☐
11. Taken as a whole, is the opinion well edited, properly formatted, professional, and polished? ☐

Below are several sample opinions.[49]

A Sample Annotated Opinion

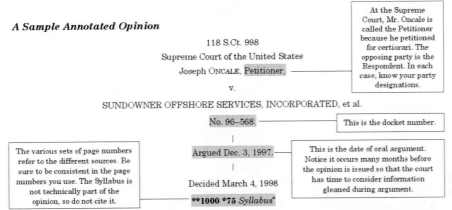

118 S.Ct. 998

Supreme Court of the United States

Joseph ONCALE, Petitioner,

v.

SUNDOWNER OFFSHORE SERVICES, INCORPORATED, et al.

No. 96–568.

Argued Dec. 3, 1997.

Decided March 4, 1998

1000 *75 *Syllabus*

At the Supreme Court, Mr. Oncale is called the Petitioner because he petitioned for certiorari. The opposing party is the Respondent. In each case, know your party designations.

This is the docket number.

The various sets of page numbers refer to the different sources. Be sure to be consistent in the page numbers you use. The Syllabus is not technically part of the opinion, so do not cite it.

This is the date of oral argument. Notice it occurs many months before the opinion is issued so that the court has time to consider information gleaned during argument.

Petitioner Oncale filed a complaint against his employer, respondent Sundowner Offshore Services, Inc., claiming that sexual harassment directed against him by respondent co-workers in their workplace constituted "discriminat[ion] . . . because of . . . sex" prohibited by Title VII of the Civil Rights Act of 1964, 42 U.S.C. § 2000e–2(a)(1). Relying on Fifth Circuit precedent, the District Court held that Oncale, a male, had no Title VII cause of action for harassment by male co-workers. The Fifth Circuit affirmed.

Held: Sex discrimination consisting of same-sex sexual harassment is actionable under Title VII. Title VII's prohibition of discrimination "because of . . . sex" protects men as well as women, *Newport News Shipbuilding & Dry Dock Co. v. EEOC,* 462 U.S. 669, 682, 103 S.Ct. 2622, 2630, 77 L.Ed.2d 89, and in the related context of racial discrimination in the workplace this Court has rejected any conclusive presumption that an employer will not discriminate against members of his own race, *Castaneda v. Partida,* 430 U.S. 482, 499, 97 S.Ct. 1272, 1282–1283, 51 L.Ed.2d 498. There is no justification in Title VII's language or the Court's precedents for a categorical rule barring a claim of discrimination "because of . . . sex" merely because the plaintiff and the defendant (or the person charged with acting on behalf of the defendant) are of the same sex. Recognizing liability for same-sex harassment will not transform Title VII into a general civility code for the American workplace, since Title VII is directed at discrimination because of sex, not merely conduct tinged with offensive sexual connotations; since the statute does not reach genuine but innocuous differences in the ways men and women routinely interact with members of the same, and the opposite, sex; and since the objective severity of harassment should be judged from the perspective of a reasonable person in the plaintiff's position, considering all the circumstances. Pp. 1001–1003.

83 F.3d 118, reversed and remanded.

■ SCALIA, J., delivered the opinion for a unanimous Court. THOMAS, J., filed a concurring opinion, *post,* p. 1003.

Attorneys and Law Firms

*76 Nicholas Canaday, III, Baton Rouge, LA, for petitioner.

Edwin S. Kneedler, Washington, DC, for U.S.

Harry M. Reasoner, Houston, TX, for respondents.

Opinion

JUSTICE SCALIA delivered the opinion of the Court.

> Notice that the judge, not you, is the author of the opinion. No opinion ever indicates which, if any clerk, assisted in drafting it, so this information must remain confidential absent your judge's permission.

This case presents the question whether workplace harassment can violate Title VII's prohibition against "discriminat[ion] ... because of ... sex," 42 U.S.C. § 2000e–2(a)(1), when the harasser and the harassed employee are of the same sex.

> The first paragraph of the opinion explains the general nature of the matter before the court. It succinctly states the hub issue in a clear, neutral way. Because an interpretation of statutory language was critical to this opinion, Justice Scalia cites it in the first paragraph.

I

The District Court having granted summary judgment for respondents, we must assume the facts to be as alleged by petitioner Joseph Oncale. The precise details are irrelevant ***77** to the legal point we must decide, and in the interest of both brevity and dignity we shall describe them only generally. In late October 1991, Oncale was working for respondent Sundowner Offshore Services, Inc., on a Chevron U.S. A., Inc., oil platform in the Gulf of Mexico. He was ****1001** employed as a roustabout on an eight-man crew which included respondents John Lyons, Danny Pippen, and Brandon Johnson. Lyons, the crane operator, and Pippen, the driller, had supervisory authority, App. 41, 77, 43. On several occasions, Oncale was forcibly subjected to sex-related, humiliating actions against him by Lyons, Pippen, and Johnson in the presence of the rest of the crew. Pippen and Lyons also physically assaulted Oncale in a sexual manner, and Lyons threatened him with rape.

> Many opinions use Roman numerals rather than the wordy, persuasive subheadings typical of many persuasive briefs. Remember that an opinion is neither persuasive or objective writing but instead a hybrid.

> Begin with facts and procedural history. In an appellate opinion, these are often combined in a section called "Background." In a trial court opinion, these may be included in a section called "Findings of Fact" if facts have been found or alternatively, "Background" if the opinion precedes fact-finding.

> The opinion makes clear that it will not recite all of the facts of the case but instead only the ones most relevant to the issue before the court.

> Notice that the Court explains why it does not recite all of the facts. This makes sure that the party understands that his story has been heard and taken into consideration rather than given short shrift.

Oncale's complaints to supervisory personnel produced no remedial action; in fact, the company's Safety Compliance Clerk, Valent Hohen, told Oncale that Lyons and Pippen "picked [on] him all the time too," and called him a name suggesting homosexuality. *Id.,* at 77. Oncale eventually quit—asking that his pink slip reflect that he "voluntarily left due to sexual harassment and verbal abuse." *Id.,* at 79. When asked at his deposition why he left Sundowner, Oncale stated: "I felt that if I didn't leave my job, that I would be raped or forced to have sex." *Id.,* at 71.

> Notice the opinion's judicious use of quotes. When you seek to emphasize something, quote it.

Oncale filed a complaint against Sundowner in the United States District Court for the Eastern District of Louisiana, alleging that he was discriminated against in his employment because of his sex. Relying on the Fifth Circuit's decision in *Garcia v. Elf Atochem North America,* 28 F.3d 446, 451–452 (1994), the District Court held that "Mr. Oncale, a male, has no cause of action under Title VII for harassment by male co-workers." App. 106. On appeal, a panel of the Fifth Circuit concluded that *Garcia* was binding Circuit precedent, and affirmed. 83 F.3d 118 (1996). We

> Here the Court briefly recounts the procedural history of the case.

granted certiorari. 520 U.S. 1263, 117 S.Ct. 2430, 138 L.Ed.2d 192 (1997).

*78 II ——————

Section Two contains the legal landscape.

[1] Title VII of the Civil Rights Act of 1964 provides, in relevant part, that "[i]t shall be an unlawful employment practice for an employer . . . to discriminate against any individual with respect to his compensation, terms, conditions, or privileges of employment, because of such individual's race, color, religion, sex, or national origin." 78 Stat. 255, as amended, 42 U.S.C. § 2000e–2(a)(1). We have held that this not only covers "terms" and "conditions" in the narrow contractual sense, but "evinces a congressional intent to strike at the entire spectrum of disparate treatment of men and women in employment." *Meritor Savings Bank, FSB v. Vinson,* 477 U.S. 57, 64, 106 S.Ct. 2399, 2404, 91 L.Ed.2d 49 (1986) (citations and internal quotation marks omitted). "When the workplace is permeated with discriminatory intimidation, ridicule, and insult that is sufficiently severe or pervasive to alter the conditions of the victim's employment and create an abusive working environment, Title VII is violated." *Harris v. Forklift Systems, Inc.,* 510 U.S. 17, 21, 114 S.Ct. 367, 370, 126 L.Ed.2d 295 (1993) (citations and internal quotation marks omitted).

It is common to begin the analysis with the statute at issue, quoting it as appropriate.

Here the opinion begins to unpack the Supreme Court's reasoning. Notice that the Court rarely uses lengthy case illustrations. More commonly, it relies upon quotes, parenthticals, and short citation sentences. Do not allow your opinion to lapse into a series of paragraphs illustrating one case after another.

[2][3][4] Title VII's prohibition of discrimination "because of . . . sex" protects men as well as women, *Newport News Shipbuilding & Dry Dock Co. v. EEOC,* 462 U.S. 669, 682, 103 S.Ct. 2622, 2630, 77 L.Ed.2d 89 (1983), and in the related context of racial discrimination in the workplace we have rejected any conclusive presumption that an employer will not discriminate against members of his own race. "Because of the many facets of human motivation, it would be unwise to presume as a matter of law that human beings of one definable group will not discriminate against other members of their group." *Castaneda v. Partida,* 430 U.S. 482, 499, 97 S.Ct. 1272, 1282, 51 L.Ed.2d 498 (1977). See also *id.,* at 514 n. 6, 97 S.Ct., at 1290 n. 6 (Powell, J., joined by Burger, C.J., and REHNQUIST, J., dissenting). In *Johnson v. Transportation Agency, Santa Clara Cty.,* 480 U.S. 616, 107 S.Ct. 1442, 94 L.Ed.2d 615 (1987), a male employee claimed that his employer discriminated against him because of his sex when it preferred a female employee for promotion. Although *79 we ultimately rejected the claim on other grounds, we did not consider it significant that the supervisor who made that decision was also a man. See *id.,* at 624–625, 107 S.Ct., at 1447–1448. If our precedents leave any doubt on the question,

This is a great example of using a quote from precedent to illustrate a point.

This is an excellent example of using two sentences to succinctly illustrate a case.

we hold today that nothing in Title VII necessarily bars a claim of discrimination "because of . . . sex" merely because the plaintiff and the ****1002** defendant (or the person charged with acting on behalf of the defendant) are of the same sex.

Courts have had little trouble with that principle in cases like *Johnson*, where an employee claims to have been passed over for a job or promotion. But when the issue arises in the context of a "hostile environment" sexual harassment claim, the state and federal courts have taken a bewildering variety of stances. Some, like the Fifth Circuit in this case, have held that same-sex sexual harassment claims are never cognizable under Title VII. See also, *e.g., Goluszek v. H.P. Smith, 697 F.Supp. 1452 (N.D.Ill.1988).* Other decisions say that such claims are actionable only if the plaintiff can prove that the harasser is homosexual (and thus presumably motivated by sexual desire). Compare *McWilliams v. Fairfax County Board of Supervisors,* 72 F.3d 1191 (C.A.4 1996), with *Wrightson v. Pizza Hut of America,* 99 F.3d 138 (C.A.4 1996). Still others suggest that workplace harassment that is sexual in content is always actionable, regardless of the harasser's sex, sexual orientation, or motivations. See *Doe v. Belleville,* 119 F.3d 563 (C.A.7 1997).

[5][6] We see no justification in the statutory language or our precedents for a categorical rule excluding same-sex harassment claims from the coverage of Title VII. As some courts have observed, male-on-male sexual harassment in the workplace was assuredly not the principal evil Congress was concerned with when it enacted Title VII. But statutory prohibitions often go beyond the principal evil to cover reasonably comparable evils, and it is ultimately the provisions of our laws rather than the principal concerns of our legislators by which we are governed. Title VII prohibits "discriminat [ion] ***80** . . . because of . . . sex" in the "terms" or "conditions" of employment. Our holding that this includes sexual harassment must extend to sexual harassment of any kind that meets the statutory requirements.

[7][8] Respondents and their *amici* contend that recognizing liability for same-sex harassment will transform Title VII into a general civility code for the American workplace. But that risk is no greater for same-sex than for opposite-sex harassment, and is adequately met by careful attention to the requirements of the statute. Title VII does not prohibit all verbal or physical harassment in the workplace; it is directed only at "*discriminat [ion]* . . . because of . . .

> Now the opinion explains how the Court has applied that overarching law to the facts of this case. This is the meat of the opinion. It contains the Court's independent analysis.

> Notice that the Court moves from plain language to precedent and finally to legislative history and policy. It places the strongest arguments first and the least compelling arguments last just as one would organize a persuasive brief. Note that the opinion may address points in a different order than the parties discussed them in the briefing.

> In deciding a case, the Justices examine all briefing, including amicus briefs.

sex." We have never held that workplace harassment, even harassment between men and women, is automatically discrimination because of sex merely because the words used have sexual content or connotations. "The critical issue, Title VII's text indicates, is whether members of one sex are exposed to disadvantageous terms or conditions of employment to which members of the other sex are not exposed." *Harris, supra,* at 25, 114 S.Ct., at 372 (GINSBURG, J., concurring).

[9][10][11][12] Courts and juries have found the inference of discrimination easy to draw in most male-female sexual harassment situations, because the challenged conduct typically involves explicit or implicit proposals of sexual activity; it is reasonable to assume those proposals would not have been made to someone of the same sex. The same chain of inference would be available to a plaintiff alleging same-sex harassment, if there were credible evidence that the harasser was homosexual. But harassing conduct need not be motivated by sexual desire to support an inference of discrimination on the basis of sex. A trier of fact might reasonably find such discrimination, for example, if a female victim is harassed in such sex-specific and derogatory terms by another woman as to make it clear that the harasser is motivated by general hostility to the presence of women in the workplace. A same-sex harassment plaintiff may also, of course, offer direct ***81** com-parative evidence about how the alleged harasser treated members of both sexes in a mixed-sex workplace. Whatever evidentiary route the plaintiff chooses to follow, he or she must always prove that the conduct at issue was not merely tinged with offensive sexual connotations, but actually constituted "*discrimina[tion]* . . . because of . . . sex."

[13][14] And there is another requirement that prevents Title VII from expanding into a general civility code: As we emphasized in *Meritor* and *Harris,* the statute does ****1003** not reach genuine but innocuous differences in the ways men and women routinely interact with members of the same sex and of the opposite sex. The prohibition of harassment on the basis of sex requires neither asexuality nor androgyny in the workplace; it forbids only behavior so objectively offensive as to alter the "conditions" of the victim's employment. "Conduct that is not severe or pervasive enough to create an objectively hostile or abusive work environment—an environment that a reasonable person would find hostile or abusive—is beyond Title VII's purview." *Harris,* 510 U.S., at 21, 114 S.Ct., at 370, citing *Meritor,* 477 U.S., at 67, 106 S.Ct., at 2405–2406. We have always regarded that requirement as crucial, and as sufficient to ensure that courts and juries do not mistake ordinary socializing in the workplace—such as male-on-male horseplay or intersexual flirtation—for discriminatory "conditions of employment."

[15][16] We have emphasized, moreover, that the objective severity of harassment should be judged from the perspective of a reasonable person in the plaintiff's position, considering "all the circumstances." *Harris, supra,* at 23, 114 S.Ct., at 371. In same-sex (as in all) harassment cases, that inquiry requires careful consideration of the social context in which particular behavior occurs and is experienced by its target. A professional football player's working environment is not severely or pervasively abusive, for example, if the coach smacks him on the buttocks as he heads onto the field—even if the same behavior would reasonably be experienced as abusive by the coach's secretary (male or female) back at the office. The ***82** real social impact of workplace behavior often depends on a constellation of surrounding circumstances, expectations, and relationships which are not fully captured by a simple recitation of the words used or the physical acts performed. Common sense, and an appropriate sensitivity to social context, will enable courts and juries to distinguish between simple teasing or roughhousing among members of the same sex, and conduct which a reasonable person in the plaintiff's position would find severely hostile or abusive.

III

> The final section contains the conclusion and disposition.

Because we conclude that sex discrimination consisting of same-sex sexual harassment is actionable under Title VII, the judgment of the Court of Appeals for the Fifth Circuit is reversed, and the case is remanded for further proceedings consistent with this opinion.

It is so ordered.

■ JUSTICE THOMAS, concurring.

> The concurring opinion is drafted separately by the author and circulated to the other judges prior to issuance of the opinion. This offers both authors an opportunity to edit their opinions to take into account statements made in the majority, dissent, etc.

I concur because the Court stresses that in every sexual harassment case, the plaintiff must plead and ultimately prove Title VII's statutory requirement that there be discrimination "because of . . . sex."

A Sample Appellate Opinion

133 S.Ct. 2107

Supreme Court of the United States

ASSOCIATION FOR MOLECULAR PATHOLOGY et al., Petitioners

v.

MYRIAD GENETICS, INC., et al.

No. 12–398.

Argued April 15, 2013.

Decided June 13, 2013

Opinion

■ JUSTICE THOMAS delivered the opinion of the Court.

Respondent Myriad Genetics, Inc. (Myriad), discovered the precise location and *2111 sequence of two human genes, mutations of which can substantially increase the risks of breast and ovarian cancer. Myriad obtained a number of patents based upon its discovery. This case involves claims from three of them and requires us to resolve whether a naturally occurring segment of deoxyribonucleic acid (DNA) is patent eligible under 35 U.S.C. § 101 by virtue of its isolation from the rest of the human genome. We also address the patent eligibility of synthetically created DNA known as complementary DNA (cDNA), which contains the same protein-coding information found in a segment of natural DNA but omits portions within the DNA segment that do not code for proteins. For the reasons that follow, we hold that a naturally occurring DNA segment is a product of nature and not patent eligible merely because it has been isolated, but that cDNA is patent eligible because it is not naturally occurring. We, therefore, affirm in part and reverse in part the decision of the United States Court of Appeals for the Federal Circuit.

I

A

Genes form the basis for hereditary traits in living organisms. See generally *Association for Molecular Pathology v. United States Patent and Trademark Office,* 702 F.Supp.2d 181, 192–211 (S.D.N.Y.2010). The human genome consists of approximately 22,000 genes packed into 23 pairs of chromosomes. Each gene is encoded as DNA, which takes the shape of the familiar "double helix" that Doctors James Watson and Francis Crick first described in 1953. Each "cross-bar" in the DNA helix consists of two chemically joined nucleotides. The possible nucleotides are adenine (A), thymine (T), cytosine (C), and guanine (G), each of which binds naturally with another nucleotide: A pairs with T; C pairs with G. The nucleotide cross-bars are chemically connected to a sugar-phosphate backbone that forms the outside framework of the DNA helix. Sequences of DNA nucleotides contain the information necessary to create strings of amino acids, which in turn are used in the body to build proteins. Only some DNA nucleotides, however, code for amino acids; these nucleotides are known as "exons." Nucleotides that do not code for amino acids, in contrast, are known as "introns."

Creation of proteins from DNA involves two principal steps, known as transcription and translation. In transcription, the bonds between DNA nucleotides separate, and the DNA helix unwinds into two single strands. A single strand is used as a template to create a complementary ribonucleic acid (RNA) strand. The nucleotides on the DNA strand pair naturally with their counterparts, with the exception that RNA uses the nucleotide base uracil (U) instead of thymine (T). Transcription results in a single strand RNA molecule, known as pre-RNA, whose nucleotides form an inverse image of the DNA strand from which it was created. Pre-RNA still contains nucleotides corresponding to both the exons and introns in the DNA molecule. The pre-RNA is then naturally "spliced" by the physical removal of the introns. The resulting product is a strand of RNA that contains nucleotides corresponding only to the exons from the original DNA strand. The exons-only strand is known as messenger RNA (mRNA), which creates amino acids through translation. In translation, cellular structures known as ribosomes read each set of three nucleotides, known as codons, in the mRNA. Each codon either tells the ribosomes which of the 20 possible amino acids to synthesize or provides a stop signal that ends amino acid production.

*2112 DNA's informational sequences and the processes that create mRNA, amino acids, and proteins occur naturally within cells. Scientists can, however, extract DNA from cells using well known laboratory methods. These methods allow scientists to isolate specific segments of DNA— for instance, a particular gene or part of a gene—which can then be further studied, manipulated, or used. It is also possible to create DNA synthetically through processes similarly well known in the field of genetics. One such method begins with an mRNA molecule and uses the natural bonding properties of nucleotides to create a new, synthetic DNA molecule. The result is the inverse of the mRNA's inverse image of the original DNA, with one important distinction: Because the natural creation of mRNA involves splicing that removes introns, the synthetic DNA created from mRNA also contains only the exon sequences. This synthetic DNA created in the laboratory from mRNA is known as complementary DNA (cDNA).

Changes in the genetic sequence are called mutations. Mutations can be as small as the alteration of a single nucleotide—a change affecting only one letter in the genetic code. Such small-scale changes can produce an entirely different amino acid or can end protein production altogether. Large changes, involving the deletion, rearrangement, or duplication of hundreds or even millions of nucleotides, can result in the elimination, misplacement, or duplication of entire genes. Some mutations are harmless, but others can cause disease or increase the risk of disease. As a result, the study of genetics can lead to valuable medical breakthroughs.

B

This case involves patents filed by Myriad after it made one such medical breakthrough. Myriad discovered the precise location and sequence of what are now known as the BRCA1 and BRCA2 genes. Mutations in these genes can dramatically increase an individual's risk of developing breast and ovarian cancer. The average American woman has a 12- to 13-percent risk of developing breast cancer, but for women with certain genetic mutations, the risk can range between 50 and 80 percent for breast cancer and between 20 and 50 percent for ovarian cancer. Before Myriad's discovery of the BRCA1 and BRCA2 genes, scientists knew that heredity played a role in establishing a woman's risk of developing breast and ovarian cancer, but they did not know which genes were associated with those cancers.

Myriad identified the exact location of the BRCA1 and BRCA2 genes on chromosomes 17 and 13. Chromosome 17 has approximately 80 million nucleotides, and chromosome 13 has approximately 114 million. *Association for Molecular Pathology v. United States Patent and Trademark Office,* 689 F.3d 1303, 1328 (C.A.Fed.2012). Within those chromosomes, the BRCA1 and BRCA2 genes are each about 80,000 nucleotides long. If just exons are counted, the BRCA1 gene is only about 5,500 nucleotides long; for the BRCA2 gene, that number is about 10,200. *Ibid.* Knowledge of the location of the BRCA1 and BRCA2 genes allowed Myriad to determine their typical nucleotide sequence.[1] That information, in turn, enabled Myriad to develop medical tests that are useful for detecting mutations in a patient's BRCA1 and BRCA2 genes and thereby assessing *2113 whether the patient has an increased risk of cancer.

Once it found the location and sequence of the BRCA1 and BRCA2 genes, Myriad sought and obtained a number of patents. Nine composition claims from three of those patents are at issue

---

[1]   Technically, there is no "typical" gene because nucleotide sequences vary between individuals, sometimes dramatically. Geneticists refer to the most common variations of genes as "wild types."

in this case.[2] See *id.*, at 1309, and n. 1 (noting composition claims). Claims 1, 2, 5, and 6 from the '282 patent are representative. The first claim asserts a patent on "[a]n isolated DNA coding for a BRCA1 polypeptide," which has "the amino acid sequence set forth in SEQ ID NO:2." App. 822. SEQ ID NO:2 sets forth a list of 1,863 amino acids that the typical BRCA1 gene encodes. See *id.*, at 785–790. Put differently, claim 1 asserts a patent claim on the DNA code that tells a cell to produce the string of BRCA1 amino acids listed in SEQ ID NO:2.

Claim 2 of the '282 patent operates similarly. It claims "[t]he isolated DNA of claim 1, wherein said DNA has the nucleotide sequence set forth in SEQ ID NO:1." *Id.*, at 822. Like SEQ ID NO:2, SEQ ID NO:1 sets forth a long list of data, in this instance the sequence of cDNA that codes for the BRCA1 amino acids listed in claim 1. Importantly, SEQ ID NO:1 lists only the cDNA exons in the BRCA1 gene, rather than a full DNA sequence containing both exons and introns. See *id.*, at 779 (stating that SEQ ID NO:1's "MOLECULE TYPE:" is "cDNA"). As a result, the Federal Circuit recognized that claim 2 asserts a patent on the cDNA nucleotide sequence listed in SEQ ID NO:1, which codes for the typical BRCA1 gene. 689 F.3d, at 1326, n. 9; *id.*, at 1337 (Moore, J., concurring in part); *id.*, at 1356 (Bryson, J., concurring in part and dissenting in part).

Claim 5 of the '282 patent claims a subset of the data in claim 1. In particular, it claims "[a]n isolated DNA having at least 15 nucleotides of the DNA of claim 1." App. 822. The practical effect of claim 5 is to assert a patent on any series of 15 nucleotides that exist in the typical BRCA1 gene. Because the BRCA1 gene is thousands of nucleotides long, even BRCA1 genes with substantial mutations are likely to contain at least one segment of 15 nucleotides that correspond to the typical BRCA1 gene. Similarly, claim 6 of the '282 patent claims "[a]n isolated DNA having at least 15 nucleotides of the DNA of claim 2." *Ibid.* This claim operates similarly to claim 5, except that it references the cDNA-based claim 2. The remaining claims at issue are similar, though several list common mutations rather than typical BRCA1 and BRCA2 sequences. See *ibid.* (claim 7 of the '282 patent); *id.*, at 930 (claim 1 of the '473 patent); *id.*, at 1028 (claims 1, 6, and 7 of the '492 patent).

C

Myriad's patents would, if valid, give it the exclusive right to isolate an individual's BRCA1 and BRCA2 genes (or any strand of 15 or more nucleotides within the genes) by breaking the covalent bonds that connect the DNA to the rest of the individual's genome. The patents would also give Myriad the exclusive right to synthetically create BRCA cDNA. In Myriad's view, manipulating BRCA DNA in either of these fashions triggers its "right to exclude others from making" its patented composition of matter under the Patent Act. 35 U.S.C. § 154(a)(1); see also § 271(a) ("[W]hoever without authority *2114 makes . . . any patented invention . . . infringes the patent").

But isolation is necessary to conduct genetic testing, and Myriad was not the only entity to offer BRCA testing after it discovered the genes. The University of Pennsylvania's Genetic Diagnostic Laboratory (GDL) and others provided genetic testing services to women. Petitioner Dr. Harry Ostrer, then a researcher at New York University School of Medicine, routinely sent his patients' DNA samples to GDL for testing. After learning of GDL's testing and Ostrer's activities, Myriad sent letters to them asserting that the genetic testing infringed Myriad's patents. App. 94–95 (Ostrer letter). In response, GDL agreed to stop testing and informed Ostrer that it would no longer accept patient samples. Myriad also filed patent infringement suits against other entities that performed BRCA testing, resulting in settlements in which the defendants agreed to cease all allegedly infringing activity. 689 F.3d, at 1315. Myriad, thus, solidified its position as the only entity providing BRCA testing.

---

[2]   At issue are claims 1, 2, 5, 6, and 7 of U.S. Patent 5,747,282 (the '282 patent), claim 1 of U.S. Patent 5,693,473 (the '473 patent), and claims 1, 6, and 7 of U.S. Patent 5,837,492 (the '492 patent).

Some years later, petitioner Ostrer, along with medical patients, advocacy groups, and other doctors, filed this lawsuit seeking a declaration that Myriad's patents are invalid under 35 U.S.C. § 101. 702 F.Supp.2d, at 186. Citing this Court's decision in *MedImmune, Inc. v. Genentech, Inc.*, 549 U.S. 118, 127 S.Ct. 764, 166 L.Ed.2d 604 (2007), the District Court denied Myriad's motion to dismiss for lack of standing. *Association for Molecular Pathology v. United States Patent and Trademark Office*, 669 F.Supp.2d 365, 385–392 (S.D.N.Y.2009). The District Court then granted summary judgment to petitioners on the composition claims at issue in this case based on its conclusion that Myriad's claims, including claims related to cDNA, were invalid because they covered products of nature. 702 F.Supp.2d, at 220–237. The Federal Circuit reversed, *Association for Molecular Pathology v. United States Patent and Trademark Office*, 653 F.3d 1329 (2011), and this Court granted the petition for certiorari, vacated the judgment, and remanded the case in light of *Mayo Collaborative Services v. Prometheus Laboratories, Inc.*, 566 U.S. ___, 132 S.Ct. 1289, 182 L.Ed.2d 321 (2012). See *Association for Molecular Pathology v. Myriad Genetics, Inc.*, 566 U.S. ___, 133 S.Ct. 694, 184 L.Ed.2d 496 (2012).

On remand, the Federal Circuit affirmed the District Court in part and reversed in part, with each member of the panel writing separately. All three judges agreed that only petitioner Ostrer had standing. They reasoned that Myriad's actions against him and his stated ability and willingness to begin BRCA1 and BRCA2 testing if Myriad's patents were invalidated were sufficient for Article III standing. 689 F.3d, at 1323; *id.*, at 1337 (opinion of Moore, J.); *id.*, at 1348 (opinion of Bryson, J.).

With respect to the merits, the court held that both isolated DNA and cDNA were patent eligible under § 101. The central dispute among the panel members was whether the act of *isolating* DNA—separating a specific gene or sequence of nucleotides from the rest of the chromosome—is an inventive act that entitles the individual who first isolates it to a patent. Each of the judges on the panel had a different view on that question. Judges Lourie and Moore agreed that Myriad's claims were patent eligible under § 101 but disagreed on the rationale. Judge Lourie relied on the fact that the entire DNA molecule is held together by chemical bonds and that the covalent bonds at both ends of the segment must be severed in order to isolate segments of DNA. This *2115 process technically creates new molecules with unique chemical compositions. See *id.*, at 1328 ("Isolated DNA . . . is a free-standing portion of a larger, natural DNA molecule. Isolated DNA has been cleaved (*i.e.*, had covalent bonds in its backbone chemically severed) or synthesized to consist of just a fraction of a naturally occurring DNA molecule"). Judge Lourie found this chemical alteration to be dispositive, because isolating a particular strand of DNA creates a nonnaturally occurring molecule, even though the chemical alteration does not change the information-transmitting quality of the DNA. See *id.*, at 1330 ("The claimed isolated DNA molecules are distinct from their natural existence as portions of larger entities, and their informational content is irrelevant to that fact. We recognize that biologists may think of molecules in terms of their uses, but genes are in fact materials having a chemical nature"). Accordingly, he rejected petitioners' argument that isolated DNA was ineligible for patent protection as a product of nature.

Judge Moore concurred in part but did not rely exclusively on Judge Lourie's conclusion that chemically breaking covalent bonds was sufficient to render isolated DNA patent eligible. *Id.*, at 1341 ("To the extent the majority rests its conclusion on the chemical differences between [naturally occurring] and isolated DNA (breaking the covalent bonds), I cannot agree that this is sufficient to hold that the claims to human genes are directed to patentable subject matter"). Instead, Judge Moore also relied on the United States Patent and Trademark Office's (PTO) practice of granting such patents and on the reliance interests of patent holders. *Id.*, at 1343. However, she acknowledged that her vote might have come out differently if she "were deciding this case on a blank canvas." *Ibid.*

Finally, Judge Bryson concurred in part and dissented in part, concluding that isolated DNA is not patent eligible. As an initial matter, he emphasized that the breaking of chemical bonds was not dispositive: "[T]here is no magic to a chemical bond that requires us to recognize a new product when a chemical bond is created or broken." *Id.,* at 1351. Instead, he relied on the fact that "[t]he nucleotide sequences of the claimed molecules are the same as the nucleotide sequences found in naturally occurring human genes." *Id.,* at 1355. Judge Bryson then concluded that genetic "structural similarity dwarfs the significance of the structural differences between isolated DNA and naturally occurring DNA, especially where the structural differences are merely ancillary to the breaking of covalent bonds, a process that is itself not inventive." *Ibid.* Moreover, Judge Bryson gave no weight to the PTO's position on patentability because of the Federal Circuit's position that "the PTO lacks substantive rulemaking authority as to issues such as patentability." *Id.,* at 1357.

Although the judges expressed different views concerning the patentability of isolated DNA, all three agreed that patent claims relating to cDNA met the patent eligibility requirements of § 101. *Id.,* at 1326, and n. 9 (recognizing that some patent claims are limited to cDNA and that such claims are patent eligible under § 101); *id.,* at 1337 (Moore, J., concurring in part); *id.,* at 1356 (Bryson, J., concurring in part and dissenting in part) ("cDNA cannot be isolated from nature, but instead must be created in the laboratory . . . because the introns that are found in the native gene are removed from the cDNA segment").[3] We granted certiorari. *2116 568 U.S. ___, 133 S.Ct. 694, 184 L.Ed.2d 496 (2012).

II

A

[1][2] Section 101 of the Patent Act provides:

"Whoever invents or discovers any new and useful . . . composition of matter, or any new and useful improvement thereof, may obtain a patent therefor, subject to the conditions and requirements of this title." 35 U.S.C. § 101.

We have "long held that this provision contains an important implicit exception[:] Laws of nature, natural phenomena, and abstract ideas are not patentable." *Mayo,* 566 U.S., at ___, 132 S.Ct., at 1293 (internal quotation marks and brackets omitted). Rather, " 'they are the basic tools of scientific and technological work' " that lie beyond the domain of patent protection. *Id.,* at ___, 132 S.Ct., at 1293. As the Court has explained, without this exception, there would be considerable danger that the grant of patents would "tie up" the use of such tools and thereby "inhibit future innovation premised upon them." *Id.,* at ___, 132 S.Ct., at 1301. This would be at odds with the very point of patents, which exist to promote creation. *Diamond v. Chakrabarty,* 447 U.S. 303, 309, 100 S.Ct. 2204, 65 L.Ed.2d 144 (1980) (Products of nature are not created, and " 'manifestations . . . of nature [are] free to all men and reserved exclusively to none' ").

[3][4] The rule against patents on naturally occurring things is not without limits, however, for "all inventions at some level embody, use, reflect, rest upon, or apply laws of nature, natural phenomena, or abstract ideas," and "too broad an interpretation of this exclusionary principle could eviscerate patent law." 566 U.S., at ___, 132 S.Ct., at 1293. As we have recognized before, patent protection strikes a delicate balance between creating "incentives that lead to creation, invention, and discovery" and "imped[ing] the flow of information that might permit, indeed spur, invention." *Id.,* at ___, 132 S.Ct., at 1305. We must apply this well-established standard to

---

[3]   Myriad continues to challenge Dr. Ostrer's Declaratory Judgment Act standing in this Court. Brief for Respondents 17–22. But we find that, under the Court's decision in *MedImmune, Inc. v. Genentech, Inc.,* Dr. Ostrer has alleged sufficient facts "under all the circumstances, [to] show that there is a substantial controversy, between parties having adverse legal interests, of sufficient immediacy and reality to warrant the issuance of a declaratory judgment." 549 U.S. 118, 127, 127 S.Ct. 764, 166 L.Ed.2d 604 (2007) (internal quotation marks omitted).

determine whether Myriad's patents claim any "new and useful . . . composition of matter," § 101, or instead claim naturally occurring phenomena.

B

[5] It is undisputed that Myriad did not create or alter any of the genetic information encoded in the BRCA1 and BRCA2 genes. The location and order of the nucleotides existed in nature before Myriad found them. Nor did Myriad create or alter the genetic structure of DNA. Instead, Myriad's principal contribution was uncovering the precise location and genetic sequence of the BRCA1 and BRCA2 genes within chromosomes 17 and 13. The question is whether this renders the genes patentable.

Myriad recognizes that our decision in *Chakrabarty* is central to this inquiry. Brief for Respondents 14, 23–27. In *Chakrabarty,* scientists added four plasmids to a bacterium, which enabled it to break down various components of crude oil. 447 U.S., at 305, and n. 1, 100 S.Ct. 2204. The Court held that the modified bacterium was patentable. It explained ***2117** that the patent claim was "not to a hitherto unknown natural phenomenon, but to a nonnaturally occurring manufacture or composition of matter—a product of human ingenuity 'having a distinctive name, character [and] use.' " *Id.,* at 309–310, 100 S.Ct. 2204 (quoting *Hartranft v. Wiegmann,* 121 U.S. 609, 615, 7 S.Ct. 1240, 30 L.Ed. 1012 (1887); alteration in original). The *Chakrabarty* bacterium was new "with markedly different characteristics from any found in nature," 447 U.S., at 310, 100 S.Ct. 2204, due to the additional plasmids and resultant "capacity for degrading oil." *Id.,* at 305, n. 1, 100 S.Ct. 2204. In this case, by contrast, Myriad did not create anything. To be sure, it found an important and useful gene, but separating that gene from its surrounding genetic material is not an act of invention.

[6] Groundbreaking, innovative, or even brilliant discovery does not by itself satisfy the § 101 inquiry. In *Funk Brothers Seed Co. v. Kalo Inoculant Co.,* 333 U.S. 127, 68 S.Ct. 440, 92 L.Ed. 588 (1948), this Court considered a composition patent that claimed a mixture of naturally occurring strains of bacteria that helped leguminous plants take nitrogen from the air and fix it in the soil. *Id.,* at 128–129, 68 S.Ct. 440. The ability of the bacteria to fix nitrogen was well known, and farmers commonly "inoculated" their crops with them to improve soil nitrogen levels. But farmers could not use the same inoculant for all crops, both because plants use different bacteria and because certain bacteria inhibit each other. *Id.,* at 129–130, 68 S.Ct. 440. Upon learning that several nitrogen-fixing bacteria did not inhibit each other, however, the patent applicant combined them into a single inoculant and obtained a patent. *Id.,* at 130, 68 S.Ct. 440. The Court held that the composition was not patent eligible because the patent holder did not alter the bacteria in any way. *Id.,* at 132, 68 S.Ct. 440 ("There is no way in which we could call [the bacteria mixture a product of invention] unless we borrowed invention from the discovery of the natural principle itself"). His patent claim thus fell squarely within the law of nature exception. So do Myriad's. Myriad found the location of the BRCA1 and BRCA2 genes, but that discovery, by itself, does not render the BRCA genes "new . . . composition[s] of matter," § 101, that are patent eligible.

[7] Indeed, Myriad's patent descriptions highlight the problem with its claims. For example, a section of the '282 patent's Detailed Description of the Invention indicates that Myriad found the location of a gene associated with increased risk of breast cancer and identified mutations of that gene that increase the risk. See App. 748–749.[4] In subsequent language Myriad explains

---

4   The full relevant text of the Detailed Description of the Patent is as follows:

"It is a discovery of the present invention that the BRCA1 locus which predisposes individuals to breast cancer and ovarian cancer, is a gene encoding a BRCA1 protein, which has been found to have no significant homology with known protein or DNA sequences. . . . It is a discovery of the present invention that mutations in the BRCA1 locus in the germline are indicative of a predisposition to breast cancer and ovarian cancer. Finally, it is a discovery of the present invention that somatic mutations in the BRCA1 locus are also associated with breast cancer, ovarian cancer and other cancers, which represents an indicator of these cancers or of the prognosis of these cancers. The mutational events of the BRCA1 locus can involve deletions, insertions and point mutations." App. 749.

that the location of the gene was unknown until Myriad found it among the approximately eight million nucleotide pairs contained in a subpart of chromosome *2118 17. See *Ibid.*[5] The '473 and '492 patents contain similar language as well. See *id.*, at 854, 947. Many of Myriad's patent descriptions simply detail the "iterative process" of discovery by which Myriad narrowed the possible locations for the gene sequences that it sought.[6] See, *e.g., id., at 750.* Myriad seeks to import these extensive research efforts into the § 101 patent-eligibility inquiry. Brief for Respondents 8–10, 34. But extensive effort alone is insufficient to satisfy the demands of § 101.

Nor are Myriad's claims saved by the fact that isolating DNA from the human genome severs chemical bonds and thereby creates a nonnaturally occurring molecule. Myriad's claims are simply not expressed in terms of chemical composition, nor do they rely in any way on the chemical changes that result from the isolation of a particular section of DNA. Instead, the claims understandably focus on the genetic information encoded in the BRCA1 and BRCA2 genes. If the patents depended upon the creation of a unique molecule, then a would-be infringer could arguably avoid at least Myriad's patent claims on entire genes (such as claims 1 and 2 of the '282 patent) by isolating a DNA sequence that included both the BRCA1 or BRCA2 gene and one additional nucleotide pair. Such a molecule would not be chemically identical to the molecule "invented" by Myriad. But Myriad obviously would resist that outcome because its claim is concerned primarily with the information contained in the genetic *sequence,* not with the specific chemical composition of a particular molecule.

Finally, Myriad argues that the PTO's past practice of awarding gene patents is entitled to deference, citing *J.E.M. Ag Supply, Inc. v. Pioneer Hi-Bred Int'l, Inc.*, 534 U.S. 124, 122 S.Ct. 593, 151 L.Ed.2d 508 (2001). See Brief for Respondents 35–39, 49–50. We disagree. *J.E.M.* held that new plant breeds were eligible for utility patents under § 101 notwithstanding separate statutes providing special protections for plants, see 7 U.S.C. § 2321 *et seq.* (Plant Variety Protection Act); 35 U.S.C. §§ 161–164 (Plant Patent Act of 1930). After analyzing the text and structure of the relevant statutes, the Court mentioned that the Board of Patent Appeals and Interferences had determined that new plant breeds were patent eligible under § 101 and that Congress had recognized and endorsed that position in a subsequent Patent Act amendment. 534 U.S., at 144–145, 122 S.Ct. 593 (citing *In re Hibberd*, 227 U.S.P.Q. 443 (1985) and 35 U.S.C. § 119(f)). In this case, however, Congress has not endorsed the views of the PTO in subsequent legislation. While Myriad relies on Judge Moore's view that Congress endorsed the PTO's position in a single sentence in the Consolidated Appropriations Act of 2004, see Brief for Respondents 31, n. 8; 689 F.3d, at 1346, that Act does not even mention genes, much *2119 less isolated DNA. § 634, 118 Stat. 101 ("None of the funds appropriated or otherwise made available under this Act may be used to issue patents on claims directed to or encompassing a human organism").

Further undercutting the PTO's practice, the United States argued in the Federal Circuit and in this Court that isolated DNA was *not* patent eligible under § 101, Brief for United States as *Amicus Curiae* 20–33, and that the PTO's practice was not "a sufficient reason to hold that isolated DNA is patent-eligible." *Id.*, at 26. See also *id.*, at 28–29. These concessions weigh against deferring to the PTO's determination.[7]

Notwithstanding Myriad's repeated use of the phrase "present invention," it is clear from the text of the patent that the various discoveries *are* the "invention."

[5]　"Starting from a region on the long arm of human chromosome 17 of the human genome, 17q, which has a size estimated at about 8 million base pairs, a region which contains a genetic locus, BRCA1, which causes susceptibility to cancer, including breast and ovarian cancer, has been identified." *Ibid.*

[6]　Myriad first identified groups of relatives with a history of breast cancer (some of whom also had developed ovarian cancer); because these individuals were related, scientists knew that it was more likely that their diseases were the result of genetic predisposition rather than other factors. Myriad compared sections of their chromosomes, looking for shared genetic abnormalities not found in the general population. It was that process which eventually enabled Myriad to determine where in the genetic sequence the BRCA1 and BRCA2 genes reside. See, *e.g., id., at 749, 763–775.*

[7]　Myriad also argues that we should uphold its patents so as not to disturb the reliance interests of patent holders like itself. Brief for Respondents 38–39. Concerns about reliance interests arising from PTO determinations, insofar as they are

C

[8][9] cDNA does not present the same obstacles to patentability as naturally occurring, isolated DNA segments. As already explained, creation of a cDNA sequence from mRNA results in an exons-only molecule that is not naturally occurring.[8] Petitioners concede that cDNA differs from natural DNA in that "the non-coding regions have been removed." Brief for Petitioners 49. They nevertheless argue that cDNA is not patent eligible because "[t]he nucleotide sequence of cDNA is dictated by nature, not by the lab technician." *Id.*, at 51. That may be so, but the lab technician unquestionably creates something new when cDNA is made. cDNA retains the naturally occurring exons of DNA, but it is distinct from the DNA from which it was derived. As a result, cDNA is not a "product of nature" and is patent eligible under § 101, except insofar as very short series of DNA may have no intervening introns to remove when creating cDNA. In that situation, a short strand of cDNA may be indistinguishable from natural DNA.[9]

III

It is important to note what is *not* implicated by this decision. First, there are no method claims before this Court. Had Myriad created an innovative method of manipulating genes while searching for the BRCA1 and BRCA2 genes, it could possibly have sought a method patent. But the processes used by Myriad to isolate DNA were well understood by geneticists at the time of Myriad's patents "were well understood, widely used, and fairly uniform insofar *2120 as any scientist engaged in the search for a gene would likely have utilized a similar approach," 702 F.Supp.2d, at 202–203, and are not at issue in this case.

Similarly, this case does not involve patents on new *applications* of knowledge about the BRCA1 and BRCA2 genes. Judge Bryson aptly noted that, "[a]s the first party with knowledge of the [BRCA1 and BRCA2] sequences, Myriad was in an excellent position to claim applications of that knowledge. Many of its unchallenged claims are limited to such applications." 689 F.3d, at 1349.

Nor do we consider the patentability of DNA in which the order of the naturally occurring nucleotides has been altered. Scientific alteration of the genetic code presents a different inquiry, and we express no opinion about the application of § 101 to such endeavors. We merely hold that genes and the information they encode are not patent eligible under § 101 simply because they have been isolated from the surrounding genetic material.

* * *

For the foregoing reasons, the judgment of the Federal Circuit is affirmed in part and reversed in part.

It is so ordered.

■ JUSTICE SCALIA, concurring in part and concurring in the judgment.

I join the judgment of the Court, and all of its opinion except Part I–A and some portions of the rest of the opinion going into fine details of molecular biology. I am unable to affirm those

relevant, are better directed to Congress. See *Mayo Collaborative Services v. Prometheus Laboratories, Inc.*, 566 U.S. ___, ___, 132 S.Ct. 1289, 1304–05, 182 L.Ed.2d 321 (2012).

[8] Some viruses rely on an enzyme called reverse transcriptase to reproduce by copying RNA into cDNA. In rare instances, a side effect of a viral infection of a cell can be the random incorporation of fragments of the resulting cDNA, known as a pseudogene, into the genome. Such pseudogenes serve no purpose; they are not expressed in protein creation because they lack genetic sequences to direct protein expression. See J. Watson et al., Molecular Biology of the Gene 142, 144, fig. 7–5 (6th ed. 2008). Perhaps not surprisingly, given pseudogenes' apparently random origins, petitioners "have failed to demonstrate that the pseudogene consists of the same sequence as the BRCA1 cDNA." *Association for Molecular Pathology v. United States Patent and Trademark Office*, 689 F.3d 1303, 1356, n. 5 (C.A.Fed.2012). The possibility that an unusual and rare phenomenon *might* randomly create a molecule similar to one created synthetically through human ingenuity does not render a composition of matter nonpatentable.

[9] We express no opinion whether cDNA satisfies the other statutory requirements of patentability. See, *e.g.*, 35 U.S.C. §§ 102, 103, and 112; Brief for United States as *Amicus Curiae* 19, n. 5.

details on my own knowledge or even my own belief. It suffices for me to affirm, having studied the opinions below and the expert briefs presented here, that the portion of DNA isolated from its natural state sought to be patented is identical to that portion of the DNA in its natural state; and that complementary DNA (cDNA) is a synthetic creation not normally present in nature.

Sample Trial Court Opinion

98 Fed.Cl. 575

United States Court of Federal Claims.

PATRIOT TAXIWAY INDUSTRIES, INC., Plaintiff,

v.

The UNITED STATES, Defendant,

and

Tactical Lighting Systems, Inc., Intervenor.

No. 11–124C.

Filed: April 22, 2011. |

Reissued: May 4, 2011.[1]

OPINION AND ORDER

■ WILLIAMS, JUDGE.

In this post-award bid protest, Patriot Taxiway Industries, Inc. ("Patriot") protests the award of a contract by the Department of the Air Force ("Air Force") to Tactical Lighting Systems, Inc. ("Tactical"), pursuant to Request for Proposals ("RFP") No. FA8533–10–R–25009. The RFP contemplated *577 a contract for the design, testing, development, and production of a portable airfield lighting system. Patriot claims that the Air Force improperly evaluated Tactical's and Patriot's past and present performance information by improperly aggregating contracts, considering future performance, not properly documenting its determination of performance confidence assessment ratings, and treating Patriot and Tactical unequally. Plaintiff also alleges that the Air Force failed to conduct a proper price reasonableness analysis and engaged in misleading discussions with Patriot regarding pricing. As such, Patriot seeks a reevaluation of the technically acceptable proposals.

Upon consideration of the Administrative Record ("AR") and the motion papers, the Court concludes that Patriot has not proven that the Air Force committed a prejudicial violation of law or deprived Patriot of a fair opportunity to compete for the contract. As such, Defendant's and Tactical's motions for judgment on the AR are granted, and Patriot's motion for a permanent injunction is denied.

Findings of Fact[2]

The Solicitation

The Air Force issued the RFP on March 2, 2010, as a small business set-aside. AR 9, 12. Amendments to the RFP were issued throughout March and April of 2010. The solicitation contemplated the design and production of a portable airfield lighting system known as Expeditionary Airfield Lighting Systems II ("EALS II"), which provides visual cues necessary for incoming aircraft to approach, land, and maneuver at night or in low-visibility conditions. The Air Force anticipated the award of a firm fixed-price, indefinite-delivery, requirements-type contract for a two-year base term and four one-year options. AR 14, 414–15. The Air Force

---

[1]   This opinion was issued under seal on April 22, 2011. The Court invited the parties to submit proposed redactions by May 2, 2011. The Opinion issued today incorporates Defendant's proposed redactions. This redacted material is represented by brackets [ ].

[2]   These findings of fact are derived from the AR and exhibits to the motion papers.

estimated the total contract value to be $44.1 million and envisioned that 24,428 airfield light fixtures would be delivered under the contract.

The procurement was conducted as a "Technically Acceptable—Performance—Price Tradeoff" best-value source selection procedure. The RFP explained the source selection procedure as follows:

(a) This acquisition will utilize the Technically Acceptable Performance-Price Tradeoff (TA-PPT) source selection procedure to make an integrated assessment for a best value award decision. A decision on the technical acceptability of each offeror's proposal will be made. For those offerors who are determined to be technically acceptable, tradeoffs will be made between past and present performance and price. Past and present performance is considered *significantly more important than price* though price remains an important consideration in the best value award decision.

(b) While the Government will strive for maximum objectivity, the tradeoff process, by its nature, is subjective; therefore, professional judgment is implicit throughout the selection process. . . . *Award will be made to one responsible offeror whose proposal conforms to all solicitation requirements . . . and provides the best value to the Government. . . .*

AR 80; *see also* AR 369, 468. Under this process, the Air Force first evaluated proposals for technical acceptability and then conducted a best value tradeoff analysis of the technically acceptable proposals based on past and present performance and price. AR 468.

To assist the Air Force in evaluating past and present performance, each offeror was to submit a FACTS Sheet, describing three "active or completed [contracts] (with preferably at least one year of performance history)" within the past six years that the offeror considered to be relevant in demonstrating its ability to perform the EALS II contract. AR 78–80, 412. Each offeror was also required to submit the same type of past and present performance information for its "critical subcontractor," defined as an entity that would be responsible for performing at least 25 percent of the production of light fixtures. *See* AR 367, 370.

*578 The RFP explained that the Air Force would consider "[t]he recency and relevancy of the [past and present performance] information, the source of the information, context of the data, and general trends in the contractor's performance." AR 81, 370. Based on its assessment, which would include analyzing the degree to which the effort involved the same "magnitude of work and complexities" as the EALS II contract, the Air Force would assign each proposal a rating of "very relevant," "relevant," "somewhat relevant," or "not relevant." AR 81–82. The RFP made clear that the " 'magnitude of effort and complexities' . . . denote[d] not only technical features and characteristics but also programmatic and logistical considerations, including but not limited to quantities produced, dollar values, type of contract, length of effort, testing requirements, type and complexity of data contractually required of the offeror, etc." AR 82.

The RFP defined each relevancy rating as follows:

RELEVANCY RATING	DEFINITION
VERY RELEVANT	A present and/or past performance effort that involved the production, testing, and installation of no less than 200 Light Emitting Diode (LED) fixtures in a commercial or military airfield, and such effort involved essentially the same magnitude of work and complexities that this solicitation requires.
RELEVANT	A present and/or past performance effort that involved the production and installation of no less than 100 LED or incandescent light fixtures in a commercial or military airfield or marine navigation application, and such effort involved much of the magnitude of work and complexities that this solicitation requires.
SOMEWHAT RELEVANT	A present and/or past performance effort that involved the production and installation of no less than 100 LED or incandescent light fixtures or other type [of] light fixtures powered by alternate energy sources including but not limited to solar, fuel cells, and wind in a commercial or military airfield, marine navigation, or industrial complex, and such efforts involved some of the magnitude of work and complexities that this solicitation requires.
NOT RELEVANT	Present and/or past performance efforts did not involve any of the magnitude of effort and complexities [that] this solicitation requires.

AR 81–82.

For the purpose of evaluating the relevancy of past and present efforts, the RFP permitted the Air Force to aggregate contracts. AR 82. Specifically, the RFP stated:

> The Government may consider an offeror's contracts in the aggregate in determining relevancy should the offeror's present and past performance lend itself to this approach. That is, an offeror's three contracts may by definition represent only a rating less than very relevant when each contract is considered as a stand-alone effort. However, when these contracts are performed concurrently (in whole or in part) and are assessed in the aggregate, the work may more accurately reflect a higher relevancy rating. In this situation, work performed in the aggregate will be considered in the assignment of a confidence assessment rating.

Id.

The RFP defined the performance confidence assessment rating as the Air Force's assessment of its confidence regarding the "offeror's ability to successfully accomplish the proposed effort based on the offeror's demonstrated present and past work record." AR 81. The RFP explained that, "considering the offeror's respective role and its work in [the] aggregate as well as the critical subcontractor(s) role, pursuant to the definition *579 of critical subcontractor, and its work in [the] aggregate, a confidence assessment rating will be assigned for the team as a whole." AR 372; *see also* AR 414.

The RFP explained that on the basis of the "recency, relevancy, and quality assessments" of the evaluated contracts, the Air Force would assign each offeror an overall performance assessment rating of substantial confidence, satisfactory confidence, limited confidence, no confidence, or unknown confidence. AR 81–83. The RFP defined each rating as follows:

RATING	DEFINITION
SUBSTANTIAL CONFIDENCE	Based on the offeror's performance record, the Government has a high expectation that the offeror will successfully perform the required effort.
SATISFACTORY CONFIDENCE	Based on the offeror's performance record, the Government has an expectation that the offeror will successfully perform the required effort.
LIMITED CONFIDENCE	Based on the offeror's performance record, the Government has a low expectation that the offeror will successfully perform the required effort.
NO CONFIDENCE	Based on the offeror's performance record, the Government has no expectation that the offeror will be able to successfully perform the required effort.
UNKNOWN CONFIDENCE	No performance record is identifiable or the offeror's performance record is so sparse that no confidence assessment rating can be reasonably assigned.

AR 83. The RFP stated that the confidence rating would serve as a basis for evaluating competing offers. AR 82.

With regard to pricing, the RFP stated that the Air Force would evaluate proposed prices for "reasonableness and balance" and calculate a total evaluated price for each proposal. AR 83. Specifically, the RFP stated:

> The existence of adequate price competition is expected to support a determination of reasonableness. Price analysis techniques may be used to further validate price reasonableness. If adequate price competition is not obtained and/or if price reasonableness cannot be determined using price analysis of Government obtained information, additional information in accordance with FAR 15.4 may be required to support the proposed price.

AR 83.

Submission of Offers

By April 29, 2010, the Air Force had received six proposals and had determined that three—those submitted by Damar AeroSystems ("Damar"), Patriot, and Tactical—were technically acceptable. AR 469, 478. The Air Force assembled a Performance Confidence Assessment Group ("PCAG") to review Damar's, Patriot's, and Tactical's past and present performance information and to assign performance confidence assessment ratings in accordance with the RFP. AR 473. The PCAG summarized its findings in the Performance Report. *See generally* AR 412–49.

The Evaluation of Patriot's Past and Present Performance

Patriot submitted past and present performance information for one of its contracts and for several contracts of its critical subcontractor. AR 437–38. For each effort, the Air Force explained why it assigned the particular relevancy rating. *See, e.g.,* AR 431, 438–39, 474–75.

In the Performance Report, the Air Force explained that Patriot's designated contract was determined to be "technically very relevant" because it involved the production, installation, and testing of over 500 LED lights—the type of lights required by the EALS II contract. AR 437–38.

However, "because the effort encompassed a significantly *580 smaller scope than the instant EALS II requirement in that it had a seven-month period of performance [for a] $7.7 [million] contract, the overall relevancy rating was determined to be somewhat relevant." AR 438. The Air Force noted that Patriot "did not show the capability to manage the logistical, programmatic, and contractual requirements associated with a long-term, high-dollar production effort." AR 439.

Patriot initially submitted four efforts of its critical subcontractor, but pursuant to the RFP, only three of these efforts were considered at the outset. AR 438. The first effort—a contract to provide 500 LED lights over three years for an estimated value of $3 million—was found to be "very relevant" from a technical standpoint. AR 431, 438, 474–75. However, the Air Force explained that, "[w]hen taking into account the scope and magnitude characteristics," the effort could only be rated "relevant" because the effort involved an estimated 500 LED fixtures, an estimated value of $3 million, and a three-year period of performance as compared to the 24,428 LED fixtures, six-year period of performance, and estimated value of $44 million of the EALS II contract. AR 438.

The second effort of Patriot's critical subcontractor was "determined to be technically relevant as it involved the production, installation, and testing of 112 portable LED airfield lighting fixtures." Id.; see also AR 433. The Air Force rated the effort as "somewhat relevant" because the "effort could not be determined [to be] very relevant as the quantities produced were not over 200" and because "this was not a long-term, high dollar contract; performance took place over a six-month period, and the contract value was $300 [thousand]." AR 438. The Air Force deemed the last two efforts "not relevant" based on the "lack of production and installation of light fixtures." AR 434–35.

Because the third submitted effort of Patriot's critical subcontractor was rated "not relevant," the Air Force considered Patriot's fourth effort, which was also rated "not relevant." AR 1484. As a result, the Air Force issued Evaluation Notice ("EN") P–P–1, which informed Patriot of the relevancy ratings of its one effort as well as the relevancy ratings assigned to the submitted efforts of its critical subcontractor. AR 435. EN P–P–1 also advised Patriot that it could submit additional efforts for those rated "not relevant" and that should Patriot possess additional information that might impact Patriot's relevancy ratings and confidence determination, it could also submit that information. Id.

In response to EN P–P–1, Patriot provided two additional efforts for consideration, but only one was considered. AR 438. This effort—an active and ongoing contract which began in 2004— was rated "very relevant" because it involved the production, installation, and testing of approximately 15,000 to 18,000 LED airfield lighting fixtures over a six-year (to date) period of performance at a value of $20 million. AR 436 (indicating that the period of performance was "2004–Present (estimated end date in 2016)"); see also AR 438, 1515–16 (listing the period of performance as "2004–ongoing" and noting that to date, 10,000 lighting fixtures had been installed and that the contract was active). The customer for this effort pointed out various strengths of the critical subcontractor, including responsiveness and on-time delivery, but also noted one weakness: "the correctness of the product when first produced." AR 438.

The Evaluation of Tactical's
Past and Present Performance

Tactical submitted past and present performance information for three of its contracts and three contracts of its critical subcontractor. AR 440. The first contract involved an ongoing effort to produce 1,988 incandescent light fixtures on a military airfield for the Taiwan Air Force. AR 440, 475–76. The contract, which was valued at $11.2 million, began in April of 2009, and was scheduled to conclude in April of 2012. Id. Although the scope and value of this contract were large, the Air Force rated it as "relevant" because the light fixtures delivered were incandescent, not LED. AR 440.

The second effort submitted by Tactical involved the production and installation of 663 incandescent light fixtures on a military *581 airfield over a period of 13 months—February of 2006 to March of 2007—at a total value of $1.7 million. AR 441. The Air Force determined that the effort was "somewhat relevant" because it did not involve the production of LED lights. *Id.* The third effort did not involve the production and installation of light fixtures and was therefore rated "not relevant." AR 442. The Air Force concluded that Tactical had "shown the capability to manage the logistical, programmatic and contractual requirements associated with long-term, high dollar production efforts relevant to this instant acquisition." AR 448.

Tactical also submitted three efforts of its critical subcontractor. AR 442–43. The first effort involved a Cooperative Research and Development Agreement ("CRADA") under which the critical subcontractor produced, tested, and installed 76 LED lights between January and December of 2005. AR 442. "There was no money involved because the effort was a CRADA." AR 442. Because the quantity of LED lights was less than 100, the effort was rated "not relevant." AR 443. The second effort, which was considered a second phase to the CRADA, involved 90 LED lights at a price of $199,983 and was performed between October and December of 2005. *Id.* Tactical represented that "[t]his effort involved the exact same lighting technology required by the EALS II." AR 2006–07. The customer feedback received on this effort "showed all exceptional ratings for all performance areas." AR 444. The Air Force observed that if reviewed on a stand-alone basis, this effort would be rated not relevant because of the small number of light fixtures produced. AR 443. Because the Air Force concluded that "these two efforts [were] so related that one [was] a direct follow-on of the first" and because the purchase order was "part of the CRADA effort according to the customer," the Air Force considered quantities and overall work involved in the CRADA with the purchase order. AR 443, 447. The Air Force rated these two efforts, collectively, as "somewhat relevant" because even considered in the aggregate, the scope and magnitude of the contracts were much smaller than the EALS II contract. *Id.* The third effort was rated "not relevant" because it did not involve production, installation, or testing. AR 444; *see also* AR 447.

The Air Force's Relevancy Ratings

After evaluating the past and present performance information that Damar, Patriot, and Tactical had submitted, the Air Force assigned the following relevancy ratings to each of the submitted contracts that it had reviewed: *[Relevancy Rating Chart Omitted]*

* * *

AR 436, 474–76. Based on these relevancy ratings, the Air Force assigned Patriot's proposal and Tactical's proposal the same overall performance confidence assessment rating of "satisfactory confidence," reflecting the Air Force's expectation that each offeror would *582 successfully perform the contract. AR 437, 448.[3]

Pricing Analysis

The Air Force compared the line item pricing found in each technically acceptable proposal and considered each proposal's initial total evaluated price. AR 450–67, 477–78. Patriot's proposal had an initial total evaluated price of $[ ]. AR 450.[4] By comparison, Tactical's proposal had an initial total evaluated price of $64,440,029. AR 450, 477. Damar's initial total evaluated price was $[ ]. *Id.*

Due to the pricing disparity, the Air Force sent an evaluation notice to the three offerors, advising them to reexamine their proposals and the RFP and to correct any errors and/or confirm their pricing. AR 454–57, 1489. EN PR–P–2 stated in pertinent part:

---

[3]   Damar's proposal received an overall performance confidence assessment rating of "limited confidence." AR 427, 474.

[4]   Elsewhere, the record indicates that Patriot's initial total estimated price was $[ ]. AR 477.

The Government's analysis of the offers received indicates that there is a disparity in prices. For each CLIN/SubCLIN, please re-examine

> Purchase Description PD08WRGBGBEA15, dated 4 February 2010, through Revision 2, dated 14 Apr 2010,
>
> Statement of Work dated 28 Dec 09,
>
> all DD Form 1423s attached to the RFP, and
>
> its pricing in the Schedule of the RFP

for both understanding and accuracy so as to ascertain if errors have been made. Offerors shall review their escalation for the option years and verify pricing. If an error is discovered, submit the replacement page(s) to the Schedule of the RFP/Proposal. If no error(s) has been made, offerors shall confirm their prices.

AR 457, 1489.

In response to this request, Patriot emailed the Air Force on May 21, 2010, and asked, "[c]ould you be more specific about the disparity [in] the findings? Is it one specific instance or multiple instances?" AR 1494. The Air Force replied, "[w]e are not pointing to any specific CLIN/SubCLIN; however, we are asking that all offerors review the requirements for understanding and that no errors were made in the pricing." AR 1496. Patriot responded:

> I realize you can't share pricing information between offerors, but is it fair to say that the disparity is an issue that one offeror has proposed pricing for some CLINs that is either much lower or much higher than the other offerors? In this case the Government has issued the EN to allow all offerors to review their pricing to be sure they have accounted for all of the tasks and effort needed to complete each CLIN or Sub CLIN. Is this a correct interpretation?

AR 1500. The Air Force replied, "[y]our interpretation is correct." AR 1503. After this exchange, Patriot confirmed its pricing and provided "background information on the methodology used to create the pricing structure submitted for the RFP." AR 1532. Tactical also confirmed its pricing. AR 2122. Due to errors discovered upon reexamination, Damar increased its total evaluated price to $[ ]. AR 478.

The total evaluated prices and the performance confidence ratings of the final proposal revisions were:

OFFEROR	PRICE	CONFIDENCE ASSESSMENT
Damar	$[ ]	Limited Confidence
Patriot	$[ ]	Satisfactory Confidence
Tactical	$64,440,029	Satisfactory Confidence

See AR 479.

Based on these findings, the Air Force determined that each offeror's proposed pricing was balanced and that each offeror's pricing was reasonable because multiple offers were submitted independently, which suggested that adequate price competition existed. AR 460–61.

*583 On August 5, 2010, the Air Force awarded the contract—No. FA8533–10–D–0010—to Tactical. AR 482. In support of this decision, the Source Selection Authority ("SSA") cited the RFP's provision that price would be an important consideration in the best value determination. AR 479–80. The SSA selected Tactical because Tactical's proposal received the same performance confidence assessment rating as Patriot's proposal, but Tactical offered to perform the EALS II contract for a significantly lower price. *Id.* As such, the SSA determined that Tactical's proposal provided the best value to the Air Force. *Id.*

GAO Decision

After receiving a written debriefing, Patriot filed an agency protest on August 10, 2010. AR 1783–85, 1788–89. The Air Force denied Patriot's protest, and on August 27, 2010, Patriot filed a protest with the United States Government Accountability Office ("GAO"). On November 9, 2011, GAO notified the parties of its intent to deny the protest. Mar. 1, 2011 Hr'g Tr. at 42. On December 6, 2010, GAO issued a decision, denying the protest on the merits, and this decision was released publicly on December 27, 2010. *Patriot Taxiway Indus., Inc.*, B–403690 Dec. 6, 2010, 2010 CPD ¶ 291; Mar. 1, 2011 Hr'g Tr. at 32.

On February 28, 2011, Patriot filed the instant action. On March 1, 2011, the Court heard argument on Patriot's application for a temporary restraining order ("TRO") and orally denied the TRO application. On April 11, 2011, this Court denied Patriot's motion for a preliminary injunction. Pending before the Court are Patriot's motion for permanent injunctive relief and Defendant's and Tactical's motions for judgment on the AR.

Discussion

Jurisdiction and Standard of Review

[1] The Court has jurisdiction over this bid protest pursuant to the Tucker Act, 28 U.S.C. § 1491(b)(1). In a bid protest, the Court reviews an agency's procurement decision under the standards enunciated in the Administrative Procedure Act ("APA"), 5 U.S.C. § 706. 28 U.S.C. § 1491(b)(4); *see also Ala. Aircraft Indus., Inc. v. United States, 586 F.3d 1372, 1373 (Fed.Cir.2009)*; *Gentex Corp. v. United States*, 58 Fed.Cl. 634, 648 (2003). Pursuant to the APA, this Court may set aside an agency action that was "arbitrary, capricious, an abuse of discretion, or otherwise not in accordance with law." 5 U.S.C. § 706(2)(A); *Ala. Aircraft Indus.*, 586 F.3d at 1373; *Gentex,* 58 Fed.Cl. at 648.

[2][3] The Court will find an agency action to be arbitrary and capricious when the agency "entirely failed to consider an important aspect of the problem, offered an explanation for its decision that runs counter to the evidence before the agency, or [the decision] is so implausible that it could not be ascribed to a difference in view or the product of agency expertise." *Ceres Envtl. Servs., Inc. v. United States,* 97 Fed.Cl. 277, 302 (2011) (citing *Ala. Aircraft Indus.,* 586 F.3d at 1375 (quoting *Motor Vehicle Mfrs. Ass'n v. State Farm Mut. Auto. Ins. Co.,* 463 U.S. 29, 43, 103 S.Ct. 2856, 77 L.Ed.2d 443 (1983))). Contracting officers are afforded considerable discretion in negotiated procurements, such as this one, where award is premised on a "best value" determination. *Id.* at 302 (citing *Banknote Corp. of Am., Inc. v. United States,* 365 F.3d 1345, 1355 (Fed.Cir.2004)). Such discretion, however, "does not relieve the agency of its obligation to develop an evidentiary basis for its findings." *Id.* (quoting *In re Sang Su Lee,* 277 F.3d 1338, 1344 (Fed.Cir.2002)). Indeed, it is well established that "the agency must examine the relevant data and articulate a satisfactory explanation for its action including a 'rational connection between the facts found and the choice made.'" *Id.* (quoting *Motor Vehicle,* 463 U.S. at 43, 103 S.Ct. 2856). A court may not substitute its judgment for that of the agency, but rather must confine its review to determining whether the agency's decision was arbitrary and capricious. *Motor Vehicle,* 463 U.S. at 43, 103 S.Ct. 2856; *Eskridge Research Corp. v. United States,* 92 Fed.Cl. 88, 97 (2010).

[4] To obtain permanent injunctive relief, a Plaintiff must show: (1) actual success on the merits; (2) it will suffer irreparable harm absent injunctive relief; (3) the balance of hardships tips in its favor; and (4) an injunction will serve the public interest. *See* *584 *PGBA, LLC v. United States, 389 F.3d 1219, 1228–29 (Fed.Cir.2004)*; *AshBritt v. United States,* 87 Fed.Cl. 344, 365 (2009).

The Grounds for Patriot's Protest

Patriot challenges the award on the following grounds:

- The Air Force failed to evaluate past performance in accordance with the RFP by aggregating consecutive but non-concurrent contracts, which led to one effort of Tactical's critical subcontractor receiving a rating of "somewhat relevant" and to Tactical obtaining a performance confidence assessment rating of "satisfactory confidence";

- In evaluating past and present performance, the Air Force improperly considered future performance;

- The Air Force assigned inconsistent weights to the determination of relevancy ratings for contracts included in the two proposals and assigned the same performance confidence assessment rating to Patriot and Tactical, despite differences in the relevancy of the contracts included in their respective proposals;

- The Air Force failed to document its determination of the performance confidence assessment ratings;

- The Air Force failed to conduct a proper price reasonableness analysis; and

- The Air Force's discussions with Patriot regarding pricing disparities were misleading and not meaningful.

Evaluation of Past and Present Performance

[5] Patriot alleges that the Air Force improperly aggregated the number of airfield light fixtures that Tactical's critical subcontractor produced under two efforts that were presented separately in Tactical's proposal. Patriot argues that the second contract was a follow-on to the first and that the contracts should not have been aggregated because they were performed consecutively, not concurrently. According to Patriot, the Air Force's improper aggregation led to Tactical's critical subcontractor receiving a rating of "somewhat relevant" on one contract, which led the Air Force to assign Tactical's proposal a performance confidence assessment rating of "satisfactory confidence"—the same rating that Patriot's proposal received.

The RFP expressly permitted the Government to "consider an offeror's contracts in the aggregate in determining relevancy should the offeror's present and past performance lend itself to this approach. . . . when these contracts are performed concurrently (in whole or in part)." AR 82, 372. Further, the RFP specified that when such contracts "are assessed in the aggregate, the work may more accurately reflect a higher relevancy rating." *Id.* Here, the periods of performance in these two contracts overlapped between October 1, 2005, and October 15, 2005, so the Air Force's aggregation of the two efforts was reasonable. *See* AR 445; AR 2002; Pl.'s Reply at 2.

Patriot further argues that the Air Force improperly considered future performance in Tactical's Taiwan Air Force contract because that contract was ongoing and Tactical had only performed one-third of the work. Patriot contends that the RFP included no provision that would allow future, promised and speculative performance to be reasonably included in the offeror's present and past work record. Pl.'s Reply at 3–4. However, Patriot itself submitted an ongoing active contract, estimated to end in 2016, as a reference for its critical subcontractor's performance. AR 436.

Because the RFP permitted the Air Force to evaluate "present" experience and "ongoing" efforts, the Air Force's evaluation of Tactical's Taiwan Air Force contract was reasonable. *See* AR 367. Tactical had been performing the Taiwan Air Force contract for more than a year when the proposals were evaluated. The Air Force confirmed that Tactical was performing satisfactorily and had delivered three of the nine airfield light systems under that contract. *See* AR 440–41.

With regard to Tactical's performance of the Taiwan Air Force contract, the Performance Report stated:

> The customer representatives reported that Tactical was the ultimate professional in its work and its customer service. Exceptional ratings were given in the areas *585 of: the extent to which the company's products met contractual requirements; the level of workmanship and quality in the products; the company's proficiency in processing the customer's order and timely deliveries' [sic] and, the company's knowledge and proficiency with industry standards and specifications.... The customer noted that [Tactical] had never provided late deliveries....

AR 440–41. Thus, although portions of the Taiwan Air Force contract had not yet been performed, the Air Force had an ample basis to consider Tactical's performance under this contract as of the evaluation. It was reasonable for the Air Force to factor both the magnitude of this ongoing contract and the quality of performance into its assessment.[5]

Patriot asserts that one of its contracts was more relevant than Tactical's Taiwan Air Force contract. The Air Force rated this Patriot contract as "somewhat relevant" because it involved only 500 LED fixtures as compared to the 24,428 lighting fixtures required by the EALS II contract, the contract's performance period was seven months as compared to six years, and the contract's estimated value was $7.7 million as compared to the $44 million estimated value of the EALS II contract. AR 430. The Air Force reasonably determined that Tactical's Taiwan Air Force contract was more relevant than Patriot's contract given that the Taiwan effort had a longer performance period, a higher estimated value, and involved delivery of significantly more airfield light fixtures.

Patriot argues that the Air Force treated Patriot and Tactical unequally in evaluating past and present performance based upon a numerical count of relevancy ratings. Patriot points out that it received one "somewhat relevant" rating for its effort, and the efforts of its critical subcontractor received one rating of "very relevant," another of "relevant," and a third of "somewhat relevant." AR 436, 474–75. By comparison, Tactical received one "relevant" rating and one "somewhat relevant" rating for its referenced contracts as well as one "somewhat relevant" rating for an effort of its critical subcontractor. AR 436, 475–76. Despite these differences, the Air Force assigned both proposals the same overall performance confidence assessment rating of "satisfactory confidence."

Patriot's argument that its relevancy ratings necessarily warranted a higher performance confidence rating than Tactical's relevancy ratings is premised on its misconception that a confidence assessment rating had to be raised if a greater number of "very relevant" or "relevant" ratings were attained. Basing a performance confidence assessment on a rote counting of the number of relevancy ratings was not what the RFP envisioned. Rather, under the RFP, confidence ratings were to be assigned based upon an assessment of the overall past and present performance, taking into account recency, relevancy, and quality. The broad category of "satisfactory confidence" could reasonably be applied to a differing array of relevancy ratings depending on the characteristics of the efforts involved. Here, both offerors were given

---

[5]   Patriot claims that in assessing relevancy the Air Force should have not have considered the total price of Tactical's Taiwan Air Force contract because a modification raising the price from roughly $8.3 million to $11.2 million had nothing to do with providing the portable airfield lighting system and instead entailed provision of 19 Mercedes Benz military vehicles. Pl.'s Reply at 4–5. However, Tactical was required to describe any changes in the dollar value and performance period of its reference contracts from the time of award until the time of its offer in the EALS II procurement. AR 87. As such, the Air Force was permitted to utilize this updated price in evaluating the effort. Moreover, the record does not reflect that the Air Force deemed the additional $3 million in the overall price of the Taiwan Air Force contract to be determinative either in rating the contract "relevant" or in assigning an overall "satisfactory confidence" rating to Tactical's proposal. Rather, in explaining the "relevant" rating for the Taiwan reference, the PCAG focused on the fact that the contract "involved the production and installation of 1,988 incandescent lights fixtures for use on a military airfield" and had received a positive customer review. AR 440, 447.

satisfactory confidence ratings, which meant that the Government had an expectation that each offeror would successfully perform the required effort. The record fully supports this expectation.

[6] Patriot further contends that Patriot's designated efforts should have been assigned at least two ratings of "very relevant," *586 without adequately articulating which efforts should have received higher ratings or why. Pl.'s Mem. at 12–13. In so arguing, Plaintiff is asking the Court to step into the shoes of the Air Force evaluators and assess past and present performance. As recognized in *AshBritt*, this Court does not sit as a super source selection authority to second guess and re-score offerors' proposals. *AshBritt*, 87 Fed.Cl. at 367 (citing *R & W Flammann GmbH v. United States*, 339 F.3d 1320, 1322 (Fed.Cir.2003)). In particular, the evaluation of offerors' past performance is generally within the agency's broad discretion. *Vantage Assocs., Inc. v. United States*, 59 Fed.Cl. 1, 22 (2003) (stating that an agency has broad discretion when evaluating past performance); *see also Clean Harbors Envtl. Servs., Inc.*, B–296176.2 Dec. 9, 2005, 2005 CPD ¶ 222 at *2. In any event, Patriot's mere disagreement with the Air Force's evaluation is insufficient to establish that the Air Force's actions were unreasonable. *See CRAssociates, Inc. v. United States*, 95 Fed.Cl. 357, 380–81 (2010).

Documentation of Patriot's Performance Confidence Assessment Rating

According to Patriot, the Air Force failed to document how it assigned a performance confidence assessment rating to the offerors based on the relevancy ratings. As Patriot argues:

> In reaching these ratings, the procurement documentation discusses at length the relevancy of the contracts and other past performance information submitted with the offers, but provides no explanation as to why a particular performance confidence rating was chosen as opposed to the other performance confidence ratings. Explanation of the final, critical step is missing.

Pl.'s Mem. at 14.

The Air Force justified its assignment of a performance confidence rating of "satisfactory confidence" to Patriot as follows:

> On the effort determined to be somewhat relevant, [Patriot] . . . demonstrated technical relevancy to EALS II, but did not show the capability to manage the logistical, programmatic, and contractual requirements associated with a long-term, high-dollar production effort. On the one very relevant, one relevant, and one somewhat relevant efforts, [Patriot's critical subcontractor] demonstrated that it can design, test, produce, and install lighting components with the same technical relevancy to EALS II. . . . Considering that the prime contractor itself offers somewhat relevant experience and its proposed critical subcontractor brings to the relationship very relevant to somewhat relevant experience, there is a satisfactory expectation that Patriot Taxiway Industries will be able to successfully perform the work required in the EALS II program.

AR 439; *see also* AR 437–38. The Air Force provided a similar explanation of the basis for Tactical's performance confidence rating. AR 447–48. These explanations belie Patriot's assertion that the Air Force did not document how it decided to assign a particular performance confidence rating.

In rejecting an argument similar to that which Patriot makes here, the court in *Precision Images, LLC v. United States* explained:

> The court does not adopt Precision's narrow construction of the [Source Selection Decision Document ("SSDD")] decision page. Rather, the court finds that the SSDD's decision page is not separate and distinct from the discussion immediately preceding it. Although the decision page does not specifically mention any of [the awardee's]

advantages or strengths and, in fact, constitutes only three paragraphs, it did not need to do so. Rather, the decision page represents the culmination of seven pages of detailed analysis of and findings related to the three offerors' proposals. Within those seven pages are individual present and past performance and cost/price evaluations for each offeror. The language of the SSDD is virtually identical to the findings contained in the PCAG final performance report, and it is apparent that the SSDD incorporated the PCAG's conclusions. . . . A review of the entire SSDD supports this conclusion. The SSDD incorporated [the awardee's] strengths or advantages into its discussion of [the awardee's] proposal, thereby rendering it unnecessary *587 and redundant to reiterate a summary of those findings in the decision page. . . . Precision's argument that these findings are absent from the agency's decision page ignores the totality of the SSDD.

79 Fed.Cl. 598, 621–22 (2007) (internal citations omitted). Here, as in *Precision Images*, the agency adequately explained why it assigned Patriot and Tactical performance confidence assessment ratings of "satisfactory confidence."

Price Reasonableness

[7][8][9] Patriot also asserts that the Air Force's price reasonableness determination was improper because it relied solely upon the existence of adequate price competition. The purpose of a price reasonableness analysis is to prevent the Government from paying too high a price for a contract. *See e.g., Ceres,* 97 *Fed.Cl.* at 303 n. 15; *DMS All-Star Joint Venture v. United States,* 90 Fed.Cl. 653, 663 n. 11 (2010). Where, as here, a firm-fixed price contract is anticipated, an agency "may use various price analysis techniques and procedures to ensure a fair and reasonable price," including the comparison of proposed prices received in response to a solicitation. FAR 15.404–1(b)(2)(i); *see also Comprehensive Health Servs., Inc.,* B–310553 Dec. 27, 2007, 2008 CPD ¶ 9 at *7. The Air Force determined that adequate price competition existed because multiple proposals were submitted independently of each other. AR 461. This approach was not erroneous. The RFP expressly provided that "[t]he existence of adequate price competition is expected to support a determination of reasonableness" and "[p]rice analysis techniques may be used to further validate price reasonableness." AR 83. As this Court recognized in *Ceres,* "[n]ormally, competition establishes price reasonableness." *Ceres,* 97 Fed.Cl. at 303; *see Comprehensive Health Servs., 2008 CPD* ¶ 9 at *7 (stating that "[a]gencies may rely upon adequate price competition alone to assess price reasonableness").

According to Patriot, because of the drastic variance among the Air Force's total program estimate of $44.1 million and the competitive offerors' total evaluated prices, the Air Force's reliance on "adequate price competition" to establish price reasonableness was arbitrary, capricious, and an abuse of discretion. However, when the Air Force's pricing analysis revealed pricing disparities, the Air Force requested that these offerors re-examine their proposals and the RFP's requirements to confirm or adjust their pricing. This request for re-examination was eminently rational and ensured that no offeror had made a mistake in its pricing. As the Air Force concluded, "[a]ll ENs for all Offerors were answered satisfactorily and are considered to be closed. . . . Adequate price competition exists." AR 460–61.

[10] To the extent Patriot alleges that Tactical's price was unreasonably low, Patriot challenges the realism of that price. *See, e.g., Ceres,* 97 *Fed.Cl.* at 302–03; *DMS,* 90 Fed.Cl. at 663 n. 11. As this Court recognized in *Ceres,* "[i]n a fixed-price procurement, the agency ordinarily does not consider the 'realism' of offerors' proposed prices because the contractor bears the risk of underpricing its offer." 97 Fed.Cl. at 303 (citations omitted). Here, as in *Ceres,* the Air Force entered into discussions to ensure that offerors' prices were accurate. Then, after confirming prices and recognizing that the contract was a fixed-price contract with the risk of an unrealistically low price falling on the contractor, the Air Force proceeded to award to Tactical with "its eyes wide open." *See Ceres,* 97 *Fed.Cl.* at 306. Patriot has not established that the Air

Force's action in awarding to the low-priced, technically acceptable contractor was arbitrary or capricious.

The Air Force's Discussions with Patriot

Patriot claims that the Air Force's discussions were misleading and not meaningful because they led Patriot to believe that the Air Force suspected that Patriot had omitted costs or failed to contemplate all of the RFP's requirements. Patriot asserts that the Air Force was obligated to convey what Patriot claims should have been the Air Force's concern, *i.e.*, that Patriot's pricing was nearly [ ] times the Air Force's estimate.

[11] Although the precise content of discussions is largely a matter of the contracting officer's judgment, generally discussions *588 must address weaknesses or deficiencies in an offeror's proposal that, unless corrected, would preclude award. *See, e.g., Ceres, 97 Fed.Cl. at 309–10.* An agency is not obligated to indicate every way that an offeror's proposal could be strengthened. *See Dynacs Eng'g Co. v. United States, 48 Fed.Cl. 124, 131 (2000).*

Where, as here, the proposed price is considered acceptable and reasonable, an agency is not required to discuss the issue at all. *See, e.g., Ceres, 97 Fed.Cl. at 309–10; Dynacs Eng'g Co.,* 48 Fed.Cl. at 132 ("[B]ecause [the agency] determined that the offeror's . . . price/cost were acceptable . . . [that point] did not require discussion."). "[U]nless an offeror's costs constitute a significant weakness or deficiency in its proposal, the contracting officer is not required to address in discussions costs that appear to be higher than those proposed by other offerors." *Ceres,* 97 Fed.Cl. at 309–10 (quoting *DMS,* 90 Fed.Cl. at 669) (citation omitted). "FAR § 15.306(e)(3) gives the contracting officer discretion to inform an offeror that 'its price is considered by the Government to be too high or too low.' But neither that provision, nor any other, requires the contracting officer to discuss a proposed price that . . . is not considered a significant weakness or deficiency." *Electronic Data Systems, LLC v. United States,* 93 Fed.Cl. 416, 434 (2010).

Patriot is Not Entitled to Permanent Injunctive Relief

To obtain permanent injunctive relief, Patriot must show that: (1) it has succeeded on the merits of the case; (2) it will suffer irreparable harm absent injunctive relief; (3) the balance of hardships tips in its favor; and (4) an injunction will serve the public interest. *See PGBA, 389 F.3d at 1228–29; AshBritt,* 87 Fed.Cl. at 365. Here, Patriot has not succeeded on the merits of its case—a circumstance which in and of itself defeats Patriot's request for injunctive relief. *See, e.g., Nat'l Steel Car, Ltd. v. Canadian Pac. Ry., Ltd., 357 F.3d 1319, 1325 (Fed.Cir.2004); Int'l Res. Recovery, Inc. v. United States,* 64 Fed.Cl. 150, 164 (2005) ("A plaintiff that cannot show that it will actually succeed on the merits of its claim cannot prevail on its motion for injunctive relief."); *Info. Tech. & Applications Corp. v. United States,* 51 Fed.Cl. 340, 357 n. 32 (2001) ("Absent success on the merits, the other factors are irrelevant."), *aff'd,* 316 F.3d 1312 (Fed.Cir.2003). As the Federal Circuit has explained:

> Although in some instances [the factors for injunctive relief], taken individually, are not dispositive because the district court's conclusion results from a process of overall balancing, a movant is not entitled to a preliminary injunction if he fails to demonstrate a likelihood of success on the merits. In other words, a court cannot use an exceptionally weighty showing on one of the other three factors to grant a preliminary injunction if a movant fails to demonstrate a likelihood of success on the merits.

Nat'l Steel Car, 357 F.3d at 1325 (internal citations omitted). Given Patriot's lack of success on the merits, injunctive relief is unwarranted.

Order

1. Defendant's Motion for Judgment on the Administrative Record is GRANTED.

2. Intervenor's Motion for Judgment on the Administrative Record is GRANTED.

3. Plaintiff's Motion for a Permanent Injunction and request for declaratory relief are DENIED.

4. Prior to the release of this opinion to the public, the parties shall review the opinion for competition-sensitive, proprietary, confidential or other protected information. The parties shall file proposed redacted versions of this decision or, in the alternative, file a notice indicating the party's intent not to file proposed redactions, on or before May 2, 2011.

5. The Clerk is directed to enter judgment on the Administrative Record in favor of Defendant and Intervenor consistent with this opinion.

A Sample Per Curiam Affirmance Without an Opinion

451 Fed.Appx. 954

This case was not selected for publication in the Federal Reporter.

Not for Publication in West's Federal Reporter See Fed. Rule of Appellate Procedure 32.1 generally

governing citation of judicial decisions issued on or after Jan. 1, 2007. See also Federal Circuit Rule 32.1 and

Federal Circuit Local Rule 32.1. (Find CTAF Rule 32.1)

United States Court of Appeals,

Federal Circuit.

JADE TRADING, LLC, by and through, Robert W. ERWIN and Laura Kavanaugh Ervin, on Behalf of Ervin Capital, LLC, Partners other than the Tax Matters Partner, Plaintiffs—Appellees,

v.

UNITED STATES, Defendant—Appellant.

No. 2011–5103.

Jan. 12, 2012.

Appeal from the United States Court of Federal Claims, No. 03–CV–2164, Mary Ellen Coster Williams, Judge.

Attorneys and Law Firms

David D. Aughtry, Chamberlain, Hrdlicka, White, Williams & Aughtry, of Atlanta, GA, argued for plaintiffs-appellees. With him on the brief was Linda S. Paine.

Joan I. Oppenheimer, Attorney, Tax Division, United States Department of Justice, of Washington, DC, argued for defendant-appellant. With her on the brief were Gilbert S. Rothenberg, Acting Deputy Assistant Attorney General, and Richard Farber, Attorney.

■ Before RADER, CHIEF JUDGE, LOURIE and LINN, CIRCUIT JUDGES.

JUDGMENT

■ PER CURIAM.

THIS CAUSE having been heard and considered, it is

ORDERED and ADJUDGED:

AFFIRMED. *See* Fed. Cir. R. 36.

E. SUPPLEMENTAL RESOURCES

1. RUGGERO J. ALDISERT, OPINION WRITING (3d ed. 2012).

2. Ruggero J. Aldisert, Meehan Rasch & Matthew P. Bartlett, *Opinion Writing and Opinion Readers*, 31 CARDOZO L. REV. 1 (2009).

3. AM. BAR. ASS'N APPELLATE JUDGES CONFERENCE, JUDICIAL OPINION WRITING MANUAL (1991).

4. William J. Brennan, Jr., *In Defense of Dissents*, 37 HASTINGS L.J. 427 (1985).

5. CALVERT G. CHIPCHASE, FEDERAL DISTRICT COURT LAW CLERK HANDBOOK (2007).

6. Tim Cobb & Sarah Kaltsounis, *Real Collaborative Context: Opinion Writing and the Appellate Process*, 5 J. ASS'N LEGAL WRITING DIRECTORS 156 (2008).

7. Jason J. Czarnezki, *The Dubitante Opinion*, 39 AKRON L. REV. 1 (2006).

8. MARY L. DUNNEWOLD, BETH A. HONETSCHLAGER, & BRENDA TOFTE, JUDICIAL CLERKSHIPS: A PRACTICAL GUIDE (2010).

9. FEDERAL JUDICIAL CENTER, JUDICIAL WRITING MANUAL (1991).

10. Thomas Gibbs Gee, *A Few of Wisdom's Idiosyncrasies and a Few of Ignorance's: A Judicial Style Sheet*, 1 Scribes J. Legal Writing 55 (1990).

11. J.J. GEORGE, JUDICIAL OPINION WRITING HANDBOOK (2007).

12. Ruth Bader Ginsburg, *Remarks on Writing Separately*, 65 WASH. L. REV. 133 (1990).

13. Gerald Lebovits et al., *Ethical Judicial Opinion Writing*, 21 GEO. J. LEGAL ETHICS 237 (2008).

14. Gerald Lebovits & Lucero Ramirez Hidalgo, *Advice to Law Clerks: How to Draft your First Judicial Opinion*, 36 WESTCHESTER B. J. 29 (2009).

15. JOSEPH LEMON, FEDERAL APPELLATE COURT LAW CLERK HANDBOOK (2007).

16. John Leubsdorf, *The Structure of Judicial Opinions*, 86 MINN. L. REV. 447 (2001).

17. ALIZA MILNER, JUDICIAL CLERKSHIPS: LEGAL METHODS IN MOTION (2011).

18. Jennifer L. Sheppard, *The "Write" Way: A Judicial Clerk's Guide to Writing for the Court*, 38 U. BALT. L. REV. 73 (2008).

19. JENNIFER L. SHEPPARD, IN CHAMBERS: A GUIDE FOR JUDICIAL CLERKS AND EXTERNS (2012).

20. Ruth Vance, *Judicial Opinion Writing: An Annotated Bibliography*, 17 J. LEGAL WRITING INST. 197 (2011).

21. Nancy A. Wanderer, *Writing Better Opinions: Communicating with Candor, Clarity, and Style*, 54 ME. L. REV. 47 (2002).

22. PAMELA CORLEY, CONCURRING OPINION WRITING ON THE U.S. SUPREME COURT (2010).

Notes

---

[1]   The author wishes to thank Professor Laura Graham of Wake Forest University School of Law and Professor Dan Brean of the University of Akron School of Law for their valuable contributions to this chapter.

[2]   FEDERAL JUDICIAL CENTER, LAW CLERK HANDBOOK 86 (Sylvan A. Sobel ed., 2d ed. 2007).

[3]   When a point of law is decided by a court, the decision is binding in all subsequent stages of the case unless subsequently overturned or vacated. *Law of the Case*, BLACK'S LAW DICTIONARY (10th ed. 2014).

[4]   Notably, Louisiana is the only state based on the Napoleonic Code rather than the English common law system.

[5]   E-Government Act of 2002, 44 U.S.C. § 3501 (2012).

[6]   Dimare Fresh v. United States, 808 F.3d 1301 (Fed. Cir. 2015).

[7]   ABIGAIL PERDUE & RANDALL LOCKWOOD, ANIMAL CRUELTY AND FREEDOM OF SPEECH: WHEN WORLDS COLLIDE 36 (2014).

[8]   18 U.S.C. § 48 (2016).

[9]   PERDUE & LOCKWOOD, *supra* note 7, at 36.

[10]   Stobie Creek Invs., LLC v. United States, 82 Fed. Cl. 636 (2008).

[11]   AMERICAN BAR ASSOCIATION, JUDICIAL OPINION WRITING MANUAL: A PRODUCT OF THE APPELLATE JUDGES CONFERENCE (West Publishing 1991).

[12]   MARY L. DUNNEWOLD, ET AL, JUDICIAL CLERKSHIPS: A PRACTICAL GUIDE (2010).

[13]   REBECCA A. COCHRAN, JUDICIAL EXTERNSHIPS: THE CLINIC INSIDE THE COURTHOUSE (1995).

[14]   FEDERAL JUDICIAL CENTER, *supra* note 2, at 81.

[15]   In some appellate courts, the 11-Day process, or an analogous procedure, allows other Chambers in the appellate court to review and provide feedback on a draft opinion before it is issued and in some cases, even place a hold on the opinion or request that the case be heard en banc. For more information on the 11-Day process, see Chapter 15.

[16]   Arthur Hellman, *Getting it Right: Panel Error and the En Banc Process in the Ninth Circuit Court of Appeals*, 34 U.C. DAVIS L. REV. 425, 435 (2000).

[17]   An *issue of first impression* refers to a novel issue that the deciding court has not squarely addressed and for which no controlling authority that is squarely on point exists. BLACK'S LAW DICTIONARY (10th ed. 2014).

[18]   FED. R. APP. P. 32.1(a)(i).

[19]   E-Government Act of 2002, 44 U.S.C. § 3501 (2012).

[20]   FEDERAL JUDICIAL CENTER, *supra* note 2, at 81.

21 Pro se litigants represent themselves and need not have legal training.

22 DUNNEWOLD, *supra* note 12, at 176–87.

23 PGA Tour, Inc. v. Martin, 532 U.S. 661, 700 (2001)(Scalia, J., dissenting).

24 Lee v. Weisman, 505 U.S. 577, 636 (1992)(Scalia, J., dissenting).

25 W. Stanfield Johnson, *The Federal Circuit's Great Dissenter and her "National Policy of Fairness to Contractors"*, 40 PUB. CONT. L.J. 275, 276 (2011).

26 Youngstown Sheet & Tube Co. v. Sawyer, 343 U.S. 579, 634 (1952)(Jackson, J., concurring); *see also* Sanford Levinson, *Why the Canon Should be Expanded to Include the Insular Cases and the Saga of American Expansionism*, 17 CONST. COMMENT. 241, 242 n.2 (2000).

27 The term "dubitante" appears to have first been used to describe Judge Blair's disposition in the 1737 case of *Bernard v. Stonehouse*, 2 Va. Colonial Dec. B60 (Va. Gen. Ct. 1737). It first appeared in American courts in the 1792 Maryland case of *Fulton v. Wood*.[24] Nearly one hundred years elapsed before the term appeared in a federal court; Judge Humphreys of the United States Court of Appeals for the District of Columbia (then known as the Supreme Court of the District of Columbia) employed the term in the 1876 case *Tuohy v. Martin*. *See* Jason J. Czarnezki, *The Dubitante Opinion*, 39 AKRON L. REV. 1, 2 (2006).

28 *Id.* at 2–3 (observing that as of 2006, only 626 American opinions mentioned the term "dubitante").

29 *See, e.g.,* Radio Corp. of Am. v. United States, 341 U.S. 412, 421 (1951)(Frankfurter, J., dubitante); O'Keeffe v. Smith Hinchman & Grylls Associates, Inc., 380 U.S. 359, 371 (1965)(Douglas, J., dubitante); Case-Swayne Co. v. Sunkist Growers, Inc., 389 U.S. 384, 403 (1967)(Douglas, J., dubitante).

30 Wi-LAN, Inc. v. LG Electronics, 684 F.3d 1364, 1374 (Fed. Cir. 2012) (Reyna J., *dubitante*).

31 *See generally* MATTHEW BUTTERICK, TYPOGRAPHY FOR LAWYERS (2d ed. 2015).

32 *See* Freeman v. Package Mach. Co., 865 F.2d 1331, 1340 (1st Cir. 1988) ("[o]nly rarely— and in extraordinarily compelling circumstances—will we, from the vista of a cold appellate record, reverse a district court's on-the-spot judgment concerning the relative weighing of probative value and unfair effect.").

33 PAMELA CORLEY, CONCURRING OPINION WRITING ON THE U.S. SUPREME COURT 5 (2010).

34 BERNARD WITKIN, MANUAL ON APPELLATE COURT OPINIONS 223 (1977).

35 CORLEY, *supra* note 33, at 2.

36 *Id.* at 6.

37 *Id.* at 10.

38 *Id.*

39 CORLEY, *supra* note 33, at 11.

40 *Id.*

41 *Id.*

42 *Id.* at 13.

43 42 U.S.C. §§ 300aa–1 to –33 (1986).

44 For an especially interesting case that did receive Supreme Court review, peruse the numerous decisions in *Cloer v. Secretary of Health and Human Services*, 133 S. Ct. 638 (2012).

45 FEDERAL JUDICIAL CENTER, *supra* note 2, at 82.

46 *Id.*

47 *Id.* at 81.

48 *Id.*

49 These opinions are taken from the Westlaw Advanced Research Database and reprinted herein with Westlaw's permission. For additional samples, see *SGS–92–X003 v. United States*, 85 Fed. Cl. 678 (2009) (involving the federal government's contractual breach arising from its failure to protect a confidential informant known as the "Princess") and *Tarasoff v. Regents of the Univ. of Cal.*,17 Cal.3d 425 (1976) (oft-cited case discussing the duty to warn).

CHAPTER 18

SPECIAL ISSUES WITH PRO SE LITIGANTS[1]

■ ■ ■

Pro se is a Latin term, which literally means "on behalf of oneself."[2] A pro se litigant is a person who represents himself or herself in a legal matter.[3] Notably, a pro se litigant need not be a licensed attorney or have any legal training whatsoever.

The concept of pro se representation derives from the idea that a person " 'can renounce a benefit[,] which the law would have introduced for his [or her] own convenience.' "[4] The origins of pro se representation can be traced to the Magna Carta, which aimed to ensure that all free Englishmen received a fair trial.[5] The import and scope of this right eroded over time, but legal scholars and parliamentarians revived it in the seventeenth century, again arguing that Englishmen be afforded the opportunity to represent themselves.[6] Although the purpose of the American Revolution was to escape British tyranny, America's founding fathers still borrowed heavily from the English legal system when establishing America's new government. Like their English counterparts, the founding fathers considered self-representation to be "a basic right of a free people" that should be fiercely safeguarded in the new republic.[7]

Thus, unsurprisingly, the modern American legal system preserves a litigant's right to proceed pro se. These protections aim to better ensure that *all* litigants, regardless of socioeconomic status or other factors, have access to justice.[8] For example, in *Faretta v. California*, the U.S. Supreme Court held that criminal litigants have the constitutional right to represent themselves.[9] In reaching its decision, the Court observed that "[i]n the federal courts, the right of self-representation has been protected by statute since the beginning of our Nation."[10] Indeed, 28 U.S.C. § 1654 states, "[i]n all courts of the United States the parties may plead and conduct their own cases personally or by counsel as, by the rules of such courts, respectively, are permitted to manage and conduct causes therein."[11]

Other provisions, including the Federal Rules of Civil Procedure and Federal Rules of Appellate Procedure, also specifically address pro se litigants.[12] Entities, such as the Administrative Office of the U.S. Courts and state judicial councils, provide further guidance and information on self-representation.[13] Some courts even produce guides for pro se litigants, which are usually available on official court websites.[14] These guides are often written in a question-and-answer format that is easily accessible to readers unfamiliar with legal terminology and procedure.

Even so, the right to self-representation is not unfettered. For instance, in 2013, the U.S. Supreme Court issued Rule 28.8, which forbids non-lawyers from arguing at the Court.[15] Nor do pro se litigants usually argue before federal appellate courts, unless they are attorneys.[16] Instead, pro se matters are generally resolved without oral argument.

A. SPECIAL CONCERNS IN PRO SE LITIGATION

The reason for such policies is that pro se litigants often pose special challenges to courts given that they usually have no formal legal training.[17] As such, they often "lack the resources, financial and other, to interpret the governing law or to marshal evidentiary and expert support for their claims."[18] Perhaps for this reason, many jurists have questioned the wisdom of proceeding pro se,[19] but some pro se litigants have no other choice. Many are low-income individuals[20] or prisoners[21] who cannot afford capable counsel or who are unable locate an attorney or legal aid organization willing or able to represent them on a pro bono basis.[22] Notably, 28 U.S.C. § 1915(e) vests a federal court with the discretion to appoint an attorney to represent an indigent litigant who presents "exceptional circumstances."[23] However, in deciding whether to exercise this discretionary power, the court must balance the interests at stake with other concerns that err against providing legal counsel.[24] In addition, prisoners proceeding pro se may request *in forma pauperis* status, which permits them to pay the court's filing fee in partial payments instead of all at once.[25]

In other instances, litigants proceed pro se simply because they mistrust attorneys, consider their cases too straightforward to necessitate counsel, or believe that, given their personal investment in the outcome, they can handle their cases more effectively than a third party.[26] On the whole, however, pro se litigants defy neat categorization, possessing differing levels of sophistication and bringing claims on diverse legal issues with distinct degrees of complexity. For example, a 2006 Utah study of pro se litigants found that 60% of litigants earned less than $36,000 per year, and 25% self-identified as minorities.[27] Yet 15% earned more than $96,000 per year.[28] Regardless of socioeconomic status or other attributes, pro se litigants who lack legal training may imperil their chance of success. According to Professor Sande L. Buhai, pro se litigants are five times likelier to lose at the district court level than their represented counterparts.[29]

In part because of their lack of legal training, pro se litigants often pose special issues for the judiciary.[30] These issues warrant significant attention given that pro se filings account for a substantial part of the docket and may be on the rise, at least in some jurisdictions.[31] For example, a 2009 study of the federal judiciary revealed that in one year, the docket included 71,543 pending pro se civil suits, or roughly 26% of the trial court docket.[32] During the same period, pro se matters accounted for 48% of the federal appellate docket, or 27,905 cases.[33] Pro se cases include criminal matters, prisoner petitions, civil cases, bankruptcy matters, administrative appeals, and original proceedings.[34] According to the National Center for State Courts, state courts have also seen a dramatic increase in pro se litigation, particularly within courts of limited jurisdiction, such as Small Claims Court and Traffic Court.[35] For example, in 2005, 4.3 million pro se litigants appeared in California state courts, bringing suits on various issues involving different degrees of complexity.[36]

The significant number of pro se cases places a heavy burden on court staff. In response, some courts have required staff to undergo training on pro se litigation, specifically discussing the types of assistance that court staff should provide. In recent years, roughly 20% of federal district courts have altered staff duties "or the organization of the clerk's office . . . to help staff handle pro se cases. These changes include designating specific staff to handle all pro se cases, rotating the responsibility for pro se cases, or referring pro se litigants to outside help."[37] According to the Federal Judicial Center, two of the most helpful measures have been designating staff for specific duties, such as hiring Pro Se Clerks who exclusively handle pro se matters[38] and providing "specially tailored information to pro se litigants (such as a package of forms or instructions for filing a case)" since some litigants struggle to locate such materials on their own.[39] For example, since 2001, the Eastern District of New York has operated a pro se office comprised of pro se staff attorneys and writ clerks whom a magistrate judge oversees.[40] This approach "reallocates the pro se caseload . . . away from all other judicial officers to a single initial decisionmaker who has multi-faceted responsibility for screening, processing, conferencing, and recommendations for disposition."[41]

Aside from the increasing number of pro se complaints filed, pro se matters pose unique challenges for other reasons as well. For instance, most pro se litigants lack access to CM/ECF and PACER, which means that they typically file paper submissions that not only often fail to comport with the court formatting guidelines but may also be illegible and incomplete.[42] Because filings do not automatically populate the case docket, individual law clerks must work very closely with the Clerk's Office to make sure that paper pleadings from pro se litigants are timely received and do not fall through the cracks. Not surprisingly, in a 2011 Federal Judicial Center survey, respondents complained that pro se submissions were "hard to read . . . incomplete . . . increas[ing] . . . [and] issues cannot be discerned."[43] Respondents also noted other issues, including "repeat filers, and frivolous filings; difficult or unstable litigants . . . and the need for improvements in the content or availability of court forms and information."[44] Respondents further reported five major issues, which plagued many pro se matters: (1) "pleadings or submissions that are unnecessary, illegible, or cannot be understood"; (2) "problems with pro se litigants' responses to motions to dismiss or for summary judgment"; (3) "pro se litigants' lack of knowledge about legal decisions or other information that would help their cases"; (4) "pro se litigants' failure to know when to object to testimony or evidence"; and (5) "pro se litigants' failure to understand the legal consequences of their actions or inaction[ ]. . ."[45] At the outset of your clerkship or as soon as you receive your first pro se matter, discuss these issues with your judge, supervising clerk, or Clerk's Office, as appropriate, to determine how to most effectively address them. As explained in more detail below, individual judges and even courts, as a whole, vary in their approaches to pro se matters. Thus, it is essential to discern your judge's preferred approach.

Given that pro se litigants generally lack familiarity with legal terminology and do not possess a strong grasp of judicial procedure, courts often afford pro se litigants special treatment, which impacts the way judges rule as well as how they write their orders and opinions. For example, Rule 8 of the Federal Rules of Civil Procedure requires a complaint to contain "a short and plain statement of the grounds for the court's jurisdiction . . . [a] showing that the pleader is entitled to relief; and . . . a demand for the relief sought . . ."[46] However, in *Haines v. Kerner*, the U.S. Supreme Court stated that the "allegations of the *pro se* complaint" are held "to less stringent standards than formal pleadings drafted by lawyers."[47] Thus, today many, if not most, courts construe pro se pleadings more liberally than those of their represented counterparts; some courts may even waive or relax technical filing requirements for pro se litigants.[48] Yet even with that liberal construction, pro se pleadings still appear less likely to withstand a motion to dismiss. Indeed, in the wake of *Twombly*[49] and *Iqbal*,[50] which heightened the standard sufficient for a pleading to satisfy Rule 8, the dismissal rate of pro se pleadings increased by 20%, twice the amount noted for pleadings not filed pro se.[51]

Notably, the liberality afforded to pro se litigants varies from one jurisdiction to another in part because *Haines*[52] "relaxed the pleading standard for the *pro se* plaintiff . . . [but] did not [expressly] define the degree of relaxation in comparison to" represented litigants.[53] As a result, jurisdictions utilize distinct approaches in pro se proceedings. For instance, Professor Michael Correll suggests that the D.C., First, Fourth, and Eighth Circuits generally do not liberally construe pro se pleadings or usually do so in a restrictive manner.[54] For example, when a pro se litigant asked the First Circuit to waive application of its administrative waiver rule merely because he proceeded pro se, the First Circuit denied his request, observing, "the Constitution does not require judges . . . to take up the slack when a party elects to represent himself."[55] Correll further contends that the Second, Fifth, Ninth, and Eleventh Circuits generally appear to take a more liberal approach.[56] For example, in *Weixel v. Board of Education of New York*, the Second Circuit stated that in a pro se matter, "the allegations . . . must be read so as to raise the strongest arguments that they suggest."[57]

Despite research regarding general approaches and trends, an individual judge may approach pro se matters differently from his or her peers on the same court; for this reason, significant variation may also exist from one judge to another. Furthermore, some courts establish local rules that specifically address pro se litigants. For example, in the Fourth Circuit, "Local Rule 34(b) requires pro se litigants to file informal briefs to serve as a sort of screening tool for the court."[58] Thus, at the outset of your clerkship or when you receive your first pro se matter, it is important to learn how your judge approaches pro se proceedings and which, if any, of your court's local rules address pro se matters. To accomplish this, simply ask your judge or supervising clerk to provide the cite to an exemplary recent opinion that your judge has authored in a pro se matter and read it to discern your judge's general approach to pro se proceedings.

B. JUDICIAL DRAFTING IN PRO SE MATTERS

For many of the reasons discussed above, drafting orders, correspondence, and opinions in pro se matters often poses unique challenges. The first rule of drafting is to understand your audience and tailor your writing appropriately. In this regard, consider the needs and level of sophistication of your pro se plaintiff. Be empathetic, remembering that you are writing directly to the litigant at the center of the lawsuit—a person whom the decision will personally impact. Ask yourself what educational level the individual likely possesses. Does the litigant appear to have any legal training? Consider these factors thoughtfully *before* you begin drafting and when later editing your work.

As you draft, take extra care to avoid making logical leaps or assuming knowledge on the part of the reader that he or she may lack. Explain things in a clear, step-by-step manner, providing more explanation and more context than you might if writing to an attorney. Avoid legalese, and if you must use it, define it either in the text or in a footnote. To see a sample of accessible writing, review the exemplary pro se opinion your judge or supervising clerk provided or review your court's *Pro Se Guide* to the extent one exists. Include an additional explanation of the court's procedure and processes, which you might typically omit when writing to an attorney. With your judge's permission, direct the party to additional helpful sources of information, such as the Clerk's Office or your court's manual for pro se litigants.[59] Maintain a patient, considerate tone. Your work product, whether a letter, order, or an opinion, must aim to educate the party, not merely inform him or her of the court's ruling.

Assuming your judge takes a more liberal approach toward construing pro se pleadings or briefing, look carefully to discern whether a party may be asserting an actionable claim or defense, albeit rather inarticulately. For instance, imagine that a pro se plaintiff's handwritten complaint states:

> My co-worker does not like me. He knows I am terrified of snakes. I have told him this often. And he also knows that I've been in and out of the hospital this year being treated for heart trouble. I had to have an ablation done last May and take heart medicine every day. But because my co-worker Dave does not like me, he deliberately left a huge rubber snake on my chair when I went to the bathroom. It looked so real! When I returned, I was so scared that I jumped and fell backward over my desk and hit the floor. The snake was knocked on top of me, and I thought it was going to bite me. I was so, so scared that my heart jumped out of my chest. I couldn't stop screaming. I pushed the snake off of me and ran out of my office. Halfway down the hall, I started having heart palpitations, and my friend Liz called 911. I had to be taken to the hospital. I am suing my coworker – David Alexander – for deliberately scaring the life out of me and causing me to suffer injuries and almost having a heart attack. And I am suing my employer, ABC Industries, for not firing Dave after I reported the incident to our Human Resources department. No one who behaves that way has any business working there.

At first glance, it may seem that the pro se plaintiff has not stated an actionable claim. After all, "deliberately scaring the life out of me" is not a cause of action. Yet because this is a pro se pleading, your judge may wish you to probe further, construing this a claim of intentional infliction of emotional distress ("IIED") or negligent infliction of emotional distress ("NIED"). Both are actionable civil tort claims. As such, rather than just dismissing the claim out of hand, your opinion might rename the claim and analyze it accordingly.

As noted above, aside from failing to clearly state the nature of the claim, pro se pleadings often present other issues as well. Some are handwritten and practically illegible.[60] Others are incoherent and contain grammatical and other errors, which make them very difficult to understand. Do your best to discern what the litigant aims to convey; with your judge's permission and as proper, seek clarification from the litigant, always including opposing counsel to avoid an impermissible ex parte communication. Even so, fully comprehending the nature and scope of a pro se pleading may prove difficult, if not impossible. As such, many pro se opinions include a helpful catch-all phrase at the end of the opinion either in the text or in a footnote. This phrase often states something to the effect of: "To the extent the party has raised additional or different arguments, those arguments have been considered and do not warrant relief."

Finally, do not assume that your judge will necessarily dispose of all pro se cases in the same manner simply because they are pro se. For example, courts dispose of cases via precedential opinions, non-precedential opinions, and non-precedential affirmances without a written opinion in certain cases. One might assume that because many pro se cases fail to state an actionable claim, pro se appeals are often disposed of via per curiam affirmances without an opinion, which are efficient and expedient. However, the courts often issue opinions in pro se matters despite the fact that pro se appeals are generally decided in the absence of oral argument. But why?

Although a full exploration of that interesting question exceeds the scope and purpose of this chapter, therapeutic jurisprudence may provide some insight. Therapeutic jurisprudence "focuses on the law's impact on emotional life and psychological well-being."[61] Advocates of therapeutic jurisprudence claim that, when thoughtfully crafted, judicial opinions can sometimes heal, or at least soothe, the emotional pain of aggrieved litigants by providing them with a meaningful opportunity to at least be heard.[62] This remains true even when the litigant ultimately does not prevail. Proponents of therapeutic jurisprudence contend that the mere act of voicing a claim to a concerned, attentive listener can sometimes be sufficient to redress an injury. Consciously or not, the underlying tenets of therapeutic jurisprudence may explain why courts often issue non-precedential opinions to dispose of pro se claims, even when those claims are meritless. At a minimum, such opinions make clear to the litigant that his or her concerns have been heard and thoughtfully considered. The opinions ideally explain the reasons underlying the disposition in plain language accessible to a non-lawyer. As one former judicial extern, Yawara Ng, astutely observed:

By avoiding Rule 36 affirmances, the court displays a form of judicial altruism. Writing opinions for meritless decisions takes time and may contravene judicial efficiency, but doing so gives appellants a sense of finality. Avoiding opinions via Rule 36 could embitter individuals pining for judicial relief and disrupt their psychological well-being. While the outcome may not be what non-lawyers sought . . . providing a reason is, in my view, more therapeutic than having them feel ignored.[63]

Below is an excerpt of a sample order of dismissal in a pro se matter. As you review it, consider how its tone and content differ somewhat from other opinions you may have read, which involved litigants represented by attorneys.

ORDER AND OPINION
GRANTING DEFENDANT'S MOTION TO DISMISS

■ ASBURY, JUDGE.

This matter comes before the Court on Defendant's motion to dismiss Plaintiff *pro se*'s complaint pursuant to Rule 12(b)(1) of the Rules of the United States Court of Federal Claims ("RCFC"). Because Plaintiff's complaint is time-barred, Defendant's motion is granted.

Background

Plaintiff *pro se*, Wyatt Heath ("Plaintiff"), served in the United States Army from April 15, 1982, until his discharge on August 6, 1990. On January 14, 2010, Plaintiff filed suit in the United States Court of Federal Claims ("Court"). He alleges that the Government violated the Due Process Clause of the Fifth Amendment when it tried him by general court-martial for alleged violations of the Uniform Code of Military Justice ("UCMJ"). Plaintiff asks the Court to rescind his discharge, correct his military records, and award him back pay as well as attorney's fees and costs.

Discussion

Plaintiff bears the burden of establishing the Court's subject-matter jurisdiction by a preponderance of the evidence. *Reynolds v. Army & Air Force Exch. Serv.*, 846 F.2d 746, 748 (Fed. Cir. 1988). In other words, Plaintiff must establish that it is more likely than not that the Court has the authority to hear and decide his case. *Id.* When considering a motion to dismiss for lack of subject-matter jurisdiction, the Court will accept the complaint's undisputed allegations as true and construe the complaint in the light most favorable to the plaintiff. *United Pac. Ins. Co. v. United States*, 464 F. 3d 1325, 1327–28 (Fed. Cir. 2006). "If the Court finds that it lacks jurisdiction over the subject-matter, it must dismiss the claim." RCFC 12(h)(3).[64]

Complaints drafted by *pro se* litigants are held to "less stringent standards than formal pleadings drafted by lawyers." *Naskar v. United States*, 82 Fed. Cl. 319, 320 (2008) (citation omitted). However, a *pro se* plaintiff must still establish the Court's subject-matter jurisdiction by preponderant evidence. *See Bernard v. United States*, 59 Fed. Cl. 497, 499 (2004) (observing that the latitude afforded to *pro se* litigants "does not relieve a pro se plaintiff from meeting jurisdictional requirements"), *aff'd*, 98 F. App'x 860 (Fed. Cir. 2004).

In the American legal system, each legal claim has an applicable statute of limitations, or specific period of time in which it can be brought before a court. "Every claim of which the United States Court of Federal Claims has jurisdiction shall be barred unless the petition thereon is filed within six years after such claim first accrues." 28 U.S.C. § 2501. Put differently, claims brought before this Court have a six-year statute of limitations that runs from the date that the cause of action accrued. *Id.* When a party brings a claim after the statute of limitations has expired, the Court lacks the authority to hear and decide the case. *See Martinez v. United States*, 333 F.3d 1295, 1303 (Fed. Cir. 2003) (observing that a court lacks subject-matter jurisdiction over claims brought outside the applicable statute of limitations). A claim accrues when all of the events have occurred that fix the alleged liability of the Government and entitle the plaintiff to institute the action. *Id.* In a case contesting a military discharge, the applicable start date for accrual of the statute of limitations is the plaintiff's date of discharge from the military. *Levy v. United States*, 83 Fed. Cl. 67, 74 (2008).

Here, Plaintiff's claim accrued on August 6, 1990—the date of his military discharge. However, he did not file a complaint arising from his discharge until January 14, 2010—approximately two decades later. Because Plaintiff filed his complaint long after the applicable six-year statute of limitations had expired, his claim is time-barred. The Court lacks the authority to hear and decide time-barred claims. Therefore, Plaintiff's complaint is dismissed.

Conclusion

For the foregoing reasons, Defendant's Motion to Dismiss is **GRANTED**.

Hoover Asbury

HOOVER ASBURY
JUDGE

Below is a sample letter to a pro se litigant.

The Honorable Maxine W. Herbert
Cabell County District Court
123 Spring Branch Road
Huntington, West Virginia 25701

April 8, 2017

Ms. Christine David
123 Lynn Oak Drive
Lavalette, West Virginia 25702

    Re: David v. Turner, No. 17–MH–5678

Dear Ms. David,

    Judge Herbert received your letter requesting that the Court grant you a three month extension to draft your response to Defendant's recent motion to dismiss your case for lack of subject-matter jurisdiction. As Defendant's motion and accompanying briefing explain, subject-matter jurisdiction refers to a court's authority to hear and decide a case. If a court lacks subject-matter jurisdiction, it must dismiss the case. In response to your letter, Judge Herbert asked me to write to you to explain that she cannot currently consider your request for an extension because you did not provide a copy of your request to opposing counsel before filing it with the Court. I have also sent a copy of this letter to Defendant.

    Judge Herbert cannot accept letters from one party to a case if the other party to the case did not also receive an identical copy of the letter by or before the same day it was mailed to the Court. In the American legal system, such a one-sided communication with the Court is called an *ex parte communication*. Ex parte communications are generally prohibited.

    If you would like Judge Herbert to consider your request for an extension, please file a *motion* with the Office of the Clerk of the Court. A motion is a request for a judge to do something. Write your request, explaining the extension you seek and why you believe the Court should grant it. On the same day that you file your motion with the Court, mail or otherwise provide an identical copy of your motion to Defendant's counsel as well so that Defendant has timely notice of your motion. This way your communication with the Court will not be a prohibited *ex parte* communication. Along with your motion to the Court, you must attach a signed affidavit, which states the date on which you mailed copies of your motion to Defendant's counsel at his current mailing address. An affidavit is a written statement in which you make an oath that you are telling the truth about the matters asserted in the statement and that you are competent to make such representations. A notary public must notarize your affidavit. To notarize the affidavit, just sign it in front of the notary, and the notary will then sign it and affix a special seal to it. Some local businesses, such as the UPS Store, offer affordable notary services.

Once the Court and opposing counsel receive your motion, opposing counsel will have a set period of time to respond to your motion. Opposing counsel may choose not to oppose the motion. However, if opposing counsel does choose to oppose your motion, he will provide you with a written copy of the opposition by mail or otherwise as well as file the opposition papers with the Court. Opposing counsel may not communicate with the Court unless he includes you on the correspondence or timely provides a copy of the filing to you.

Then Judge Herbert will carefully read and consider both sets of papers from both parties and make a decision. Judge Herbert will write out her decision and issue an Order explaining her decision to both parties at the same time. If she grants your request for an extension, she will also include the new extended deadline when she issues her Order so that you know by when you must file your response to Defendant's Motion to Dismiss your complaint. For more information on filing motions with the Court, please visit "Pro Se Resources" on our court website, which is available for free at http://www.wvcourts.gov. If you have any additional concerns or questions, please feel free to contact our Clerk's Office at (304) 867-5308. You may not telephone our Chambers directly unless you have opposing counsel on the line as well.

Sincerely,

Kenneth Hope

Law Clerk to the Honorable Maxine W. Herbert

In addition to crafting accessible orders, opinions, and correspondence in pro se matters, courts also assist pro se litigants in other meaningful ways. According to a 2011 report from the Federal Judicial Center:

The clerk's office provides a variety of services to help reduce the burden of pro se cases. The most common form of direct assistance provided to pro se litigants is procedural help by clerk's office staff as part of their regular duties; such assistance is provided by 76 (84%) of the 90 responding districts. Almost all of the districts offer at least one of the programs or services listed in the questionnaire, which included electronic filing through CM/ECF, dissemination outside the courthouse of information about pro se services, a mediation program, and a bar-sponsored program to help pro se litigants prepare their submissions.

Almost all of the districts offer at least one service to assist non-prisoner pro se litigants in obtaining legal representation. More than half of the districts appoint counsel to represent a pro se litigant for the full case or in limited circumstances (e.g., in mediation or at trial). Most districts help pro se litigants find counsel, pay for counsel, or both. Nearly half the district courts pay costs, and an additional quarter pay costs and some or all attorneys' fees. Additionally, a majority of district courts have taken steps to encourage attorneys to provide pro bono legal counsel for pro se litigants.[65]

In addition, many judges have employed other strategies to effectively resolve issues inherent in pro se proceedings while still preserving self-represented litigants' access to justice. For example, some judges construe submissions broadly, accept "letters as motions or pleadings, appoint counsel as appropriate, refer "pretrial matters to a magistrate judge," become more heavily involved in pro se proceedings "than in represented cases," and take a more relaxed stance toward "compliance with deadlines."[66]

C. SUPPLEMENTAL RESOURCES

1. Beth Zeitlin Shaw, *Please Ignore this Case: An Empirical Study of Nonprecedential Opinions in the Federal Circuit*, 12 GEO. MASON L. REV. 1013 (2004).

2. Michael Correll, *Finding the Limits of Equitable Liberality: Reconsidering the Liberal Construction of Pro Se Appellate Briefs*, 35 VT. L. REV. 863 (2011).

3. *Unbundling Resources by State*, Am. Bar Assoc., http://www.americanbar.org/groups/delivery_legal_services/resources/pro_se_unbundling_resource_center/pro_se_resources_by_state.html.

4. *Self-Representation Resource Guide*, National Center for State Courts, http://www.ncsc.org/Topics/Access-and-Fairness/Self-Representation/Resource-Guide.aspx.

5. Donna Stienstra, Jared Bataillon, & Jason A. Cantone, *Assistance to Pro Se Litigants in U.S. District Courts: A Report on Surveys of Clerks of Court and Chief Judges* (2011), http://www.fjc.gov/public/pdf.nsf/lookup/proseusdc.pdf/$file/proseusdc.pdf.

Notes

1   The author wishes to acknowledge the significant contributions of Professor Dan Brean of the University of Akron School of Law to this chapter. The author is also grateful to the intellectual contributions of Yawara Ng, Vanessa Garrido, and Cate Berenato. Mr. Ng and Ms. Garrido drafted excellent scholarly papers exploring the pro se phenomenon in federal courts as part of their summer clerking course. As a result of this happy coincidence, discussions regarding this chapter and their papers proved especially enriching and mutually beneficial.

2   *Pro Se*, BLACK'S LAW DICTIONARY (10th ed. 2014) ("For oneself; on one's own behalf; without a lawyer").

3   *Id.*

4   Michael Correll, *Finding the Limits of Equitable Liberality: Reconsidering the Liberal Construction of Pro Se Appellate Briefs*, 35 VT. L. REV. 863, 864 (2011) (quoting HERBERT BROOM, A SELECTION OF LEGAL MAXIMS 200 (1845)).

5   Claire Breay & Julian Harrison, *Magna Carta: An Introduction*, BRITISH LIBRARY (Jan. 1, 2017), http://www.bl.uk/magna-carta/articles/magna-carta-an-introduction.

6   Faretta v. California, 422 U.S. 806, 821–22 (1975) (discussing the historical origins of pro se representation).

7   *Id.* (holding that criminal litigants have a constitutional right to represent themselves).

8   In *Griffin v. Illinois*, the U.S. Supreme Court stated that "there is no meaningful distinction between a rule which would deny the poor the right to defend themselves in a trial court and one which effectively denies the poor an adequate appellate review according to all who have money enough to pay the costs in advance." 351 U.S. 12, 18 (1956).

9   Faretta, 422 U.S. at 836. *But see* Martinez v. Court of Appeals of Cal., Fourth App. Dist., 528 U.S. 152, 158–63 (2000) (concluding that there is no constitutional right to self-representation in criminal appeals because self-representation is unnecessary to a fair appellate proceeding partly due to "scant historical evidence pertaining to the issue of self-representation on appeal[s]" given that appeals were unavailable during the first part of the nation's history).

10   Faretta, 422 U.S. at 812 (1975).

11   28 U.S.C. § 1654 (2016).

12   *See generally* CODE OF CONDUCT FOR UNITED STATES JUDGES, Canon 4, § A(2)(c); FED. R. CIV. P. 11; FED. R. CRIM. P. 11; FED R. APP. P. 3.

13   *See, e.g., Preparing for Court*, CAL. COURTS, http://www.courts.ca.gov/1002.htm.

14   *See, e.g., Pro Se Litigant Guide*, UNITED STATES DIST. COURT FOR THE DIST. OF UTAH 1 (Apr. 2014), http://www.utd.uscourts.gov/forms/prose_guide.pdf (advising readers that "self-representation carries certain responsibilities and risks that pro se litigants should be aware of before they proceed. The court encourages all individuals who are thinking about pro se or self-representation to carefully review the risks associated with self-representation and to inform themselves of the potential consequences."). According to a 2011 study by the Federal Judicial Center:

> The most common sources of information are the district's local rules, principal forms, and courthouse or courtroom locations, followed by handbooks developed specifically for pro se litigants. Eighty-four percent of the districts have such a handbook for non-prisoner pro se litigants, and 77% have one for prisoner pro se litigants. The courts' websites are the most likely place to find rules, forms, and courthouse locations, while the public area of the clerk's office is the most common place to acquire a nonprisoner handbook. Pro se litigants with access to neither must depend on getting the appropriate materials from court staff through the mail or by finding some other source. The prisoner pro se handbook, for example, is most accessible by mail. While 84% of district courts provide free public access to computers in the clerk's office and 67% provide access to CM/ECF, only 6% provide software to assist pro se filers in preparing pleadings or other submissions.

Donna Stienstra, Jared Bataillon, & Jason A. Cantone, *Assistance to Pro Se Litigants in U.S. District Courts: A Report on Surveys of Clerks of Court and Chief Judges* (2011), http://www.fjc.gov/public/pdf.nsf/lookup/proseusdc.pdf/$file/proseusdc.pdf; *see also Pro Se Information*, UNITED STATES COURT OF FED. CLAIMS, http://www.uscfc.uscourts.gov/pro-se-information.

15   *See* SUP. CT. R. 28.8.

[16] *Filing Your Appeal—Pro Se—Motions, Arguments & Decisions*, THE UNITED STATES COURT OF APPEALS FOR THE TENTH CIRCUIT, https://www.ca10.uscourts.gov/clerk/filing-your-appeal/pro-se/motions-arguments (stating that "[o]ral arguments are rarely conducted in cases with pro se litigants").

[17] Correll, *supra* note 4, at 865. Indeed:

> The *pro se* litigant thus places the conscientious judge on the horns of a dilemma: the court can ignore the claimant's obvious position of disadvantage, adhering as a formal matter to ethical norms; or the court can intervene in ways that attempt to ensure a fair and accurate result but deviate from the norm of passivity.

Lois Bloom & Helen Hershkoff, *Federal Courts, Magistrate Judges, and the Pro Se Plaintiff*, 16 ND J.L. ETHICS & PUB. POL'Y 475, 513 (2002).

[18] *Id.* at 483.

[19] In his dissenting opinion in *Faretta*, Justice Harry Blackmun quipped, " 'one who is his own lawyer has a fool for a client.' " 442 U.S. at 852 (Blackmun, J., dissenting) (citation omitted). This well known saying has been attributed to British attorney and scholar Henry Kett who in 1814 wrote, "I hesitate not to pronounce, that every man who is his own lawyer, has a fool for a client." Ted Brooks, *He Who Is His Own Lawyer Has a Fool for a Client*, COURT TECH. TRIAL PRESENTATION (Sept. 19, 2011), http://trial-technology.blogspot.com/2011/09/he-who-is-his-own-lawyer-has-fool-for.html.

[20] *See generally* Emergy G. Lee III, *Law Without Lawyers: Access to Civil Justice and the Cost of Legal Services*, 69 U. MIAMI L. REV. 499, 503 (2015); Michelle N. Struffolino, *Taking Limited Representation to the Limits: The Efficacy of Using Unbundled Legal Services in Domestic-Relations Matters Involving Litigation*, 2 ST. MARY'S J. LEGAL MAL. & ETHICS 166, 202 (2012) (stating that only 1 out of 6,415 low-income individuals has access to legal aid and that less than 1% of America's legal expenditure aids impoverished persons); Sande L. Buhai, *Access to Justice for Unrepresented Litigants: A Comparative Perspective* 42 LOY. L.A. L. REV. 979, 983 (2009); Stephan Landsman, *Celebrating the 40th Anniversary of the Federal Judicial Center: The Growing Challenge of Pro Se Litigation*, 13 LEWIS & CLARK L. REV. 439, 444 (2009) (asserting that 80% of low-income individuals and 60% of those categorized as "middle class" cannot afford legal representation). *But see* Drew A. Swank, Esq., *The Pro Se Phenomenon*, 19 BYU J. PUB. L. 373, 378 (2005) (discussing one survey, which revealed that only 31% of pro se litigants chose to self-represent because they could not afford an attorney).

[21] According to a study conducted by the Administrative Office of U.S. Courts, prisoners initiated 68% of the pro se cases filed between September 30, 2008, and September 30, 2009; put differently, pro se prisoner matters constituted 18% of *all* civil suits filed in the federal district courts during that time period. James C. Duff, *Judicial Business of the United States Courts: 2009 Annual Report of the Director* 75, 127 (2009), http://www.uscourts.gov/Statistics/JudicialBusiness/JudicialBusiness2009.aspx. According to Bloom and Hershkoff:

> [n]ationwide, prisoner petitioners comprised only one percent of federal civil filings in 1958; by 1989, these petitions constituted eleven percent of all civil filings. The number of habeas corpus petitions, the federal mechanism by which prisoners challenge their custody by the government, rose 1800% nationwide from 1945 to 1989. Similarly, the federal courts have witnessed a surge in § 1983 cases filed by inmates challenging the conditions of their confinement, including the denial of medical care, physical abuse, and improper placement in administrative segregation.

Bloom & Hershkoff, *supra* note 17, at 479–80.

[22] Correll, *supra* note 4, at 867 (attributing the rise in pro se litigation to "the cost of legal services, decreased availability of legal aid programs," and a stronger interest in being more actively engaged in one's own legal representation) (citation omitted).

[23] 28 U.S.C. § 1915(e)(1) (2016). As the Maryland District Court explained in *Bailey-El v. Housing Authority of Baltimore City, et al.*:

> A federal district court judge's power to appoint counsel under 28 U.S.C. § 1915(e)(1) is a discretionary one and may be considered where an indigent claimant presents exceptional circumstances. The question of whether such circumstances exist in a particular case hinges on the characteristics of the claim and the litigant. Where a colorable claim exists but the litigant has no capacity to present it, counsel should be appointed.

No. RDB–15–2063, 2016 WL 2649550, at *4 (May 9, 2016) (internal citations omitted).

[24] 28 U.S.C. § 1915(a)(1) states in pertinent part:

Subject to subsection (b), any court of the United States may authorize the commencement, prosecution or defense of any suit, action or proceeding, civil or criminal, or appeal therein, without prepayment of fees or security therefor, by a person who submits an affidavit that includes a statement of all assets such prisoner possesses that the person is unable to pay such fees or give security therefor. Such affidavit shall state the nature of the action, defense or appeal and affiant's belief that the person is entitled to redress.

[25]   *Id.* § 1915(a)(1)-(c).

[26]   *See, e.g.*, Roger J. Miner, *Dealing with the Appellate Caseload Crisis: The Report of the Federal Courts Study Committee Revisited*, 57 N.Y.L. SCH. L. REV. 517, 521 (2013); Chris Johnson, *Leveraging Technology to Deliver Legal Services*, 23 HARV. J.L. & TECH. 259, 261, 268 (2009) (explaining how litigants who distrust attorneys sometimes use legal websites to perform their own legal services); Swank, *supra* note 20, at 375 (discussing one survey in which 45% of the pro se respondents stated that they chose to represent themselves because their cases were easy and straightforward).

[27]   Correll, *supra* note 4, at 868.

[28]   *Id.* at 869 ("these figures illustrate . . . [a] lack of demographic uniformity. No single group makes up an overwhelming majority of the pro se population . . . pro se litigants operate with varying degrees of sophistication. . .").

[29]   Buhai, *supra* note 20, at 986.

[30]   For general information regarding concerns inherent in pro se litigation, see Daniel H. Brean, *Pro Se Patent Appeals at the Federal Circuit* (unpublished manuscript on file with author).

[31]   *See* LEGAL SERVICES CORP., DOCUMENTING THE JUSTICE GAP IN AMERICA: THE CURRENT UNMET CIVIL LEGAL NEEDS OF LOW-INCOME AMERICANS 1, 26, 27 (Sep. 2009), http://www.lsc .gov/sites/default/files/LSC/pdfs/documenting_the_justice_gap_in_america_2009.pdf (noting a perceived rise in pro se litigation corresponding with America's recent mortgage crisis and recession).

[32]   Duff, *supra* note 21, at 75.

[33]   *Id.* at 75, 127.

[34]   *Id.* at 43, 75, and 127.

[35]   *See generally* CHARLES L. OWEN, RONALD W. STAUDT, & EDWARD B. PEDWELL, ACCESS TO JUSTICE: MEETING THE NEEDS OF SELF-REPRESENTED LITIGANTS (2002), https://www.kentlaw.iit.edu/Documentsänd%20Centers/CAJT/access-to-justice-meeting-the-needs.pdf.

[36]   Correll, *supra* note 4, at 868.

[37]   STIENSTRA, BATAILLON, & CANTONE, *supra* note 14, at vi.

[38]   Bloom & Hershkoff, *supra* note 17, at 495–97.

[39]   STIENSTRA, BATAILLON, & CANTONE, *supra* note 14, at vi; *see also Guide for Pro Se Petitioners and Appellants*, UNITED STATES COURTS, http://www.cafc.uscourts.gov/rules-of-practice/pro-se.

[40]   Bloom & Hershkoff, *supra* note 17, at 495–97.

[41]   *Id.* at 497.

[42]   STIENSTRA, BATAILLON, & CANTONE, *supra* note 14, at vi.

[43]   *Id.*

[44]   *Id.*

[45]   *Id.* at vii.

[46]   FED. R. CIV. P. 8.

[47]   92 S. Ct. 594, 596 (1972). In *Haines v. Kerner*, the plaintiff *pro se* was an inmate at the Illinois State Penitentiary who sued state officers and prison officials, alleging physical injuries sustained and the deprivation of rights endured when the plaintiff was forcibly placed in solitary confinement. *Id.* at 595–96. When the Eastern District of Illinois dismissed his complaint, he appealed, and the Seventh Circuit affirmed. *Id.* The U.S. Supreme Court reversed and remanded. *Id.*

[48]   *See, e.g.*, Estelle v. Gamble, 429 U.S. 97, 106 (1976) (stating that *Haines* allows courts to apply less stringent standards to pro se pleadings than other pleadings); In re McFadden, 477 B.R. 686, 689 (Bankr. N.D. Ohio 2012) (same); Pro-Concepts, LLC v. Resh, 2014 U.S. Dist. LEXIS 18416, at *9 (E.D. Va. Feb. 11, 2104) (same).

⁴⁹ *See generally* Bell Atl. Corp. v. Twombly, 550 U.S. 544 (2007).

⁵⁰ *See generally* Ashcroft v. Iqbal, 129 S. Ct. 1937 (2009).

⁵¹ *See* Rory K. Schneider, *Illiberal Construction of Pro Se Pleadings*, 159 U. PA. L. REV. 585, 618 (2011).

⁵² Robert Bacharach & Lyn Entzeroth, *Judicial Advocacy in Pro Se Litigation: A Return to Neutrality*, 42 IND. L. REV. 19, 26–27 (2009) (noting that because the Supreme Court provided no express guidance regarding *how* courts should liberally construe pro se pleadings, circuits have articulated their own unique standards for doing so); *see also* Correll, *supra* note 4, at 885. Correll critiques the common practice of liberally construing pro se pleadings because doing so is "unsupported by an express procedural mandate . . . [was] never promulgated through a judicial rule-making process . . . and never expanded to reach represented parties." *Id.* at 875. He further observes that "what began as a general rule derived from the basic tenets of notice pleading has transformed . . . [into] a far narrower rule on appeal affording additional appellate rights to a discrete subclass of litigants." *Id.* at 887.

⁵³ Bacharach & Entzeroth, *supra* note 52, at 29.

⁵⁴ Correll, *supra* note 4, at 876.

⁵⁵ Eagle Eye Fishing Corp. v. U.S. Dept. of Commerce, 20 F.3d 503, 506 (1st Cir. 1994).

⁵⁶ Correll, *supra* note 4, at 879.

⁵⁷ 287 F.3d 138, 146 (2d. Cir. 2002) (quoting McPherson v. Coombe, 174 F.3d 276, 280 (2d Cir. 1999)) (internal quotation marks omitted).

⁵⁸ Correll, *supra* note 4, at 878. An exhaustive discussion of local rules specific to pro se litigants exceeds the scope of this chapter.

⁵⁹ The American Bar Association provides a comprehensive listing of pro se resources by state, which is available at http://www.americanbar.org/groups/delivery_legal_services/resources/pro_se_unbundling_resource_center/pro_se_resources_by_state.html. The National Center for State Courts provides additional guidance at http://www.ncsc.org/Topics/Access-and-Fairness/Self-Representation/Resource-Guide.aspx and http://www.publiccounsel.org/featured?id=0003 (a website, which provides guides and tutorials on how to draft a complaint, motion, etc.).

⁶⁰ *See* Haines v. Kerner, 404 U.S. 519 (1972) (per curiam), *reh'g denied*, 405 U.S. 948 (1972).

⁶¹ David B. Wexler, *Therapeutic Jurisprudence and Legal Education: Where Do We Go from Here?*, 71 REV. JUR. U.P.R. 177, 178 (2002).

⁶² David B. Wexler, *Two Decades of Therapeutic Jurisprudence*, 24 TOURO L. REV. 17, 20 (2008).

⁶³ *But see* Brean, *supra* note 30 (advocating for the Federal Circuit to dispose of more pro se patent appeals via Rule 36 in part because of the case subject matter as well as the sophistication and legal familiarity of litigants filing such appeals).

⁶⁴ This is a local rule of the Court, which is available on the court's website.

⁶⁵ STIENSTRA, BATAILLON, & CANTONE, *supra* note 14, at v.

⁶⁶ *Id.* at vii.

CHAPTER 19

LIFE AFTER CLERKING

■ ■ ■

All good things must come to an end.[1] The same is true of clerkships. But you can rest assured that your time spent clerking will be one of the most rewarding and formative stages in your legal career. As one former appellate clerk observed:

> I came out of my clerkship a better reader, writer, and overall lawyer. I had acquired five years' worth of experience and skills in a single year. My clerkship also opened the door for me to do more of the appellate work that I desired, and it even helped me obtain an academic position. Not to mention the many wonderful friends and colleagues that I met while clerking. What more could you want out of a job?[2]

I could not agree more. No matter where you go and what you ultimately do, you will never forget the important lessons learned and unbreakable bonds forged during your clerkship. You will emerge a stronger, smarter attorney and hopefully, a more empathetic and well-rounded human being.

Unfortunately, however, your clerkship does not last forever. It is usually the beginning, not the end, of your professional career. With the exception of career clerks, law clerks are typically hired for a set term of one to two years.[3] Although this constant turnover requires judges to recruit and retrain new clerks, it also periodically injects Chambers with fresh perspectives and diverse insights. The short clerkship term also enables more new lawyers to enjoy the tremendous benefits of clerking— lessons that they will hopefully take with them into the practice and impress upon others. While some judges may permit you to extend your clerkship, other judges may not due to court or Chambers rules or because the judge has already hired an incoming replacement. It is important to understand the scope of your clerkship term at the outset and whether a possibility of extending the clerkship exists. As your clerkship term ends, you must begin to wind down.

A. WINDING DOWN

As you prepare for your departure, take measures to make the transition as smooth as possible. Assist your judge in selecting a replacement clerk. With your judge's permission, notify your alma mater and attorney-colleagues of the clerkship opening and post the opening on OSCAR and law school job posting sites. Review applications, speak to references, and participate in clerk interviews, providing an honest and reasoned assessment of each candidate. Focus on selecting a good fit for Chambers, both personally and professionally. Choose someone will also be a nice complement to the other clerks with whom the new hire will work.

In addition, begin winding down your open assignments, clearing as much as possible from the docket that your new hire will inherit. If possible, take on fewer new matters unless you can resolve them before your clerkship concludes. The longer you clerk, the easier the job becomes because you grow more familiar and adept at drafting opinions in your judge's voice and understanding recurring legal issues that come before the court. Your expertise grows, but a new hire will be starting fresh. Make things as easy as possible for your replacement. Given the incoming clerk's lack of expertise and training, it may take him or her longer to complete tasks, so the less you leave behind the better.

In that regard, draft a short exit memo for each open case, leaving clear instructions to your successor regarding what remains to be done and preferably, in what order. For your convenience, a sample exit memo is provided below. Leave an exit memo in the electronic folder of each corresponding case so that the new clerk can easily locate them. In addition, draft a single overarching exit memo that directs the new clerk to each of the case-specific exit memos and provides other general guidance. After your clerkship concludes, the new clerk will likely be unable to contact you to ask questions about the cases you previously handled since doing so might violate Chambers confidentiality. Thus, it is important that you leave written, clear instructions. Out of an abundance of caution, also provide a copy of your overarching exit memo to your judicial assistant or a co-clerk who will remain behind to provide guidance to your successor. Meet with your judge during the last week of your clerkship to review the status of open cases and provide an updated copy of your case status chart.

Below is a sample exit memo.

CONFIDENTIAL

To: Janet Lynn

From: Mary Lycans

Date: December 7, 2017

Re: Hoover v. David, 17–1234

This case involves an allegation of unlawful termination due to age in violation of the Age Discrimination in Employment Act ("ADEA"). Plaintiff (Hoover) is a sixty-two year old man who claims that despite receiving positive performance evaluations and meeting his deliverables, he was fired and replaced by a thirty-year old female with less industry experience. Defendant (David) claims that Hoover's position was eliminated for budgetary reasons and that Hoover was not replaced with a younger employee; the female Hoover references in the complaint absorbed a few of Hoover's former responsibilities, while two other employees, both over forty, absorbed the remainder. This is a complex case.

Defendant moved for summary judgment on November 1, 2017, and Plaintiff opposed the motion on November 30, 2017. Defendant's reply brief is due on December 10, 2017. Be on the lookout for the reply brief or any motions for an extension of time. Judge has scheduled oral argument in the matter for January 8, 2018. (See the updated case chart and Chambers calendar, which reflect these deadlines. Revise them as necessary should Judge grant any motion for an extension of time. Defendant is prone to request them.) I have used the available briefing to begin drafting a bench memo in preparation for oral argument. (See the sample bench memo in the electronic folder called "Samples" for guidance on format.) The most recent draft is located in the electronic folder and labeled as "Hoover v. David Mot. for SJ Bench Memo Version Three 12.5.17." Work from this draft. Ask your co-clerk Rachel if you have any questions. She has ADEA experience and thus, may be able to assist you. Since this will likely be the first bench memo you submit to Judge, do not be afraid to ask Rachel to review it. Judge will be out of town December 20 through January 3, so be sure to get her the bench memo no later than December 17 so you have time to meet with her and do any supplemental research before she leaves town. Talk to our JA, Trudy, to get a meeting on the schedule now for December 17 because Judge's schedule fills up quickly. Get started on this bench memo soon as it is a difficult case. Good luck!

Your successor may also appreciate additional tips or guidance that you have gleaned during your clerkship term, particularly if he or she has no prior clerkship experience. Amass helpful books and guides from

Chambers or the court's library, such as *Maintaining the Public Trust*, and leave those behind in your office for the new clerk to peruse. Create a computer folder called "Samples" with samples of your best 11-Day, order, opinion, and bench memo that the new clerk can use as a guide. Provide a short list of fun places to eat, exercise, or attend happy hour in or near the court to help the new clerk acclimate, particularly if he or she has relocated to the city for the clerkship. Draft a short welcome note or letter to the new clerk, perhaps with a small gift such as a mug, to make the new clerk immediately feel at home. In this way, you are mentoring your replacement and better ensuring a smooth transition for Chambers. You are also setting a collegial tone for your replacement from the outset. Leave your new contact information with the judicial assistant, your former co-clerks, and your successor. In short, be thoughtful in your departure and do for your successor what you wish had been done for you.

For your convenience, a sample Chambers departure checklist is included below. It is non-exhaustive and may require revision given the nature of your clerkship responsibilities. Consult your Chambers to determine if it possesses a Chambers-specific checklist but feel free to supplement that list with the one included below.

Clerkship Departure Checklist

1. Have I reminded my judge, judicial assistant, and co-clerks of my end date at least three weeks in advance? (Unless the judge instructs otherwise, an outgoing clerk has no obligation to notify parties or their counsel of the clerk's impending departure.) ☐

2. Have I notified clerks from other Chambers with whom I am working on a pending case? ☐

3. Have I completed my conflicts list and obtained permission to remove it from Chambers so long as I keep it confidential? ☐

4. Have I avoided accepting any compensation, gifts, or expenses, such as a signing bonus or moving expenses, from my prospective employer that would violate ethical rules and guidelines? ☐

5. Have I updated all status charts in each case as well as the court calendar to reflect any pending dates and deadlines? ☐

6. Have I completed as much as is practicable on each pending case to leave the clearest docket possible for the incoming clerk? ☐

7. Have I prepared exit memos for each pending case and placed them in the appropriate case folder? ☐

8. Have I completed an overarching exit memo that provides general instructions and guidance for my replacement? ☐

9. Have I provided a copy of this general memo to the judicial assistant and/or left a copy on my desk for the new clerk? ☐

10. Have I left the new clerk a welcome greeting, such as a card or letter, on my desk? ☐

11. Have I removed all personal items from my office making sure to leave behind court office supplies and equipment? ☐

12. Have I returned all Chambers or Court property, such as keys, badges, key cards, etc.? ☐

13. Have I provided my new contact and employment information to my Chambers, such as a personal email or telephone number where I can be reached after my clerkship concludes? ☐

B. NEXT STEPS

The remainder of the chapter discusses additional next steps you may consider or encounter as your clerkship concludes.

Will I automatically be admitted to appear before my court at the conclusion of my clerkship?

It depends. In some courts, it is customary for your judge to move for your admission to appear before the court near the end of the clerkship. The admission ceremony is a momentous occasion. It is not unusual for a clerk's friends and family to attend. It is your responsibility to prepare the proper application for admission to the bar. It is only granted to clerks who are in good standing; other requirements also apply. During the ceremony, some judges even provide personal remarks about each law clerk before moving for their admission. It is a highlight and fitting end to a remarkable professional experience and an event that no clerk will forget.

To what extent may I discuss my clerkship or my judge during my search for post-clerkship positions?

It depends. As noted in Chapter 6, as you pursue post-clerkship employment, take care to avoid ethical issues, such as potential breaches of confidentiality. After your clerkship concludes, Canon 4C(4) of the *Code of Conduct for Judicial Employees* no longer applies, so you may accept signing bonuses, travel expenses, lunches, etc.[4] Yet other ethical obligations, such as your continuing duty to maintain Chambers confidentiality and avoid conflicts of interest, last a lifetime. Thus, before your clerkship concludes, vet your resume with your judge to obtain approval and seek permission to include a reference to your clerkship on your professional and social media profiles. During interviews with prospective employers, never divulge confidential information gleaned as a result of your clerkship duties, such as insight regarding the judge's decision-making process or predictions on how the judge will rule in a pending case. Exercise an abundance of caution and discuss any concerns with your judge *before* taking action. Even after the clerkship concludes, it is inappropriate to use your special relationship with your judge to influence prospective employers, such as by implying that if a firm that frequently appears before your former judge offers you employment, the judge is likelier to rule more favorably in the firm's cases that are pending before the judge. That being said, it is usually permissible to ask your judge to serve as a reference or to state that you are well-suited for a position given your clerkship experience. Prospective employers look favorably upon former clerks given the invaluable training and experience that clerking provides.

May I ask my judge to serve as a reference or provide a recommendation?

It depends. Judges often form a close relationship with their clerks and as such, are uniquely well suited to serve as references or draft letters of recommendation, not only for your first post-clerkship position but for subsequent positions as well. Some judges may even telephone prospective employers on your behalf. This is especially true if you apply for other clerkships. That being said, judges vary in their willingness to actively participate in your job search.

Thus, at the outset of your clerkship, ask more senior clerks or former clerks whether your judge customarily serves as a reference, writes recommendation letters, or speaks to prospective employers on a former law clerk's behalf. As noted above, some judges play an active role in their law clerk's post-clerkship development while others do not. This is often a product not only of your judge's personal preferences but also your performance as a clerk and your relationship with your judge and Chambers family.

If your judge does offer to serve as a reference or recommender, promptly provide the judge with any material that he or she may need to do so, such as an updated resume and a description of the job for which you are applying; some judges may even ask you to take a first cut at drafting the recommendation letter. Always provide your judge with a handwritten thank you note for assisting you in the job search, even if you do not ultimately obtain the position. After all, your judge has taken time out of his or her extremely hectic schedule to advocate on your behalf.

After my clerkship concludes, may I use clerkship work product as a writing sample?

It depends. Some Chambers may permit you to use material produced during your clerkship as a writing sample, but typically, you must seek permission to do so *before* your clerkship concludes. Determine whether this is permissible at the outset of your clerkship and express your interest in taking advantage of this unique opportunity. To the extent you do use such material as a writing sample, vet the intended sample with your judge *prior* to the end of your clerkship and redact any confidential or identifying information from the sample. Include an excerpt at the beginning of the writing sample, which makes clear that "the sample has been redacted to preserve Chambers confidentiality and is being used with the permission of Chambers." If you apply for subsequent clerkships, a judicial writing sample produced during your prior clerkship may be especially helpful.

Do the ethical rules applicable to me during my clerkship apply with equal force after my clerkship concludes?

It depends. As noted above, the ethical rules discussed in this book primarily apply to *current* clerks, but some rules, including a clerk's duty of loyalty and confidentiality, remain in effect throughout a clerk's lifetime. Other rules, such as the prohibition on receiving gifts during a clerkship, cease to apply after your clerkship concludes. Yet the applicable rules of professional responsibility still govern your professional conduct so long as you practice law.

As noted earlier, the duty to maintain Chambers confidentiality is a lifelong obligation. It is often tested during interviews or in the practice. For example, an interviewer may ask a former clerk or extern to discuss the judge's decision-making process or to predict how the judge will rule in a pending case. A partner may ask a former clerk to disclose which types of arguments the judge might find most compelling. In both instances, the former clerk must simply explain that due to his or her ethical obligation to maintain Chambers confidentiality, he cannot comment and politely suggest that the judge's issued opinions will provide sufficient insight into such questions.

How may I avoid post-clerkship conflicts of interest?

During your clerkship, familiarize yourself with the rules regarding conflicts of interest. Prepare a conflicts list of any cases on which you work and ask permission to remove the list from Chambers for your personal, albeit confidential, use. Once you commence post-clerkship employment, advise your new employer that you may not work on any case that you worked on as a clerk, that was pending before your court during your clerkship (whether you worked on it or not), or any case of which you have special knowledge as a result of your clerkship. Nor may you typically write scholarly articles, client advisories, blogs, etc., about cases that were pending at your courts during your clerkships absent your judge's permission. With Chambers permission, however, you may reference a publicly issued decision so long you do not divulge any information about the decision not available to the public and gained as a direct result of your clerkship. In everything you do, be sure to avoid actual conflicts as well as the appearance of impropriety. As soon as you become aware of an actual or potential conflict of interest, alert your employer so that the employer can remove you from the matter as necessary. The necessity of doing so is generally determined on a case-by-case basis.

May I appear before my former court or judge?

It depends. Appearing before your former judge or court may give rise to the appearance of impropriety and thus raises special ethical considerations. When filing a brief before a court, the court will require the brief drafter to list any potential issues that might give rise to a conflict, such as whether or not the attorney externed, interned, or clerked for any judges on the court. At that point, your former judge can recuse himself or herself from the matter.

Judges and courts differ widely in this respect. Some courts may provide guidance regarding a time limit before which a former clerk may appear in the court or in which the former clerk may appear before his or her former judge. Judges may also have Chambers-specific policies, whether written or unwritten, establishing a certain number of years before which a former clerk may appear before them; until those years elapse, the judge will recuse himself or herself from any cases involving the former clerk. Other judges have no such rules or limitations, although it is important for the former clerk to note any potential conflicts not only when filing the brief but also when accepting the case from the client or partner.

If you do argue before your former judge, be professional. Never imply to your client, colleagues, opposing counsel, etc., that the court will likely rule in your favor because you formerly clerked for the judge. Nor is it appropriate for you to contact your judge before or after the appearance to receive feedback from the judge or discuss the case with him or her, at least not while the case is pending. Never expect or imply special treatment or abuse your special relationship with your judge. Conduct yourself in the same manner you would if appearing before a judge whom you had never met.

How do I maintain a relationship with my former judge and co-clerks?

It is critical to maintain a strong relationship with your Chambers family after your clerkship concludes. Yet attorneys lead busy, hectic lives, and law clerks often end up living and working in a different city than where they clerked. Thus, building and maintaining close relationships takes effort and dedication. However, it is well worth the effort.

Even after your clerkship ends, make concerted efforts to keep in touch with Chambers. Keep abreast of Chambers and court events, such as bar receptions, clerk reunions, and informal clerk send-offs. Attend when you can, even if your schedule only permits you to make an appearance. There is no substitute for an in-person visit. When you cannot attend, send an email declining the invitation and explaining why. In addition, send occasional emails when a case pending before the court during your clerkship is issued or affirmed. Stay connected on social media as appropriate. Email or send a card around the holidays or on birthdays. Send congratulatory notes or cards for important new life developments, such as engagements, marriages, births, publications, or new jobs. Show a sincere interest in your fellow co-clerks' personal and professional lives; after all, they are family. When you learn that you will be in town, email Chambers or your fellow co-clerks well in advance to schedule a short visit or better yet a lunch, coffee break, or happy hour. Do not just remain in touch with your judge but also with your judicial assistant and former co-clerks and externs, each of whom are an integral part of your Chambers family.

Most importantly, make sure that your relationships remain a two-way street where you are *giving* guidance and assistance as much as you are receiving it. Never let a relationship feel parasitic. Help others whenever and however you can, within ethical bounds. Serve as a reference or recommender for your former co-clerks or externs. Advise Chambers of a potential strong clerkship applicant whom you believe would be a great fit. Suggest your judge for speaking engagements, teaching or writing opportunities, or honors and awards for which he or she is well suited. Assist your colleagues in their own job searches or connect them with colleagues that may be well positioned to do so. Be a friend, a helper, and a mentor however and whenever you can, expecting nothing in return. In other words, be sincere and treat others as you would like to be treated. Never maintain a relationship purely for strategic reasons; to the contrary, having friends means being a friend in good times and in bad.

How can I mentor others?

Clerking is a privilege and an honor. It truly is a once-in-a-lifetime experience, so if you have had the privilege to clerk, pay it forward.[5] Without running afoul of your ethical obligations, share the important lessons learned from your clerkship with others. Indeed, it was my strong desire to inspire my students to clerk that prompted me to develop my judicial externship program, my clerkship course, and ultimately to write this book. Upon joining the faculty at my law school, I also volunteered for the Clerkship Committee and in my efforts to assist others in obtaining clerkships, I frequently review clerkship applications, conduct mock interviews, and draft recommendation letters for former students.

You need not be a law school professor to assist others in obtaining a clerkship. To the contrary, there are countless ways to mentor the next generation of law clerks. First, contact your alma mater to alert them of your clerkship and willingness to speak to prospective clerks, conduct mock interviews, or participate on panels about judicial clerking. In particular, speak to your law school's Clerkship Committee, Director of Clerkships, and Office of Career and Professional Development, many of whom have a designated Clerkship Advisor or Director of Clerkships. Advise them of your current contact information and employer; update this information whenever you change locations or positions so they can remain in touch with you. Also contact former professors who assisted you in obtaining your clerkship to thank them and explain how much you benefited from the experience. Talk about your clerkship with attorney friends and colleagues and as appropriate, encourage them to clerk. Speak on panels or to classes at your law school about your clerkship experience.

Most importantly, throughout your career continue to exemplify the honor and integrity expected of you during your clerkship. Remember that even after your clerkship concludes, your professional conduct will always reflect upon your judge as well as yourself. In everything you do, avoid conduct that might diminish the dignity of the court and judge you served. Aim to uphold the highest ethical standards, both professionally and personally. And most importantly, do good in the world around you.

Notes

1   GEOFFREY CHAUCER, TROILUS AND CRISEYDE—BOOK V 192 (1385), http://triggs.djvu.org/djvu-editions.com/CHAUCER/TROILUS/Download.pdf.

2   A former clerk at the United States Court of Appeals for the Federal Circuit provided this quote, and it is used here with his permission.

3   In the rare instance that your judge has not defined the term of your clerkship, then assume that you will clerk for at least one year and do not seek post-clerkship employment until you have obtained your judge's permission. Plan to provide your Chambers with as much notice as possible of your departure, but by no means less than six weeks so that the judge has ample time to find a replacement clerk.

4   CODE OF CONDUCT FOR JUDICIAL EMPLOYEES (2013), http://www.uscourts.gov/rules-policies/judiciary-policies/code-conduct/code-conduct-judicial-employees (last visited July 22, 2016).

5   PAY IT FORWARD (Warner Bros. 2000).

CHAPTER 20

REFLECTIONS ON CLERKING

■ ■ ■

A clerkship is often the most formative stage in an attorney's career. Its countless benefits last a lifetime. Clerks amass a remarkable amount of knowledge and experience in an incredibly short period of time. More than that, they gain wisdom, maturity, and discernment, which prove invaluable in their subsequent professional endeavors. Clerks evolve from analytical surface-dwellers to deep thinkers who probe issues from every angle. Perhaps more importantly, they often forge lifelong bonds with their judges and with one another. For all of these reasons and many more, a positive clerkship experience is an incomparable opportunity for both personal growth and professional development.

Yet to optimize the benefits of clerking, it is essential to practice mindfulness. During your clerkship, make concerted efforts to be present in the moment, and when the moment passes, meaningfully reflect upon what you learned from the experience. Below are some suggested ways that you can create a more mindful clerkship experience.[1]

A. MINDFULNESS AND REFLECTION

1. **Set goals**: Before your clerkship commences, think deeply about the professional and personal goals you hope to accomplish both *during* and *after* your clerkship. For example, if your long-term goal is to argue in front of the U.S. Supreme Court, ask yourself how your federal appellate clerkship can help make that dream a reality. List your goals and for each one, brainstorm an action plan. Jot down tangible steps to accomplish each goal. Review and revise the list, as necessary, during your clerkship, adding and removing goals and action items as necessary. Consistently track your progress to ensure that you are making your clerkship count.

2. **Meditate:**[2] Clerkships can be stressful, and stress sometimes impedes performance. To better manage daily stress, begin each day with a *mindfulness minute*, devoting at least one minute to meditation. Use a mindfulness meditation script that you locate online or create a script tailored to you and your needs. As your day begins, close your eyes. Concentrate on your breathing. Breathe deeply in through your nose and out through your mouth. Imagine that you are breathing in relaxation and focus and breathing out tension and distraction. Consider each of the things weighing heavily on your mind that are unrelated to your tasks for

the day. Now imagine yourself pushing each of those distractions away and clearing space in your mind for deep thinking and concentration. When you open your eyes, write down things that require attention after work but then put the list away.

3.   **Eliminate unnecessary distractions:** To further enhance your productivity, turn off your smartphone and other personal electronic devices and put them away before you commence work. Close your email system. Turn off any instant messaging and other devices on your work computer. Remove and put away any accessories that make noise, such as digital watches. Close each window on your computer except the one in which you are working. Close your door or wear earplugs to eliminate distracting noises. If Chambers culture permits you to do so, consider wearing headphones and listening to classical music or any lyric-free background noise that facilitates deep concentration. Promise yourself that you will work in this distraction-free, uninterrupted setting for at least one hour before taking a break.

4.   **Take periodic mental and physical breaks:** For every one to two hours of intense concentration or whenever you switch to a new task, allow yourself a ten to fifteen minute mental break to reset, refresh, and refocus. During this break, stand up and walk away from your computer. Step outside for fresh air. Use the restroom. Grab a coffee. Talk to a co-clerk. Walk away from your work and return with fresh eyes.

5.   **Consistently engage in meaningful self-reflection:** After each new task, reflect upon what you learned and how you can apply those lessons to future assignments. Consider what worked well and what you would do differently next time. As appropriate, request feedback on each project from your supervising clerk or judge. Take notes during these feedback sessions so that you can incorporate the suggestions on subsequent assignments. Consider saving your notes in an electronic *feedback file* on your computer for future reference. Below is a sample new project reflection.

New Project Reflection

Reflection enhances the educational value of an experience. It also increases the likelihood that the lessons learned from the experience will be stored in your long-term memory. With that in mind, please complete the following short reflection. Be honest and thoughtful. Edit your responses carefully and write in complete sentences.

1. Briefly describe the nature of this project. What were your general impressions of the project?

2. How much time did you expect this project to take at the outset? How long did you actually take to complete the project? Did you work efficiently? Why or why not?

3. List three ways to improve your efficiency the next time you complete a similar project.

4. List the three most important lessons you learned from this project. How will you apply them going forward?

5. With respect to your completion of this project, what strategies worked? Why?

6. If you could do this project again, what would you do differently? Why?

7. What, if any, feedback did you receive regarding this project? How will you incorporate that feedback on the next similar project?

8. What advice, if any, would you give to a new clerk commencing this project in the future?

Customized reflections are particularly useful. For example, complete the following reflection after observing your first oral argument.

Reflections on Oral Argument

Reflection enhances the educational value of an experience. It also increases the likelihood that the lessons learned from the experience will be stored in your long-term memory. With that in mind, please complete the following short reflection. Be honest and thoughtful. Edit your responses carefully and write in complete sentences.

1. Based on your experience, including your conversations with your judge and fellow clerks, what are three hallmarks of effective advocacy?

2. In three sentences or less, please share your general impressions of how effectively you prepared your judge for oral argument. Were any points raised at argument that you had not included in your bench memo?

3. Did anything surprise you about the oral argument? If yes, what and why?

4. Which question(s) did you expect to hear that you did not hear? Why do you believe no judge asked the question(s)?

5. Based on your observation, which advocate was strongest? List three reasons why.

6. Which advocate was weakest? List three reasons why or three errors that the advocate made.

7. Based on your experience observing the oral argument, what are three hallmarks of effective oral advocacy?

8. List one way you plan to develop or hone this skill or attribute.

At the conclusion of your clerkship or externship experience, engage in the meaningful reflection below.

Final Reflection

As your clerkship or externship comes to a conclusion, reflect upon what you learned and how you can apply these lessons to subsequent positions. Reflection enhances the educational value of an experience. It also increases the likelihood that the lessons learned from the experience will be stored in your long-term memory. With that in mind, please complete the following short reflection. Be honest and thoughtful. Edit your responses carefully and write in complete sentences.

1. As your clerkship or externship draws to an end, please share the three most important pieces of wisdom that you learned. How will you apply them going forward?

2. Please share three important skills that you acquired or honed. How will you apply them going forward?

3. Please share the three most important pieces of advice that you gained from your judge. Why did this advice resonate with you?

4. What was your favorite project and why?

5. What was your favorite matter and why?

6. What was your favorite aspect of clerking and why?

7. With regard to writing specifically, list three things you learned.

8. With regard to oral communication specifically, list three things you learned.

9. With regard to professionalism specifically, list three things you learned.

> 10. With regard to time management specifically, list three things you learned.
>
> 11. In a few sentences, please share your general reflections of your clerkship. Did you learn and grow? Are you a stronger thinker, writer, editor, and speaker? Do you have a greater understanding of what it means to be an ethical professional and a clearer sense of how to successfully achieve your goals?
>
> 12. Do you feel better prepared to hit the ground running in your next legal position?

B. PERSONAL REFLECTIONS

At the conclusion of both of my clerkships, I reflected upon the most important lessons I had learned. Although those lessons are too many to count, I have synthesized some of my most important observations below:

1. **Choose wisely:** Not all clerkships are equally beneficial. Self-assess and research courts and judges so that you select a clerkship that meets or exceeds your expectations. Find the best fit both personally and professionally. Because individuals differ in their interests, aspirations, and aptitudes, a clerkship that is a perfect fit for one person may be ill-suited for another.

2. **Cast a wide net:** You have nothing to lose and everything to gain by applying broadly even to positions for which you may feel underprepared or unqualified. Do not sell yourself short. You never know how something in your application might resonate with a judge. Despite the prevailing wisdom that judges only hire candidates who were on law review or in the top of the class, this is not always the case. Nor do all judges require clerks to have connections to the clerkship locale.

3. **Be open-minded:** All clerkships have value. Whether you clerk at a federal court, state court, or even with an administrative law judge, you will acquire knowledge and gain skills. The skills and knowledge may differ by clerkship, but each experience is enriching. Do not assume that only the most prestigious clerkships will yield lasting benefits.

4. **Seize opportunities that come your way:** A clerkship might require you to move to a new place, leave a loved one behind, or submerge yourself in an entirely new practice area, but great risk often yields great reward. Go all in.

5. **You can never do enough to prepare:** Thoughtfully reading this book is an excellent starting point to prepare for

a clerkship, but your preparation cannot end there. Once you obtain a clerkship, confer with your judge and the existing law clerks regarding how to best prepare. Read seminal cases from the court. Visit Chambers or observe a hearing if and when you are in town before your clerkship commences. Read the five cases of which your judge is most proud to discern his or her voice, writing style, and ideology. Study practice areas common to the court with which you are unfamiliar. Learn the court rules. Take a judicial drafting course or complete a judicial externship to the extent possible. No matter how much you prepare, you will still have a tremendous amount to learn once the clerkship commences. However, thoughtful preparation will make the learning curve less steep and likely improve your initial confidence and ultimate performance.

6. **Be intentional:** Before your clerkship commences, create a list of goals that you hope to accomplish during your clerkship. Then create an action plan to accomplish each goal. During your clerkship, execute your action plan, supplement it as necessary, and track which goals you have accomplished.

7. **Do not procrastinate:** Never procrastinate on an assignment. As soon as you get the assignment, begin working on it even if the deadline is far in the future. In my experience, many projects take far longer than one might expect. Furthermore, unforeseeable circumstances occasionally arise, such as an illness or unexpected death in the family. However, if you have planned for contingencies and built in wiggle room, then you will typically be able to meet deadlines even when events take a surprising turn.

8. **Be flexible:** No day ever goes exactly as planned. Do plan out your day, preferably the evening before, but be flexible as the day progresses, adjusting your schedule and work as necessary. Rigidity adds stress and impedes efficiency.

9. **Grow a thick skin:** No one enjoys receiving criticism, especially on a project to which we have devoted significant time. An effective clerk must be resilient, but mental toughness seems to be in short supply. Possessing it will immediately set you apart from your peers. However, realize that no one emerges from law school as a writing expert; even law clerks with years of practice experience still receive feedback, often significant, from their judges on drafts. Never take this feedback personally regardless of how it is delivered. Judges are not legal writing professors. They will usually not have time to sit down with you and patiently coach you on

how to improve your writing. They may not even have time to deliver the feedback in person or explain in detail the positive aspects of your work product. Typically, they will only suggest revisions often with little or no explanation. Thus, it is important to grow a thick skin and understand that feedback helps you grow and develop as a writer. Do not feel defeated or upset. Embrace feedback and learn from the revisions as you incorporate them.

10. **Anticipate and take initiative:** A clerk's job is to make the judge's job easier however possible. For this reason, the most effective clerks anticipate their judge's needs even without the judge having to express them. Put differently, they do what needs to be done even without being asked.

11. **Do not take shortcuts:** Use your time wisely but do not take intellectual or other shortcuts. Failing to read a case that you cite or to verify a Record quote may allow you to produce a draft more quickly, but in so doing, you may have sacrificed the draft's thoroughness and credibility, which is impermissible. Never sacrifice quality for speed. Take the time you need to produce a high-quality draft.

12. **Never forget the people who paved the way:** During your clerkship, reach out to the recommenders and professors who helped you obtain the clerkship and prepared you to perform it well. Show gratitude. Provide them with helpful guidance regarding how to better assist and prepare the next generation of law clerks.

13. **Remember just how privileged you are:** Clerking is a privilege. Recognizing that will give you the strength to endure on difficult days. Never take the honor and importance of your position for granted.

14. **Be sincere:** Even before your clerkship commences, make efforts to be polite, courteous, and collegial. Form meaningful relationships, not strategic ones. Be kind to everyone all the time. Developing meaningful relationships is one of the most important benefits of clerking, but doing so is impossible if you act insincerely. Your judge and fellow clerks will quickly spot individuals who merely forge strategic friendships. Those relationships will not endure, and such dishonorable conduct will tarnish your reputation with others. So just practice the golden rule, being kind to everyone from the janitor to the judge, regardless of whether those relationships will ever prove professionally helpful. Treating everyone equally regardless of station is simply the right thing to do.

To act otherwise demeans the integrity and dignity of your judge and yourself.

15. **Be realistic and resilient:** Like every other position, clerkships have ups and downs. Although clerking is generally a wonderful experience, there will also be difficult days. Manage your expectations of the clerkship and of your performance therein. Accept that you will make mistakes from time to time and not always receive positive feedback on your work. Strive to maintain a positive attitude. If you must vent, do so outside the office to your significant other, friends, or family to avoid damaging Chambers morale; yet never divulge confidential information. Understand that the feedback you receive will only strengthen your work product. Learn from your mistakes and do not repeat them. As noted earlier, such resilience, while rare, is a hallmark of professionalism and will serve you well in any post-clerkship position.

16. **A reputation is hard to build and easy to lose:** It often takes a very long time and very hard work to earn the respect and esteem of your judge and fellow clerks. But a single act of poor judgment or carelessness can destroy that reputation in an instant; sometimes the harm done is irreparable. Moreover, the name you make for yourself during your clerkship will follow you. Years later, your fellow clerks will remember you as the person who always worked tirelessly to produce a job well done or the undedicated person who always clocked out early despite missing deadlines. How do you want to be remembered?

17. **Exercise an abundance of caution:** Given the gravity of your position and your special relationship with your judge, take special care in everything you do so as to avoid inadvertently making ethical or other errors.

18. **Treat every draft you submit to your judge as if it were final:** Take pride in your work. Invest 100% in each draft and only submit your best effort. Never convince yourself that because it is merely a draft, you may submit a version that is late, incomplete, unedited, or otherwise unpolished. Doing so is highly unprofessional as well as unproductive. It is better to request an extension reasonably in advance than to submit incomplete or inaccurate work.

19. **Edit everything, including your speech and ideas:** Think before you speak. Your communication, both oral and written, reflects your credibility. People will neither respect

nor believe you if you have poor communication skills. So edit your writing and your speech carefully. This applies to every professional email you send as well as to more formal communications, such as bench memoranda. Do not rely on spellchecking software exclusively. In addition, thoughtfully consider an idea, including its long-term and short-term implications on the body of law, before sharing it. Express it tactfully, choosing your words carefully.

20. **Make every moment count:** Savor every moment of your clerkship and brainstorm thoughtful ways to make each moment count. For example, during a hearing, write down the hallmarks of effective oral advocacy you observe. Be an intellectual sponge, learning from everything. If there is a skill you wish to acquire or knowledge you wish to gain, ask your judge for work that will help you accomplish that goal. Be proactive.

21. **Do triage:** Not all issues are equal, so do not treat them as such. Develop good judgment in deciding which cases, issues, and assignments take priority and which do not. But never base that determination on the identity of the parties, only on the nature of the issue.

22. **Give your best effort to everything you do, whether large or small:** Sometimes a single, small act has a profound impact on another. For example, your judge may never forget how you stepped up to take the reins of answering the phones, booking travel, etc., when her judicial assistant had to unexpectedly take a month off due to an unexpected illness. Your simple act of stepping up and assuming more responsibility might be the most memorable thing you do during the clerkship. Moreover, it is incredibly important to remember that no matter how small or insignificant a case seems to you, that case may mean the world to someone else. Indeed, the outcome might alter the course of a litigant's life in ways you cannot even imagine. The beauty of our justice system is that, ideally, each person, no matter his or her sex, skin color, socioeconomic status, or any other trait, is supposed to be equal in the eyes of the law. Although this notion may seem aspirational, we can only hope to achieve it if each participant in the judicial system, especially law clerks, strives to make that notion a reality. Because you are part of the system, you can change it.

23. **Say thank you:** Understand that working side-by-side a brilliant jurist day in and day out for any length of time is an

incredible privilege that few attorneys enjoy. Be grateful and show it each day by thanking your judge for his or her feedback and guidance. Thank your co-clerks and your judicial assistant for the wonderful contributions they make to your clerkship experience. Thank the Marshals for risking their lives to keep you safe. Thank the janitors for ensuring that your work environment is clean and comfortable. Be gracious and grateful in every interaction.

24. **Practice the Golden Rule:** In everything, treat others, regardless of station, with the respect, patience, and consideration with which you wish to be treated.

25. **Pay it forward:** Be a force for good in the world. After your clerkship concludes, share the lessons you learned with others and apply them to effect positive change in your field. Pass along your wisdom to the next generation of attorneys and law clerks. Help your judge and former co-clerks whenever and however you can. Be an active, helpful member of your extended Chambers family. Educate others on the value of clerking and assist them in obtaining and preparing for clerkships.

C. OTHER REFLECTIONS ON CLERKING[3]

There is perhaps no better way to demonstrate the benefits of clerking than to hear from former clerks. You have already heard my story. Indeed, my passion for clerking and deep admiration for the judiciary has seeped into every page of this book. For this reason, the section that follows showcases reflections of *other* former law clerks and judicial externs who served federal and state judges across America. Taken together, they handled a diverse array of matters, and today, they utilize the lessons learned and skills honed during their clerkships in a vast array of legal positions, including public service, private practice, and even Academia. To inform and inspire the next generation of law clerks, they generously share their experiences below.

My year as a clerk for a judge on the United States Court of Appeals for the Third Circuit taught me more than I could have imagined. I applied for a clerkship because that is what ambitious law students did. What I did not realize was how much I would learn through the clerkship. The lessons I learned have carried through my professional career. And so, in no particular order, here are the lessons I learned:

1. A strong mentor is the most important thing for a young attorney. The judge I clerked for prided himself in mentoring young attorneys. His tutelage made me seek out strong mentors when I joined a law firm.

2. Clerking is the best job ever. You get to work for someone who has selected you because he or she believes you will fit the chambers. And, that makes it likely that you will. At the same time, you are exposed to a variety of different legal issues, learn how to learn the law quickly, how to evaluate arguments, and how judges think.

3. I learned judges truly want to reach the right decision under the law, but they (and their clerks) have limited time. . . . [T]he key to successful advocacy was to explain to the judge why the law supported my position and to do so as succinctly as possible. . . .

4. And the judge taught me the most important lesson of my life: "you don't want to be known as often wrong, seldom in doubt. It is much better to be known as often in doubt, seldom wrong."

—*Former Law Clerk at the United States Court of Appeals for the Third Circuit*

Judicial clerkships give new lawyers tremendous responsibility, help them understand the judicial process from the inside, and take their skills to a whole new level. First, a new lawyer at a private law firm of any size will not have the responsibilities given to a law clerk for years. Next, from working closely with a judge, a law clerk gains insight into adjudication that is unavailable outside judicial chambers. Finally, due to the pace and load of cases, a law clerk by necessity becomes a much more efficient researcher and writer.

—*Former Law Clerk at the United States Court of Appeals for the Fourth Circuit*

Regardless of your post-clerkship plans or your portfolio in Chambers, I see only upsides to clerking. Your day-to-day tasks—evaluating different styles of oral and written advocacy, interfacing with a judge, and actually exercising "judgment" (in many senses of that word)—are likely to be once-in-a-lifetime, enlightening, gratifying, and applicable to virtually all components of your practice. Clerking is the Swiss Army Knife of the profession in that it prepares you for virtually anything that comes your way.

—Former Law Clerk at the United States Court of Federal Claims (now a government attorney)

Clerking was a marvelous experience. I cannot imagine a better, more intensive, or more fun way to understand the ins and outs of the judicial process. Everywhere you turn there is more to learn, and you are learning something from every judge and clerk on the court. Everybody has the same mission of administering justice and reaching the right conclusions, so it is remarkably collegial.

The job is thus very rewarding, but also very challenging. It is not about picking winners, though that is part of it. You must understand the law, the procedure, and the facts as well as or better than the parties themselves do. Sometimes parties do not brief the issues that really matter and might dispose of the case, or they fail to consider whether the court even has jurisdiction to hear the case or award the relief requested. Your responsibility to see those issues and reach the right judgment is weighty, and it has important real-world consequences for the parties. So take your time, read carefully, keep an open mind while you read and research, and routinely debate the tricky issues in cases with your colleagues.

I came out of my clerkship a better reader, writer, and overall lawyer. I had acquired five years' worth of experience and skills in a single year. My clerkship also opened the door for me to do more of the appellate work that I desired, and it even helped me obtain an academic position. Not to mention the many wonderful friends and colleagues that I met while clerking. What more could you want out of a job?

—Former Law Clerk at the United States Court of Appeals for the Federal Circuit (now in Academia)

Clerking has provided me with the tremendous and rare opportunity to refine my analytical and writing abilities under the guidance of a federal judge. I have had exposure to many areas of law and have learned to digest and analyze complex matters in short timeframes. As these skills would prove highly beneficial in any area of legal practice, I would strongly encourage both those interested in litigation and transactional work alike to pursue a judicial clerkship early in their careers.

—*Former Law Clerk at the United States District Court for the Southern District of Georgia (now in private practice)*

Clerkships are an invaluable experience for lawyers to hone their research and writing skills. By providing a window into the judicial system, clerkships offer opportunities for law clerks to learn how to best approach legal issues with a thorough and persuasive analysis. Clerkships are also an incredible opportunity to develop long lasting professional relationships with fellow law clerks, judicial administrative staff, and judges who have a wealth of experience in the judicial system and critical career advice to share. My clerkship was most certainly the best job to launch my legal career after graduating from law school.

—*Former Law Clerk at the District of Columbia Court of Appeals*

The surface benefits of a clerkship are readily apparent: an opportunity to see the inner workings of the judiciary, hone legal research and writing skills on a daily basis, and gain exposure to a variety of substantive and procedural issues.

But the value of a clerkship goes deeper. The skeleton of a case, which often remains illusory while in law school, takes life as you dig into the work. You see cases from their infancy to their resolution. You will be challenged. Moreover, the constant exposure to new substantive and procedural issues sparks a type of "sixth sense" or "legal intuition" that will be invaluable in practice going forward.

My judge has been a teacher, a mentor, and a friend. Now, I am now part of a network of former clerks who have clerked for my judge specifically, and I am part of a network of former clerks across the judiciary. My writing skills have undoubtedly improved since law school, and I now work more intelligently and efficiently. As a direct result of the clerkship, I feel more prepared to begin my practice. It is an honor and a privilege to clerk. If the opportunity arises, seize it.

—*Former Law Clerk at the United States District Court for the Eastern District of Pennsylvania*

Clerking is one of the best experiences a new lawyer can have, for many reasons, but a key one is really getting to understand how a judge approaches various issues and decisions. Knowing the person behind the black robe helps to make you a much more effective advocate.

—*Former Law Clerk at the United States Court of Appeals for the Eleventh Circuit (now in Academia)*

Clerking is a wonderful experience, which helps improve not only your own writing, but your organization of information and advocacy skills. . . . [M]y interactions with my judge forced me to articulate my thoughts and reasons clearly and concisely and to see the case from all sides. Furthermore, my judge possessed a vast breadth of knowledge, from which I learned so much. Lastly, another great advantage of clerking is that you become a part of the "family" of clerks who have served your judge.

—*Former Law Clerk at the United States Court of Appeals for Veterans Claims (now working as a government attorney)*

It will be hard to return to law school after externing at the D.D.C. Every day we were scrambling to help the judge resolve a never-ending tide of issues. The diversity of cases really fast-tracks legal education because you are not only adapting to a variety of cases, you have to learn to teach yourself and teach others. It is also a humbling experience to realize how little you know and how much you have to rely on others. Also, because Chambers is so small, there is very little time to proofread and double check what you write before the judge reviews it and it goes out the door. Overall, I cannot speak highly enough about my time in Chambers and the accelerated track on which it set me.

—*Former Judicial Extern at the United States District Court for the District of Columbia*

My clerkship has been one of the best experiences of my career and gave me an opportunity to learn from one of the most distinguished attorneys and jurists I have ever met. Thanks to my judge's mentorship, I have become a better writer, analytical thinker, and advocate. Perhaps most importantly, my judge taught me to never forget the very real impacts that the law can have on people from all walks of life, for better or worse.

—*Former Clerk at the United States Court of Appeals for the Federal Circuit (now working as in-house counsel)*

Although it has been over 20 years since I clerked, I am still in contact with my judge, and I look back on that year as one of the best experiences of my career. One benefit of clerking is the opportunity to research and write at the highest level every day, helping to develop the law in interesting cases. My advice to incoming law clerks is to savor every minute of your clerkship experience and get the most out of the opportunity that you can, critically reading briefs, articulately discussing legal issues with your judge, observing advocates, and writing to the best of your ability. It can seem overwhelming and daunting at first, the awesome responsibility entrusted to you as a clerk, but you are up to the task or the judge would not have chosen you to be there. Overall, clerking is a unique and wonderful learning experience that you should thoroughly enjoy!

—*Former Law Clerk at the Maine Supreme Judicial Court (now in Academia)*

[Clerking] changed my life, my career, and my understanding of the law in many ways. . . . [My judge] truly believes that the legal profession is a family that ought to help each other rather than pounce on each other's missteps . . . [and] taught me that attorneys and judges should have a heart. . . . [He] never loses sight of the fact that, even though a case is about applying the law to facts, it impacts people's lives. . . . [In conclusion], clerking . . . helped me to connect-the-dots of lawyering—links that often remained a mystery to me even after graduating law school and passing the bar. In addition, I learned about how to live an honorable life in what can be a not-so-honorable profession. I guess you could say I got my masters in the way that the law works and also how the life of a lawyer should look. In sum, I learned how to see myself, how to write, how to be a professional, and how to treat others. I think that's pretty much all you could ask for from any clerkship.

—*Former Law Clerk at the United States Court of Appeals for the Eighth Circuit (now in Academia)*

Spending the summer after my first year of law school as a judicial extern was remarkably beneficial in my legal education and career path. As my first legal job, it gave me an opportunity to learn from my judge, his assistant, and his clerks, who were all brilliant and eager to help me learn and grow as a soon-to-be attorney. My writing, communication, and presentation skills notably improved as a direct result of their feedback and encouragement. I learned by example while working closely with talented attorneys on a daily basis. Chambers was a wonderful environment for learning. The judge and his clerks were intellectually curious and passionate about the law. I am grateful to have had the opportunity to grow professionally under their guidance.

—*Former Judicial Extern at the United States Court of Appeals for the Federal Circuit (now in private practice)*

I externed at the Office of Special Masters after my first year of law school. Whereas many law students spend their first summer merely watching lawyers work, I spent my summer working alongside them under the tutelage of an experienced jurist. Subsequent employers told me that my meaningful, substantive work during my first summer set me apart. The externship also propelled me into the fall semester where I earned my highest grades of law school. Through the connections I made during my externship, I was able to secure an internship for the following summer at the Department of Justice. In addition to improving my writing and helping me secure a subsequent internship, my judicial externship also solidified my desire to clerk after graduation. In large part due to the skills learned and experience gained during my judicial externship, I secured a federal clerkship upon graduation. In sum, my judicial externship profoundly impacted every aspect of my law school experience and opened doors that might have otherwise remained closed to me.

—*Former Judicial Extern at the Office of Special Masters (now clerking for a federal magistrate judge)*

Notes

[1]   These suggestions are largely inspired by the excellent scholarship of Professor Shailini J. George at Suffolk University Law School. *See generally* Shailini J. George, *The Cure for the Distracted Mind: Why Law Schools Should Teach Mindfulness*, 53 DUQ. L. REV. 215 (2015).

[2]   These suggestions are adapted from Shailini J. George, *Easy Ways to Incorporate Mindfulness in the Legal Writing Classroom*, 29 THE SECOND DRAFT 2, 34–35 (Fall 2016).

[3]   All reflections are quoted with each author's express permission. Each author was advised to obtain his or her former judge's consent before supplying a quote. Quotes were included in full or in part at my discretion and with the author's prior consent. Some quotes were also used in full or in part elsewhere in the book.

APPENDIX

EXCERPT OF *COURTING CLERKSHIPS: THE NALP JUDICIAL CLERKSHIP STUDY*

■ ■ ■

Introduction and Rationale for Study[1]

Judicial clerkships open doors to satisfying legal careers—yet the profession's understanding of who is applying for clerkships, why they do so, and how the process can be managed effectively is little understood. Motivated by several critical concerns about clerkships and diversity in the legal profession, the National Association for Law Placement (NALP) and the American Bar Association (ABA) undertook a comprehensive study of judicial clerkships as employment opportunities for law graduates.

The study, conducted in several phases, sought input from three significant populations: law school administrations/career service professionals, third-year students, and alumni law clerks. It has captured information on student perceptions about the clerkship application and selection processes; the value students perceive in clerkships; data on the presence of women graduates and graduates of color in federal, state, and local clerkships; the influence of clerkships on attorney careers; and the roles that law school faculty and administration assume in the student clerkship application processes.

Methodology

This study compiled data from four sources. The first portion of the study analyzed retrospective empirical data compiled by NALP for five years (1994–1998) to refute or substantiate anecdotal evidence about differences in the frequency of judicial clerk positions among men, women and graduates of color. The data, collected by NALP annually on the employment experiences of new law graduates, produces information on 86–90% of all graduates from ABA-accredited law schools each year and thus offers the most comprehensive insights regarding graduate employment as judicial clerks through these detailed analyses.

For the subsequent phases of the study, NALP designed and implemented three comprehensive surveys to elicit critical information from each of the three target groups: law school administrations/career service professionals, third-year students, and alumni law clerks. The collective goals of these questionnaires, respectively, were:

- To determine the roles that law school administration and faculty assume in the student clerkship application process;

- To identify law school student perceptions regarding judicial clerkships and the application process; and

- To evaluate former and present law clerk perceptions regarding the application process, the value of the clerkship experience, and its impact on their future careers.

A joint letter from William Paul, President of the ABA, and Patricia Bass, President of NALP, notified the deans of all ABA-accredited law schools of the purposes of this study and invited each to participate in the administrative law school survey. One hundred and forty-seven law school career services offices, or 81%, returned their completed surveys to NALP.

Using standard survey selection methods, 61 law schools were identified to form a pool of schools for the law student and alumni inquiries. This pool included a representative sample of law schools that have a high number of federal clerkships, those with a high number of non-federal (state and/or local) clerkships, and some randomly selected from the remainder. As a result, the schools in the sample pool represent a diverse cross-section nationally of school characteristics (public, private, size, geographic region and reputation), with varying levels of students and graduates pursuing federal, state and local clerkships. These schools were invited to participate in an effort to survey all current third-year students, regardless of whether they have applied for or accepted a judicial clerkship, and graduates from the classes of 1998 and 1999 who pursued a clerkship following graduation.

A letter notifying the law schools in the sample pool was sent out by NALP in early December 1999 asking the schools to indicate their agreement to participate in the next phase of the study and to provide information as to the number of surveys needed for their third-year students and alumni from the classes of 1998 and 1999 who are serving or had served as law clerks, as well as their preferred method of distribution to the students and alumni.

Survey questionnaires were subsequently distributed to approximately 14,000 third-year students and 4,000 alumni law clerks in January 2000. Of the roughly 14,000 law students to whom the law student surveys were distributed, 1660 students, or 11%, returned their completed surveys to NALP. The law clerk survey was distributed to approximately 4,000 alumni, and 931 alumni returned their completed surveys—an extraordinary return rate that approaches 24%.

Overview of the Findings:

Analysis of Employment Statistics

- **Minority representation among the clerkship population is generally lower than in the law school population.** Historically, the representation of Hispanic and Black/African American law clerks has been significantly lower than the representation of these groups in the general law school population, with some variation observed by court types. In contrast, Asian-Pacific Islanders in the federal clerk population, particularly in certain circuit courts, increasingly maintain a representation equivalent or even exceeding their numbers in the law school class. The data show a trend towards a slightly decreasing percentage of white law clerks, from 87.1% in the Class of 1994 to 85.1% in the Class of 1998.

- **For the last four of the five years included in the study, women comprised a majority of the law clerk population.** However, there is a disproportionately high percentage of women serving as local and state clerks and a greater percentage of men than women as federal clerks, although the gap has decreased slightly through the years. Vastly different patterns emerge within each federal circuit, both with the relative percentages of men in comparison to women and with the degree of variation in these distributions from year to year.

- **Different patterns of clerkship populations emerge based on law school characteristics.** Federal clerkships comprise a significant percentage of the judicial clerkships taken by graduates of private law schools. In contrast, for public schools the distribution is sharply skewed towards state clerkships. Both school types show a relatively small, constant proportion of local clerks. When the law schools are aggregated according to their total J.D. enrollment, other patterns can be observed. As a whole, the law schools in all of the size categories report a higher percentage of state clerks than federal clerks, with the smallest portion being local clerks. However, in the smallest school size (500 or fewer students), prevalence of state clerkships significantly outweighs the other levels; the percentage of federal clerks is highest in the intermediate school size (501–750 students), where it approaches most closely the state clerk population.

Findings from the Administrative Survey of Law Schools

- **Nearly all law schools offer programs on judicial clerkships, but the number and range of subjects vary**

widely. One of the most visible indicators of support for, or efforts devoted to, the judicial clerkship process is evident in the number and scope of programs on this subject. Almost all of the responding law schools conduct a program on an introduction or overview of clerkships, with most of them sponsored by the career services office. However, notably absent are specialized informational/support programs in this area for women and students of color—only about a quarter of the responding schools provide such programs. Also missing were programs on preparing for a clerkship, which are not offered by 64% of the law schools.

- **The vast majority of law schools offer a formal internship or externship program with local judges.** The schools with an externship or internship program generally believe that this has positively affected the number of clerkship applications, and the majority also perceive a positive effect on clerkship offers.

- **As a group, law schools allocate considerable resources to the judicial clerkship process.** Postings of letters from judges seeking clerks proved to be the most highly valued resource. Also highly valued by the schools are the clerkship handbooks published by their career services offices; however, 23% of schools, mostly the smaller schools, do not publish a clerkship handbook. Among the other resources most valued are the NALP Federal and State Judicial Clerkship Directory, the Almanac of the Federal Judiciary, and the WESTLAW® and LEXIS® resources.

- **Equally notable are the resources that the majority of schools do not have.** More than 71% reported that they do not have a judicial clerkship section on their Web site; of those that did have this resource, most found it to be useful. Largely missing as well were collections of written comments from faculty, and more than half of the schools did not have written feedback from alumni law clerks even though those who have such resources regarded them as valuable. Another significant resource, the Directory of Minority Judges of the United States, was not present at 49% of law schools, and the percent appeared even higher among certain school types; for example, 68% of the smallest school size and 52% of the public schools did not have this publication.

- **Universally, the law schools cited a need for more comprehensive resources regarding clerkship hiring procedures.** In the absence of a uniform comprehensive source on the timing of applications, hiring, contents of application packages, terms of clerkships, biographical and general information on judges, most schools maintain their own database of judges to which they allocate considerable time and resources.

- **Law schools in every category type and size of school indicated that the lack of uniform guidelines hinders the clerkship application process.** In their qualitative comments, this issue overshadowed all others, as the respondents addressed the problem this creates in their efforts to provide effective support for their students in the clerkship application process without draining the resources of their offices. Many schools commented that the clerkship applicant pool for the judges has been negatively impacted as well. Roughly half of the reporting schools noted that their schools are making programmatic changes in response to this issue, by moving up clerkship programming for second year students to earlier in the fall semester and by including first year students in their clerkship programming.

- **About half of the schools have a faculty clerkship committee.** Faculty generally are supportive of students applying for clerkships in terms of providing recommendations, but one-quarter of the schools experienced difficulty in getting the faculty to send letters of recommendation in a timely fashion.

- **Career services offices generally provide counseling or advising in connection with judicial clerkship applications but fewer offer clerical support.** A little more than half of the career services offices provide some kind of clerical support for students in connection with the processing of the clerkship applications, ranging from supplying students with a list of judges on a disk to mail merge to collecting and mailing the application package. These services, when provided by a career services office, are generally available to all students who would like to apply for judicial clerkships, although some schools select the students to which they will provide other kinds of support.

- **Financial assistance in connection with the clerkship application and interview process is limited at best.** Moreover, no school offers any other financial assistance for the judicial clerkship term except for a few schools that include clerkships within their loan forgiveness programs.

- **In their perceptions of student success, the career services professionals followed traditional expectations.** They named as the top criteria for success high class ranks, the law review/law journal credential, support of top faculty, and a summer or academic year judicial internship or externship. In the experience of career service professionals, a special connection to a judge does not emerge as a primary factor in acquiring federal and state clerkships.

- **Schools that offer more resources to students tend to have a higher percentage of graduates in clerkships.** Law schools that provide academic programs designed to support or encourage judicial clerkships had a higher percentage of their graduates obtaining clerkships than their counterparts without these programs and those schools that maintain a judicial database showed a similar tendency. In addition, the law schools with a faculty clerkship committee tended to have more of their graduates entering clerkships than those that did not have this committee; however, this positive correlation did not exist where the committee included a screening function. On a cautionary note, a causative link has not been established between these factors from the law schools and the clerkship rates of their students, nor can this be ascertained from the present data.

Findings from the Law Student Survey

- **Clearly students recognize the value of the clerkship relative to one's legal career.** For those who did apply for a clerkship, the factors that most influenced their decision to apply were the desire to gain the work experience of a clerkship; the impact of a clerkship on their future career; the prestige of clerkships; and discussions with others, primarily lawyers in practice.

- **The desire to clerk in the geographic locale or court of their future practice was the factor that most influenced the decision to apply to particular courts.** More than one-half of the students looked to the level of the court (trial/appellate), while almost as many focused on the type of court (federal/state/local). The reputation of the judge was also ranked by students as extremely significant in their decision where to apply. Other significant factors included the length of the clerkship term (one year versus two year); the atmosphere in chambers/ working conditions; and that the judge previously hired clerks from their law school.

Considerably de-emphasized by the students were factors such as personal connection to the judge and the race/ethnicity, gender, sexual orientation or disability status of the judge.

- **A substantial number of students cited the financial differential of a clerkship salary as a component of their decision not to apply for a clerkship at all.** While the financial burdens of applying for a judicial clerkship did not appear to play as large a role as expected for those students who chose to apply for a clerkship, the expense of the application and interview process did surface as a concern among some students.

- **The data do not support a finding that students chose not to apply for clerkships due to a perception of bias toward their gender, race or ethnicity.** Respondents who did not apply for a clerkship cited most often as a reason for not applying that they preferred a different post-graduation option. A substantial percent of the students indicated that they did not think their applications would be competitive. More than one-third of the non-applying students stated as a reason that they lacked the finances to apply or interview for a clerkship and emphasized as a deterrent the financial differential of the clerkship salary given their considerable educational debt. Almost one-third of these students stated that they felt discouraged by some aspect of the application process; of these, most pointed to the timing or the arduousness of the process. Most of those students who did not apply for a clerkship reported that they would have done so if one or more of these factors were different.

- **The racial and ethnic patterns of judicial clerks appear to be a reflection of these patterns in the student applicant population of our study, rather than a difference in the success of their applications.** The overall success rate of those applying for a clerkship was quite high at 69.5%, and two of these groups, Asian/Pacific Islander and Hispanic/Latino, had even higher success rates. In order to increase minority representation among law clerks, efforts should focus on the need to increase the number of minority students who apply in the first instance, particularly among certain groups, such as Hispanics and African-Americans.

- **A gender differential in success rates emerged.** Sixty-six percent of the women who applied received a clerkship offer, in contrast to 74% of the male students in our study.

The gender patterns in judicial clerks and applicants, while favorable when viewed in the context of the overall law school class, tend to vary with the type of court (federal versus state and local) and may also reflect a differential in the success rate of their applications.

- **A much lower percentage of students in the upper age category (36 and older) received an offer.** Moreover, more than any other demographic group, students in this category perceived their age to be a disadvantage leading to unsuccessful clerkship applications.

- **The results do not support the hypothesis of connections to judge as a significant component in obtaining a clerkship.** This fact contrasts with the perceptions among many of the students who offered as a reason for not applying for a clerkship, or for not succeeding with their clerkship applications, that they did not have the right "connections" to acquire a clerkship.

- **Grades, law review, and the academic record all play the largest roles in both the perceptions of students and the reality of a successful clerkship application.** These perceptions largely coincide with those of the career services personnel of their law schools.

- **Roughly one in ten applications at the federal level resulted in an invitation to interview, and one in four applications at the state level did so.** However, these numbers may not accurately reflect the practice common in some courts of submitting one application to a pool for distribution to many judges in that court. About one in three of the interviews with a state or federal judge resulted in an offer, although for state appellate courts the yield rate appeared somewhat higher at 43%.

- **The time given by judges to respond to a clerkship offer may not be as limited as has been widely believed and previously reported, but it is still a problem.** The response time most often described—identified by approximately one-third of the students—was "two days to one week." Still, a substantial proportion of students reported the prevalence of "on the spot" responses. Many students expressed frustration with the time pressure they experienced both in scheduling their interviews and responding to an offer.

- **One of the most problematic aspects of the application process for students was the obtaining and control of**

references. Most strikingly, over one-third of the students indicated that they experienced difficulties in finding people to provide these references and an even greater percentage (36%) reported problems with the content of the letters. A large number of students expressed the concern that their professors did not know them well enough to write meaningful recommendations, due in part to the part to the earlier timing of the application process. In addition, almost one-third of the students experienced problems with the timely submission of these letters.

- **Students were generally satisfied with the assistance provided by their law schools.** In describing the level of assistance provided by their law schools overall, most of the students felt that they received adequate or very useful assistance in obtaining information or advice about their cover letter, resume, writing sample or letters of recommendation, and received adequate assistance in the area of interviewing. However, almost one-half of the students would have liked additional assistance from their law schools in collecting information or advice about the judges.

- **The lack of timing guidelines and standard application procedures makes the process chaotic and encumbered their experiences.** The absence of these uniform procedures, along with a lack of information about individual judges' application procedures and requirements, emerged repeatedly as significant factors in students' dissatisfaction with the clerkship application process.

Findings from the Alumni Law Clerk Survey

- **The respondents to the alumni law clerk survey represented clerkships from a wide variety of types and levels of courts and judges nationwide.** In their demographic composition, the racial/ethnic and gender distributions were closely similar to the demographics observed for the student respondents who applied for a judicial clerkship, as well as the general law clerk population.

- **The qualifications of the clerks mirrored the perceptions of students as to the qualifications of successful candidates.** A significant percent of these law clerks reported that they had top grades/high class rank, had been a teaching or research assistant, were on the law review/ law journal, and/or had significant professional work experience prior to law school. Nearly one-third had a summer or academic year judicial intern/externship.

- **Only a relatively small percentage of the alumni law clerks reported having a special connection to a judge while in law school.** This fact provides further support for the findings of the student survey that, contrary to the perceptions among many of the students who did not apply for or receive a clerkship, very few of the students who applied and received an offer actually had a special connection to a judge.

- **The majority of law clerks responded that costs did not affect their choices during the application process.** A relatively small percentage applied to fewer judges as a consequence of the cost. Once again, the financial factor does not appear most significant for the choices made by applicants during the clerkship application process. However, some alumni did complain of the expense and, as noted above, some students pointed to financial considerations (i.e., the salary differential) as a reason for their decision not to apply for a judicial clerkship in the first instance.

- **The views of the law clerks did not entirely coincide with those of the students and career services professionals with regard to the important factors in judges' selections of law clerks.** Based on their past application experience and their observations as a law clerk, these alumni identified most often as "extremely important" to the judge the evaluation of the interview—even more highly than the academic record, which had received the strongest weight from their student counterparts. (Of course, it must be recognized that grades are an important component in obtaining this crucial interview.) According to the law clerks, second in importance were personal character traits. Not very important in the clerks' view were demographic characteristics and personal connection to the judge.

- **Almost one-third of the law clerks indicated that in retrospect they would have done something differently in the application process.** Many of them would have applied to more judges or more widely across the courts, applied sooner or started the application process earlier, built stronger recommendations from the faculty, pursued the clerkship more aggressively through phone calls to chambers, and/or researched additional information about the judicial ideology and the atmosphere of different judges' chambers, particularly by talking to former clerks.

- **Overall, the law clerks reported that their clerkship helped them acquire and improve a wide variety of legal and professional skills.** The substantial majority felt that the skills gained in their clerkships met or exceeded their initial expectations. Generally, clerks in trial courts (whether federal or state) ranked their skill development somewhat higher than those in appellate courts. The same pattern holds true with regard to the clerks' perception of the development of the relationship with their judges; most agreed that the relationship met or exceeded their expectations but trial court clerks ranked this slightly higher than appellate clerks.

- **When asked to characterize the degree to which their clerkship affected the ease of success in handling their post-clerkship duties, the former law clerks answered positively.** Significant variation appeared by court type, with the most positive response from law clerks in state trial and local trial courts, followed by federal trial courts, and a moderately positive response in federal appellate and state appellate courts.

- **Many respondents commented that their clerkship made them rethink their long-term goals and gave them a greater awareness of opportunities within the field.** They also cited an emphasis on quality of life issues, as well as consideration of personal happiness and the value of job satisfaction. In addition, many addressed their need for increased financial compensation and a pressure to enter private practice at the outset. Several indicated that the exposure to a variety of attorneys and law firms helped them decide which firm to join. As a result of their clerkship, some reported a heightened interest in government service or academia.

- **Almost half of the law clerks responded that their clerkship helped a great deal in obtaining their first post-clerkship position.** Almost one-quarter stated that it helped somewhat and over one-quarter believed that the clerkship did not substantially affect this factor. In essence, no one reported that the clerkship negatively affected the post-clerkship employment search.

- **In rating their clerkships, the law clerks resoundingly gave their overall experience high marks.** When asked whether they would clerk again, a remarkable 97% responded in the affirmative. In addition, their narrative comments reflect the strong positive feelings these alumni carry with them from their judicial clerkship experiences, as well as the valuable impact this professional experience has had on their future careers.

* * *

III. Students

- **Students are encouraged to find out more information about the judges.** Using the growing availability of resources (see appendix), students should research the atmosphere and relationships in chambers, particularly through information from former law clerks. Since web sites are continually growing and changing, students should explore the many on-line resources that are available.

- **Students should apply widely.** They should remain open minded and flexible as to the types of courts and judges. There are many opportunities available for a valuable judicial clerkship. Students should not be discouraged by their lack of connections to a judge in applying for a clerkship, since the data demonstrate that only a small percentage of students and law clerks have such connections.

- **Students should take advantage of all the resources offered by their law schools.** They should work on developing their relationships with faculty though writing, class participation, and serving as research assistants so that they can enhance their law school experiences and obtain more meaningful faculty recommendations. Students should take advantage of the programs on judicial clerkships provided by their law schools (and ask for more, if needed).

- **Almost one-third of the law clerks indicated that in retrospect they would have done something differently in the application process.** As general advice to students from the alumni respondents, their substantive narratives revealed that many of them would have applied to more judges or more widely across the courts, applied sooner or started the application process earlier, built stronger recommendations from the faculty, pursued the clerkship more aggressively through phone calls to chambers, and/or researched more to try to obtain additional information about the judicial ideology and the atmosphere of different judges' chambers, particularly by talking to former clerks.

Note

---

1   This is an excerpt of *Courting Clerkships: The NALP Judicial Clerkship Study* (2000). The full report is available at http://www.nalp.org/courtingclerkships. The study is a publication of the National Association for Law Placement ("NALP") and is copyrighted by NALP. The excerpt is reprinted herein with NALP's permission.

INDEX

References are to pages